Strategies for
Building Multicultural
Competence
in Mental Health and
Educational Settings

Strategies for Building Multicultural Competence

in Mental Health and Educational Settings

Edited by

Madonna G. Constantine and Derald Wing Sue

WILEY

John Wiley & Sons, Inc.

Library of Congress Cataloging-in-Publication Data:

Strategies for building multicultural competence in mental health and educational
    settings / edited by Madonna G. Constantine and Derald Wing Sue.
        p. cm.
    ISBN 0-471-66732-3 (pbk.)
        1. Psychiatry, transcultural—United States.   2. Cross-cultural counseling—
United States.   3. Educational counseling—United States.   4. Multiculturalism—
United States.   I. Constantine, Madonna G.   II. Sue, Derald Wing.
RC455.4.E8S77 2005
616.89′00973—dc22

                                                                                2004042298

Printed in the United States of America.

10   9   8   7   6   5   4   3   2   1

To the many courageous women and men working in mental health and educational settings who tirelessly promote social justice issues to bring about necessary changes. We applaud your strength and dedication in trying to make this world a better place for all of us.

Contents

Part V   Concluding Thoughts

Foreword

Psychology is the handmaiden of the status quo.
—Derald Wing Sue

IN 2002, THE American Psychological Association's Council of Representatives unanimously approved the "Guidelines on Multicultural Education, Training, Research, Practice, and Organizational Change for Psychologists," culminating a multi-decade effort by a dedicated and persistent group of psychologists who saw much of psychology as culture bound. I will not cite the history of this journey, but simply note that resistance over the years to these ideas was strong. The predominant resistance was a refusal to face the fact that the "tried and true" was grounded in a worldview not shared by three quarters of the world's population. The title of Robert Guthrie's book, *Even the Rat Was White,* brings to the forefront that traditional psychology is biased toward Western European cultures, that the knowledge base, theories, and practices of psychology may not be applicable to the lives of an increasingly diverse population, and that imposing this worldview on people of color, for example, represents cultural oppression. Attempts to get members of our profession to question their assumptions of cultural reality have been difficult, and some of the battles leading up to the approval of the "Guidelines" were not pleasant.

Although the "Guidelines" have now become official policy of the American Psychological Association, in truth, they have no teeth. Practitioners, researchers, and professors are not required to use them. The "Guidelines" do, however, provide an important moral authority that should not be ignored but that many may try to forget. The challenge before us is to gain the attention of the psychological community and develop awareness and action around the "Guidelines."

Strategies for Building Multicultural Competence in Mental Health and Educational Settings is a major step in that direction. It is given to us at a critical time that may lead to culturally relevant theories and practices. We might actually see our field begin to change from a monocultural to a multicultural profession. The editors and authors have not been content just to see the "Guidelines" approved. They have provided many specifics that show us that cultural competence is an opportunity for a revitalized and restored psychology and with it a new paradigm that can bring equality and new standards for research and practice. The change might even be enjoyable.

What specifically can this book do for you, the practitioner, professor, student, or researcher? It provides specifics for culturally sensitive assessment, counseling, and therapy, and organizational change. Ideas for integrating indigenous methods into psychological practice are provided. Independent practitioners can learn about culturally relevant issues and approaches that will make them more effective not only with persons of color, but with all of their clients. Professors will find ideas for improving their teaching and a new excitement in sharing them with students in the classroom. Organizational change is stressed as essential if institutional racism is to be addressed. Finally, although psychology is a research-based profession, it has consistently failed to examine underlying assumptions of research. These false and limiting assumptions need serious challenge, and the reader will find three lively and critical chapters that can change the way research is taught and practiced.

A text like this is needed for several reasons: (1) to aid psychologists in adapting the "Guidelines" to their work and roles, (2) to challenge traditional psychology and to advocate for the inclusion of culture in the entire profession, (3) to encourage psychologists to understand themselves as racial and cultural beings and how that affects their roles and practice, and (4) to indicate how psychology may become culturally obsolete unless it acknowledges that race, culture, and ethnicity are functions of each of us. Truly, the assumptions emanating from this text may literally change the face of psychology. If psychology fails to meet the challenge of multiculturalism, the alternative is to become irrelevant and obsolete.

I offer my most sincere thanks and appreciation to the editors and authors of this important volume for showing us the future. A commitment to multiculturalism can help us remake ourselves into better human beings and professionals. No one can read this text and honestly continue to practice in the old monocultural ways.

ALLEN E. IVEY, EdD, ABPP
Counseling and Social Justice Program
University of South Florida
Distinguished University Professor (Emeritus)
University of Massachusetts, Amherst

Preface

IN AUGUST 2002, the American Psychological Association's (APA) Council of Representatives approved the "Guidelines on Multicultural Education, Training, Research, Practice, and Organizational Change for Psychologists." These "multicultural competencies" were developed in recognition of the fact that the mental health needs of many culturally diverse groups were unmet via traditional forms of counseling. The "Guidelines" were subsequently published in 2003 and generally focus on helping psychologists and other mental health professionals to understand themselves as racial/cultural beings in clinical, training, educational, research, and organizational settings.

In our work as educators, trainers, consultants, and practitioners, we know that many mental health professionals are eager to take a multiculturally centered perspective in working with diverse individuals, but they often lack the knowledge and expertise to achieve this goal. As such, this book presents myriad ways to operationalize the "Guidelines" so that practitioners, trainers, educators, clinical supervisors, researchers, and administrators can be multiculturally effective in their work. We believe the audience for this book will include mental health professionals who hunger for specific hands-on strategies and concrete suggestions that will enable them to implement specific interventions intended to promote their multicultural competence in the twenty-first century. These professionals are being increasingly challenged to serve as agents of social change in a multicultural society.

Chapters in this book identify concrete strategies to help mental health professionals increase their multicultural competence. The authors include well-known scholars, practitioners, researchers, and administrators in the area of multicultural counseling who are employed in a variety of work settings.

The book is divided into five general parts. The first part provides an overview of the "Guidelines," along with operational definitions of terms used throughout the "Guidelines." The following two sections address the application of the "Guidelines" in clinical practice, educational, training, and organization settings. The fourth section of the book discusses considerations in conducting culturally sensitive research in light of the "Guidelines." The final section provides concluding thoughts and future considerations for fostering multicultural competence by expanding the social justice efforts of mental health professionals in organizations, institutions, and societies.

Our work on this book would not have been possible without the love and support of our families, friends, and colleagues around the globe. We also are especially indebted to the contributors of the chapters in this book. These individuals have generously agreed to donate the proceeds from the sale of this book to future multicultural conferences and projects in the field of applied psychology. We appreciate you and the outstanding work you have done!

We hope that you enjoy reading *Strategies for Building Multicultural Competence in Mental Health and Educational Settings.* May it stimulate your mind and nourish your spirit!

Contributors

Michelle Anderson, MA
Ohio State University
Columbus, Ohio

Jessica Barfield, BA
Indiana University
Bloomington, Indiana

Sarah J. Brazaitis, PhD
Teachers College
Columbia University
New York, New York

Janet Chang, MA
University of California, Davis
Davis, California

Devika Dibya Choudhuri, PhD
Eastern Michigan University
Ypsilanti, Michigan

Nancy C. Coleman, PhD
University of Florida at
  Gainesville
Gainesville, Florida

Madonna G. Constantine, PhD
Teachers College
Columbia University
New York, New York

Edward A. Delgado-Romero, PhD
Indiana University
Bloomington, Indiana

Benetta Fairley, MS
Indiana University
Bloomington, Indiana

Lisa Y. Flores, PhD
University of Missouri–Columbia
Columbia, Missouri

Jairo N. Fuertes, PhD, ABPP
Fordham University at
  Lincoln Center
New York, New York

Mary A. Fukuyama, PhD
University of Florida
  at Gainesville
Gainesville, Florida

Tamara Godfrey, MEd
Ohio State University
Columbus, Ohio

David E. Greenan, EdD
The Minuchin Center for the
  Family
New York, New York

George V. Gushue, PhD
Teachers College
Columbia University
New York, New York

Sally M. Hage, PhD
Teachers College
Columbia University
New York, New York

Yu-Ping Huang, BEd
University of Missouri–Columbia
Columbia, Missouri

Monica Jefferson, MA
Ohio State University
Columbus, Ohio

Mai M. Kindaichi, MA, MEd
Teachers College
Columbia University
New York, New York

Naa Oyo A. Kwate, PhD
Mailman School of Public Health
Columbia University
New York, New York

Yi-Jiun Lin, MEd
University of Missouri–Columbia
Columbia, Missouri

Rebecca S. Martínez, PhD
Indiana University
Bloomington, Indiana

Sharon Mintz, MSEd
Fordham University at
    Lincoln Center
New York, New York

Jeffery Scott Mio, PhD
California State Polytechnic
    University at Pomona
Pomona, California

Alexa Mislowack, BA
Fordham University at
    Lincoln Center
New York, New York

Marie L. Miville, PhD
Teachers College
Columbia University
New York, New York

Linda James Myers, PhD
Ohio State University
Columbus, Ohio

Ezemenari M. Obasi, MA
Ohio State University
Columbus, Ohio

Ruperto M. Perez, PhD
University of Florida
    at Gainesville
Gainesville, Florida

Jason Purnell, MA
Ohio State University
Columbus, Ohio

Dinelia Rosa, PhD
Teachers College
Columbia University
New York, New York

Gargi Roysircar, PhD
Antioch New England
    Graduate School
Keene, New Hampshire

Derald Wing Sue, PhD
Teachers College
Columbia University
New York, New York

Stanley Sue, PhD
University of California, Davis
Davis, California

Shawn O. Utsey, PhD
Virginia Commonwealth
  University
Richmond, Virginia

Melba J. T. Vasquez, PhD, ABPP
Independent Practice
Austin, Texas

Rheeda L. Walker, PhD
University of South Carolina
Columbia, South Carolina

PART I

Overview of the American Psychological Association's Multicultural Guidelines: Implications for Multicultural Competence

The American Psychological Association's Guidelines on Multicultural Education, Training, Research, Practice, and Organizational Psychology: Initial Development and Summary

Madonna G. Constantine and Derald Wing Sue

People of color, including those of multiracial and multiethnic heritage, represent an increasing proportion of the U.S. population (Jones & Smith, 2001; U.S. Census Bureau, 2003). According to the 2000 U.S. Census (U.S. Census Bureau, 2003), approximately 40% of the nation's population consists of people of color (Jones & Smith, 2001). The landscape of racial and ethnic diversity across the United States indicates particularly high cultural diversity in coastal and border states, especially California, Texas, Arizona, New Mexico, Washington, Florida, New York, and Louisiana, and a general growth in cultural diversity in the midwestern, northwestern, and southern regions of the United States (U.S. Census Bureau, 2003). These demographic statistics underscore the need for professional psychologists to have a vested interest in addressing cultural diversity issues as practitioners, educators, researchers, and policymakers. Thus, it behooves psychologists and the larger field of psychology to reflect on potential monocultural biases to foster cultural relevance in research, practice, education, and training (Sue, 2001).

Recently, the American Psychological Association (APA) as a professional organization has responded to the increased diversification of the United States, in part, with explicit statements endorsing the importance of cultural competence for psychologists. Specifically, the "Guidelines on Multicultural Education, Training, Research, Practice, and Organizational Change for Psychologists" (APA, 2003), herein referred to as the APA Multicultural Guidelines, is a compilation of six prescriptive statements that reflect the evolution of the psychology profession with regard to recognizing that cultural competence is necessary in meeting the varied needs of individuals belonging to diverse cultural groups or historically marginalized groups. These multicultural competencies reflect a response to several APA divisions' calls for recognition and integration of multicultural initiatives within the larger psychological community, as well as the exponentially growing representation of people of color in the United States (Sue, Bingham, Porche-Burke, & Vasquez, 1999). As a living document, this set of competencies was designed to be expanded alongside future empirical and conceptual psychological contributions and as broader social movements influence public interests.

RELEVANT BACKGROUND

The APA Multicultural Guidelines (APA, 2003) were published with the goal of affecting current and future psychological practice, training, education, and research and had been preceded by nearly 40 years of attention to multicultural issues in certain subfields of applied psychology. Social movements such as the Civil Rights Movement in the 1950s and 1960s represented forums for political action and subsequent public policy initiatives that addressed explicit differential access to human rights and power based on race and ethnicity. In the social context of change, structural and functional changes occurred within the psychology profession that affected the development of organizational bodies focused on cultural diversity issues. Specifically, momentum from the sociopolitical activism in the late 1960s created an atmosphere in which leading African American psychologists mobilized to increase representation of Black people in psychology and in leadership roles in professional psychological organizations, eliminate racially biased research from professional journals, and establish training programs in which cultural issues were included (Robinson & Morris, 2000). This kind of activism marked the beginning of the Association of Black Psychologists (ABP); other subgroups of psychologists of color, such as the Asian American Psychological Association (AAPA), were formed in the early 1970s.

Greater visibility of psychologists of color in the profession facilitated the development and disbursement of research related to people of color

(APA, 2003). For example, in 1971, the National Institute of Mental Health (NIMH) established an Office of Minority Research; NIMH reorganized 15 years later to support research that included populations of color in all research. With financial and instrumental support from NIMH, organizations such as ABPsi and AAPA were able to support and publish research pertinent to populations of color. Additionally, interfacing with NIMH gave psychologists of color the opportunity to represent and increase visibility for multicultural issues within the profession.

Significant contributions to the multicultural psychology literature emerged from several counseling psychologists' commitment to enhancing mental health professionals' competence in working with clients of color (Constantine, 2002; Robinson & Morris, 2000). Sue and his colleagues' seminal work and development of a tripartite model of multicultural counseling competence (i.e., Sue et al., 1982) has laid the foundation for much of the existing literature on multicultural counseling (Constantine & Ladany, 2001). Sue and his colleagues defined the tripartite model in terms of counselors' (1) recognizing their personal attitudes and values around race and ethnicity, (2) developing their knowledge of diverse cultural worldviews and experiences, and (3) identifying effective skills in working with clients of color.

Ten years later, under the leadership of Dr. Thomas Parham, members of the Professional Standards Committee of the Association for Multicultural Counseling and Development (i.e., Sue, Arredondo, & McDavis, 1992) expanded the tripartite model to include three desired characteristics of multiculturally competent counselors: awareness of personal assumptions, values, and biases; understanding the worldviews of culturally diverse clients; and developing abilities to use and create culturally appropriate intervention strategies. The three counselor characteristics were crossed with the three dimensions of competence from the first iteration of the tripartite model to yield nine competency areas in which 31 total statements were offered. Arredondo and her colleagues (1996) produced a supplement to Sue et al.'s competencies that served to formally define constructs and competencies that had been hard to implement in the previous version.

The third major revision of the multicultural competencies (Sue et al., 1998) reflected major empirical and theoretical emphases in the literature, namely, research in racial and ethnic identity models (see Helms & Cook, 1999), and expanded the range of professional helping roles, such as social change agent and advocate (Atkinson, Thompson, & Grant, 1993). This was evident in the inclusion of three new competencies under the skills dimension, two of which speak to racial and cultural identity models and the third to adopting helping roles other than those of counselor or psychotherapist. Further, characteristics of multiculturally-competent organizations were described and operationalized (Sue et al., 1998). Eleven operationalization statements concerning multiculturally inclusive organizations stressed commitment to diversity in all levels of personnel (including formal and informal mentorship), mission statements, and action plans. These competencies promoted the inclusion of diversity agendas in all facets of organizational management such that culture was now regarded as central rather than peripheral in multicultural organizational settings. The third iteration of the tripartite model of multicultural counseling competence also underscored the role of psychologists in addressing the effects of interpersonal and institutional racism from meso-cosmic levels, including therapy and the classroom, to systemic levels that include the field of psychology itself (Sue et al., 1998).

FOUNDATIONAL PRINCIPLES OF THE MULTICULTURAL GUIDELINES

The APA Multicultural Guidelines are grounded in six principles that "articulate respect and inclusiveness for the national heritage of all groups, recognition of cultural contexts as defining forces for individuals' and groups' lived experiences, and the role of external forces such as historical, economic, and socio-political events" (APA, 2003, p. 382). In their philosophical underpinnings, the principles of the APA Multicultural Guidelines encourage psychologists to see themselves as potential leaders of social justice in teaching, research, and clinical capacities and as active advocates of multiculturalism against the deleterious effects of racism, discrimination, and oppression. The principles are designed to influence the planning and actualization of education, research, practice, and organizational change informed by multiculturalism. Although all of the principles encourage psychologists to reflect on their own professional stances, Principles 5 and 6 specifically address organizational and social change roles that psychologists may engage to benefit clients, students, trainees, and the broader society.

> *Principle 1:* Ethical conduct of psychologists is enhanced by knowledge of differences in beliefs and practices that emerge from socialization through racial and ethnic group affiliation and membership and how those beliefs and practices will necessarily affect the education, training, research, and practice of psychology.

In accordance with ethical principles related to respecting all individuals (APA, 1992: Principle D; APA, 2002: Principle E) and social responsibility (APA, 1992: Principle F; APA, 2002: Principle D), it is clear that greater knowledge of cultural differences will guide psychologists' understanding of their roles as teachers, trainers, researchers, and practitioners, such that their behavior in these capacities would reflect multicultural sensitivity. In particular, psychologists who engage social justice work that derives from knowledge of contextual influences on a group of marginalized individuals may exhibit appreciation and respect for others' broader social and cultural conditions.

> *Principle 2:* Understanding and recognizing the interface between individuals' socialization experiences based on ethnic and racial heritage can enhance the quality of education, training, practice, and research in the field of psychology.

Psychologists should be aware of how their own cultural identities might affect interpersonal dynamics in practice, teaching, training, and research contexts. Additionally, psychologists' understanding of collective experiences based in race and ethnicity may contribute to greater sensitivity to intra- and intercultural group dynamics.

> *Principle 3:* Recognition of the ways in which the intersection of racial and ethnic group membership with other dimensions of identity (e.g., gender, age, sexual orientation, disability, religion/spiritual orientation, educational attainment/experiences, and socioeconomic status) enhances the understanding and treatment of all people.

An appreciation of how cultural identities interface, in addition to recognition of within-group differences along varied dimensions of identity, can inform research, treatment, and organizational interventions for given cultural groups. The integration of various dimensions of identity may lead to richer understandings of individuals' experiences and contribute to complex and innovative research in psychology.

> *Principle 4:* Knowledge of historically derived approaches that have viewed cultural differences as deficits and have not valued certain social identities helps psychologists to understand the underrepresentation of ethnic minorities in the profession and affirms and values the role of ethnicity and race in developing personal identity.

Historical knowledge of the institutional uses of psychology to promote oppressive systems, such as academic segregation, institutionalization in mental illness facilities, slavery, and immigration restrictions, may lead psychologists to reflect on the systemic implications of research, treatment, conceptualization, and education models. Additionally, recognizing that traditional models of psychology and psychotherapy were derived in specific social contexts that may not have validated the humanity of people of color can allow psychologists to adopt or create novel approaches to psychology that may better suit clients' concerns.

> *Principle 5:* Psychologists are uniquely able to promote racial equity and social justice. This is aided by their awareness of their impact on others and the influence of their personal and professional roles in society.

Sensitivity to racism, oppression, and mechanisms of social injustice related to race and ethnicity affords psychologists opportunities to address inequality at individual, group, and political levels. For example, at the individual level, psychologists may work with clients in naming certain experiences as discriminatory and finding personal advocacy resources. Psychologists may be able to address injustices at the group level through encouraging collegial faculty members to recruit prospective graduate students of color into majority-White graduate programs. At the political level, psychologists may develop research programs that address psychological and academic benefits of affirmative action and use this research to promote public policy and law.

> *Principle 6:* Psychologists' knowledge about the roles of organizations, including employers and professional psychological associations, are potential sources of behavioral practices that encourage discourse, education and training, institutional change, and research and policy development that reflect rather than neglect cultural differences. Psychologists recognize that organizations can be gatekeepers or agents of the status quo, rather than leaders in a changing society with respect to multiculturalism.

Psychologists may be able to utilize their connections to organizations, specifically professional psychological associations, to promote multicultural initiatives and contribute to ongoing pushes for integrating multiculturalism. For example, groups of psychologists may become involved as consultants with secondary school educational boards to increase retention, graduation, and college enrollment rates of students of color. Further, psychologists may be involved in psychological organizations, such as the Society for the Psychological Study of Ethnic Minority Issues (APA, Division 45), to develop professional strategies that explicitly target enrollment, retention, and graduation rates of students of color at secondary and postsecondary educational levels.

THE MULTICULTURAL GUIDELINES

Guideline 1: Psychologists are encouraged to recognize that, as cultural beings, they may hold attitudes and beliefs that can detrimentally influence their perceptions of and interactions with individuals who are ethnically and racially different from themselves.

The APA Multicultural Guidelines state that interactions between any two people are multicultural in that individuals' cultural perspectives shape perceptions of life experiences (Arredondo et al., 1996; Sue & Sue, 2003). Knowledge of cultural influences on worldview orientations may inform psychologists' understanding of how their norms and values may contrast with those of clients, trainees, and research participants. Additionally, primary awareness of personal race-based stereotypes may allow psychologists the opportunity to reflect on the origin and reinforcement of these stereotypes on social and psychological levels, addressing how, when, and to whom stereotypes are conjured; this may be a critical step in developing cultural sensitivity. Psychologists are not immune from tendencies to differentiate in-groups from out-groups; however, it is when power is distributed unequally, favoring psychologists, that psychology may be a medium for exploitation, insult, and ignorance. Mental health professionals may de-emphasize racial and ethnic group membership through the adoption of color-blind approaches or the focus on universal aspects of human behavior over racial or ethnic differences. Values endorsing assimilation with the White majority group may be masked by a color-blind approach, though psychologists may be unaware of pernicious effects of color blindness, including maintaining a harmful status quo and ignoring potentially salient race-related factors (Ridley, 1995). Once aware of attitudes and values related to race, ethnicity, and culture, psychologists may process and reduce their biases through various strategies, including building a "we" conceptualization of human interaction from an "us versus them" conceptualization (Gaertner & Dovidio, 2000) or increasing contact with people of color to foster connection and empathy.

Guideline 2: Psychologists are encouraged to recognize the importance of multicultural sensitivity/responsiveness to, knowledge of, and understanding about ethnically and racially different individuals.

Cultural empathy for the experiences of people of color may foster psychologists' understandings of clients', students', and research participants' worldviews and perspectives. In particular, appreciation of others' perceptions of psychologists as cultural beings may facilitate their understanding of others' willingness to seek help and their level of trust (Terrell & Terrell, 1981). Knowledge of racial identity (e.g., Atkinson, Morten,

& Sue, 1998; Cross, 1971; Helms, 1984; Root, 1998), ethnic identity (e.g., Phinney, 1990, 1992), and spiritual identity (e.g., Myers et al., 1991) models may provide insight into the psychological experiences of people of color. Additionally, psychologists are encouraged to research the history of and legislative attention to culturally diverse populations to build contextual knowledge of potential experiences of clients, students, and research participants of color. The development of a cultural knowledge base in concert with cultural self-awareness may in turn facilitate cross-cultural communication between psychologists and clients, peers, students, research participants, and organizations.

Guideline 3: As educators, psychologists are encouraged to employ the constructs of multiculturalism and diversity in psychological education.

Psychologists as educators may not adequately address multiculturalism and diversity in psychological education out of fear of perpetuating stereotypes of portraying themselves as racist (Ridley, 1995), discomfort with multiculturalism (Helms & Cook, 1999; Sue & Sue, 2003), or the belief that multiculturalism is not a legitimate area of psychological study. Psychologists who operate from these beliefs may take a color-blind approach to race and culture, exhibit ethnocentric monoculturalism, or willfully omit the role of culture in psychological development and theory, respectively. Because multicultural training has been associated with the development of multicultural competence (e.g., Constantine & Gainor, 2001; Constantine, Juby, & Liang, 2001), trainees' competence in working with culturally diverse people may be compromised when educators do not address multicultural issues in psychology. Although training programs in applied fields of psychology increasingly have included multiculturalism in their curricula (Bernal & Castro, 1994; Hills & Strozier, 1992; Suarez-Balcazar, Durlak, & Smith, 1994), psychology educators may take steps toward comprehensive integration of multiculturalism in the classroom.

Support for multiculturalism and diversity in psychological education may be exhibited through the process, as well as the content, of education. Model programs of minority retention efforts can encourage psychologists to develop strategies to increase enrollment and retention of students of color in training programs. Psychology educators may include explicit statements valuing multiculturalism and diversity in the syllabi, offer experiential opportunities related to cultural diversity, and employ various modalities of teaching to reach students' varied learning styles. Last, psychology educators may participate in faculty committee searches for prospective faculty of color.

Guideline 4: Culturally sensitive psychological researchers are encouraged to recognize the importance of conducting culture-centered and ethical psychological research among persons from ethnic, linguistic, and racial minority backgrounds.

Psychologists are encouraged to pursue and respect research that is relevant to national demographic changes. Populations that are increasing rapidly include bilingual individuals and non-English speakers, aging people of color, and multiracial individuals (U.S. Census Bureau, 2003). However, limitations to multicultural research include the omission of culture as a nuisance variable, predominance of White participants or overuse of culturally diverse convenience samples, and the ignorance of within-group differences among populations of color (Quintana et al., 2001). To address these limitations, psychologists are encouraged to be mindful of potential culture-boundness in research design, assessment procedures, and interpretation of data (Quintana et al., 2001). Culture-centered researchers are encouraged to ground research design in theories that complement the worldview and experiences of the population of study. Additionally, culture-centered researchers use assessment strategies with specific cultural populations for which sound psychometric evidence is available and have knowledge of linguistic, conceptual, and functional equivalence of measurement constructs across diverse cultures (Rogler, 1999). Moreover, culture-centered researchers are encouraged to incorporate relevant cultural value-based hypotheses into interpretations of research results (Quintana et al., 2001). Last, culture-centered researchers report the racial, gender, and age characteristics of their sample and address possible limitations to the generalizability of their results based on sample characteristics.

Guideline 5: Psychologists are encouraged to apply culturally appropriate skills in clinical and other applied psychological practices.

Cultural self-awareness and knowledge about worldview variables and experiences of people of color predicate the application of culturally appropriate skills in psychological practice (Sue et al., 1992; Sue et al., 1998). Although formulaic skill sets specific to cultural groups may be counterproductive (Helms & Cook, 1999; Sue & Sue, 2003), the development of a multiculturally informed skill set may facilitate psychologists' adaptations of traditional interventions to suit clients' needs more appropriately. Eager practitioners who are motivated to implement culture specific interventions might find that a certain dimension of cultural identity is not necessarily salient for their clients in a certain therapeutic context. Similarly, visible group membership (e.g., race or ethnicity) may overshadow within-group variations (e.g., racial identity status) that may require further psychological processing. Moreover, psychological literature may not provide detailed intervention strategies for specific cultural populations, such as multiracial individuals or aging people of color. Psychologists are thus encouraged to adopt holistic and ecological perspectives of their clients, with reference to cultural and sociopolitical factors such as gender, generational status, language ability, parental migration histories, neighborhood of origin, educational attainment, and availability of community resources (Root, 1998) when considering potential intervention strategies. Additionally, it may be valuable for psychologists to include indigenous healers and community support networks, such as herbalists, religious groups, and respected elders, in intervention strategies (Atkinson et al., 1993).

> *Guideline 6:* Psychologists are encouraged to use organizational change processes to support culturally informed organizational (policy) development and practices.

The parameters of psychologists' roles may shift in accordance with the interests of the diversifying population of the United States. Psychological services that are constrained to an office setting might not adequately meet the mental health needs of individuals who are unfamiliar with social institutions (including mental health services), have limited English proficiency, or have experienced systematic discrimination or oppression in social institutions (Atkinson et al., 1993; Sue et al., 1998). Evidenced in the history of the multicultural movement in particular (Arredondo & Perez, 2003), psychologists have been instrumental in the development of professional and public policy changes related to experiences of people of color through their involvement in professional organizations. Culture-centered psychologists are encouraged to participate in local, state, and national legislative efforts devoted to promoting equality across dimensions of identity (Vera & Speight, 2003). However, despite the availability of models of multicultural organizational development (e.g., Sue, 2001; Sue et al., 1998), many psychologists have limited experience and training in social justice and organizational development issues (Prilleltensky & Prilleltensky, 2003). The APA Multicultural Guidelines provide examples of "best practice" approaches to organizational change, although the reflection of such approaches in organizational settings may be gradual.

CONCLUSION

The APA Multicultural Guidelines represent a hallmark in the movement toward including multicultural initiatives in the field of psychology. These

Multicultural Guidelines imply that all psychologists should engage in culturally relevant education, training, research, practice, and organizational development. Therefore, psychologists who traditionally had not endorsed these practices may experience direct or indirect pressure to do so; in other words, psychologists who endorse more traditional models of training, research, and practice may be taken out of their comfort zones. Training institutions also might need to employ multicultural consultants to address potential professional resistance. Further, it behooves psychologists to become more adept at understanding how to impact large organizational bodies with regard to multicultural organizational issues.

REFERENCES

American Psychological Association. (1992). *Ethical principles of psychologists and code of conduct.* Retrieved June 23, 2003, from http://www.apa.org/ethics /code1992.html.

American Psychological Association. (2002). *Ethical principles of psychologists and code of conduct.* Washington, DC: Author.

American Psychological Association. (2003). Guidelines on multicultural education, training, research, practice, and organizational change for psychologists. *American Psychologist, 58,* 377–402.

Arredondo, P., & Perez, P. (2003). Expanding multicultural competence through social justice leadership. *Counseling Psychologist, 31,* 282–289.

Arredondo, P., Toporek, R., Brown, S. P., Jones, J., Locke, D. C., Sanchez, J., et al. (1996). Operationalization of the multicultural counseling competencies. *Journal of Multicultural Counseling and Development, 24,* 42–78.

Atkinson, D. R., Morten, G., & Sue, D. W. (1998). *Counseling American minorities* (5th ed.). New York: McGraw-Hill.

Atkinson, D. R., Thompson, C. E., & Grant, S. K. (1993). A three-dimensional model for counseling racial/ethnic minorities. *Counseling Psychologist, 21,* 257–277.

Bernal, M. E., & Castro, F. G. (1994). Are clinical psychologists prepared for service and research with ethnic minorities? Report of a decade of progress. *American Psychologist, 49,* 797–805.

Constantine, M. G. (2002). Predictors of satisfaction with counseling: Racial and ethnic minority clients' attitudes toward counseling and ratings of their counselors' general and multicultural counseling competence. *Journal of Counseling Psychology, 49,* 255–263.

Constantine, M. G., & Gainor, K. A. (2001). Emotional intelligence and empathy: Their relation to school counselors' multicultural counseling knowledge and awareness. *Professional School Counseling, 5,* 131–137.

Constantine, M. G., Juby, H. L., & Liang, J. J.-C. (2001). Examining multicultural counseling competence and race-related attitudes among White marital and family therapists. *Journal of Marital and Family Therapy, 27,* 353–362.

Constantine, M. G., & Ladany, N. (2001). New visions for defining and assessing multicultural counseling competence. In J. G. Ponterotto, J. M. Casas, L. A. Suzuki, & C. M. Alexander (Eds.), *Handbook of multicultural counseling* (2nd ed., pp. 482–498). Thousand Oaks, CA: Sage.

Cross, W. E. (1971). The Negro-to-Black conversion experience: Toward a psychology of Black liberation. *Black World, 20,* 13–27.

Gaertner, S. L., & Dovidio, J. F. (2000). *Reducing intergroup bias: The common ingroup identity model.* Philadelphia: Brunner/Mazel.

Helms, J. E. (1984). Toward a theoretical explanation of the effect of race on counseling: A Black and White Model. *Counseling Psychologist, 12,* 153–165.

Helms, J. E., & Cook, D. A. (1999). *Using race and culture in counseling and psychotherapy: Theory and process.* Boston: Allyn & Bacon.

Hills, H. I., & Strozier, A. L. (1992). Multicultural training in APA-approved counseling psychology programs: A survey. *Professional Psychology: Research and Practice, 23,* 43–51.

Jones, N. A., & Smith, A. S. (2001). *Census 2000 brief: Two or more races.* U.S. Census Bureau. Retrieved May 30, 2003, from http://www.census.gov/prod/2001pubs/c2kbr01-6.pdf.

Myers, L. J., Speight, S. L., Highlen, P. S., Cox, C. I., Reynolds, A. L., Adams, E. M., et al. (1991). Identity development and worldview: Toward an optimal conceptualization. *Journal of Counseling and Development, 70,* 54–63.

Phinney, J. S. (1990). Ethnic identity in adolescents and adults: Review of research. *Psychological Bulletin, 198,* 499–514.

Phinney, J. S. (1992). The Multigroup Ethnic Identity Measure: A new scale for use with diverse groups. *Journal of Adolescent Research, 7,* 156–176.

Prilleltensky, I., & Prilleltensky, O. (2003). Synergies for wellness and liberation in counseling psychology. *Counseling Psychologist, 31,* 273–281.

Quintana, S. M., Troyano, N., & Taylor, G. (2001). Cultural validity and inherent challenges in quantitative methods for multicultural research. In J. G. Ponterotto, J. M. Casas, L. A. Suzuki, & C. M. Alexander (Eds.), *Handbook of multicultural counseling* (2nd ed., pp. 604–630). Thousand Oaks, CA: Sage.

Ridley, C. R. (1995). *Overcoming unintentional racism in counseling and therapy: A practitioner's guide to intentional intervention.* Thousand Oaks, CA: Sage.

Robinson, D. T., & Morris, J. R. (2000). Multicultural counseling: Historical contexts and current training considerations. *Western Journal of Black Studies, 29,* 235–249.

Rogler, L. H. (1999). Methodological sources of cultural insensitivity in mental health research. *American Psychologist, 54,* 424–433.

Root, M. P. P. (1998). Resolving "other" status: Identity development of biracial individuals. In P. B. Organista, K. M. Chun, & G. Marin (Eds.), *Readings in ethnic psychology* (pp. 100–122). New York: Routledge.

Suarez-Balcazar, Y., Durlak, J. A., & Smith, C. (1994). Multicultural training practices in community psychology programs. *American Journal of Community Psychology, 22,* 785–798.

Sue, D. W. (2001). Multidimensional facets of cultural competence. *Counseling Psychologist, 29,* 790–821.

Sue, D. W., Arredondo, P., & McDavis, R. J. (1992). Multicultural counseling competencies and standards: A call to the profession. *Journal of Multicultural Counseling and Development, 20,* 64–88.

Sue, D. W., Bernier, J. B., Durran, M., Feinberg, L., Pedersen, P., Smith, E., et al. (1982). Position paper: Cross-cultural counseling competencies. *Counseling Psychologist, 10,* 45–52.

Sue, D. W., Bingham, R. P., Porche-Burke, L., & Vasquez, M. (1999). The diversification of psychology: A multicultural revolution. *American Psychologist, 54,* 1061–1069.

Sue, D. W., Carter, R. T., Casas, J. M., Fouad, N. A., Ivey, A. E., Jensen, M., et al. (1998). *Multicultural counseling competencies: Individual and organizational development.* Thousand Oaks, CA: Sage.

Sue, D. W., & Sue, D. (2003). *Counseling the culturally diverse* (4th ed.). Hoboken, NJ: Wiley.

Terrell, F., & Terrell, S. L. (1981). An inventory to measure cultural mistrust among Blacks. *Western Journal of Black Studies, 5,* 180–184.

United States Census Bureau. (2003). *National population estimates: Characteristics.* Retrieved June 28, 2003, from http://eire.census.gov/popest/data/national/tables/asro/NAEST2002-ASRO-.04.php.

Vera, E. M., & Speight, S. L. (2003). Multicultural competence, social justice, and counseling psychology: Expanding our roles. *Counseling Psychologist, 31,* 253–272.

PART II

Applying the Multicultural Guidelines in Clinical Practice

CHAPTER 2

Culturally Sensitive Assessment, Diagnosis, and Guidelines

GARGI ROYSIRCAR

THE COST CONSCIOUSNESS of a medical model frequently offers homogenization as a cheap substitute for efficiency. In fact, a recent review of managed care practices affecting professional psychology acknowledged preoccupation with diagnosis, suggesting that symptom checklists may replace testing and assessment (Sanchez & Turner, 2003). Multicultural assessment, on the other hand, decries cookbook procedures and superficial formulations because these are more likely to generate stereotypes than usable psychological profiles of racial and ethnic minority individuals. When multicultural assessment accompanies standard tests and test batteries, it reduces bias and maintains relevancy for all clients. However, to conduct multicultural assessment, psychologists have to be knowledgeable of culturally sensitive assessment research (see Lonner, 1985; Okazaki & Sue, 1995) and apply multicultural assessment practice models (e.g., Hays, 1996; Ridley, Li, & Hill, 1998; Roysircar-Sodowsky & Kuo, 2001). This chapter is organized around three primary issues: (1) the use of cultural data in the assessment process; (2) validity issues in the use of standardized tests with culturally diverse individuals, given that the validity of tests for people of color is a major controversy in professional psychology; and (3) brief descriptions of multicultural assessment practice models.

PSYCHOLOGISTS' MYTHS ABOUT ASSESSMENT

Psychologists' myths about assessment need to be addressed at the outset. Multicultural assessment and measurement is held responsible for research deficiencies, which, detractors argue, lead to a lack of main-stream consensus on the value of multicultural training. This blame attribution ignores the acknowledged operation of bias in individual professional judgment (Turk & Salovey, 1988) and flagrant racism among practitioners and in institutional structures (e.g., Rollock & Gordon, 2000). This blame orientation arises from a resistance to multicultural theory's premise that clients come with values-based assumptions, world-views, cultural socialization, racism experiences, acculturation versus enculturation conflicts, and culture-bound mental health issues and help-seeking attitudes.

Sometimes a distinction is made between assessment that is taught in the standard objective, projective, and intelligence testing courses and multicultural assessment, which is taught in a diversity course. In the standard training, the underlying assumption is that there is some capacity that psychologists possess that is not culturally based; that is, psychologists are universalists. On the other hand, the diversity course covers the thoughts of social scientists (e.g., Dovidio, 2001; Steele, 1997) and psychologists of color, in particular (e.g., Malgady, 1996; Trimble, Helms, & Root, 2003), who consider the work of all psychologists to be cultural, with mainstream methods and constructs representing one particular set of cultural perspectives, the Euro-American worldview or Western biological perspectives that have overlooked the effects of racial and cultural influences. From this point of view, all human behavior must be understood in a cultural context. The ensuing corollary is that multicultural issues are not simply an "add-on" to a "noncultural" foundation of human behavior. All assessment questions are influenced by the psychologist's culture and feelings of comfort with his or her own reference group. Multiculturally competent psychologists know that their worldview is neither universal nor objective, and therefore, they are always aware of their own cultural assumptions (Ibrahim, Roysircar-Sodowsky, & Ohnishi, 2001; Roysircar-Sodowsky & Frey, 2003; D. W. Sue, Arredondo, & McDavis, 1992). Psychologists examine the theories or models they use that bias their assessment and interpretations in a particular direction (Roysircar, 2003) and incorporate assessment methods that complement diverse worldviews and lifestyles of their clients.

Stanley Sue (1999) says that selective attention is paid to a limited set of scientific principles that overemphasize the importance of internal validity consideration in research. Methodological foci define elegance by the clarity of causal effects of one variable on another, being relatively negligent of external validity or the generality of findings to specific settings and populations. Thus, there is an overreliance on comparative methodology in psychology's experimental designs. A balanced attention to quantitative and qualitative sources of data, with neither privileged over the other, is underutilized in assessment but is remedied in the practice models presented here.

BARRIERS TO MULTICULTURAL ASSESSMENT

There are four elements of the assessment and diagnosis process that affect the assessment of diverse individuals in the United States. First, the *Diagnostic and Statistical Manual of Mental Disorders,* fourth edition, text revised (American Psychiatric Association, 2000), outlines the psychiatric nosology that forms the foundation on which diagnoses are contingent in the United States. A narrow orientation toward *DSM* diagnoses can be an obstacle in the assessment of people who have marginalized status. Second, the generalizability of the widely used standardized test, the Minnesota Multiphasic Personality Inventory-2 (MMPI-2; Graham, 2000), is questionable with regard to its empirically keyed correlates relative to cultural diversity. Similarly, the multicultural applications of the Rorschach Comprehensive System (CS) and the Thematic Apperception Test (TAT) have not been adequately addressed. Third, the clinician, who always faces the risk of being influenced by bias, is a potential barrier to accurate assessment. Finally, the multiple socially constructed identities of clients and their related cultural and sociopolitical experiences can also present a challenge in assessment.

The American Psychological Association's landmark document, the "Guidelines on Multicultural Education, Training, Research, Practice, and Organizational Change for Psychologists" (APA, 2003), legitimizes a psychologist's professional role as engaged in promoting racial equity and social justice and provides six guidelines for implementation. General research issues relevant to the acquisition of an adequate and sufficient ethnic minority knowledge basis are emphasized as well as issues more specific to assessment research and practice. For instance, psychologists should be knowledgeable about the linguistic equivalence of instruments used with individuals who have limited English-language proficiency and also report cultural equivalence data when using instruments across diverse populations, thus attesting to the instrument's generalizability. When making interpretations, psychologists should consider cultural hypotheses as possible explanations for test findings.

Similarly, psychologists should examine the effects of acculturation, racism experience, and racial identity, using such information for descriptive purposes that become an important part in conceptualizing problems and perhaps in selecting tests (Roysircar-Sodowsky & Kuo,

2001). Assessing the client's perception of the source of the problem and cultural acceptability of the symptom is also part of a more multiculturally competent assessment process. When diversity is seen as extraneous to someone's personality, behavior is misidentified and mistakenly pathologized. Or, if diversity becomes an exclusive focus, people of color are assumed to be similar, within-group differences are ignored, and behavior is misidentified and underpathologized.

THE *DIAGNOSTIC AND STATISTICAL MANUAL*

A concern has been expressed (Fox, 1994) that a narrowing focus on *DSM* diagnosis would curtail the use of a full array of instruments and that "the continued growth and development of professional psychology may ultimately stand or fall on the integrity of the educational system that prepares future generations of practitioners" (p. 200). The *DSM-IV-TR* (American Psychiatric Association, 2000) has the capacity to perpetuate false assumptions in its relative lack of a comprehensive delineation of multicultural variability. This lack leaves the *DSM* vulnerable to aiding in the misdiagnosis, misprognosis, and mistreatment of minority clients. The manual exemplifies the cliché of trying to fit a square peg in a round hole. Many of the *DSM* diagnostic criteria are based on Euro-American social norms, making it difficult to use to identify psychopathology in someone from another culture. For instance, a Muslim woman may be misdiagnosed Agoraphobic because she does not leave her home, which is likely the result of generational influences of conservative Islamic societies in the Saudi Arabian Peninsula and Northern Africa (e.g., Saudi Arabia, Sudan, Somalia) forbidding women to leave the house unescorted. Cultures cope differently with internal and external stressors (Kuo, Roysircar, & Newby-Clark, 2004). Anxiety content varies across cultures; not knowing this, an *ataque de nervios* of a Latina might be misdiagnosed as panic attacks. Asians express anxiety through somatic symptoms and European Americans through cognitive-behavioral symptoms. Japanese and Koreans may develop persistent and excessive fears of offending others in social situations instead of feeling embarrassed, shy, or lacking in assertiveness. Loss of face may result in suicidal attempts by a Chinese owing to status loss or social humiliation rather than because of self-concept and interpersonal concerns. To compensate for the *DSM*'s delimited nosology, clinicians can include in their assessment the framework of ADDRESSING (Age and generational influences, Developmental and acquired Disabilities, Religion and spiritual orientation, Ethnicity, Socioeconomic status, Sexual orientation, Indigenous heritage, National origin, and Gender), as proposed by Hays (1996). Hays suggested that each of these sociocultural contexts of clients should be noted in assessment to arrive at a comprehensive report.

On the other hand, uneducated sensitivity to cultural variations can lead to underpathologizing (Type II error) when psychopathology is, in fact, the cause of behavior but is incorrectly labeled as normative for the client's culture. Take the case of an adult, U.S.-born, well-educated, second-generation Asian Indian woman who financially depends on her immigrant parents while living an expensive city life. She lies to and manipulates her parents and is either confrontational or attention seeking with her extended relatives. She makes psychosomatic and malingering presentations that prevent her from seeking employment. She appears to be envious or complaining of her second-generation cousins, who lead productive and successful lives and who also keep away from her, outside of family events. Determining that this person's family-related issues stem from systemic interdependence in Asian Indian family centeredness is an underdiagnosis.

Although underdiagnosis does occur, overpathologizing is far more common in multicultural assessment. A female Vietnamese refugee appears to a clinician to be suffering from depression. The clinician is failing to take into account cultural variations that exist in Buddhist culture, wherein women are taught to be modest, reticent, and low-keyed, especially in the presence of men. This woman's worldview includes a spiritual belief in fatalism and is, at the same time, silently resistant to Western psychotherapy because of her faith in indigenous herbal medicines, acupuncture, and prayer. She is reluctant to divulge information about her trauma because of her political immigrant status and fears that she may be sent back to her former country if she reveals mental illness (Huynh & Roysircar, 2004). In addition, she cannot speak English, has no medical insurance, and is worried about health care costs, transportation to the hospital, and child care during hospital visits. This client is experiencing the stressors of cultural barriers, low income, and limited health care access. She is not necessarily depressed. On the other hand, an adolescent Croatian refugee who was a child soldier in ethnic-cleansing wars is trapped in his lived experience of many cultures and identities, which is causing conflict in his family of first-generation immigrant parents and his refugee community, who have been his primary sources of support and grounding through war, escape, and relocation (Roysircar, 2004). He takes pride in his previous undesirable behaviors and hatred of Serbian Muslims. In this case, cultural identity issues are related to Posttraumatic Stress Disorder (PTSD) and depression (Roysircar). Internal cultural conflicts, confusions, or alienation, as well as the rejection of one's family over value preferences, are also related to depression and low self-esteem in Asian Americans (Roysircar-Sodowsky & Maestas, 2000).

The *DSM* describes 25 forms of behaviors that are locality-specific troubling experiences, delimited to certain societies; these are known as culture-bound syndromes. There are also symptoms that may be related to a particular cultural context (e.g., fainting spells, aches and pains), but the related *DSM* disorder (V-codes, e.g., acculturation problems, noncompliance with treatment, religious or spiritual problems, parent-child relation problem; Axis I disorder, e.g., PTSD) may not be a culture-bound syndrome. The challenge for the clinician is to be able to distinguish psychopathology from culture-related conditions and psychopathology that is expressed through cultural symptoms. The first step is to become familiar with the culture-bound syndromes and then to learn culturally appropriate questioning for the person being interviewed by consulting with ethnic experts.

The *DSM* guidelines for screening cultural variants and its cultural formulation outline are also not easily accessible. These are presented in an appendix, not in the traditional multiaxial system. Managed care companies expect a diagnosis in the first session, leaving the clinician very little time to differentiate psychopathology from culture-related conditions. Another obstacle is that many instruments do not require an assessment of cultural variables. Cultural variables are not routinely screened for in the typical clinical setting. A final obstacle is that insurance companies do not reimburse clinicians who do assessment of cultural variables or who request long-term therapy for the treatment of the complex interface of psychotherapy and culture (S. Sue, 1998). The cultural formulation outline is helpful in distinguishing cultural variables, but there are many barriers to the use of this *DSM* outline (Paniagua, 2000).

CULTURAL VALIDITY OF PERSONALITY TESTING

The fact that the MMPI-2 has been the most widely used structured test of personality or psychopathology for the past 60 years makes it understandable that its use as a multicultural assessment tool is of interest. Although the effort to re-standardize the MMPI-2 in 1989 was ostensibly aimed at increasing the representativeness of the normative sample, important discrepancies still exist. With the rate of immigration in this country and the high birthrate of racial and ethnic minority groups, the 1980 census data, in which 82% of the population was White, do not even approximate current census data (U.S. Census, 2003). Thus, the 1989 re-standardization of the MMPI-2 did not eliminate bias.

For example, there is evidence of bias at the level of mean score differences between African Americans and Whites on clinical, validity, and content scales of the MMPI-2 (Handel & Ben-Porath, 2000). However, the

MMPI-2 clinical interpretation is not based on normative differences, but rather on the empirical/external correlates of the test's scales, high-point pairs, and code types. Therefore, the prediction of significant variance in relevant extra-test criteria (i.e., empirical correlates) would be the gold standard of evidence of consistent absence of bias. Such a prediction would descriptively take into account the acculturation and heterogeneity of subgroups within an ethnic group.

Let's first examine the empirical correlates themselves. The construct validity of the empirical correlates is limited. The external correlates have been guided by the European American dominant culture's psychiatric nosology. To the extent that external correlates are reflective of the nosology of the U.S. culture, findings that suggest generalization of external correlates (or for that matter, cross-cultural differences between mean scores) are simply pointing to the correlation between the test and the system of thinking and categorization that the test has been validated by. For example, an external criterion is therapist ratings, and the *DSM-IV-TR* and standard textbooks of psychopathology presumably guide the ratings of therapists whose training included such literature. Because the interpretation of the scores on the MMPI-2 is based on the same system of understanding psychopathology, we would expect that the therapist ratings would validate the test scores in question. The generalizability of those ratings would likely not be across cultures, in which the manifestation and categorization of mental illness may be quite different. The first priority of establishing the generalizability of a measure to a culture other than the one for which it was constructed should be the demonstration of the equivalence of psychiatric nosology (Nichols, Padilla, & Gomez-Maqueo, 2000). Current multicultural thought, which argues the lack of construct equivalency of psychiatric constructs specifically (e.g., panic attacks, social phobia, depression, PTSD) and psychological constructs (e.g., self-esteem) in general (Roysircar-Sodowsky & Kuo, 2001), makes it seem likely that the use of the MMPI-2 with minority individuals will require knowledge of such disparities and a related capacity to know when it is appropriate to use the test and how interpretation must be informed by client contexts.

A common recommendation in multicultural research is the use of moderator variables as sources of cultural information affecting test interpretation (APA, 2003). "Correction of Culture," suggested by Cuellar (2000), was derived by comparing acculturation scores with normative data to provide evidence of the magnitude of statistical difference occurring as a function of cultural adaptation issues. These suggested statistical controls, however, need to be presented as formulae, as in the case of the MMPI-2 K scale, which practitioners can use for profile corrections and interpretation. Research is needed so that cultural corrections are possible to calculate accurately. Given the initial status of suggested statistical controls, the present author focuses instead on practice steps that may be taken to make assessment more valid with racial and ethnic minorities with corresponding justifications.

MULTICULTURAL TESTING STANDARDS

Psychological testing is frequently used in school systems to determine placement, to screen for learning disabilities, and to assess for psychopathology. Pedersen and Carey (2003) found that often schools administer tests that have the potential to influence a child's academic placement and other important decisions regarding a child's education. The authors thus refer to this as "high-stakes" testing. The multicultural issue in this setting is that many times there are no accommodations, such as language accommodation for non-English-speaking children, in the testing process. As a result of the lack of accommodation, the child receives poor test scores that are not accurate indicators of the child's true abilities or potential. Part of the reason minority students are at risk for dropout, suspension, and special education identification is the common mismatch between the student's and the test's cultures.

Projective tests, such as the TAT and the Rorschach, rely on storytelling and verbal articulations that rely on language. This response format is biased against individuals who speak English as a second language (ESL). Research shows that Hispanic and Black children have been evaluated as being less verbally fluent, less behaviorally mature, and more pathological than White children related to their performance on projective tests; however, there is strong research indicating that minority children are articulate when tested with culturally oriented instruments, such as Tell Me a Story (Constantino & Malgady, 1996).

When clinicians use standard tests in assessment, they need to be concerned with fairness in testing. A crucial component for multicultural assessment training is the development of multicultural assessment practice standards. The following standards assist with fairness in testing:

- To thoroughly explore fairness in testing, a clinician must consider the technical properties of the tests used; the various ways test reports are written; case law, regulations, and statutes that govern test use; and remedies for harmful practices such as biased testing.
- Because reports and inferences resulting from test findings can significantly impact an individual's life, the interactions between the

clinician and the client and the clinician's test interpretation are as important as the technical aspects of testing.

- Fairness in testing includes consideration of possible test bias (due to test content, test responses, and a lack of correlation between test and criterion scores), equitable treatment during the testing process, and evaluation of the meaning of outcome differences across groups.
- Testing individuals who have insufficient proficiency in the language of the test will introduce construct-irrelevant components into the testing process and will thus necessitate a cautious approach to the interpretation of test results.
- When testing bilingual individuals, an individual's level of acculturation can have an impact on test results; individuals who know two languages may test poorly in both (e.g., an ESL student who is not formally educated in his or her native language); the cultural and linguistic background of the examiner will affect the performance of an examinee; only a professionally trained bilingual examiner should test individuals with limited proficiency in the language of the test.
- A computer-generated interpretation of test results is acceptable when a clinician is familiar with the test and is able to evaluate the computer report and when the clinician is certain that the test norms and empirical correlates are appropriate for the client tested.
- When interpreting reported scores for a given test, it is particularly important to know the date of administration relative to the established norms for the test and whether the client gives feedback that the test score is an accurate reflection of his or her abilities.
- Even when traditional assessment tools are used with caution, they are used in combination with a clinical interview and observation.

For more specific standards on the prevention of bias in assessment, readers are referred to *Standards for educational and psychological testing* (American Educational Research Association, American Psychological Association, & National Council on Measurement in Education, 1999). Clinicians without such specific standards for how to take culture into account in the diagnostic process develop their own notions, which are often inaccurate and biased (Ridley, Hill, Thompson, & Ormerod, 2001; Roysircar-Sodowsky & Kuo, 2001).

In addition to providing multiculturally appropriate testing, it is suggested that the initial assessment of cultural issues be done on the intake form that the clinician completes after the first interview. Such an intake form is illustrated in the Appendix on page 33. The suggested sample represents a response to the need for standard forms that can evaluate culture in assessment.

CLINICIAN BIAS

To comprehend the gravity of bias, it is important to discuss the prevalence of racial discrimination in society. Klonoff, Landrine, and Ullman (1999) investigated discrimination as well as generic stressors experienced by African Americans. Racial discrimination was a more powerful predictor of psychiatric symptoms than were generic stressors. A structural equation model supported racial discrimination as being a latent construct consisting of three indicators: recent racist events, lifetime racist events, and appraised racist events. A common perception of psychologists regarding race variability is that low social class accounts for significant variance in Black mental health. In the Klonoff et al. study, the participants belonged to various class levels, and class was not a significant predictor. Gender, however, played a significant role in who presented with symptoms.

Racism in the general society is paralleled by race bias in clinical judgment. African American and Hispanic patients were less likely than White patients to be diagnosed as having a psychotic disorder but, in a contradictory way, were also more likely than Whites to be diagnosed with Schizophrenia (Garb, 1997). This finding was consistent even when measures of psychopathology indicated that a diagnosis of Schizophrenia was not warranted (Garb, 1997). Compared to other patients, African Americans received prescriptions for psychiatric medication significantly more often (Garb, 1997). Even though race was not significantly correlated with violence, Black and America Indian inmates were predicted to be more violent than White inmates (Garb, 1997). Clinicians were less apt to diagnose clients when they were of upper-socioeconomic status. High socioeconomic status was also predictive of a better prognosis than low socioeconomic status, even when data did not support this finding. Not surprising, middle-class clients were more likely to be referred to insight therapy, and lower-class clients were more likely to be referred for supportive therapy (Garb, 1997). Finally, when clinicians were unaware of the effect of multicultural bias, the likelihood increased that they would misunderstand and misrepresent their clients' presenting problems.

Bias creates a range of countertransference in the clinician. Biases may predispose the clinician to minimize issues of importance to the client, experience difficulty maintaining boundaries, avoid setting appropriate limits, enable the client to continue maladaptive ways of functioning, and avoid discussing areas that make the therapist uncomfortable. Some proposed areas of focus in bias prevention are awareness of historical influences (oppression of minority groups, counseling theory being based on European American culture), experiential learning through exposure-immersion experiences with culturally diverse individuals and in minority communities (Roysircar, 2004b), recognition of the client's uniqueness within his or her culture, understanding cultural and individual differ-ences as strengths, and developing a social justice advocacy orientation for work with minority clients (Roysircar, 2004a; Roysircar-Sodowsky & Kuo, 2001; Sodowsky, Kuo-Jackson, & Loya, 1996).

SOCIALLY DEFINED IDENTITIES AND RELATED EXPERIENCES OF CLIENTS

Race, ethnicity, and culture are salient group-specific factors in individual identities. Each context creates stresses and conflicts owing to the domi-nant culture's interface with a minority person's internalized identities. The conflicts that arise between a client's diversity and the mainstream Euro-American culture undoubtedly will emerge during assessment and treatment. Therefore, it is critical that clinicians understand the effects of the socially constructed meanings of race, ethnicity, and culture (APA, 2003) on clients and include these in assessment if suggestive of client stresses (e.g., in the *DSM* Axis IV). Or the clinician could make clinical hy-potheses regarding the relationship between the client's expressed racial or ethnic identity concerns or acculturation difficulties with the obtained clinical profile. Briefly, race is the meaning one gives to physical constructs, such as skin color; ethnicity is an individual's belonging to a specific group and abiding by that group's traditions; and culture is the values, morals, customs, and beliefs that are transmitted generationally among a group of people (APA, 2003).

Clinicians must certainly understand various models of ethnic identity (Roysircar-Sodowsky & Maestas, 2000) and racial identity (Atkinson, Morten, & Sue, 1998; Choney & Behrens, 1996; Cross, 1995; Helms, 1995) to discover the extent to which individuals can be differentially de-scribed, relative to their reference group identity, as well as to determine which identity schemas are dominant and recessive for a client in partic-ular contexts. The goal of standard assessment is to capture individual differences. Therefore, reporting a minority client's identity characteris-tics, whether congruent or discrepant with each other or whether gener-alizable or uniquely particular, is the employment of "dynamic sizing," as recommended by S. Sue (1998). This is the ability to recognize "when to generalize and be inclusive and when to individualize and be exclusive" (p. 466). For example, a client may see her status as a lesbian as a betrayal of her ethnic identity or of her identification with a religion that accords higher status to reproductive sexuality (Greene, 1994). If unaware of a client's internalization of criticisms from his or her own ethnic group and of conflicts among the client's various group-related identities, it will be difficult, if not impossible, to do accurate assessment and, conse-quently, to promote positive development. At the same time, although a racial or ethnic minority client is vulnerable to conflicts related to minority-majority societal exchanges, the client may have developed certain strengths and resilience due to his or her status as a member of multiple oppressed groups (Greene, 1994). These potential strengths and level of resilience need to be qualitatively assessed.

PRACTICE GUIDELINES FOR MULTICULTURAL ASSESSMENT

In multicultural assessment training, trainees first practice applying multicultural professional guidelines (e.g., APA, 2003; Council of National Psychological Associations for the Advancement of Ethnic Minority Issues, 2002) to published research and the testing reports that they review. Then, when doing their assessment assignments, they follow the professional guidelines as well as the assessment procedures provided by multicultural practice models. Several independent sources of multicultural assessment guidelines and recommendations are now available (Ponterotto, Gretchen, & Chauhan, 2001; Roysircar-Sodowsky & Kuo, 2001; Ridley et al., 1998; Ridley et al., 2001). These are comprehensive assessment initiatives. The consequences for not obtaining adequate data increase the risk of diagnostic error and, in the end, are costly for the client, the family, and the health care system.

Ridley et al. (1998) propose the use of the Multicultural Assessment Procedure (MAP), which has four phases. Phase 1 includes the clinical interview and the Person-in-Culture Interview, which asks clients about their cultural background. It is important during Phase 1 for clinicians to be aware of transference, countertransference, ethical obligations, and their own cultural bias and experiences. Phase 2 consists of interpreting information that is evidence of actual cultural differences of the client, as well as information that is idiographic to the client. The clinician comes up with working hypotheses about the effects of the client's culture on presenting issues and where the two (culture and mental health) converge. The clinician examines which behavior is representative or adaptive in an individual's culture and which is not. Phase 3 involves psychological testing and rules out medical conditions to further differentiate cultural bias. All collected data are incorporated and compared to clinical impressions and the *DSM* criteria. Phase 4 involves an assessment decision. It is important for a clinician to be open to more information on the client's culture to be incorporated into the clinical picture later on. Ridley et al. emphasize that to minimize bias in the assessment process, it is important to recognize the role of the clinician and assessment tools as contributing to assessment bias, but also that the clinician be willing to recognize the cultural experience of each individual and how it affects the clinician's approach to the assessment process. However, the MAP does not address the *DSM*'s culture-bound syndromes, guidelines for cultural formulations, culturally sensitive V-codes, and the inclusion of Axis IV diagnosis on issues of discrimination.

Elaborating further on their practice model, Ridley et al. (2001) emphasized an idiographic assessment perspective for evaluating clinical hypotheses. Client evaluation is done in terms of core salient and subsidiary multiple identities related to gender, class, race or ethnicity, age, and sexual orientation. A holistic appraisal is done of the client's assets, limitations, resources, vulnerabilities, and coping styles. There is recognition of trauma effects and psychological systems from a variety of sources, including physical factors and other psychological conditions, which is similar to the approach of the biopsychosocial model. Attention is paid to the impact of bias on clinical judgment and differential diagnosis, particularly concerning race, gender, and social class.

Roysircar-Sodowsky and Kuo (2001) include in their hierarchical assessment procedures the importance of establishing rapport, explaining assessment methods to the client, consulting with professionals from the client's ethnic background to interpret and explain obtained results, and seeking feedback from clients on the assessment results. Roysircar-Sodowsky and Kuo's procedures emphasize a critical attitude to standard tests, eschew computerized reports, and advocate the use of multiple methods, including self-description, behavioral ratings, record reviews, and interviews with family members. Psychologists pretest for the appropriate use of standard instruments for hypothesis generation and testing, as well as for the selection of specific tests for referral problems and constructs of interest. For translated tests, an examination of response formats and validity issues is recommended. Use of extra-assessment information available in the research literature to understand and interpret test results is mandated, which procedure is illustrated through an extensive case example. Sodowsky et al. (1996) discuss psychologists' internal desire for self-exploration in the context of their own culture as well their professionally based searches for a politically based ideology because social justice and consciousness are fundamental to multicultural counseling competencies.

Ponterotto et al. (2001) say that multicultural assessment training is synonymous with cultural identity assessment, using quantitative and qualitative tools. The quantitative tools include standard nomothetic instruments with accompanying guidelines for the selection, use, and application of approximately 100 self-report measures of cultural identity. The authors provide a review of qualitative, idiographic cultural identity stage assessment models, using the *DSM-IV* cultural formulation outline

(American Psychiatric Association, 2000), as well as five semistructured interview models. The contents, order, and numbers of stages in identity assessment models varied considerably with regard to conceptual origins, level of abstraction, degree of comprehensiveness, breadth, and inclusiveness. Ponterotto et al. integrated these models into a descriptive context of provider responsibilities and awareness of power differentials as a consequence of clinician self-exploration and self-scrutiny consistent with the multicultural counseling competencies. This holistic idiographic framework can be used for a culturally relevant diagnostic interview process organized by major areas of client worldview/perception of problem, client's family background, cultural explanations of the presenting illness, and cultural elements of the provider-client relationship. Ponteroto et al. suggested that cultural identity is related to symptom manifestation, diagnosis, and test bias, which has received some initial support in the research (e.g., Cuellar, 2000; Cuellar & Roberts, 1997; Hovey & King, 1997; Klonoff & Landrine, 1999; Kwan & Sodowsky, 1997; Rodriguez, Myers, Morris, & Cardoza, 2000) and in this chapter's case examples. While awaiting generalizability evidence both in research and in case studies, the present author suggests that cultural identity descriptive information is an important part of conceptualizing problems and in selecting tests (see the Appendix for an intake form that includes cultural information).

Does the existence of systematic procedures guarantee that professionals will be committed to using them and will utilize them fully? Their use will probably increase if assessment instructors train and supervise students in their use. Research is needed to test the outcome of multicultural assessment procedures, that is, the extent to which diagnostic error is reduced or prevented and the extent to which the decision-making process is informed and enhanced.

CONCLUSION

Multicultural assessment is a necessary supplement or complement that extends the range and credibility of standard assessment. Assessment competence training needs to include a wider variety of assessment methods, focusing on clinical judgment to move beyond instrument-based technology efficiency, as well as legitimizing a role for multicultural assessment. It is the responsibility of assessment instructors to understand and respect cultural differences and understand multicultural competence as a multifaceted construct (APA, 2003; D. W. Sue et al., 1992); increase awareness in trainees of bias sources and strategies for bias reduction; increase familiarity with psychometric and generalizability information relevant to tests used with multicultural and international clients; expose students to standard and multicultural assessment simultaneously; and supervise practice with multicultural assessment.

APPENDIX

Clinician Intake Form

Clinician: _____ Intake date: _____ Time: _____

Client Name: _____ Prefers to be called: _____

Address: _____ DOB: _____ Sex: ( ) Male   ( ) Female

Phone (Home): _____ (Work): _____

Referral source: _____

Reason for referral or self-referral:

_____

_____

Treatment history (Have you been in therapy before? Recently? Treatment status? Currently taking medication? Name and dosage):

_____

_____

Impression of risk: ( ) No/Low   ( ) Medium   ( ) High

(Explain) _____

_____

Impression of fit, including attitudinal fit, with you, the clinician:
( ) Yes   ( ) No   ( ) Unsure

(Explain) _____

_____

Treatment options discussed (circle):

Individual   Family   Couple   Group   Home care   Psychoeducational program

Assessments to be completed at intake: _____

Other suggested assessment measures: _____

Family history important to client

Education: _____

Parents: _____

Siblings: _____

Extended family: _____

Physical abuse: _____

Sexual abuse: _____

Immigration: _____

Relocations: _____

Trauma survival: _____

Relationships important to client: _____

Qualitative assessments/descriptions:

1. English language fluency: _____
2. Individualistic-collectivistic worldview orientation: _____
3. Acculturation adaptation (integrated/bicultural; assimilated; traditional/ separated; marginalized): _____
4. Acculturative stress: _____
5. Perceived discrimination/racism: _____
6. Family/extended family concerns: _____
7. Intergenerational issues: _____
8. Dating concerns: _____
9. Intimacy concerns: _____
10. Interpersonal relationship concerns: _____
11. Gender role concerns: _____
12. GLBT concerns: _____
13. Education concerns: _____
14. Work concerns: _____
15. Coping style: _____
16. Social/network resources: _____
17. Loss of face issues: _____
18. Issues of privacy/confidentiality: _____
19. *DSM-IV* culture-bound syndromes: _____
20. Cultural symptoms of *DSM-IV* disorders: _____
21. *DSM-IV* cultural V-codes: _____
22. *DSM-IV* Axis IV cultural stressors: _____

Case conceptualization: _____

_____

_____

Comments: _____

_____

_____

Clinician Name: _____ Signature: _____ Date: _____

REFERENCES

American Educational Research Association, American Psychological Association, & National Council on Measurement in Education. (1999). *Standards for educational and psychological testing.* Washington, DC: Authors.

American Psychiatric Association. (2000). *The diagnostic and statistical manual* (4th ed., text rev.). Washington, DC: Author.

American Psychological Association. (2003). Guidelines on multicultural education, training, research, practice, and organizational change for psychologists. *American Psychologist, 58,* 377–402.

Atkinson, D. R., Morten, G., & Sue, D. W. (1998). *Counseling American minorities* (5th ed.). New York: McGraw-Hill.

Choney, S. K., & Behrens, J. T. (1996). Development of the Oklahoma Racial Attitudes Scale Preliminary Form (ORAS-P). In G. R. Sodowsky & J. C. Impara (Eds.), *Multicultural assessment in counseling and clinical psychology* (pp. 225–240). Lincoln, NE: Buros Institute of Mental Measurements.

Constantino, G., & Malgady, R. (1996). Development of the TEMAS, a multicultural thematic apperception test: Psychometric properties and clinical utility. In G. R. Sodowsky & J. C. Impara (Eds.), *Multicultural assessment in counseling and clinical psychology* (pp. 85–136). Lincoln, NE: Buros Institute of Mental Measurements.

Council of National Psychological Associations for the Advancement of Ethnic Minority Issues. (2002). *Guidelines for cultural competence in the treatment of ethnic minority populations.* Washington, DC: APA.

Cross, W. E. (1995). The psychology of nigrescence: Revising the Cross model. In J. G. Ponterotto, J. M. Casas, L. A. Suzuki, & C. M. Alexander (Eds.), *Handbook of multicultural counseling* (pp. 93–122). Thousand Oaks, CA: Sage.

Cuellar, I. (2000). Acculturation as a moderator of personality and psychological assessment. In R. H. Dana (Ed.), *Handbook of cross-cultural and multicultural personality assessment* (pp. 113–129). Mahwah, NJ: Erlbaum.

Cuellar, I., & Roberts, R. (1997). Relations of depression, acculturation, and socioeconomic status in Latino sample. *Hispanic Journal of Behavioral Sciences, 19*(2), 230–238.

Dovidio, J. F. (2001). On the nature of contemporary prejudice: The third wave. *Journal of Social Issues, 57*(4), 829–849.

Fox, R. E. (1994). Training professional psychologists for the twenty-first century. *American Psychologist, 49,* 200–206.

Garb, H. N. (1997). Race bias, social class bias, and gender bias in clinical judgment. *Clinical Psychology: Science and Practice, 4*(2), 99–120.

Greene, B. (1994). Lesbian women of color: Triple jeopardy. In L. Comaz-Diaz & B. Greene (Eds.), *Women of color: Integrating ethnic and gender identities in psychotherapy* (pp. 389–427). New York: Guilford Press.

Graham, J. (2000). *MMPI 2: Assessing personality and psychopathology.* New York: Oxford University Press.

Handel, R. W., & Ben-Porath, Y. S. (2000). Multicultural assessment with the MMPI-2: Issues for research and practice. In R. H. Dana (Ed.), *Handbook of cross-cultural and multicultural assessment* (pp. 229–245). Mahwah, NJ: Erlbaum.

Hays, P. A. (1996). Culturally responsive assessment with diverse older clients. *Professional Psychology: Research and Practice, 27*(2), 188–193.

Helms, J. E. (1995). An update of Helms's white and people of color racial identity models. In J. G. Ponterotto, J. M. Casas, L. A. Suzuki, & C. M. Alexander (Eds.), *Handbook of multicultural counseling* (pp. 181–198). Thousand Oaks, CA: Sage.

Hovey, J. D., & King, C. A. (1997). Suicidality among acculturating Mexican Americans: Current knowledge and directions for research. *Suicide and Life Threatening Behavior, 27*(1), 92–103.

Huynh, U., & Roysircar, G. (2004). Community health promotion curriculum: A case study on Vietnamese and Cambodian refugees. In R. Toporek, L. H. Gerstein, N. A. Fouad, G. Roysircar, & T. Israel (Eds.), *Handbook for social justice in counseling psychology.* Thousand Oaks, CA: Sage.

Ibrahim, F. A., Roysircar-Sodowsky, G., & Ohnishi, H. (2001). Worldview: Recent developments and needed directions. In J. G. Ponterotto, M. C. Casas, L. A. Suzuki, & C. M. Alexander (Eds.), *Handbook of multicultural counseling* (2nd ed., pp. 425–455). Thousand Oaks, CA: Sage.

Klonoff, E., & Landrine, H. (1999). Acculturation and alcohol use among Blacks: The benefits of remaining culturally traditional. *Western Journal of Black Studies, 23*(4), 211–216.

Klonoff, E., Landrine, H., & Ullman, J. B. (1999). Racial discrimination and psychiatric symptoms among Blacks. *Cultural Diversity and Ethnic Minority Psychology, 5,* 329–339.

Kwan, K. L., & Sodowsky, G. R. (1997). Internal and external ethnic identity and their correlates: A study of Chinese American immigrants. *Journal of Multicultural Counseling and Development, 25,* 52–68.

Kuo, B. C. H., Roysircar, G., & Newby-Clark, I. R. (2004). *Development of the Cross-Cultural Coping Scale: Collective, avoidance, and engagement coping in three cohorts of Chinese-Canadian Adolescents.* Submitted for publication.

Lonner, W. J. (1985). Appraisal and assessment in cross-cultural counseling. *Counseling Psychologist, 13,* 599–614.

Malgady, R. G. (1996). The question of cultural bias in assessment and diagnosis of ethnic minority client: Let's reject the null hypothesis. *Professional Psychology: Research and Practice, 27,* 101–105.

Nichols, D. S., Padilla, J. E., & Gomez-Maqueo, E. L. (2000). Issues in the cross-cultural adaptation and use of the MMPI-2. In R. H. Dana (Ed.), *Handbook of cross-cultural and multicultural assessment* (pp. 247–292). Mahwah, NJ: Erlbaum.

Okazaki, S., & Sue, S. (1995). Methodological issues in assessment research with ethnic minorities. *Psychological Assessment, 7,* 367–375.

Paniagua, F. A. (2000). Culture-bound syndromes, cultural variations, and psychopathology. In J. Cuellar & F. A. Paniagua (Eds.), *Handbook of multicultural mental health: Assessment and treatment of diverse populations* (pp. 139–169). New York: Academic Press.

Pedersen, P. B., & Carey, J. C. (2003). *Multicultural counseling in schools: A practical handbook* (2nd ed., pp. 270–289). Boston: Allyn & Bacon.

Ponterotto, J. G., Gretchen, D., & Chauhan, R. V. (2001). Cultural identity and multicultural assessment: Quantitative and qualitative tools for the clinician. In L. A. Suzuki, J. G. Ponterotto, & P. J. Meller (Eds.), *Handbook of multicultural assessment: Clinical, psychological, and educational practices* (2nd ed., pp. 67–99). San Francisco: Jossey-Bass.

Ridley, C. R., Hill, C. L., Thompson, C. E., & Omerod, A. J. (2001). Clinical practice guidelines in assessment: Toward an idiographic perspective. In D. Pope-Davis & H. Coleman (Eds.), *The intersection of race, class, and gender: Implications for multicultural counseling* (pp. 191–211). Thousand Oaks, CA: Sage.

Ridley, C. R., Li, L. C., & Hill, C. L. (1998). Multicultural assessment: Reexamination, reconceptualization, and practice application. *Counseling Psychologist, 26*, 810–827.

Rodriguez, N., Myers, H. F., Morris, J. K., & Cardoza, D. (2000). Latino college student adjustment: Does an increased presence offset minority status and acculturative stress? *Journal of Applied Social Psychology, 30*(7), 1523–1550.

Rollock, D., & Gordon, E. W. (2000). Racism and mental health into the 21st century: Perspectives and parameters. *American Journal of Orthopsychiatry, 70*(1), 5–13.

Roysircar, G. (2003). Counselor awareness of own assumptions, values, and biases. In G. Roysircar, P. Arredondo, J. N. Fuertes, J. G. Ponterotto, & R. L. Toporek (Eds.), *Multicultural counseling competencies 2003: Association of Multicultural Counseling and Development* (pp. 17–38). Alexandria, VA: AMCD.

Roysircar, G. (2004a). Child survivor of war: A case study. *Journal of Multicultural Counseling and Development, 32*(3), 168–180.

Roysircar, G. (2004b). Cultural self-awareness assessment: Practice examples from psychology training. *Professional Psychology: Research and Practice, 35*(6), 1–9.

Roysircar-Sodowsky, G., & Frey, L. L. (2003). Children of immigrants: Their worldviews value conflicts. In P. Pedersen & J. C. Carey (Eds.), *Multicultural counseling in schools: A practical handbook* (pp. 61–83). Boston: Allyn & Bacon.

Roysircar-Sodowsky, G., & Kuo, P. Y. (2001). Determining cultural validity of personality assessment: Some guidelines. In D. Pope-Davis & H. Coleman (Eds.), *The intersection of race, class, and gender: Implications for multicultural counseling* (pp. 213–239). Thousand Oaks, CA: Sage.

Roysircar-Sodowsky, G., & Maestas, M. V. (2000). Acculturation, ethnic identity, and acculturative stress: Evidence and measurement. In R. H. Dana (Ed.), *Handbook of cross-cultural and multicultural assessment* (pp. 131–172). Mahwah, NJ: Erlbaum.

Sanchez, J. M., & Turner, S. M. (2003). Practicing psychology in the era of managed care: Implications for practice and training. *American Psychologist, 58*, 116–129.

Sodowsky, G. R., Kuo-Jackson, Y. P., & Loya, G. J. (1996). Outcome of training in the philosophy of assessment: Multicultural counseling competencies. In D. Pope-Davis & H. Coleman (Eds.), *Multicultural counseling competencies:*

Assessment, education and training, and supervision. Thousand Oaks, CA: Sage.

Steele, C. M. (1997). A threat in the air: How stereotypes shape intellectual identity and performance. *American Psychologist, 52*(6), 613–629.

Sue, D. W., Arredondo, P., & McDavis, R. J. (1992). Multicultural counseling competencies and standards: A call to the profession. *Journal of Counseling and Development, 70,* 477–486.

Sue, S. (1998). In search of cultural competence in psychotherapy and counseling. *American Psychologist, 53,* 440–448.

Sue, S. (1999). Science, ethnicity, and bias: Where have we gone wrong? *American Psychologist, 53,* 440–448.

Trimble, J. E., Helms, J. E., & Root, M. P. (2003). Social and psychological perspectives on ethnic and racial identity. In G. Bernal, J. E. Trimble, A. K. Burlew, & F. T. L. Leong (Eds.), *Handbook of racial and ethnic minority psychology* (pp. 219–275). Thousand Oaks, CA: Sage.

Turk, D. C., & Salovey, P. (1988). *Reasoning, inference, and judgment in clinical psychology.* New York: Free Press.

United States Census. (2003). *Migration by race and Hispanic origin.* Retrieved July 19, 2004, from http://www.census.gov/prod/2003pubs/censr-13.pdf.

CHAPTER 3

Using the Multicultural Guidelines in Individual and Group Counseling Situations

EDWARD A. DELGADO-ROMERO, JESSICA BARFIELD, BENETTA FAIRLEY, AND REBECCA S. MARTÍNEZ

Case Example 1

Gareth is a psychologist in private practice in a rural setting. He graduated with his doctorate in counseling psychology approximately 10 years ago and is intrigued by the recent focus in the profession on multicultural issues. While in graduate school, he participated in one 6-week seminar on multicultural counseling but had minimal additional training outside of that seminar. Gareth eagerly reads the May 2003 issue of *American Psychologist* hoping to learn more about multicultural issues. Although he enjoys reading the article, he begins to feel overwhelmed by the many concepts, suggestions, and guidelines that he is now faced with. He is not sure where to begin, but he feels that at least he is not alone in wanting to address the issue of multicultural sensitivity and responsiveness in his practice.

HISTORICALLY IN PSYCHOLOGY, the perspectives of racial, ethnic, cultural, and sexual minorities have been marginalized or ignored in mainstream theoretical and empirical work (e.g., Guthrie, 1976; Holliday & Holmes, 2003) and the dominant Anglo perspective has been presented as universal. Consequently, theoretical perspectives and empirical research regarding working effectively with groups and individuals in therapy have frequently been culturally bound rather than universal and often inappropriately applied to non-White populations. Fortunately, the field of psychology has recognized the need to incorporate cultural, racial, and ethnic perspectives into case conceptualizations, clinical practice, research, and the training of psychologists. The publication of "Guidelines on Multicultural Education, Training, Research, Practice, and Organizational Change for Psychologists" (American Psychological Association [APA], 2003) represents the culmination of more than 40 years of effort by many individuals and organizations within APA and related professional organizations (e.g., the American Counseling Association and the Association for Multicultural Counseling and Development). The document covers a broad range of topics, and when considered alongside the growing literature on multicultural counseling competence (e.g., Pope-Davis, Coleman, Liu, & Toporek, 2003; Roysircar, Arredondo, Fuertes, Ponterotto, & Toporek, 2003; Roysircar, Sandhu, & Bibbins, 2003; Sue, 2001), it might be overwhelming for the individual and group counseling practitioner to know where to begin to effectively apply the APA Multicultural Guidelines to her or his clinical work. The aim of this chapter is to provide some guidance for individual and group counselors who represent the front line of service provision.

In this chapter, the authors present the elements of the APA Multicultural Guidelines (referred to hereafter as the Multicultural Guidelines) considered most salient to individual therapy and group work. We summarize recent empirical and conceptual research related to the Multicultural Guidelines and discuss concrete strategies that mental health professionals can use to develop their multicultural awareness, knowledge, and skills. Although the Multicultural Guidelines do not specifically address individual and group therapy, they do refer to "applied psychological practices" (APA, 2003, p. 390); therefore, in this chapter the authors apply the specific Multicultural Guidelines to these two modes of clinical practice, considering commonalities in and then differences between how the Multicultural Guidelines are applied to individual and group counseling. Readers should note that the Multicultural Guidelines are intended as suggested or recommended professional behavior and do not take precedence over the professional clinical judgment of practitioners.

MULTICULTURAL GUIDELINES THAT APPLY TO INDIVIDUAL AND GROUP COUNSELING

The first two guidelines are designed to apply to all psychologists working in clinical settings. Both fall under the general category of "Commitment to Cultural Awareness and Knowledge of Self and Others" (APA, 2003, p. 382). Guideline 1 calls for psychologists to (1) develop a greater understanding of how different cultures shape worldviews, (2) become more aware and sensitive about their attitudes toward others, (3) acknowledge the potential biased nature of their attitudes, (4) explore their own worldview, (5) recognize the resistant nature of individuals' potential preferences for within-group similarity, and (6) understand their assumptions about improving multicultural interactions and potential issues associated with different therapeutic approaches.

Guideline 1 also offers specific strategies for reducing stereotypical attitudes about clients. These strategies include: (1) awareness of one's attitudes and values, sometimes referred to as worldview; (2) effort and practice in changing the automatically favorable perception of the in-group; and (3) effort and practice in changing the automatically negative perceptions of the out-group. Also under the purview of Guideline 1 are suggestions for increased contact with members of groups other than one's own, actively viewing others as individuals rather than as members of a group, changing perceptions of "us versus them" to "we," and actively increasing tolerance and trust of racial/ethnic and sexual minority groups.

Guideline 2 encourages psychologists to recognize the importance of multicultural sensitivity as well as knowledge and understanding of ethnically and racially different individuals. Sensitivity implies more than knowledge about historical, societal, and professional prejudice and other forms of devaluation and dehumanization; it also implies an *empathic* understanding of this experience. Counselors who convey multicultural empathic understanding recognize (1) the stigmatizing aspects of being a member of a devalued group, (2) the experience of overt and covert prejudice and racism, and (3) the differential consequences of race and ethnicity for people of color, the experience of stereotype threat, and specific racial/ethnic identity development models. Empathic understanding cannot be gained without experience and personal risk taking, and Guideline 2 suggests ways to gain experience and understanding of oppressed or stigmatized groups. Empathic understanding and multicultural sensitivity have the potential to inform and enrich the therapeutic relationship. Therefore, optimally the counselor will seek to understand the cultural worldview of the client while simultaneously growing and taking steps toward personal and professional prejudice reduction.

Guideline 5 specifically addresses practice issues, regardless of setting (e.g., community, agency, school) or modality (e.g., individual or group therapy, consultation). This guideline addresses the challenges that psychologists face in working with increasingly diverse U.S. and international populations in therapy. Guideline 5 suggests that psychologists focus on the client in the context of her or his culture, use culturally appropriate assessment tools and procedures, and have a broad and flexible range of interventions. These three aspects of Guideline 5 are discussed in detail next.

Guideline 5 advises psychologists to connect individual, family, cultural, and societal issues as they relate to cultural issues and the presenting psychological concerns. To effectively do this, psychologists need to consider the client in relevant contexts (e.g., generational history, English-language fluency, acculturative stress, sexual orientation) so that they can understand the subjective world of the client and eliminate the potential of personalizing societal and institutional problems (e.g., blaming the victim). Guideline 5 also advises psychologists to become more aware of the environmental contexts (e.g., office decorations, administrative procedures) in treatment settings so that they reflect the counselor's cultural sensitivity. Finally, psychologists are advised to be aware of the role that culture plays in establishing and maintaining the therapeutic relationship, as client expectations and perceptions of the role of the therapist are influenced by cultural experiences. For example, a psychologist may interpret a client's deference and lack of initiative in therapy as resistance when deference to authority might be an integral part of the worldview of the client. If a psychologist is explicit about his or her expectations and assumptions in the therapeutic relationship and explores the expectations and assumptions of the client, a stronger therapeutic alliance will be established.

Issues relative to unbiased multicultural assessment are discussed elsewhere in this volume. We want to emphasize that psychologists ought to demonstrate sensitivity and critical judgment in the choice and implementation of assessment procedures. For individual and group therapists, this includes intake or group screening procedures as well as assessments administered during the course of therapy.

Culturally sensitive practitioners are encouraged to develop skills and practices that are sensitive and responsive to the worldviews and cultural backgrounds of clients. Psychologists are also advised to participate in culturally diverse and culture-specific activities to learn about alternative helping practices and nontraditional interventions outside of Western cultures. Along these lines, psychologists are encouraged to evaluate the cultural appropriateness of Western-based therapies for culturally diverse clientele and work toward expanding these principles to include culture-specific strategies. Mental health practitioners can add these skills to their practice repertoires by explicitly integrating client diversity into therapy. Note that the Multicultural Guidelines consider this practice as an additive process rather than a call to replace old skills or develop entirely new skills.

INDIVIDUAL COUNSELING

Case Example 2

Elizabeth is a school psychologist in a Midwestern town where the state university is the main employer. The college of education has recently partnered with Seoul National Teachers College and the result has been an influx of Korean families into the community. Most of the families speak little English, and there have already been some miscommunications at the local school due to the lack of bilingual teachers.

Elizabeth has been asked to provide family therapy to the family of an elementary-age child who has been described by school personnel as disruptive, inattentive, and aggressive. Before her first session, a colleague confides that the child has been singled out by classmates and been the target of racist slurs and harassment. Elizabeth has never worked with a Korean family and is unsure how to proceed. She is especially uneasy about addressing the recent allegations of racism with the family.

Case examples are a practical method frequently used to illustrate the need for multicultural sensitivity and responsiveness. They also provide applied examples of culturally sensitive therapeutic interventions. Numerous published case examples focus on the integration and implementation of effective multicultural interventions in individual therapy. For example, Roysircar and colleagues (2003) asked counselor trainees to report cases illustrating how they understood multicultural competencies in working with several diverse clients: a Colombian immigrant woman (Wilczak, 2003), a client with multiple sclerosis and cerebral palsy (Sweet & Estey, 2003), and a Jewish American adolescent (DeFrino, 2003). The trainees in all of these case reports identified pertinent literature and information about the multicultural aspects of their therapy and were able to discuss how working with these clients challenged their assumptions and biases.

Similarly, Kwan (2001), in a special issue of the *Journal of Mental Health Counseling,* presented case examples in reaction to a hypothetical counseling scenario involving covert and overt racism toward a client whose race or ethnicity was not stated. Several authors reacted to the scenarios supposing the client was Asian American (Alvarez & Kimura, 2001), Latino (Delgado-Romero, 2001), African American (Hargrow, 2001), biracial (Aldarondo, 2001), or White (Daniels, 2001). In their clinical vignettes, these authors specified the cultural knowledge and culturally sensitive and responsive skills appropriate for effective therapy. Culturally centered case conceptualizations are also available from the perspective of specific theoretical orientations (e.g., existentialism; M. P. Evans & Valadez, 2003), specific clinical specialties (e.g., vocational rehabilitation counseling; Bellini, 2003), and specific presenting issues (e.g., separation/individuation with a Haitian American client; Field, 2001). Case examples have also been used to illustrate multicultural principles by other authors (e.g., Liu & Clay, 2002; Ridley, Li, & Hill, 1998; Semmler & Williams, 2000; Toporek & Reza, 2001). Consequently, individual therapists may find many practical and case-focused examples of applying multicultural principles to their clinical work.

A significant amount of research has concentrated on understanding multicultural competence from the perspectives of counselors and counselors in training (e.g., Constantine, Ladany, Inman, & Ponterotto, 1996).

However, psychologists have only recently begun to recognize that comparatively limited attention has been given to the client's perspective concerning effective and competent multicultural practice and virtually no measures are available to assess clients' perceptions of what multiculturally competent counselors do in therapy (Fuertes, Bartolomeo, & Nichols, 2001; Pope-Davis, Liu, Toporek, & Brittan-Powell, 2001). Pope-Davis and colleagues (2002) conducted a qualitative study to investigate a client's self-identified needs and the extent to which these needs were met by the counselor and which needs were perceived as the most significant to the client's overall experience. Clients' perceptions of counselor multicultural competence were strongly correlated with their perceptions of counselor trustworthiness, expertness, and empathy (Fuertes & Brobst, 2002). Similarly, Constantine (2002) found that racial and ethnic minority clients' ratings of their counselor's multicultural competence accounted for significant variance in their satisfaction ratings beyond that accounted for by ratings of general counseling competence. Clearly, the client's perspective on what constitutes multicultural competence needs to be addressed in therapy.

One limitation in the current multicultural competence literature is that, by design, many of the studies involve intake sessions only (e.g., Pope-Davis et al., 2002) or a single session only (e.g., Thompson & Jenal, 1994) or focus solely on the therapist (Fuertes, Mueller, Chauhan, Walker, & Ladany, 2002). Consequently, there is limited research (e.g., Thompson et al., 2003; Thompson et al., 2004; Tsang, Bogo, & George, 2003) that examines the process of multicultural competence over the course of the therapeutic relationship. Research that focuses on process and outcome in multicultural therapy is a promising area for future study, and practitioners are encouraged to examine multicultural issues throughout the entire therapeutic relationship.

In summary, despite some limitations, there is a great deal of practical information regarding multiculturally sensitive individual therapy available in the literature. The Multicultural Guidelines provide a way to focus this information; however, the Multicultural Guidelines need to continue to evolve as workable strategies. This task is challenging, as many scholars have pointed out the inherent difficulty in defining multicultural competence (Ridley, Baker, & Hill, 2001).

GROUP COUNSELING

Case Example 3

Jane is a psychologist who is an expert in leading substance abuse recovery groups. A large part of her practice includes court-mandated substance abuse recovery groups offered by the county government as an alternative to incarceration. Jane has been asked to run a group for recent Mexican immigrants, many of whom do not speak English. Jane does not speak Spanish and initially declines to run the group, citing her concern that she might not run the group effectively due to her inability to speak or comprehend Spanish and her lack of familiarity with Mexican culture. She later finds out that if she does not run the group, this group of Mexican immigrants will not be offered alternative diversion programs and will instead be sent directly to jail.

Group counseling is distinct from individual counseling. Although the same Guidelines (1, 2, and 5) are relevant to individual and group therapists, the application of the Multicultural Guidelines will differ as treatment modalities differ. In group therapy, for example, there are (often) co-leaders and the therapist's focus is not solely on the individual but also on the group process and dynamics. As was the case with individual therapy, it was previously thought that group principles were universal rather than culturally bound (e.g., Gazda, Ginter, & Horne, 2001). However, it is now recognized that an individual's race, ethnicity, culture, and sexual orientation are not abandoned when he or she joins a therapy group. Therefore, it is important for the group leader to actively address multicultural issues in group counseling because of the overt and covert reciprocal impact that these issues may have on the group dynamics. Group counseling is in itself a cross-cultural phenomenon (Gazda et al., 2001; Leong, Wagner, & Kim, 1995) that has its own socially and culturally relevant beliefs, assumptions, and behavior patterns which are candidly exhibited by each group member (regardless of his or her race or ethnicity).

As was the case for individual therapy, there are several examples of the application of multicultural principles to group work. For example, Shechtman, Hiradin, and Zina (2003) highlighted how cultural differences may be actively considered in therapeutic group interventions with different ethnic populations. There are also several case examples of the application of multicultural considerations to group work available to group leaders. For example, Elligan and Utsey (1999) described an African-centered support group for African American men; Holcomb-McCoy (2003) described multicultural group counseling in K–12 schools; Gloria (1999) described a support group for Chicana college students; and Portman (2003) provided a qualitative experiential perspective of herself as an American Indian applying Native American values (e.g., collectivism) to group work. In each of these examples, the issue of integrating culturally responsive group leadership, knowledge, and skills was discussed in relation to the given population.

One particular text stands out in the way that the authors comprehensively address multicultural group work issues. DeLucia-Waack and Donigian (2004) in *The Practice of Multicultural Group Work* featured cultural, social, and familial contextual information on the 11 multicultural group experts who take turns as both group leaders and group members throughout the course of the text. Here, relevant multicultural contextual information is infused in both group leadership and group membership. The work highlighted here is crucial because it reinforces the idea that multicultural group leadership competence is not a collection of techniques but the integration of multicultural beliefs, knowledge, and skill, as filtered through and transformed by the unique experiences of the group leader. Nevertheless, with the vast available multicultural literature, understanding how to effectively utilize and conceptualize the information may prove to be, at best, overwhelming and, at worst, discouraging.

However, in group work there is a highly useful resource to assist group leaders in becoming multiculturally sensitive. The Association for Specialists in Group Work (ASGW, 2003) published a set of principles for diversity-competent group workers (Haley-Banez, Brown, & Molina, 1999) that provides specific guidance to group therapists. In the following, we point out how the ASGW Guidelines represent a specific application of multicultural practice (separate from but parallel with the APA Multicultural Guidelines).

Both the APA and ASGW Guidelines provide guidance for group leaders. The APA Multicultural Guidelines suggest that group leaders attain knowledge about social policy (APA, 2003), and the ASGW principles suggest that diversity-competent group workers be knowledgeable about the characteristics of and resources in the communities in which their group members live. The ASGW principles further emphasize that psychologists be aware of overt and covert discriminatory practices at social and community levels. Clearly, the documents are parallel in many ways.

Other points of convergence include an emphasis on culturally appropriate assessment and testing related to group work, identifying awareness, knowledge, and skills for effective and culturally sensitive group leadership, the need for personal and professional awareness of self, the need for awareness of the worldview of group members, the need for diversity-sensitive group intervention strategies, and the need to demonstrate clear and explicit knowledge of group work and theory and how it may conflict with specific cultural beliefs, values, and traditions. We believe it is a useful exercise for psychologists who facilitate therapy groups to examine the ASGW principles as an example of how to apply multicultural issues specifically to group leadership. Group psychologists may be guided by the ASGW principles in their efforts to adapt and delineate their own perspectives of multicultural group work.

Within the realm of group counseling, addressing multicultural concerns must begin before a therapy group even forms. Questions regarding recruitment, location, group focus, and group makeup need to be negotiated before developing a group. Smith, Li-Chen, Inman, and Hudson-Findling (1999) recommend collaborating with community resources to discuss issues regarding recruitment and appropriate group locations for persons of color. It is also important for the group counselor to consider factors beyond simple demographic diversity when forming a new group. For example, Asian Americans differ substantially in their racial/ethnic identity and acculturation (Leong et al., 1995; Shechtman et al., 2003), and, therefore, homogeneity among Asian Americans cannot be assumed. For any group member, identity and acculturation have a significant effect on attitude toward group counseling, thoughts regarding seeking professional psychological help, and level of self-disclosure in the group counseling setting. Racial/ethnic identity is not unique to people of color: Whites also have racial and ethnic identities (e.g., Helms, 1995), and group counselors should be prepared to help all group members explore cultural assumptions, beliefs, and behaviors.

CONCRETE STRATEGIES TO DEVELOP MULTICULTURAL COMPETENCE

Some of the Multicultural Guidelines are fairly straightforward and self-explanatory; others require introspection (professional and personal) and work to challenge insensitive or prejudicial beliefs such as color blindness. For example, knowledge-based guidelines are easier to address than guidelines that call for personal and professional self-examination of beliefs, attitudes, and behaviors. In other words, to become knowledgeable about ethnic identity theories (Guideline 2), one must commit the time and effort to becoming familiar with this literature. However, becoming aware of one's worldview, increasing contact with members of other racial/ethnic groups, building trust in others, and increasing tolerance for others (Guideline 1) call for a substantial amount of personal courage, risk taking, and potential awkwardness or emotional pain. There seems to be no way of avoiding the fact that developing multicultural competence is not a passive, academic, or knowledge-based endeavor. Parallel to the expectations of clients in individual and group therapy, developing multicultural competence is an active, awkward, challenging, and growth-inducing process on the part of mental health providers.

As discussed earlier, the APA Multicultural Guidelines are a culmination of 40 years of work; fortunately, individual and group therapists can benefit from a large body of concrete and specific strategies for building multicultural competence. In particular, Patricia Arredondo (1999; Arredondo & Arciniega, 2001; Arredondo et al., 1996; Roysircar et al., 2003) and her colleagues have systematically provided concrete examples and strategies for mental health professionals to achieve multicultural competence and have offered over one hundred specific ideas that articulate the application of multicultural competence in clinical practice. For example, Arredondo and Arciniega provide strategies and learning exercises such as structured written activities where participants are asked to investigate educational experiences that have historically been available or not available to members of their cultural group. They are then asked to analyze how the effects of these educational experiences have impacted their own and others' behavior, allowing for the identification of biases and assumptions about educational and institutional barriers. Other diversity-enhancing experiences include role playing, where participants are placed into uncomfortable, difficult, and possibly emotionally taxing conversations regarding multiculturalism; examining media imagery pertaining to the journeys of immigrants or refugees, with the goal of providing information that will increase awareness and knowledge of, empathy for, and insight into the experience of oppressed populations; and reviewing articles and critically analyzing research findings from the perspectives of multiculturalism and diversity (in terms of population sample, language variables, and societal factors such as economic status and residency).

In addition to the more general practical application of the Multicultural Competence Guidelines, several authors have articulated concrete approaches to working with specific populations, such as Latinas (Aviles, 2003) and Latino families (Santiago-Rivera, Arredondo, & Gallardo-Cooper, 2002), Native Americans (Frey, 2003), South Asians (Inman & Tewari, 2003), African Americans (Parham, 2002), GLBT clients (McLean, 2003), and women of color (e.g., Madison-Colemore & Moore, 2003). Others have addressed race/ethnicity and spirituality (K. M. Evans, 2003; Fukuyama & Sevig, 1999), race/ethnicity and sexual identity (Stanley, 2004), and issues relevant to the elderly of color (e.g., González, 1995).

As all practitioners in the mental health field are being asked to address their competence in working with diverse client populations, one response is for mental health professionals to take this task on individually. Although multicultural competence is ultimately the responsibility of individuals, group approaches may provide the necessary support and challenge for optimal growth. Therefore, we suggest that psychologists seek out or develop a network of other mental health professionals in their local area who are committed to implementing the Multicultural Guidelines in their clinical work. These cultural competence groups might revolve around discussing readings, inviting guest speakers, and planning activities to increase contact with marginalized groups in the community. This type of professional support group can provide didactic and experiential learning, consultation, feedback, and encouragement and reduce feelings of isolation. These support groups should be careful to attend to issues of the diversity within the group membership as well as prevent the exclusion or tokenization of mental health professionals from diverse backgrounds.

Once a cultural competence focus group is formed, a group leader might be appointed to moderate the group's activities. One example of an activity is a reading club. The readings could fluctuate between the academic literature, focusing on the exploration of the historical perspectives and theories that describe ethnic and racial identity development, to more personal narratives and biographies that vividly depict the experiences of diverse people. The ultimate goal of the group would be to foster discussion, debate, and multicultural growth. Group members may consider designing homework assignments for the group based on the application of the Multicultural Guidelines. These assignments might then serve as a foundation for dialogue or activities in subsequent meetings. Additionally, group leaders may plan field trips to participate in local, state, and national events, festivals, celebrations, and conferences.

Given advances in technology, multicultural competence groups might also form through Internet web sites, newsgroups, and online chat rooms. Many therapists may find it exceptionally difficult to find the time to commit to traveling to weekly or monthly meetings. A possible remedy to such a dilemma could involve utilizing the Internet as a resource for gathering with other practitioners. This option affords the benefits of group interactions in the convenience of homes or offices. Moreover, the Internet provides endless possibilities in terms of international contacts and resources that enrich the diversity of group membership.

Building the awareness, sensitivity, and relevance of multiculturally competent practice is only the beginning, however. Considerable work must also be devoted to taking into account clients in context. It might be useful to utilize case examples or videotapes focused on cultural competence with specific populations (e.g., see www.emicrotraining.com), which could be reviewed as a group to provide a more calculated approach to understanding the client's perspective.

Regardless of the approach, mental health practitioners should also recognize that the process of becoming a multiculturally competent counselor is not a linear path toward a concrete end. Given increases in internationalization, globalization, and immigration, dynamic and fluid cultural changes, and the increased demographic diversity of the United

States, multicultural competence cannot be considered a fixed or static end state. Rather, it should be viewed as an ongoing and dynamic process that occurs over the lifetime of one's career.

As a conclusion to this chapter, we revisit our case examples.

Case Example 1 Revisited

Gareth decided to take some proactive steps to becoming culturally competent. He sought CEU opportunities for multicultural training and formed a cultural competence group along with some other practitioners in the community. He consulted a colleague knowledgeable in multicultural issues and selected *Education of a WASP* by Lois M. Stalvey (1970) as the first book for the cultural competence group. The book focuses on the journey toward confronting personal and societal racism. Gareth could relate to the story of the author although it was written many years ago. Furthermore, Gareth's group has made it a goal to invite guest speakers and to attend local multicultural events together. Gareth finds that attempting to implement the Multicultural Guidelines has been a challenging yet invigorating experience. He is convinced (and so are we) that his new emphasis on multicultural sensitivity has improved his work in therapy with all clients.

Case Example 2 Revisited

Elizabeth decided to raise the issue of the racism and harassment experienced by the child at school during the family session. The family members were angry and embarrassed, but they agreed to come back the next week. Elizabeth took the time between appointments to begin to learn more about Korean families and found a helpful chapter in the book *Ethnicity and Family Therapy* (Kim, 1996). She consulted with the minister of a local church that serves a large Korean contingent to learn more about the growing Korean community. In addition, she arranged an appointment with the principal of the school to discuss the possibility of an in-service for teachers about Korean culture. She also discussed ways of incorporating prejudice-reduction efforts with the staff and student body. During the next family session, the parents confided that they had also experienced incidents of racism and were surprised that an American therapist would talk about racism. Although she realizes that she has much more work to do in building up her multicultural competence, Elizabeth feels that she is off to a good start.

Case Example 3 Revisited

Jane is shocked about the social injustice that the Mexican immigrants face as a consequence of her decision not to provide group therapy. A secretary in the county government office volunteers to be a translator for the group, but Jane declines again, realizing that this arrangement is not ethically appropriate. Although it may place her employment with the county in jeopardy, Jane decides to meet with the local leaders of the Mexican immigrant community and representatives of the National Council of La Raza to explain her concerns: ensuring that competent group therapy and incarceration diversion is provided and the ethical, moral, and legal responsibility of the county to provide trained interpreters or find bilingual group leaders. Jane is uncomfortable with her new role as social activist, and not all members of the Mexican immigrant community have been receptive to her concerns; however, the alternative of unfair incarceration based on language is too terrible for her to contemplate.

REFERENCES

Aldarondo, F. J. (2001). Racial and ethnic identity models and their application: Counseling biracial individuals. *Journal of Mental Health Counseling, 23,* 238–255.

Alvarez, A. N., & Kimura, E. F. (2001). Asian Americans and racial identity: Dealing with racism and snowballs. *Journal of Mental Health Counseling, 23,* 192–206.

American Psychological Association. (2003). Guidelines on Multicultural Education, Training, Research, Practice, and Organizational Change for Psychologists. *American Psychologist, 58,* 377–402.

Arredondo, P. (1999). Multicultural counseling competencies as tools to address oppression and racism. *Journal of Counseling and Development, 77,* 102–108.

Arredondo, P., & Arciniega, G. M. (2001). Strategies and techniques for counselor training based on the multicultural counseling competencies. *Journal of Multicultural Counseling and Development, 29,* 263–273.

Arredondo, P., Toporek, R., Brown, S., Jones, J., Locke, D., Sanchez, J., et al. (1996). Operationalization of multicultural counseling competencies. *Journal of Multicultural Counseling and Development, 24,* 42–78.

Association for Specialists in Group Work (ASGW). *Principles for diversity-competent group workers.* Retrieved December 12, 2003, from http://www.asgw.org.diversity.htm.

Aviles, R. M. D. (2003). Multicultural issues in assessment: Assessment procedures with a Latina. In G. Roysircar (Ed.), *Multicultural competencies: A guidebook of practices (pp. 81–95).* Alexandria, VA: Association for Multicultural Counseling and Development.

Bellini, J. (2003). Counselors' multicultural competencies and vocational rehabilitation outcomes in the context of counselor-client racial similarity and difference. *Rehabilitation Counseling Bulletin, 46,* 164–173.

Constantine, M. G. (2002). Predictors of satisfaction with counseling: Racial and ethnic minority clients' attitudes toward counseling and ratings of their counselors' general and multicultural counseling competence. *Journal of Counseling Psychology, 49,* 255–263.

Constantine, M. G., Ladany, N., Inman, A. G., & Ponterotto, J. G. (1996). Students' perceptions of multicultural training in counseling psychology programs. *Journal of Multicultural Counseling and Development, 24,* 241–253.

Daniels, J. A. (2001). Conceptualizing a case of indirect racism using the White Racial Identity Development model. *Journal of Mental Health Counseling, 23,* 256–268.

DeFrino, B. (2003). Multicultural interactions with Jewish American adolescents. In G. Roysircar, P. Arredondo, J. N. Fuertes, J. G. Ponterotto, & R. L. Toporek (Eds.), *Multicultural competencies 2003: Association for Multicultural Counseling and Development* (pp. 121–130). Alexandria, VA: Association for Multicultural Counseling and Development.

Delgado-Romero, E. A. (2001). Counseling a Hispanic/Latino client: Mr. X. *Journal of Mental Health Counseling, 23,* 207–221.

DeLucia-Waack, J. L., & Donigian, J. (2004). *The practice of multicultural group work: Visions and perspectives from the field.* Belmont, CA: Brooks/Cole, Thompson Learning.

Elligan, D., & Utsey, S. (1999). Utility of an African-centered support group for African American men confronting societal racism and oppression. *Cultural Diversity and Ethnic Minority Psychology, 5,* 156–165.

Evans, K. M. (2003). Including spirituality in multicultural counseling: Overcoming counselor resistance. In G. Roysircar (Ed.), *Multicultural competencies: A guidebook of practice.* (pp. 161–171). Alexandria, VA: Association for Multicultural Counseling and Development.

Evans, M. P., & Valadez, A. A. (2003). Culture-centered counseling from an Existential perspective: What does it look like and how does it work for an African American woman client. In G. Roysircar, P. Arredondo, J. N. Fuertes, J. G. Ponterotto, & R. L. Toporek (Eds.), *Multicultural competencies 2003: Association for Multicultural Counseling and Development* (pp. 149–160). Alexandria, VA: Association for Multicultural Counseling and Development.

Field, L. D. (2001). Separation/individuation in a cultural context: The case of a Haitian-American student. *Journal of College Student Psychotherapy, 16,* 135–151.

Frey, L. L. (2003). Use of narratives, metaphor, and relationship in the assessment and treatment of a sexually reactive Native American youth. In G. Roysircar (Ed.), *Multicultural competencies: A guidebook of practices* (pp. 119–128). Alexandria, VA: Association for Multicultural Counseling and Development.

Fuertes, J. N., Bartolomeo, M., & Nichols, C. M. (2001). Future research directions in the study of counselor multicultural competencies. *Journal of Multicultural Counseling and Development, 29,* 3–12.

Fuertes, J. N., & Brobst, K. (2002). Clients' ratings of counselor multicultural competency. *Cultural Diversity and Ethnic Minority Psychology, 8,* 214–223.

Fuertes, J. N., Mueller, L. N., Chauhan, R. V., Walker, J. A., & Ladany, N. (2002). An investigation of European American therapists' approach to counseling African American clients. *Counseling Psychologist, 30,* 763–788.

Fukuyama, M. A., & Sevig, T. D. (1999). *Integrating spirituality into multicultural counseling.* Thousand Oaks, CA: Sage.

Gazda, G. M., Ginter, E. J., & Horne, A. M. (2001). *Group counseling and group psychotherapy: Theory and application.* Boston: Allyn & Bacon.

Gloria, A. (1999). Apoyando Estudiantes Chicanas: Therapeutic factors in Chicana college student support groups. *Journal for Specialists in Group Work, 24,* 246–259.

González, G. M. (1995). Cuban-Americans. In N. A. Vacc, S. B. DeVaney, & J. Wittmer (Eds.), *Experiencing and counseling multicultural and diverse populations* (pp. 293–316). Bristol, PA: Accelerated Development.

Guthrie, R. V. (1976). *Even the rat was White: A historical view of psychology.* New York: Harper & Row.

Haley-Banez, L., Brown, S., & Molina, B. (1999). Association for specialists in group work principles for diversity-competent group workers. *Journal for Specialists in Group Work, 24,* 7–14.

Hargrow, A. M. (2001). Racial identity development: The case of Mr. X as an African American. *Journal of Mental Health Counseling, 23,* 222–237.

Holcomb-McCoy, C. (2003). Using multicultural literature to enhance peer helping training. *Peer Facilitator Quarterly, 18,* 45–48.

Holliday, B. G., & Homes, A. L. (2003). A tale of challenge and change: A history and chronology of ethnic minorities in psychology in the United States. In G. Bernal, J. E. Trimble, A. K. Burlew, & F. T. L. Leong (Eds.), *Handbook of racial and ethnic minority psychology* (pp. 15–64). Thousand Oaks, CA: Sage.

Inman, A. M., & Tewari, N. (2003). The power of context: Counseling South Asians within a family context. In G. Roysircar (Ed.), *Multicultural competencies: A guidebook of practices* (pp. 97–107). Alexandria, VA: Association for Multicultural Counseling and Development.

Kim, B.-L. C. (1996). Korean families. In M. McGoldrick, J. Giordando, & J. K. Pearce (Eds.), *Ethnicity and family therapy* (2nd ed., pp. 281–294). New York: Guilford Press.

Kwan, K. K. (2001). Models of racial and ethnic identity development: Delineation of practice implications. *Journal of Mental Health Counseling, 23,* 269–278.

Leong, F. T. L., Wagner, N. S., & Kim, H. H. (1995). Group counseling expectations among Asian American students: The role of culture-specific factors. *Journal of Counseling Psychology, 42,* 217–222.

Liu, W. M., & Clay, D. L. (2002). Multicultural counseling competencies: Guidelines in working with children and adolescents. *Journal of Mental Health Counseling, 24,* 177–187.

Madison-Colemore, O., & Moore, J. L. (2003). Women of color and substance abuse: A counseling model for an African American woman client. In G. Roysircar (Ed.), *Multicultural competencies: A guidebook of practices* (pp. 67–80). Alexandria, VA: Association for Multicultural Counseling and Development.

McLean, R. (2003). Deconstructing Black gay shame: A multicultural perspective on the quest for a healthy ethnic and sexual identity. In G. Roysircar (Ed.), *Multicultural competencies: A guidebook of practices* (pp. 109–118). Alexandria, VA: Association for Multicultural Counseling and Development.

Parham, T. A. (2002). *Counseling persons of African descent: Raising the bar of practitioner competence.* Thousand Oaks, CA: Sage.

Pope-Davis, D. B., Coleman, H. L. K., Liu, W. M., & Toporek, R. L. (Eds.). (2003). *Handbook of multicultural competencies in counseling and psychology.* Thousand Oaks, CA: Sage.

Pope-Davis, D. B., Liu, W. M., Toporek, R. L., & Brittan-Powell, C. S. (2001). What's missing from multicultural competency research: Review, introspection, and recommendations. *Cultural Diversity and Ethnic Minority Psychology, 7*, 121–138.

Pope-Davis, D. B., Toporek, R. L., Ortega-Villalobos, L., Ligiéro, D. P., Brittan-Powell, C. S., Liu, W. M., et al. (2002). Client's perspectives of multicultural counseling competence: A qualitative examination. *Counseling Psychologist, 30*, 355–393.

Portman, T. A. A. (2003). Multicultural competence and group work: A collectivistic view. In G. Roysircar, P. Arredondo, J. N. Fuertes, J. G. Ponterotto, & R. L. Toporek (Eds.), *Multicultural competencies 2003: Association for Multicultural Counseling and Development* (pp. 141–147). Alexandria, VA: Association for Multicultural Counseling and Development.

Ridley, C. R., Baker, D. M., & Hill, C. L. (2001). Critical issues concerning cultural competence. *Counseling Psychologist, 29*, 822–832.

Ridley, C. R., Li, L. C., & Hill, C. L. (1998). Multicultural assessment: Reexamination, reconceptualization, and practical application. *Counseling Psychologist, 26*, 827–910.

Roysircar, G., Arredondo, P., Fuertes, J. N., Ponterotto, J. G., & Toporek, R. L. (Eds.). (2003). *Multicultural competencies 2003: Association for Multicultural Counseling and Development.* Alexandria, VA: Association for Multicultural Counseling and Development.

Roysircar, G., Sandhu, D. S., & Bibbins, V. E. (Eds.). (2003). *Multicultural competencies: A guidebook for practices.* Alexandria, VA: Association for Multicultural Counseling and Development.

Santiago-Rivera, A. L., Arredondo, P., & Gallardo-Cooper, M. (2002). *Counseling Latinos and la familia: A practical guide.* Thousand Oaks, CA: Sage.

Semmler, P. L., & Williams, C. B. (2000). Narrative therapy: A storied context for multicultural counseling. *Journal of Multicultural Counseling and Development, 28*, 51–62.

Shechtman, Z., Hiradin, A., & Zina, S. (2003). The impact of culture on group behavior: A comparison of three ethnic groups. *Journal of Counseling and Development, 81*, 208–216.

Smith, T. B., Li-Chen, C., Inman, A. G., Hudson-Findling, J. (1999). An outreach support group for international students. *Journal of College Counseling, 2*, 188–190.

Stanley, J. L. (2004). Biracial lesbian and bisexual women: Understanding the unique aspects and interactional processes of multiple minority identities. *Woman and Therapy, 27*, 159–172.

Stavley, L. M. (1970). *The education of a WASP.* New York: William Morrow.

Sue, D. W. (2001). Multidimensional facets of cultural competence. *Counseling Psychologist, 29*, 790–821.

Sweet, S. G., & Estey, M. (2003). A step toward multicultural competencies: Listening to individuals with multiple sclerosis and cerebral palsy. In G. Roysircar, P. Arredondo, J. N. Fuertes, J. G. Ponterotto, & R. L. Toporek (Eds.), *Multicul-*

tural competencies 2003: Association for Multicultural Counseling and Development (pp. 103–120). Alexandria, VA: Association for Multicultural Counseling and Development.

Thompson, C., Berrian, A., Cumberlander, N., Brown, T., Chow, J., Murry, S., et al. (2004). *An instrumental case study of a cross-racial therapy relationship involving a client with racial identity conflicts.* Manuscript under review.

Thompson, C., Delgado-Romero, E. A., Korth, B., Issacs, K., Hwang, B. J., & Vandiver, B. (2003). *Psychotherapy research using critical methodology: A focus on racism.* Symposium presented at the American Psychological Association, Toronto, Canada.

Thompson, C., & Jenal, S. T. (1994). Interracial and intraracial quasi-counseling interactions when counselors avoid discussing race. *Journal of Counseling Psychology, 41,* 484–491.

Toporek, R. L., & Reza, J. V. (2001). Context as a critical dimension of multicultural counseling: Articulating personal, professional, and institutional competence. *Journal of Multicultural Counseling and Development, 29,* 13–30.

Tsang, A. K. T., Bogo, M., & George, U. (2003). Critical issues in cross-cultural counseling research: Example of an ongoing project. *Journal of Multicultural Counseling and Development, 31,* 63–78.

Wilczak, C. (2003). A counselor trainee's conversations with a Colombian immigrant woman. In G. Roysircar, P. Arredondo, J. N. Fuertes, J. G. Ponterotto, & R. L. Toporek (Eds.), *Multicultural competencies 2003: Association for Multicultural Counseling and Development* (pp. 89–101). Alexandria, VA: Association for Multicultural Counseling and Development.

CHAPTER 4

Using the Multicultural Guidelines in Couples and Family Counseling

GEORGE V. GUSHUE, DAVID E. GREENAN,
AND SARAH J. BRAZAITIS

COUPLES AND FAMILY counseling emphasizes systems and context. Individual behavior is not examined in isolation, but rather is seen as inextricably linked to the familial context in which it is expressed. That is, individual behavior and dysfunction are seen to be representations of family dynamics; therefore, adequate assessment and treatment can occur only in a family context. For family theorists and practitioners, the family unit, not the individual seeking treatment (or for whom treatment is sought), is the client (S. Minuchin, 1974).

The field of couples and family therapy came into being over 50 years ago, in part in response to psychiatry's singular focus on individual psychodynamics (Broderick & Schrader, 1981) and the realization through field theory (Lewin, 1951) and group dynamics (Bion, 1948) that human behavior is both interactive and interconnected. With the introduction of feminist concepts into family therapy (Walters, Carter, Papp, & Silverstein, 1988), the field became more sensitive to the impact of larger systems (i.e., gender and culture) on the family's interactions. More recently, numerous authors have called attention to the importance of race, ethnicity, and sexual orientation as influences on the interactions between families and larger systems (Greenan & Tunnell, 2003; McGoldrick, Pearce, & Giordano, 1996; P. Minuchin, Colapinto, & Minuchin, 1998; Sciarra, 1999; Sue & Sue, 2003). In this view, culture is a superordinate construct that affects how families are organized, how they interact, and what is judged to be healthy family functioning.

56

The recent "Guidelines on Multicultural Education, Training, Research, Practice, and Organizational Change for Psychologists" proposed by the American Psychological Association (APA, 2003) have important implications for couples and family practitioners. This chapter provides a brief overview of the existing literature on cultural dimensions of family counseling, relates four of the APA's Multicultural Guidelines explicitly to couples and family counseling, provides an illustrative case example, and suggests strategies for acquiring multicultural competence in couples and family counseling.

CULTURE AND FAMILIES

Over the past 30 years, a growing body of research has addressed the various ways in which culture affects family functioning. This research can be grouped into three general trends: between-group cultural differences, within-group cultural differences, and how culture affects the interactions between the therapist and the family.

BETWEEN-GROUP CULTURAL DIFFERENCES

Perhaps the first serious attention given to culture by family therapists was in the form of describing differing cultural and ethnic patterns of family functioning. For example, how are Irish families different from Vietnamese families? To date, the most frequent type of research on families and culture examines the varying patterns of family organization and interaction for different cultural groups. Perhaps the best known and most frequently cited example of this approach is McGoldrick, Pearce, and Giordano's (1982) *Ethnicity and Family Therapy,* the most recent edition of which (1996) describes the family interactional patterns of some 40 racial, ethnic, and religious groups.

Multicultural scholars have highlighted a number of domains as important for understanding the cultural context of families. One emphasizes understanding a family's cultural values and, by extension, understanding what is considered "normal" in a given family (e.g., Brown, 1997; Ho, 1987; Kluckhohn & Strodtbeck, 1961; Sue & Sue, 2003). For instance, a family from a collectivistic culture may define individuation and autonomy differently from a family whose culture values individualism. Leong (1993) offers an example of this when he cautions career counselors that for Asian American clients, a career decision may be based not on what is best for the individual but on what is best for the family. A number of authors have noted cultural variations on the definition of "family" itself (e.g., Falicov, 1996; Garcia-Preto, 1996). For some cultures, family means primarily the nuclear family of parents and children. For others, it means an extended family of those related by important kinship bonds. In addition, a number of authors have observed that relationship roles for heterosexual couples (e.g., egalitarian vs. hierarchical) may vary from culture to culture (e.g., Sue & Sue, 2003). Others have noted the importance of examining the impact of larger sociopolitical systems on the continuity or disruption of a family's cultural patterns. For instance, what are the lasting effects of slavery and racism on Black family systems? How might racial privilege influence the dynamics of a White family? How are immigrant families affected when parents need to depend on their children who are more English-proficient? Finally, as with individual therapy, family counselors must decide what constitutes a culturally appropriate intervention. Which members of the family are invited to come in for treatment? What is the value placed on direct communication, emotional expression, and open conflict? In sum, differences in worldviews, social location, and history among cultural groups result in important differences in the meaning and dynamics of family life.

Within-Group Cultural Differences

One potential danger in delineating culture-based differences in families is stereotyping. For example, although the structure and interactional styles of a Mexican American family may be different in a number of important ways from those of an Asian American family, it is also true that there is substantial variation among Mexican American and Asian American families. Thus, another important trend in the literature on culture and families has drawn attention to significant cultural differences among families of the same culture. In addition to idiosyncratic differences that may be attributed to the unique personalities that make up any particular family, four systematic ways of thinking about within-group cultural differences among families have been proposed. The first is to note the national differences that underlie some of the broad categories used to talk about culture. For instance, more than 32 distinct cultural groups are subsumed under the heading of "Asian and Pacific American" in the United States (Sue & Sue, 2003). However, there are substantial cultural differences between, say, a Japanese American family and a Malaysian American family. A second within-group moderator is socioeconomic status. To what extent does social class influence family functioning and roles in ethnic, cultural, or racial groups? Although there is some literature on this point, it is not extensive (e.g., Aponte, 1976; Baer, 1999; Fulmer, 1988; Hines, 1988; S. Minuchin, Montalvo, Guerney, Rosman, & Schumer, 1967; Uttal, 1999).

A third perspective used to make within-group family cultural distinctions is that of acculturation (e.g., Santisteban & Mitrani, 2003). This construct has particular relevance for families who have immigrated to the United States. There are numerous models to measure acculturation, but essentially, these constructs consider the extent to which individuals endorse the values, beliefs, and behaviors of their traditional culture as well as the extent to which they endorse the values, beliefs, and behaviors of the dominant culture in which they are presently living. Typically, children of immigrant families acculturate more rapidly than their parents, creating the potential for cultural conflict between traditional parents and their more "Americanized" children. In cases such as these, a counselor needs to be cognizant of cultural differences that exist within the same family (Gushue & Sciarra, 1995; Szapocznik & Kurtines, 1993).

Finally, some authors have noted the potential for differences in racial-cultural identity within families. The racial-cultural identity paradigm (Atkinson, Morton, & Sue, 1998; Helms, 1995) describes differences in psychological orientation to race and culture based on individuals' various experiences of and responses to racism and the sociopolitical context of the United States. The importance of these models for family counseling (as with acculturation) is that they delineate another domain of potential synergy or conflict within families as well as between differing members of the family and the counselor based on similarities or differences in racial-cultural orientation (Gushue, 1993).

COUNSELOR'S CULTURE AND TRAINING

Many of the studies cited earlier also note the importance of counselors' awareness of their own cultural biases regarding family functioning (e.g., Sue & Sue, 2003). Some authors have endeavored to delineate the impact of racial-cultural differences between therapists and the families they treat (Banks, 2001; Bean, Perry, & Bedell, 2002; Falicov, 1988, 1995; Gushue, 1993; Gushue & Sciarra, 1995). Some empirical research has endeavored to study the effects of family counselors' racial or cultural attitudes or awareness on family treatment (Constantine, Juby, & Liang, 2001; Gushue, Constantine, & Sciarra, 2004); however, overall, the empirical research on the impact of family counselors' worldviews is scant. Clearly, it is essential that counselors be aware of their own worldviews, insofar as those constellations of beliefs and values will in turn influence assessment, goals, and strategies for working with families that present for treatment. To date, although much has been written about the development of multicultural competence for mental health practitioners, little has been written about how this might apply specifically to family training.

MULTICULTURAL GUIDELINES AND COUPLES AND FAMILY COUNSELING

This section outlines how four of the APA's (2003) recent Multicultural Guidelines can be applied to couples and family counseling. In brief, these Multicultural Guidelines urge a commitment to (1) cultural awareness and knowledge of self, (2) cultural awareness and knowledge of others, (3) culturally appropriate skill in psychological practice, and (4) advocacy of organizational change to bring about culturally sensitive organizational practices, including policy.

CULTURAL AWARENESS AND KNOWLEDGE OF SELF

The first Guideline refers to counselors' knowledge and awareness of their own worldviews and potential biases. Indeed, counselors must become aware of their own culturally based assumptions rather than allowing them to operate implicitly. Specifically, in couples and family counseling it is essential that counselors be aware of their implicit assumptions about what "normal" families look like. For instance, do they expect partners or spouses to have an egalitarian or hierarchical relationship? Is "good communication" direct or indirect? Is expression of emotion encouraged? In the counselor's definition of optimal family functioning, how rigid or permeable should the boundaries between the subsystems in the family be? What is considered the optimal level of autonomy for individuals within the family? Some of these assumptions may reflect the dynamics in counselors' own family of origin. Others may be reflections of training. However, all reflect culturally based assumptions that are the products of socialization. The first guideline requires family counselors to work to become aware of the cultural basis inherent in their own beliefs (whatever they may be) regarding optimal family functioning.

CULTURAL AWARENESS AND KNOWLEDGE OF OTHERS

The second Guideline encourages counselors to acquire knowledge and awareness of the culturally informed values, beliefs, and behaviors of their clients. Couples and family counselors must be knowledgeable about the impact of histories of marginalization and stigmatization or of privilege and domination (where applicable), and they must have insight into the meaning of the family's presenting symptoms as well as the significance of the couple's or family's seeking or being referred for counseling at all. In essence, the counselor must be able to take the client family's point of view.

Furthermore, as was noted in the literature earlier, a family counselor cannot assume that cultures are monolithic. To what extent does the Puerto Rican family sitting in the consulting room resemble or diverge from the family patterns of a "typical" Puerto Rican family? Part of knowing about other cultures, according to the second guideline, is recognizing intracultural variations. Therapists must take into account the extent to which individual variation, level of acculturation, racial-cultural identity status, and socioeconomic status affect the ways a particular family embodies a larger cultural pattern. Also, a multiculturally competent family counselor must be able to identify and work with cultural differences within the same family. For instance, the children in an immigrant family may be taught in school to speak up and ask challenging questions; however, this behavior may not be what is expected in their familial relationships. In this case, a counselor may be dealing with two or more cultural worldviews within the same family.

PRACTICE

Multicultural competence in psychological practice is critical. We have already suggested a number of important elements for considering families in their cultural context. The following considers how the Multicultural Guidelines might apply to two other crucial dimensions of practice: family assessment and interventions used in treatment.

ASSESSMENT

At the heart of any good family assessment are the following questions: What's wrong and what's right? Where is this family stuck? What are its strengths? As counselors listen to and observe their client families, they are also making judgments, comparing what they see to what they expect based on their beliefs about optimal functioning. Counselors note both areas of strength and the dynamics that appear to be related to the family's distress; goals for treatment will be based on the counselor's perceptions of the family's problem. Critical to the process of culturally centered family assessment is the standard counselors use to arrive at their judgments.

Judgments about what is optimal, what is normal, and what is dysfunctional are all made with reference to culturally derived standards. Thus, it is critical for counselors to use paradigms that are culturally appropriate for the family they are assessing. Behavior that is seen as potentially pathological in one cultural context may be viewed as adaptive in another. For an Irish American adult man to call his mother every day might point to an enmeshed family system; for a Dominican American this behavior would be considered within normal limits. In fact, from a Dominican cultural perspective, not to do so might signify a family system that is disengaged. This point highlights the challenge of culturally centered family assessment. On one hand, it has become commonplace to say that counselors should not impose their own cultural biases on their clients; on the other hand, not imposing one's own values is not sufficient. Counselors also need to know enough about the client family's worldview to begin to formulate hypotheses about what is and is not normative from the family's cultural perspective. Otherwise, family counselors run the risk of dismissing potentially destructive behavior as simply "culturally different."

TREATMENT

Once the goals of family treatment are clarified, counselors must also adopt culturally centered interventions to achieve them. That is, treatment strategies as well as goals must be consonant with the family's worldview. For instance, how will the family therapist choose to join the family? If the family is from a culture that favors a "doing" orientation, it may behoove the counselor to articulate a diagnosis and a plan quickly, to show agency. If the family's culture is more relational in nature, it may be more important for the therapist to take more time to establish a working relationship with the family before actively intervening. If the culturally derived family structure is egalitarian, the therapist may choose to ally with the weaker of the two members of the couple. On the other hand, if an authoritarian structure is culturally syntonic, the counselor might seek initial rapport with the person viewed as the head of the family. How confrontational should the counselor be in challenging the dynamics that have led a family to seek treatment? What might this look like in a culture that favors indirect or high-context communication? The same oral communication that might be perceived as refreshingly honest in one culture may be considered disrespectful in another.

A number of other areas should also be considered. Who from an extended family should be attending the sessions? With an immigrant family, how will the therapist manage the question of language and what it suggests about the potential cultural divisions within the family? Should counselors agree to see families if they do not speak the family's primary language? Whereas families from cultures with a future orientation to time may be comfortable with an open-ended treatment plan, those with a present orientation may need goals that are more immediate. To ask family members how it feels to be talking to an outsider presumes that it would be culturally appropriate for them to say. How will a counselor trained to work with clients from an egalitarian stance modify that approach when working with a family whose cultural expectation is that he or she be an expert? These are only some of the choices family counselors must make in choosing culturally appropriate intervention strategies to implement their plan for a given family.

ORGANIZATIONAL CHANGE

Finally, the APA Multicultural Guidelines advocate for organizational development and change so as to promote culturally sensitive and relevant organizational structures, policies, and procedures. For couples and family educators, researchers, and counselors, this is a call to advocate for cultural awareness and knowledge of self and others throughout their organizations as well as to promote culturally sensitive training, research, and practice at every organizational level, including the organization's top leadership. Cultural knowledge, awareness, sensitivity, and appropriateness should be woven into the organization's vision, mission, policies, procedures, and day-to-day behaviors. For example, if part of an organization's mission is to provide high-quality child care for immigrant families, is such child care accessible to those communities? Are child care teachers and administrators multilingual? Is the site easily reachable via public transportation? Is it open early in the morning, late in the evening, and even overnight to accommodate parents who have shift work, including night shifts? That is, are the organizational policies and procedures culturally appropriate and sensitive given the organization's particular family constituency groups? This Guideline encourages couples and family educators, researchers, and counselors to use their family systems perspective to recognize their role as change agents in the very systems in which they work.

Case Example: A Multisystemic Family Consultation

The case of Tanya and her family is used as an example of how one might implement the Multicultural Guidelines previously mentioned and to illustrate the culturally appropriate use of multisystemic interventions. Names and specific information that might identify individuals have been altered to protect their privacy.

The setting for this case study was a prenatal clinic for high-risk pregnant women located in a large, public, urban hospital that primarily serves patients who are of color and poor. Historically, the prenatal clinic had been an all-women's environment. The founder and director of the clinic was a Black woman, as was the head nurse. Nearly all of the other clinic staff (e.g., nurses' aides, social workers, administrators, and support staff) was female and most were of color. The clinic had recently received a grant to enhance services for pregnant women who were at high risk for premature or low birth weight babies due to histories of substance abuse. As part of the grant, a family therapist/consultant was hired, a White male psychologist with advanced training in family therapy and extensive experience in working with poor families of color with histories of substance abuse.

First Referral: From an Individual to a Systemic Perspective

Tanya, a patient in the clinic, was a 25-year-old Black woman in the beginning of her second trimester of pregnancy. The staff complained that Tanya was medically non-compliant and difficult, an "in-your-face" kind of patient. She frequently was confrontational and short-tempered with the clinic staff. Although drug-free for over a year, Tanya had a history of polysubstance abuse since early adolescence. Soon after the family therapist/consultant joined the clinic, Tanya was referred to him for individual psychotherapy. The staff told the therapist that they feared she was at risk for relapse as she neared her delivery date. Reflecting the clinic's individualistic medical model philosophy, the social worker and nurse had referred Tanya for therapy sessions with the stated goals of helping her learn stress management skills and increasing her compliance with her medical care.

Tanya was a tall woman, bright, direct, and emotionally expressive; she was polite but guarded in her first meeting with the therapist. She told the therapist that she had a two-and-a-half-year-old-son, Anthony, and she needed to get back home to him. Home for her was a residential drug treatment program. When the therapist asked if she had family or friends who supported her, she dismissed him with an affirmative nod but offered no further elaboration. In an attempt to be responsive to Tanya's needs, the therapist said, "Tanya, it's obvious that you're stressed and that what we are doing isn't helping you to alleviate that. What could we do to make this place more accommodating to you?" With little prompting, Tanya said the clinic environment wasn't friendly and she had to wait too long to be seen for her appointments.

In response to Tanya's feedback, the therapist talked with the unit social worker and the head nurse about ways to make the Ob/Gyn clinic more family-oriented. As adequate nutrition was an issue for these women, they agreed to organize a food pantry. The director was able to reserve a room adjacent to the clinic that was large enough for both the pregnant women and their families. On the next clinic day, cheese, bread, fruit, hard-boiled eggs, and juices were set out in the waiting room. As the pregnant women arrived, they were delighted and surprised. This began what later came to be called "the breakfast club."

Although not traditional family therapy, the therapist's first intervention was a successful one. Rather than imposing his White middle-class version of individual psychotherapy, he had elicited from Tanya her assessment of what the problem was. If he had begun the session by being hierarchical (e.g., "Tanya, your yelling at the staff is inappropriate"), she would likely have responded angrily or perhaps left treatment. By being respectful and inquisitive about her needs, he began to build trust as he joined with her. By minimizing his role as the psychologist focused on psychopathology, he also identified himself as a potential advocate and resource for Tanya.

Further Clinical Interventions: Reconnecting

On the next clinic day, the therapist was aware of a sense of community in the waiting room that had not existed on prior clinic days. These women were often isolated from their traditional support systems; many had not spoken to their family of origin in many years. Yet, the women had taken the initial steps in this group to begin reconnecting to community, not a traditional family as defined by the staff but their own version of family. An important, potentially reparative experience had happened during this brief time, illustrating the need for family therapists to be self-aware and creative, particularly when working with clients who are poor and marginalized. The therapist had minimized his role, allowing the collective resources of the group to emerge. Rather than viewing themselves as incompetent crack addicts, the women began to have an experience of empowerment as they became "the experts" by helping one another.

However, the family therapist still faced several challenges in developing useful interventions for these women. Specifically, he would need to create a forum that addressed the staff's fears that women with histories of substance abuse were unable to parent their children. Equally significant, in this traditionally all-female environment, fathers of the babies were often viewed by staff as disruptive and potentially treacherous; this was a cultural devaluing of poor men of color that was shared by many of the pregnant women in the clinic. The therapist would need to challenge this belief if the fathers of the babies were to be part of the solution for family preservation. Finally, the White family therapist would need to monitor his own racism regarding stereotypes about poor men of color, including that they were unreliable, unhelpful, or dangerous.

Systemic Interventions: Multidisciplinary Collaboration

To address the staff's fears that the mothers were incompetent and to address the devaluing of men within the clinic, the family therapist met with the Ob/Gyn director and suggested she form a biweekly interdisciplinary team meeting. She agreed and in addition asked that the therapist present at grand rounds on these issues. In attendance at rounds and the team meetings were the medical staff of the women's prenatal services and representatives of psychiatry and psychology, social work, the drug treatment programs, child welfare, and pediatrics. This multidisciplinary group was invited to discuss their concerns and to suggest what would make their jobs easier in providing services for these patients. The staff concurred that the biggest challenge in working with pregnant women with histories of substance abuse was the number of missed appointments. The family therapist raised the possibility that if the clinic invited the patients to include supportive members of their family in treatment, perhaps their compliance with medical appointments would improve.

Out of these meetings, the cultural norm held by many of the staff, that women are the exclusive caretakers of families, was examined and a concept of family was developed that expanded many of the staff members' definition. New policy guidelines were implemented. A woman would now be able to invite to the clinic anyone whom she considered to be supportive of her delivering and raising a healthy baby. The clinic staff arranged tours of the clinic and delivery floor for the patients and their families; this was an opportunity to acquaint the women's support network with the clinic's services and to introduce fathers of the babies to the Ob/Gyn staff. With the patients' permission, the family therapist invited staff occasionally to sit in and observe the breakfast club so that they might have a deeper understanding of the pregnant women's lives.

It was enlightening to see how this new treatment philosophy affected Tanya. During the following breakfast clubs, Tanya began to share with the group some of the stresses she was experiencing. She told the group she was involved with a man who was the father of the baby she was about to deliver. She had two children by different men; one child was in foster care, and she cared for the other. Recently, child welfare had notified Tanya that because she was doing so well in her recovery, they were going to return her daughter to her. Tanya said that her boyfriend was stressing out and not showing up when he said he would. "I don't need any man pulling me down," she declared. The other women in the group nodded in agreement. The family therapist questioned Tanya's position. Like many women in the group, she had become accustomed to being "Supermom," minimizing her support system. "Maybe he has potential to be part of your support system?" the therapist wondered aloud.

The following week, Tanya showed up for group with her boyfriend, Eddie, and her son, Anthony. Eddie was a tall man, neatly groomed, dressed in hip-hop-style clothes. He did not appear to be overjoyed by this visit. During the breakfast club he sat beside Tanya but said little beyond introducing himself. The group appeared interested in Eddie and asked him if he was nervous about becoming a new dad. They wanted to know if he intended to be in the delivery room. Eddie shyly responded that he would like to be in the delivery room. Carmen, one of the more vocal women, called out, "Be careful you don't pass out," and the other women all laughed. But in a reversal of the group's prior position that men were not a resource, the women praised Eddie for wanting to be involved in the birth of his baby. Taking in this feedback, Tanya gave Eddie a broad smile.

The therapist began meeting with Tanya, Eddie, and Anthony for family therapy sessions. In these meetings, the sources of Tanya's stress became clearer as the fragmenting effects of the multiple systems involved in the couple's life emerged. Eddie had been in the same drug treatment program as Tanya, and they had broken the no-dating rule there. They would need to take responsibility for that violation if Tanya was to graduate. Tanya's family heritage of single women raising the children also emerged. After multiple relapses, she had become disconnected from most of her family. As the sessions progressed, Eddie gradually became more involved and active with Anthony. At the end of one session, the therapist shared his impressions that they were a couple in transition, struggling on their own to become a family.

Family Empowerment and Family Preservation

Tanya and Eddie's problems were not magically resolved. In many ways, they were just beginning to cope with the challenges of becoming a family. They would need to negotiate their different parenting styles when their baby was born. Over the course of several family meetings, with the support of Tanya's extended family, the couple made their first difficult decision. Tanya shared that her daughter, Tameka, was in a very good foster home and that she never had played a part in raising her. Although she loved her and had always kept her visitation appointments, she felt that Tameka would do better if she stayed with her foster parents, whom she now considered her family. They were all tearful as the couple discussed what was best for their family.

After Tanya graduated from her drug treatment program, she and Eddie moved into her grandmother's apartment. Anthony became less anxious in the family meetings. Tanya reported letting Eddie take care of him when he wasn't working so she could rest more as her delivery time approached. When the therapist asked, "What's changed? You never used to let him?" she laughed, put her feet up on a stool and said, "Oh, he's a natural father. I was just being a control freak before!"

The Multicultural Guidelines Exemplified in a Family Therapy Case

Tanya's case illustrates a number of the multicultural competencies applied to a family intervention. First, the counselor, a White American male, was aware of his own implicit cultural family paradigm (emphasis on nuclear family, individualism, differentiation, autonomy, etc.) and his own internalized racism (e.g., exposure to and internalization of stereotypes about poor men of color) and worked to prevent these culturally learned values and societal stereotypes from predetermining his treatment. Second, he was sensitive to the possibility that the women of color presenting for treatment might have different cultural values reflected in different definitions of family (more inclusive, collectivistic) and expectations for clinical services (e.g., less detached, more informal, more person-focused). He also noted class-based within-group cultural differences (bordering on antagonism) between the clinic's predominantly middle-class women of color staff and its predominantly poor women of color clients.

Third, the counselor included an education/training dimension to his treatment as part of his advocacy work for the clients. He presented at grand rounds and encouraged the clinical staff to reflect on the cultural values underlying the philosophy of treatment at the clinic and how this was different from the cultural values of the clients. He led the staff in an exploration of their own cultural biases and expectations about family structure and dynamics, pregnancy, and child rearing and how these might influence their work with the clients. He asked the staff to consider their internalized racism and stereotypes about people with histories of substance abuse and suggested ways in which these were embedded in the clinic's policies.

Finally, he also assessed the cultural values underlying the institutional policies in the clinic. In this case, he suspected that the treatment protocol reflected a vision of family rooted in the values of the dominant culture. He noted the clinic's predisposition to treat the mother as an individual rather than as part of a family unit. This was evident in the lack of accommodation for children in the waiting room, Tanya's referral for individual psychotherapy, and the reluctance to include fathers in general in the medical care. He suspected that the staff's reluctance to engage the fathers and expressed concerns about safety might have been influenced by racist stereotypes. In addition, he noted how the pristine and formal atmosphere of the clinic might have reflected a dominant culture model of treatment, focusing on scientific, clinical, and symptom-focused delivery of service.

Accordingly, the therapist attempted to adapt both his own perspective and the clinic's practice to better reflect the expectations of the people it served. He took on an advocate role. He worked to make the clinic less formal and more welcoming to the women and families it served. In response to what he perceived as an overly individualized model of treatment, he invited the clients' children and lobbied the clinic staff to include in their treatment partners or people whom the clients defined as family. In addition, rather than work from the interfamily group model he had initially planned, he formed "the breakfast club," a less formal, more inclusive, more personal approach. Finally, in conducting family therapy, the counselor explored not only the dynamic between the couple, but also the multiple systems in which the family was embedded (e.g., cultural context, drug treatment programs, medical, and child welfare). This case demonstrates how the Multicultural Guidelines can be applied to family counseling, particularly with regard to knowledge of self and others, training, practice, and organizational development and change.

STRATEGIES FOR ACQUIRING MULTICULTURAL FAMILY COMPETENCE

This section suggests some strategies for developing multicultural competence in the four areas discussed earlier. First, family practitioners and trainees need to engage in self-assessment regarding their own cultural assumptions about family structure and functioning. Practica courses that promote critical self-reflection regarding patterns in one's family of origin should also encourage students to consider the cultural dimensions of their own family's dynamics, making explicit the cultural assumptions they may have inherited about families (e.g., boundaries, intimacy, conflict resolution, communication). Practitioners and trainees alike can interview members of their family of origin, with special attention to cultural influences in the family's functioning. Culture should also be an explicit component of family genograms.

Second, a starting point for increasing knowledge and awareness of a variety of family cultural patterns is reading, taking courses, and participating in workshops that feature information about families from different cultural contexts. It is especially important for counselors to acquire knowledge and awareness about the culture of families with whom they are likely to work, particularly culturally centered perspectives on optimal and suboptimal family functioning. Didactic information is essential; exposure to and interaction with families from a variety of cultural backgrounds is equally critical. Students should be required to obtain practica experiences in a variety of settings with various populations. Multiculturally competent supervision as part of these practica experiences is also necessary. Trainees and others wishing to develop multicultural competence in this area would do well to have a mentor who can help them attend to the cultural nuances of a given family's dynamics while also helping them explore their own culturally biased reactions to the family.

Third, couples and family counselors (as all counselors) should engage in continuing education to assess and refine their multicultural competence. Even experienced counselors should seek out supervision with colleagues and mentors to continually increase awareness of their own cultural biases and blind spots in treating couples and families. Counselors should participate in case conferences, grand rounds, and symposia and workshops at professional conferences where multicultural competence in couples and family therapy is featured. If such opportunities are not readily available, counselors should advocate developing them.

Finally, those working in couples and family counseling should consider a multisystems perspective in their own organizations. That is, they should examine sub- and suprasystem dynamics and consider whether these systems promote a culture-centered framework. Couples and family counselors with multicultural competence should be encouraged to seek organizational leadership positions and to influence culture-centered policies and procedures. Additionally, as the case example shows, positive organizational change toward multicultural competence is possible at various levels of the organization: A counselor providing direct clinical service, an educator training the next generation, and a researcher in a lab are all potentially capable of encouraging organizations to inculcate multicultural competence into their vision, mission, and day-to-day operations.

CONCLUSION

The recent APA Multicultural Guidelines draw attention to several areas of knowledge, awareness, and skill required to adequately understand clients, taking into account the cultural contexts and the sociopolitical realties that inform their worldviews—and the perspectives of those who treat them. This chapter has suggested a number of ways the Multicultural Guidelines might be applied to work with families and couples. The recent psychological literature on culture and families was used to frame the discussion, a case example was provided, and strategies were offered regarding developing competence in the areas noted in the Multicultural Guidelines. Just as individuals are embedded in family systems, cultural contexts shape family organization and dynamics. This chapter has highlighted how race and culture influence both clients' and therapists' assumptions about optimal family functioning and about what constitutes dysfunction. In a society currently concerned with "defending marriage and the family," psychologists will have ample opportunity though their practice, teaching, research, and advocacy to attest to the multiplicity of ways in which healthy families can be constituted.

REFERENCES

American Psychological Association. (2003). Guidelines on multicultural education, training, research, practice, and organizational change for psychologists. *American Psychologist, 58,* 377–402.

Aponte, H. (1976). Underorganization in the poor family. In P. J. Guerin (Ed.), *Family therapy: Theory and practice.* New York: Gardner.

Atkinson, D. R., Morten, G., & Sue, D. W. (Eds.). (1998). *Counseling American minorities* (5th ed.). Dubuque, IA: McGraw-Hill.

Baer, J. (1999). The effects of family structure and SES on family processes in early adolescence. *Journal of Adolescence, 22,* 341–354.

Banks, A. (2001). Tweaking the Euro-American perspective: Infusing cultural awareness and sensitivity into the supervision of family therapy. *Family Journal: Counseling and Therapy for Couples and Families, 9,* 420–423.

Bean, R. A., Perry, B. J., & Bedell, T. M. (2002). Developing culturally competent marriage and family therapists: Treatment guidelines for non-African-American therapists working with African-American families. *Journal of Marital and Family Therapy, 28,* 153–164.

Bion, W. R. (1948). Experience in groups. *Human Relations, 1,* 314–329.

Broderick, C. B., & Schrader, S. S. (1981). The history of professional marriage and family therapy. In A. S. Gurman & D. P. Kniskern (Eds.), *Handbook of family therapy.* New York: Brunner/Mazel.

Brown, D. (1997). Implications of cultural values for cross-cultural consultations with families. *Journal of Counseling and Development, 76,* 29–35.

Constantine, M. G., Juby, H. L., & Liang, J. J.-C. (2001). Examining multicultural counseling competence and race-related attitudes among White marital and family therapists. *Journal of Marital and Family Therapy, 27,* 353–362.

Falicov, C. J. (1988). Learning to think culturally in family therapy training. In H. A. Liddle, D. C. Breunlin, & R. C. Schwartz (Eds.), *Handbook of family therapy and training supervision* (pp. 335–357). New York: Guilford Press.

Falicov, C. J. (1995). Training to think culturally: A multidimensional comparative framework. *Family Process, 34,* 373–388.

Falicov, C. J. (1996). Mexican families. In M. McGoldrick, J. Giordano, & J. K. Pearce (Eds.), *Ethnicity and family therapy* (2nd ed., pp. 66–84). New York: Guilford Press.

Fulmer, R. (1988). Lower-income and professional families: A comparison of structure and life cycle process. In E. Carter & M. McGoldrick (Eds.), *The changing family life cycle* (2nd ed., pp. 545–578). New York: Gardener.

Garcia-Preto, N. (1996). Puerto Rican families. In M. McGoldrick, J. Giordano, & J. K. Pearce (Eds.), *Ethnicity and family therapy* (2nd ed., pp. 66–84). New York: Guilford Press.

Greenan, D. E., & Tunnell, G. (2003). *Couple therapy with gay men.* New York: Guilford Press.

Gushue, G. V. (1993). Cultural-identity development and family assessment: An interaction model. *Counseling Psychologist, 21*(3), 487–513.

Gushue, G. V., Constantine, M. G., & Sciarra, D. T. (2004). *The impact of culture, self-reported multicultural counseling competence, and shifting standards of judgment on perceptions of family functioning.* Manuscript submitted for publication.

Gushue, G. V., & Sciarra, D. T. (1995). Culture and families: A multidimensional approach. In J. G. Ponterotto, J. M. Casas, L. A. Suzuki, & C. M. Alexander (Eds.), *Handbook of multicultural counseling* (pp. 586–606). Thousand Oaks, CA: Sage.

Helms, J. E. (1995). An update of Helms's White and People of Color racial identity models. In J. G. Ponterotto, J. M. Casas, L. A. Suzuki, & C. M. Alexander (Eds.), *Handbook of multicultural counseling* (pp. 181–198). Thousand Oaks, CA: Sage.

Hines, P. M. (1988). The family cycle of poor black families. In E. Carter & M. McGoldrick (Eds.), *The changing family life cycle* (pp. 513–544). New York: Gardner.

Ho, M. K. (1987). *Family therapy with ethnic minorities.* Newbury Park, CA: Sage.

Kluckhohn, F. R., & Strodtbeck, F. L. (1961). *Variations in value orientations.* Evanston, IL: Row, Patterson.

Leong, F. T. (1993). The career counseling process with racial-ethnic minorities: The case of Asian Americans. *Career Development Quarterly, 42,* 26–40.

Lewin, K. (1951). *Field theory in social science.* New York: Harper.

McGoldrick, M., Pearce, J. K., & Giordano, J. (1982). *Ethnicity and family therapy* (1st ed.). New York: Guilford Press.

McGoldrick, M., Pearce, J. K., & Giordano, J. (1996). *Ethnicity and family therapy* (2nd ed.). New York: Guilford Press.

Minuchin, P., Colapinto, J., & Minuchin, S. (1998). *Working with families of the poor.* New York: Guilford Press.

Minuchin, S. (1974). *Families and family therapy.* Cambridge: MA: Harvard University Press.

Minuchin, S., Montalvo, B., Guerney, B., Jr., Rosman, B. L., & Schumer, F. (1967). *Families of the slums: An exploration of their structure and treatment.* New York: Basic Books.

Santisteban, D. A., & Mitrani, V. B. (2003). The influence of acculturation processes on the family. In K. M. Chun, P. B. Organista, & G. Marín (Eds.), *Acculturation: Advances in theory, measurement, and applied research* (pp. 121–135). Washington, DC: American Psychological Association.

Sciarra, D. T. (1999). *Multiculturalism in counseling.* Itasca, IL: F. E. Peacock Publishers.

Sue, D. W., & Sue, D. (2003). *Counseling the culturally diverse: Theory and practice* (4th ed.). New York: Wiley.

Szapocznik, J., & Kurtines, W. M. (1993). Family psychology and cultural diversity. *American Psychologist, 48,* 400–407.

Uttal, L. (1999). Using kin for child care: Embedment in the socioeconomic networks of extended families. *Journal of Marriage and the Family, 61,* 845–857.

Walters, M., Carter, B., Papp, P., & Silverstein, O. (1988). *The invisible web: Gender patterns in family relationships.* New York: Guilford Press.

CHAPTER 5

Applying the Multicultural Guidelines to Career Counseling with People of Color

Lisa Y. Flores, Yi-Jiun Lin, and Yu-Ping Huang

MULTICULTURAL CAREER COUNSELING and research has gained prominence in the vocational psychology literature over the past several decades. In the 1970s and 1980s, few publications in counseling, psychology, and vocational journals focused on career development or career counseling practice with persons of color; however, we have seen an increasing trend of publications in this area of research since the early 1990s (Flores, Leal-Muniz, Berkel, & Nilsson, 2003; Perez, Constantine, & Gerard, 2000). Researchers have identified salient issues that influence the career development of persons of color, such as experiences of discrimination, the importance of family and friends in the decision-making process, and gender role socialization within one's culture. The scholarly literature pertaining to the vocational development of diverse racial and ethnic groups is on the rise, and this literature offers critical information for career counseling practice with persons of color.

This chapter addresses career development issues among persons of color in the United States. We outline the ways in which the new "Guidelines on Multicultural Education, Training, Research, and Organizational Change for Psychologists" (American Psychological Association [APA], 2003) apply to multicultural career counseling practice. Next, we present two case examples and provide suggestions for applying the Multicultural Guidelines in career counseling. Also in this section, we integrate findings from the most recently published articles that pertain to the career development of persons of color. Finally, we conclude by providing concrete strategies that career counseling practitioners can implement to develop multicultural competencies for career counseling practice with persons of color.

ELEMENTS OF THE MULTICULTURAL GUIDELINES RELEVANT TO CAREER COUNSELING WITH PEOPLE OF COLOR

The "Guidelines on Multicultural Education, Training, Research, Practice, and Organizational Change for Psychologists" (APA, 2003) set the standard for culturally competent career counseling practice. While all of the Multicultural Guidelines can be tied in one way or another to career counseling practice with people of color, Guidelines 1, 2, and 5 are particularly relevant to the practice.

In accordance with Guideline 1, psychologists are encouraged to recognize personal attitudes and beliefs that may negatively influence their assessment of and work with culturally diverse clients. Career counseling practitioners can possess a range of attitudes that, if left unexamined, can impede the career counseling process. In particular, career counselors must understand their attitudes about work and what work/career means to their lives. For some individuals, work may be viewed as a central element of their lives and to their identity. Conversely, others may perceive work as a means to provide for the family; it may serve only a minor, if any, role in their self-identity. Additionally, career counselors should assess their personal definition of success and beliefs about failure and ensure that they are not pushing their clients toward a path that the career counselor alone considers worthy. These, along with other career-related attitudes (e.g., formal education, decision-making process), should be thoroughly evaluated and understood by career counseling practitioners.

As mental health professionals, having awareness of our own assumptions, values, and beliefs is important but not sufficient. Guideline 2 encourages psychologists to understand their culturally diverse clients. Our knowledge and sensitivity to individuals who are racially and ethnically different from us is another critical element for effective career counseling. In conjunction with the first Guideline, developing skills in this area may help to improve career counseling services to people of color. In particular, career counselors must be aware of and sensitive to the history of people of color in the United States. Specifically, past and current experiences with institutional systems (e.g., public schools, higher education, workplace) may help to inform the career counselor about the career decision making of people of color. Moreover, career counselors should be cautious against assuming that all individuals from a certain racial or ethnic group have had similar life experiences and are alike in their perceptions about work.

Finally, Guideline 5 calls for psychologists to employ culturally appropriate clinical intervention skills in practice. Career counseling practitioners working with culturally diverse clients are encouraged to conceptualize the client's presenting career issues within the client's cultural context. Other culturally appropriate skills relevant to career counseling may include educating the client about social barriers, providing concrete help such as developing a resume or interviewing for a job, discussing strategies used and reasons for utilizing these strategies, and inviting immediate family or extended family members to be involved in the process.

In summary, adherence to these Multicultural Guidelines and continued work on the part of the career counselor to assess personal attitudes, to understand their culturally diverse clients, and to implement culturally sensitive strategies in their career practice with persons of color will ensure the effective delivery of career counseling services.

CASE EXAMPLES IN MULTICULTURAL CAREER COUNSELING

In this section, we present two counseling scenarios, one with a Korean American woman and one with a Native American adolescent boy, presenting with career-related concerns. After describing their situations and dilemmas, we offer suggestions for counseling interventions with these clients. We believe that a critical component to culturally competent career counseling is that practitioners understand the most recent research findings and use this knowledge to inform their career practice. Thus, when discussing potential counseling interventions, we incorporate findings from studies that are closely linked to the Multicultural Guidelines and that we believe may facilitate successful career counseling with persons of color. In addition, we address issues that may serve as a barrier to effective counseling. Finally, we apply Guidelines 1, 2, and 5 to the following case examples.

Case Example: The Case of Angela

I am 31 years old, married, and the mother of a 3-year-old girl. I am a first-generation Korean American raised in California. Both of my parents were born in Korea. Although they have lived in the United States for several years, their interactions are still what I consider traditional or conservative. My father is basically in charge of almost everything except house chores and the children's education, which are considered the main responsibilities of my mother. My mother is a housewife and has never worked outside of our family.

My husband is Korean. He originally came to the United States to pursue his PhD in biochemistry. We met in college in 1992 and married after dating for 4 years. He is currently completing his postdoctoral training, and I am an elementary school teacher. Recently, my husband has been talking about the possibility of going back to Korea because his mother has been very ill for the past year. As the oldest son, he is responsible for caring for his elderly parents. My parents think that I should go back to Korea with my husband because a married woman is expected to take her husband's family as her main family. I visited Korea several times with my parents when I was young and three times with my husband after we got married, so I feel I have a certain level of connection with this country. However, I also have a couple of concerns about going to Korea. First, if we went back, we would be expected to live with my husband's parents. I left home when I was 18 years old to attend college and have never lived with my parents since, so I don't know if I can adjust to living with two elderly people. Second, my father-in-law has implicitly suggested that for the whole family's sake, I should not continue working and should stay at home to take care of my mother-in-law and my daughter. Even if I wanted to work, one of my Korean friends told me that in Korea it is not easy for a married woman to get a job. Most Korean women are encouraged to stay at home to raise children and take care of the family, and this is not appealing to me.

I have been arguing with my husband for weeks about this. I don't know if I am capable of taking care of an ill person. I don't want to quit working because work has become a part of my identity. However, I see how upset my husband gets after these disagreements, and I feel bad. We have talked about several alternatives, such as a temporary separation, inviting his parents to come to the United States, and paying a nurse to take care of his mother. However, it seems that none of these alternatives works for both of us. This is the first time I have realized how different it is between us in terms of family and work values. I love my husband and my family, and I am afraid that I will lose my marriage if we aren't able to work this out. What should I do?

Case Example: The Case of Mahkah

I am starting my last year in high school. I was born in Arizona and lived in the reservation community for several years. To give my older brother and me a better education, my parents decided to move to the city. Right now, I feel confused about what I can and want to do after high school. My father was a carpenter working in a furniture factory. He was laid off 3 years ago and has not been employed since. Some of my uncles and relatives stay at home and enjoy their lives with family members.

Recently, one of my teachers asked us to think of our future career. Personally, I really can't see that I have many choices. I know I am pretty good at science, but I don't know what my options are in this area. My teacher suggested that I talk to the career counselor in my school, but I'm not sure this is necessary. How can they understand what I really want? Our school counselors are White people who don't understand me; I just don't feel they can do anything for me.

At least I have my family supporting my decisions. My brother told me college is not for everyone. College is only for people who are rich and brilliant. I always believe what he tells me, even though he didn't finish high school. Now he is working in a big factory near our home. He seems to really like his job. I guess I could be like him in the future.

PROPOSED COUNSELING INTERVENTIONS

In understanding and conceptualizing Angela's and Mahkah's career concerns, we suggest that the struggles they are encountering invite intervention at three levels: (1) internal values in terms of gender roles, work, and family; (2) potential interpersonal conflicts; and (3) potential conflicts resulting from cultural differences. The race/gender ecological model of career development of women of color and White women (Cook, Heppner, & O'Brien, 2002) suggests that the subsystems of the macrosystem and microsystem developed by Bronfenbrenner (1977) in interaction with the individual are particularly useful in explaining career behavior. The goal of the intervention in both cases is to integrate each client's unique personal, environmental, and cultural characteristics into the career decision-making process.

The proposed interventions are discussed in detail later. First, we want to highlight that an assessment of the personal-environmental barriers is crucial in the course of career counseling with both Angela and Mahkah. Researchers have reported that ethnic minority college students perceived more education- and career-related barriers and less coping self-efficacy than their European American counterparts (Luzzo & McWhirter, 2001). In another study, Asian Americans indicated time management, and African Americans, Latinos/as, and Native Americans cited personal finances as barriers to achieving career goals (Perrone, Sedlacek, & Alexander, 2001).

At the individual level of Cook et al.'s (2002) model, a multiculturally competent career counselor can assist Angela and Mahkah in exploring their essential values in work, family, and gender roles. Because of Angela's role as a woman and a first-generation Korean American, it is critical to take her gender and cultural contexts into account. Findings across studies indicate that racial identity attitudes (Carter & Constantine, 2000), orientation toward culture (Montgomery, Miville, Winterowd, Jeffries, & Baysden, 2000; Niemann, Romero, & Arbona, 2000), feminist attitudes (Zook, 2001), and acculturation (F. T. L. Leong, 2001; Tang, Fouad, & Smith, 1999) may account for differences in the career development process for persons of color. Therefore, integrating an assessment of feminist attitudes and acculturation may be helpful while conceptualizing Angela's presenting issues and developing effective interventions.

In Mahkah's case, career counselors should be aware that Native American adolescents indicated high levels of interest for 2 years or less of postsecondary education (Turner & Lapan, 2002) and that people of color may attribute success more to effort and less to ability (Phinney, Baumann, & Blanton, 2001; Weaver, 2000). Determining Mahkah's career dreams and educational aspirations, assessing if he believes he can achieve these dreams, and determining how he attributes successes in his life are important areas for exploration. In addition, the career counselor should note his limited knowledge of career choices and negative attitude toward career counseling. To address these issues, the counselor can clarify the function of career counseling by authentically responding to Mahkah's concerns and can help him expand his global knowledge of work by using sources of occupational information. Furthermore, an assessment of Mahkah's career interests and career self-efficacy may reveal important aspects of his career decision making. Researchers have found that ethnicity moderated the relationships of interest and abilities with career choice among a nationally representative sample of high school students (Tracey & Hopkins, 2001). It is possible that even though he has exhibited skills in science, he may not have been encouraged to pursue these skills through employment. Finally, the career counselor can emphasize Mahkah's strengths in science to increase his self-esteem.

Second, interpersonal interactions within the microsystem, such as home, school, and work setting, have been suggested as a vehicle providing information related to an individual's career behaviors (Cook et al., 2002). Several studies have found a relationship between family/social support or involvement and the educational and career aspirations of people of color (Flores & O'Brien, 2002; Gloria & Ho, 2003; Gloria & Kurpius, 2001; Juntunen et al., 2001; Kenny, Blustein, Chaves, Grossman, & Gallagher, 2003; Montgomery et al., 2000; Otto, 2000; Schultheiss, Palma, Predragovich, & Glasscock, 2002; Trusty, 2002; Turner & Lapan, 2002). Common salient factors across qualitative studies of American Indians (Juntunen et al., 2001), professional Latinas (Gomez et al., 2001), and professional African American women (Pearson & Bieschke, 2001) included value of education and social support. These studies suggest that relational factors may be especially important in the career development of individuals from diverse racial and ethnic groups who place high value on interdependence and community connection. Thus, assessing support among family (e.g., mother, father, siblings, extended family) and non-family members (e.g., teachers, peers) and including important members of the family in the career counseling should be considered.

In the case of Angela, couple counseling may be helpful in terms of resolving potential conflicts between her and her husband. The dilemma that Angela is facing obviously involves not only her personal interests but also those of her husband and the whole family. Therefore, while empowering Angela during her decision-making process, encouraging mutual understanding and dialogue between Angela and her husband will optimize the effects of career counseling.

Due to Mahkah's frequent and close interaction with family members, strategies aimed at understanding the support and role of family in his career development is essential. The career counselor should seek information about Mahkah's roles and responsibilities in his immediate and extended family. The career counselor can help Mahkah become aware of the messages he has received pertaining to career and how he perceives the career development of his father, brother, and other male extended family members as having an influence on his current career options. As noted, Mahkah's parents moved to the city to improve their children's education. The career counselor might help Mahkah talk about his feelings regarding his parents' decision. Moreover, Mahkah's parents and other family members may be consulted to gather input regarding Mahkah's career decisions.

A proposed intervention at this level might include asking the client and other family members to construct a family career genogram to gather information regarding family members' occupations, work values, and gender roles and to discuss patterns in their families across generations. Through comparison of their respective career genograms, topics such as worldviews, personal-work-family role conflict, male and female role expectations, and acculturation can be presented and discussed naturally. A discussion of possible career options and the pros and cons associated with each option, the possible adjustment difficulties, transition barriers, and support needs is recommended.

Finally, career clients need to be aware of the social factors influencing their career development process. For example, researchers have found that institutional cultural congruity (Constantine & Watt, 2002; Gloria & Ho, 2003; Gloria & Kurpius, 2001) and college racial composition (Flowers, 2002) were related to the academic success and persistence of students of color. One of Angela's concerns is the perceived difference between the two cultures and the potential adjustment difficulties resulting from these cultural differences. The macrosystem of the ecological model gives us a framework for approaching issues related to the ideological components of a given society such as norms and values (Cook et al., 2002). Unfamiliarity and ambiguity can easily trigger anxieties. Thus, clarifying the cultural norms, values, and expectations of the specific cultural context (i.e., Korea) may be helpful for Angela. Specifically, information regarding Koreans' cultural values and practices, expectations of their elderly parents, vocational gender stereotypes, job opportunities, and the social support system she may encounter in Korea should be gathered and explored. Talking with her husband, parents, parents-in-law, and Korean friends are potential avenues to access practical information. If possible, talking with other women who have gone through similar struggles may also be helpful.

As a Native American student, Mahkah has expressed some concerns about being understood by the White career counselor. An exploration of his views toward Whites in general may illuminate beliefs regarding occupational and educational segregation, and an effective multicultural career counselor can help Mahkah understand how his beliefs were shaped and how they may influence his career decisions. With this awareness, his career counselor can provide more effective interventions by helping him identify and practice skills to cope with the environment. For example, if Mahkah decides to enter the workforce after graduation from high school, his career counselor might teach him job search skills, such as interviewing and resume writing. Alternatively, if he decides to continue his education, the career counselor might provide resources that may help him gain admission, seek financial support, and develop a social support network. Also, the career counselor may connect Mahkah to programs targeted to improving the academic achievement of people of color, such as Upward Bound, McNair Scholars prep program, and other college access programs. Researchers have found that these and other programs that serve youth at risk for educational failure have yielded positive outcomes for program participants (Hathaway, Nagda, & Gregerman, 2002; Linnehan, 2001; O'Brien et al., 2000; Perna, 2002; Sorge, Newsom, & Hagerty, 2000).

Potential Barriers to Effective Counseling

It is important that career counselors consider issues that may prevent effective career counseling with these clients. In both cases, family members' attitudes toward help-seeking behavior and participating in career counseling are significant elements in effective counseling. The absence of family members' involvement and support in the decision-making process may compound the presenting issues and possibly weaken a client's self-efficacy in dealing with career issues. Second, concerns regarding premature termination may arise. Perceived effectiveness of the counseling and working alliance are crucial elements for a client to continue sessions. Thus, it is important to establish a strong working alliance with culturally diverse clients in the initial sessions. Clarifying Angela's and Mahkah's expectations of career counseling, the career counseling process, and suggested interventions may be necessary.

APPLICATION OF GUIDELINE 1 TO CASE EXAMPLES

As evidenced in the case examples, there are many areas that a multiculturally competent career counselor will need to explore to be effective with these clients. If career counselors are unaware of their personal attitudes toward women, vocational gender expectations, values about the relative importance of work and family, attitudes about work-bound high school students, beliefs about achievement and success, and personal attributions related to unemployment, they might unwittingly impose their own values, assumptions, and beliefs on the client. Possible outcomes may include unknowingly steering the client's decision in a direction that the career counselor prefers and that reflects the career counselor's values and beliefs. On the other hand, premature termination may result due to the counselor's lack of awareness. Career counselors are encouraged to be aware that they are also cultural beings shaped by cultural factors and should recognize their own worldview so that they can understand others' frame of cultural reference.

APPLICATION OF GUIDELINE 2 TO CASE EXAMPLES

Culturally competent career counselors should be aware of the variables that may account for within-group differences among people of color. Specifically, worldview, racial/ethnic identity, acculturation, and cultural values are a few dimensions to assess when working with persons of color. Each of these variables may play a significant role in the career decision making among persons of color, and career counselors are encouraged to consider their relative influence on both the career development process as well as the career counseling process and relationship. Culturally skilled career practitioners will assess Angela's and Mahkah's worldview, racial/ethnic identity, and acculturation level and their potential influence on their career development and decision making. In addition, failing to understand the career and educational patterns across their families and within their respective cultures and potential environmental barriers to career-related behaviors of these clients will make effective counseling and positive outcome less possible.

Because knowledge is one way to reduce bias and stereotypes of people from culturally different backgrounds, career counselors should increase their understanding and knowledge of career-related issues when working with clients who might have preferences, values, and attitudes that are different from their own. This understanding may be obtained by learning the history of government treatment of and employment laws for culturally diverse populations. Also, counselors should be aware of the recent literature on the career development of people of color.

APPLICATION OF GUIDELINE 5 TO CASE EXAMPLES

Culturally appropriate interventions include assessing environmental barriers, career and educational patterns across generations, and acculturation level of the clients. The flexibility of the format of career counseling, such as inviting family members to counseling sessions, can also be considered a cultural technique. Effective career counselors help their culturally diverse clients clarify questions by talking about family and the meaning of specific terms in their own cultural context.

Career practitioners may also consider utilizing career assessment measures that have recently been validated with diverse groups. Specifically, the factor structure of the Vocational Identity Scale of My Vocational Situation suggested a one-factor model for African American college students (Toporek & Pope-Davis, 2001). In another study, the validity of the Career Maturity Inventory was questioned when used with nonacculturated Asian Americans (Hardin, Leong, & Osipow, 2001), and the researchers suggested that career counselors assess acculturation and self-construal in relation to these clients' career decision making. Finally, researchers (Betz & Gwilliam, 2002; Chung, 2002; Gwilliam & Betz, 2001) provided validity evidence for several career self-efficacy measures, including the short version of the Career Decision-Making Self-Efficacy Scale (Betz, Klein, & Taylor, 1996), the Skills Confidence Inventory (Betz, Borgen, & Harmon, 1996), the Self-Efficacy Questionnaire (Lenox & Subich, 1994), and the Self-Efficacy Rating Scale (Lapan, Boggs, & Morrill, 1989) with diverse college students. Vocational counselors may consider following the recommendations of culturally suitable career assessment models in their practice with people of color (e.g., Bingham & Ward, 1994, 1997; Flores, Spanierman, & Obasi, 2003; Ward & Bingham, 1993).

The results of a series of process and outcome studies by Kim and his associates can illuminate important aspects of career counseling with Asian Americans. Kim, Li, and Liang (2002) reported that Asian American clients positively rated the working alliance with their counselors when counseling focused on immediate problem resolution. However, clients who adhered to Asian values rated their counselor higher on cross-cultural counseling skills when the counselor focused on insight attainment. In another study, researchers found that neither clients' adherence to Asian cultural values nor counselors' self-disclosure were related to session outcome (Kim et al., 2003). These clients evaluated counselor disclosures that were related to strategies as more helpful than disclosures that were related to approval/reassurance, facts/credentials, and feelings.

It is clear that effective career counseling with people of color does not occur in a cultural or contextual vacuum and that various factors need to be taken into account while working with racially/ethnically diverse clients. The era of monocultural intervention has become history. Multiculturally competent career counselors and vocational psychologists should continuously educate themselves with empirical research and literature regarding career development of racially/ethnically diverse clients and apply their knowledge and skills to clinical practice.

SUGGESTIONS FOR CONTINUED DEVELOPMENT OF MULTICULTURAL CAREER COUNSELING COMPETENCIES

Cross-cultural competencies identify the skills necessary to work effectively with diverse clients. They were first operationalized by Sue and his colleagues (1982) to include awareness, knowledge, and skills. A decade later, Sue, Arredondo, and McDavis (1992) expanded the competencies to encompass awareness, knowledge, and skills in the following areas: counselor awareness of own cultural values and beliefs, counselor awareness of client's worldview, and culturally appropriate intervention strategies. Based on the earlier versions of multicultural competencies and the new set of Multicultural Guidelines (APA, 2003), a number of concrete strategies related to multicultural career counseling are identified and discussed next and center on the competency areas of awareness, knowledge, and skills.

AWARENESS

Because multicultural sensitivity is an ongoing and lifelong process (Kiselica, 1999), increasing one's awareness of how one's own and others' cultural backgrounds influence worldview and behaviors is an essential process of career counselors' multicultural professional development. In addition to gaining factual knowledge about the populations we work with, it is equally important to acknowledge how our own racial/cultural heritage and racial identity development affect our values, beliefs, and assumptions related to career behaviors. Career counselors can develop multicultural competencies in this area by:

- Reflecting and understanding how their career development has been shaped by their own cultural background.
- Clarifying their assumptions about the career development process.
- Understanding that each client lives in a unique sociocultural context that may espouse values unlike those reflected by European American culture, such as individualism and autonomy, affluence, the structure of opportunity open to all, the centrality of work in people's lives, and the linearity, progressiveness, and rationality of the career development process (Gysbers, Heppner, & Johnston, 2003).
- Developing awareness of how discrimination and oppression affect worldview, and how these acts influence the perception of the world of work for their culturally diverse clients.

KNOWLEDGE

To be a culturally competent mental health professional, Sue and Sue (2003) suggested that it is crucial to equip ourselves with specific knowledge and information about the particular group with which we are working, to understand how the sociopolitical system in the United States operates with respect to the treatment of marginalized groups in our society, and to be aware of institutional barriers that prevent some culturally diverse clients from using mental health services. Career counselors can develop multicultural competencies in this area by:

- Remaining updated on the latest vocational psychology literature and empirical findings specifically pertaining to culturally diverse groups.
- Understanding important legislation and sociocultural forces that have shaped the career development of culturally diverse groups in the United States.
- Understanding issues related to the norms of career-related instruments and how these instruments may be biased and distort the results of culturally diverse clients' career behaviors.
- Considering the influence of contextual and environmental factors on an individual's career decision-making process (i.e., Lent, Brown, & Hackett's social-cognitive career theory, 1994; Cook et al.'s race/gender ecological approach to career development, 2002).
- Interviewing people across various marginalized groups about their career development and the factors that they feel have helped or hindered the process, specifically focusing on the roles of culture, racism, sexism, and classism in their career decision making, selection of careers, and career-related beliefs.
- Understanding how culturally diverse individuals define career and their work-related experiences (interviewing, hiring, negotiating, work relations).
- Attending conferences that focus on racial/cultural issues in counseling (e.g., National Multicultural Conference and Summit, Teachers College Winter Roundtable) and enrolling in continuing education workshops that focus on some aspect of cross-cultural competencies (e.g., assessment, counseling specific groups).

Given that there is greater variation within cultural groups than between groups, counselors must be careful to distinguish between fundamental understanding and overgeneralization or stereotyping of individuals from racially or ethnically diverse groups.

SKILLS

Writing of culturally appropriate intervention strategies, Sue et al. (1992) emphasized interventions on not only the individual but also the organizational and societal levels. Career counselors can develop skill competencies at the individual level by:

- Clarifying the process of career counseling, expectations and goals of career counseling, and purposes of assessment instruments to decrease anxiety related to ambiguity of the process on the part of culturally diverse clients (Leong & Gim-Chung, 1995) and to avoid premature termination.
- Expanding flexibility of locations (e.g., home visit, assessment of workplace) to conduct career counseling (Sue & Sue, 2003).
- Conducting a thorough assessment, including worldview, racial/ethnic identity, acculturation, parents' educational and occupational backgrounds, and personal aspirations.
- Equipping themselves with a variety of nonstandardized assessment techniques and strategies that may be useful in career counseling with racially/ethnically diverse clients, including the Missouri Occupational Card Sort, Career Genogram, Career-O-Gram (Thorngren & Feit, 2001), and storytelling (Brott, 2001).
- Administering and interpreting assessment instruments developed for specific racial/ethnic groups (i.e., acculturation scales, racial identity instruments).
- Becoming involved with culturally diverse groups outside of work roles, such as through community events and celebrations (Sue et al., 1992).
- Receiving consultation/supervision from other professionals who have expertise in working with clients of diverse racial/ethnic backgrounds.
- Creating a multicultural welcoming space for diverse clients (Heppner & Duan, 1995) that includes reading materials and decor that is appealing to culturally diverse clients.

Career counselors can develop skill competencies at the organizational and societal level by:

- Promoting collaboration between vocational psychology researchers and career counseling practitioners.
- Initiating and developing outreach programs to make career services more accessible to racial/ethnic minority groups.

- Increasing the service utilization of underrepresented minority groups by offering services in diverse formats.
- Becoming a devoted advocate for social justice (O'Brien, 2001).

CONCLUSION

Our society is becoming increasingly diverse, and projection estimates indicate that these trends will continue into the next several decades. The fabric of our society will look markedly different in the year 2050 than it does today, according to government projections, which take into account international migration rates, fertility rates, and mortality rates of each racial and ethnic group (Day, 1996). We believe that it is the ethical responsibility of current and future career counselors and vocational psychologists to work effectively with people who are representative of the U.S. population and not merely one segment of the population, which has historically been the focal point of career counseling research and training. To assist in this endeavor, we highlighted career development issues encountered by persons of color in the United States, provided a brief summary of the career development literature on persons of color published from 2000 to 2004, provided suggestions for applying the Multicultural Guidelines in career counseling using two case examples, and suggested concrete strategies that career counseling practitioners can implement to continue to develop multicultural competencies for career counseling practice with persons of color.

REFERENCES

American Psychological Association. (2003). Guidelines on multicultural education, training, research, practice, and organizational change for psychologists. *American Psychologist, 58,* 377–402.

Betz, N. E., Borgen, F. H., & Harmon, L. W. (1996). *Skill Confidence Inventory applications and technical guide.* Palo Alto, CA: Consulting Psychologists Press.

Betz, N. E., & Gwilliam, L. R. (2002). The utility of measures of self-efficacy for Holland themes in African American and European American college students. *Journal of Career Assessment, 10*(3), 283–300.

Betz, N. E., Klein, K. L., & Taylor, K. M. (1996). Evaluation of a short form of the career decision-making self-efficacy scale. *Journal of Career Assessment, 4,* 47–57.

Bingham, R. P., & Ward, C. M. (1994). Career counseling with ethnic minority women. In W. B. Walsh & S. H. Osipow (Eds.), *Career counseling for women: Contemporary topics in vocational psychology* (pp. 165–195). Hillsdale, NJ: Erlbaum.

Bingham, R. P., & Ward, C. M. (1997). Theory into assessment: A model for women of color. *Journal of Career Assessment, 5*(4), 403–418.

Bronfenbrenner, U. (1977). Toward an experimental ecology of human development. *American Psychologist, 32,* 513–531.

Brott, P. E. (2001). The storied approach: A postmodern perspective for career counseling. *Career Development Quarterly, 49,* 304–313.

Carter, R. T., & Constantine, M. G. (2000). Career maturity, life role salience, and racial/ethnic identity in Black and Asian American college students. *Journal of Career Assessment, 8,* 173–180.

Chung, Y. B. (2002). Career decision-making self-efficacy and career commitment: Gender and ethnic differences among college students. *Journal of Career Development, 28*(4), 277–284.

Constantine, G. M., & Watt, S. K. (2002). Cultural congruity, Womanist identity attitudes, and life satisfaction among African American college women attending historically Black and predominantly White institutions. *Journal of College Student Development, 43,* 184–194.

Cook, E. P., Heppner, M. J., & O'Brien, K. M. (2002). Career development of women of color and White women: Assumptions, conceptualization, and interventions from an ecological perspective. *Career Development Quarterly, 50,* 291–305.

Day, J. C. (1996). *Population projections of the United States by age, sex, race, and Hispanic origin: 1995–2050.* U.S. Bureau of the Census, Current Population Reports, P25–1130. Washington, DC: U.S. Government Printing Office.

Flores, L. Y., Leal-Muniz, V., Berkel, L. A., & Nilsson, J. E. (2003, August). *Racial/ethnic minority vocational research: A trend analysis across three decades.* Poster session presented at the annual meeting of the American Psychological Association, Toronto, Canada.

Flores, L. Y., & O'Brien, K. (2002). The career development of Mexican American adolescent women: A test of social cognitive career theory. *Journal of Counseling Psychology, 49,* 14–27.

Flores, L. Y., Spanierman, L. B., & Obasi, E. M. (2003). Ethical and professional issues in career assessment with diverse racial and ethnic groups. *Journal of Career Assessment, 11*(1), 76–95.

Flowers, L. A. (2002). The impact of college racial composition on African American students' academic and social gains: Additional evidence. *Journal of College Student Development, 43,* 403–410.

Gloria, A. M., & Ho, T. A. (2003). Environmental, social, and psychological experiences of Asian American undergraduates: Examining issues of academic persistence. *Journal of Counseling and Development, 81,* 93–105.

Gloria, A. M., & Kurpius, S. E. R. (2001). Influences of self-beliefs, social support, and comfort in the university environment on the academic nonpersistence decisions of American Indian undergraduates. *Cultural Diversity and Ethnic Minority Psychology, 7,* 88–102.

Gomez, M. J., Fassinger, R. E., Prosser, J., Cooke, K., Mejia, B., & Luna, J. (2001). Voces abriendo caminos (Voices forging paths): A qualitative study of the career development of notable Latinas. *Journal of Counseling Psychology, 48,* 286–300.

Gwilliam, L. R., & Betz, N. E. (2001). Validity measures of math- and science-related self-efficacy for African Americans and European Americans. *Journal of Career Assessment, 9,* 261–281.

Gysbers, N. C., Heppner, M. J., & Johnston, J. A. (2003). *Career counseling: process, issues, and techniques* (2nd ed.). Boston: Allyn & Bacon.

Hardin, E. E., Leong, F. T. L., & Osipow, S. H. (2001). Cultural relativity in the conceptualization of career maturity. *Journal of Vocational Behavior, 58,* 36–52.

Hathaway, R. S., Nagda, B. A., & Gregerman, S. R. (2002). The relationship of undergraduate research participation to graduate and professional education pursuit: An empirical study. *Journal of College Student Development, 43,* 614–631.

Heppner, M. J., & Duan, C. (1995). From a narrow to expansive world view: Making career centers a place for diverse students. *Journal of Career Development, 22,* 87–100.

Juntunen, C. L., Barraclough, D. J., Broneck, C. L., Seibel, G. A., Winrow, S. A., & Morin, P. M. (2001). American Indian perspective in the career journey. *Journal of Counseling Psychology, 48,* 274–285.

Kenny, M. E., Blustein, D. L., Chaves, A., Grossman, J. M., & Gallagher, L. A. (2003). The role of perceived barriers and relational support in the educational and vocational lives of urban high school students. *Journal of Counseling Psychology, 50,* 142–155.

Kim, B. S. K., Hill, C. E., Gelso, C. J., Goates, M. K., Asay, P. A., & Harbin, J. M. (2003). Counselor self-disclosure, East Asian American client adherence to Asian cultural values, and counseling process. *Journal of Counseling Psychology, 50*(3), 324–332.

Kim, B. S. K., Li, L. C., & Liang, C. T. H. (2002). Effects of Asian American client adherence to Asian cultural values, session goal, and counselor emphasis of client expression on career counseling process. *Journal of Counseling Psychology, 49*(3), 342–354.

Kiselica, M. S. (1999). Preparing Anglos for the challenges and joys of multiculturalism. *Counseling Psychologist, 26,* 5–21.

Lapan, R. T., Boggs, K. R., & Morrill, W. H. (1989). Self-efficacy as a mediator of investigative and realistic general occupational themes on the Strong-Campbell Interest Inventory. *Journal of Counseling Psychology, 36*(2), 176–182.

Lenox, R. A., & Subich, L. M. (1994). The relationship between self-efficacy beliefs and inventoried vocational interests. *Career Development Quarterly, 42*(4), 302–313.

Lent, R. W., Brown, S. D., & Hackett, G. (1994). Toward a unifying social cognitive theory of career and academic interest, choice, and performance. *Journal of Vocational Behavior, 45,* 79–122.

Leong, F. T. L. (2001). The role of acculturation in the career adjustment of Asian American workers: A test of Leong and Chou's. (1994). Formulations. *Cultural Diversity and Ethnic Minority Psychology, 7,* 262–273.

Leong, F. T. L., & Gim-Chung, R. H. (1995). Career assessment and intervention with Asian Americans. In F. T. L. Leong (Ed.), *Career development and vocational behavior of racial and ethnic minorities* (pp. 193–226). Mahwah, NJ: Erlbaum.

Linnehan, F. (2001). The relation of a work-based mentoring program to the academic performance and behavior of African American students. *Journal of Vocational Behavior, 59,* 310–325.

Luzzo, D. A., & McWhirter, E. H. (2001). Sex and ethnic differences in the perception of educational and career-related barriers and level of coping efficacy. *Journal of Counseling and Development, 79,* 61–67.

Montgomery, D., Miville, M. L., Winterowd, C., Jeffries, B., & Baysden, M. F. (2000). American Indian college students: An exploration into resiliency factors revealed through personal stories. *Cultural Diversity and Ethnic Minority Psychology, 6,* 387–398.

Niemann, Y. F., Romero, A., & Arbona, C. (2000). Effects of cultural orientation on the perception of conflict between relationship and education goals for Mexican American college student. *Hispanic Journal of Behavioral Sciences, 22,* 46–63.

O'Brien, K. M. (2001). The legacy of Parsons: Career counselors and vocational psychologists as agents of social change. *Career Development Quarterly, 50,* 66–76.

O'Brien, K. M., Bikos, L. H., Epstein, K. L., Flores, L. Y., Dukstein, R. D., & Kamatuka, N. A. (2000). Enhancing the career decision-making self-efficacy of upward bound students. *Journal of Career Development, 26*(4), 277–293.

Otto, L. B. (2000). Youth perspectives on parental career influence. *Journal of Career Development, 27,* 111–118.

Pearson, S. M., & Bieschke, K. J. (2001). Succeeding against the odds: An examination of familial influences on the career development of professional African American women. *Journal of Counseling Psychology, 48,* 301–309.

Perez, R. M., Constantine, M. G., & Gerard, P. A. (2000). Individual and institutional productivity of racial and ethnic minority research in the Journal of Counseling Psychology. *Journal of Counseling Psychology, 47*(2), 223–228.

Perna, L. W. (2002). Precollege outreach programs: Characteristics of programs serving historically underrepresented groups of students. *Journal of College Students Development, 43,* 64–82.

Perrone, K. M., Sedlacek, W. E., & Alexander, C. M. (2001). Gender and ethnic differences in career goal attainment. *Career Development Quarterly, 50,* 168–178.

Phinney, J. S., Baumann, K., & Blanton, S. (2001). Life goals and attributions for expected outcomes among adolescents from five ethnic groups. *Hispanic Journal of Behavioral Sciences, 23,* 363–377.

Schultheiss, D. E. P., Palma, T. V., Predragovich, K. S., & Glasscock, J. M. J. (2002). Relational influences in career paths: Siblings in context. *Journal of Counseling Psychology, 49*(3), 302–310.

Sorge, C., Newsom, H. E., & Hagerty, J. J. (2000). Fun is not enough: Attitudes of Hispanic middle school students toward science and scientists. *Hispanic Journal of Behavioral Sciences, 22,* 332–345.

Sue, D. W., Arredondo, P., & McDavis, R. J. (1992). Multicultural counseling competencies and standards: A call to the profession. *Journal of Multicultural Counseling and Development, 70*(4), 477–486.

Sue, D. W., Bernier, J. B., Durran, M., Feinberg, L., Pedersen, P., Smith, E., et al. (1982). Position paper: Cross-cultural counseling competencies. *Counseling Psychologist, 10*(2), 45–52.

Sue, D. W., & Sue, D. (2003). *Counseling the culturally diverse: Theory and practice* (4th ed., pp. 3–27). New York: Wiley.

Tang, M., Fouad, N. A., & Smith, P. L. (1999). Asian Americans' career choices: A path model to examine factors influencing their career choices. *Journal of Vocational Behavior, 54*, 157–192.

Thorngren, J. M., & Feit, S. S. (2001). The career-o-gram: A postmodern career intervention. *Career Development Quarterly, 49*, 291–303.

Toporek, R. L., & Pope-Davis, D. B. (2001). Comparison of vocational identity factor structures among African American and White American college students. *Journal of Career Assessment, 9*, 135–151.

Tracey, T. J. G., & Hopkins, N. (2001). Correspondence of interests and abilities with occupational choice. *Journal of Counseling Psychology, 48*, 178–189.

Trusty, J. (2002). African American's educational expectations: Longitudinal causal models for women and men. *Journal of Counseling and Development, 80*, 332–345.

Turner, S., & Lapan, R. T. (2002). Career self-efficacy and perceptions of parent support in adolescent career development. *Career Development Quarterly, 51*, 44–55.

Ward, C. M., & Bingham, R. P. (1993). Career assessment of ethnic minority women. *Journal of Career Assessment, 1*(3), 246–257.

Weaver, C. N. (2000). Work attitudes of Mexican Americans. *Hispanic Journal of Behavioral Sciences, 22*, 275–295.

Zook, C. E. (2001). The predictive influence of academic achievement, career exploration, self-esteem, and feminist identity to the career self-efficacy and outcome expectations of college women. *Dissertation Abstracts International. Section B: The Sciences & Engineering, 61*(09-B). (UMI No. 95006-396)

CHAPTER 6

Independent Practice Settings and the Multicultural Guidelines

MELBA J. T. VASQUEZ

THE "GUIDELINES ON Multicultural Education, Training, Research, Practice, and Organizational Change for Psychologists" (American Psychological Association [APA], 2003), hereinafter referred to as the Multicultural Guidelines, were developed because racial and ethnic diversity among clients presents challenges for all of us. We tend to relate most easily, in our lives as well as in our practices, to those most similar to us, including with regard to the major variables of gender, ethnicity, and social class. In this chapter, I identify the importance of multicultural competence in psychotherapy with members of racial/ethnic minority groups, including immigrant and international groups. I also identify potential obstacles as well as positive strategies that I believe to be relevant for the independent practitioner wishing to provide competent ethical services to ethnic minority populations and use case examples to demonstrate key issues.

A goal of this chapter is to promote increased understanding about working with those different from us, which leads to increased competence. Learning to work with those different from us is an ongoing process. A basic assumption is that most of us must be reminded about the importance of having compassion toward a variety of clients, for whom such feelings do not necessarily come naturally for various reasons. At times, simple differences to which we have not been exposed may raise anxieties and render us cautious or distant. At other times, we may have had negative experiences or may have been taught negative stereotypes or generalizations and may behave in negative ways. It is important to note that many of these stereotypes and generalizations and the ensuing behaviors are often, if not usually, subconscious. No one is immune from these processes, including ethnic minority psychologists, even about our own ethnic group members. Internalized racism is a dynamic that we all work against but that can be subtle, unconscious, and powerfully destructive.

CULTURALLY APPROPRIATE INDEPENDENT PRACTICE

Guideline 5 states, "Psychologists are encouraged to apply culturally appropriate skills in clinical and other applied psychological practices" (APA, 2003, p. 390). In this chapter, I limit the discussion to psychotherapy in independent practice.

Psychologists are encouraged to use a "cultural lens" as a central focus of professional behavior. The term "culture-centered" is used in the Multicultural Guidelines to refer to the recognition that all individuals are influenced by different contexts, including historical, ecological, sociopolitical, and disciplinary contexts. It is not necessary to develop an entirely new repertoire of psychological skills to practice in a culture-centered manner. It may be helpful to consider an "overlay" of additional issues and challenges in our work with racial/ethnic minority clients and others different from us. In other words, there will likely be situations where culture-centered conceptualizations and adaptations in interventions and practices will be more effective. Racial/ethnic minority and immigrant clients typically present with very similar problems, relative to other clients. Mental illnesses affect individuals of all ages, colors, and ethnic backgrounds, and all individuals have the right to seek a better quality of life through psychotherapy treatment (U.S. Department of Health and Human Services, 2001). Yet, variations in conceptualization and interventions may be important in providing effective services. A basic assumption is that a more culturally competent psychologist is flexible and adaptable in generating alternative conceptualizations and interventions with a variety of problems with a variety of clients (Pedersen, Draguns, Lonner, & Trimble, 2002).

Although the population of the United States is more culturally and linguistically diverse than it has ever been (U.S. Census Bureau, 2004), racial/ethnic minority and immigrant populations continue to be underrepresented in seeking and utilizing psychological service. The surgeon general's report on mental health (U.S. Department of Health and Human Services, 2001) underlined this concern and identified various disparities in health and mental health services. An ethical responsibility for psychologists is to try to provide equitable services to clients. Given the disparities in mental health services, it is incumbent upon our profession to try to understand the obstacles that would keep anyone with mental health problems and/or who wanted to improve the quality of their life from seeking or receiving effective psychotherapy services in our independent practices. What can we, as individual private practitioners, do to contribute to developing equal access to effective mental health services?

KNOWLEDGE OF SELF AND OTHERS

The first two Multicultural Guidelines inform the other four and are designed to apply to all psychologists. The first Guideline states, "Psychologists are encouraged to recognize that, as cultural beings, they may hold attitudes and beliefs that can detrimentally influence their perceptions of and interactions with individuals who are ethnically and racially different from themselves" (APA, 2003, p. 382). Our worldviews, including the way we perceive our lives and our experiences and those of others, are shaped in large part by our cultural experiences. Every one of us has a set of cultural experiences and backgrounds, both conscious and subconscious.

The second Multicultural Guideline states, "Psychologists are encouraged to recognize the importance of multicultural sensitivity/responsiveness to, knowledge of, and understanding about ethnically and racially different individuals" (APA, 2003, p. 385). Psychologists and counselors are encouraged to learn how cultures differ in basic premises that shape the worldview of individuals from those cultures. The risk in not being aware of one's worldview as well as that of a racial/ethnic minority client is that one may unconsciously and automatically judge the client negatively, and perhaps in a pathological manner. For example, one common example is the value of independence in White, Western culture (which has influenced the evolution of theory and practice of psychotherapy) compared to other cultures, such as Asian American or Latina/o. A cultural facet of mainstream American culture is a preference for individuals who are independent and focused on achievement and success, who have determined and are in control of their own personal goals, and who value rational decision making (APA, 2003; Fiske, 1998). From this perspective, a basic developmental task for all individuals, based on our psychological theories, is the individuation process. We often assess whether a young adult, for example, is appropriately involved in the process of individuation or separation from his or her primary family; clients may be labeled pathologically dependent if we judge that they are still relying on their family of origin to an abnormal degree. By contrast, individuals whose culture is not largely characterized by Western worldviews, such as Latina/o cultures, tend to have a preference for those who have a group or community identity and tend to be very family and cooperatively oriented. Latina/o sons and daughters tend to live at home longer than their

White counterparts (Vasquez & de las Fuentes, 1999). They also make many decisions based on the primacy of family identity and closeness. This includes choosing to live at home or not move far away to attend college and prioritizing the amount of vacation time spent with family. These choices do not necessarily constitute pathological dependency.

Other examples of White culture that may lead to inappropriate negative pathological conceptualizations include strict adherence to time schedules and a priority of achievement and success. For various cultural groups, including Latinas/os, the value of *personalismo*, or personal relationships and connections, is more important than time orientation, success, and achievement; this is related as well to the value of being cooperatively oriented. Latina/o children, for example, may have tendencies to be more focused and motivated when competing as a group than when competing as individuals. Several studies have indicated that Mexican American children develop stronger group enhancement and altruism motives (in completing a number of games) than Anglo-American children, who develop stronger competitive motives (Kagan, 1977). Research has identified the mechanisms, socialization, and ethnic identity by which children's ethnic behaviors are socialized; such studies reconfirm that the ethnic identity of Mexican American children, taught by mothers teaching about Mexican culture, is related to more cooperative and less competitive preferences compared to samples of Anglo-American children (Knight, Cota, & Bernal, 1993).

The issue is not that there is lack of time orientation or value of achievement and success, but that at times, relationships and relationship-oriented activities may take priority, perhaps to a greater extent for some racial/ethnic minorities than in the dominant White culture. At the same time, it is important to remember that there is great heterogeneity within racial/ethnic groups. Many Latina/o individuals, while very cooperation-oriented and great team players, can also be as achievement/success-oriented and competitive as their White colleagues. The key message here is that one should not automatically pathologize such a person. Instead, look for the cultural differences and variations. In addition to being aware of one's own values and worldview and that of diverse clients, an important strategy is to listen to the client's narrative to determine the extent of cultural value versus degree and nature of the problem.

For example, a Latina graduate student who reports frustration with getting negative feedback about her chronic lateness may be conceptualized as being passive-aggressive and/or ambivalent in her behavior. An alternative perspective, applying a cultural lens, would lead to exploring her daily experiences and priorities and supporting her in her perspective (if this is the case) that attending to her children and other family members is more important to her than being on time for class and appointments in certain circumstances. A therapist could also help her explore the consequences for her in the world of academia or in the work world and consider whether those consequences are worth her choices or whether she might wish to adjust to the expectations in that world. Focusing on skills of adaptability and flexibility in moving in and out of her family values and expectations and those of the White work/academic world might be a helpful conceptualization for her. I would suggest that this is a subtle but significantly important difference in conceptualization and intervention from a cultural context.

GETTING SPECIFIC: WHAT DO PRACTITIONERS DO TO HURT AND TO HELP?

A number of social psychological studies are now available to inform us of some human processes that contribute to problems and issues in intergroup relationships. Here I briefly review some potential solutions to these problems, especially those referenced in the Multicultural Guidelines, and apply these to psychotherapy.

CATEGORIZATION: A CONSTRUCTIVE AND DESTRUCTIVE STRATEGY

One of the things we do when we perceive others is place them in a category. This is a psychological process that helps to organize and reduce the often overwhelming amount of information about an individual into manageable chunks that go together (Allport, 1954). This normal process leads to associating various traits and behaviors with particular groups, even if they are inaccurate for most individuals from those groups. Stereotyping and generalizing are consequences of this process.

Opotow (1990), a social psychologist, described how we tend to further form groups in a we/they dichotomy. When we do so, people are able to treat "they" as objects, in insensitive ways, even to the extreme of lynching and the Holocaust. People in our own in-groups are more highly valued and more trusted and engender greater cooperation as opposed to competition. We have more compassion for those in our in-group than for those in the out-groups. For example, Democrats would have a tendency to have more compassion for Bill Clinton's problems than would Republicans; right-wing conservatives would have a tendency to have more compassion for Rush Limbaugh's prescription drug addictions than would liberals and to be more supportive of when and how George W. Bush decided to go to war in Iraq. A White male therapist would have a tendency to have more compassion for a White male client who perceived that he

did not get a promotion due to affirmative action policies. A Latina therapist may have a tendency to have more compassion for a Latina client who
perceived that she did not get a promotion because of biased evaluations.

One of the basic assumptions in much of the multicultural counseling
literature is that ethnic similarity between counselor and client increases
the probability of a positive outcome (Pedersen et al., 2002). What happens
when a White male therapist has an African American woman professing
discrimination? It is quite common to have automatic biases, stereotypic
attitudes, and negative attributions and interpretations about people in
the out-group. Unfortunately, for most psychologists and other mainstream health providers, individuals in racial/ethnic minority groups are
viewed as out-group members. Furthermore, when a person of color or a
woman in the public eye does something wrong, those negative stereotypes are often reinforced. Selective perception of racial/ethnic minorities
in key positions causes many of us to notice the negative exception and
generalize, as opposed to when European White men make major mistakes. These reinforced negative stereotypes unfortunately encourage us
to keep people in the out-group in our categorization schema.

The fact is that it is impossible to be color-blind; as much as we perceive
ourselves to be egalitarian, we are not *subconsciously* color-blind. Dovidio,
Gaertner, Kawakami, and Hodson (2002) have demonstrated in a series of
studies that contemporary racism among Whites is subtle, often unintentional, and unconscious, but that its effects are systematically damaging
and foster miscommunication and distrust. Dovidio et al. acknowledged
that many Whites often give off negative body language (less eye contact,
voice tone not as warm or natural) in response to those different from
themselves. Although these Whites are not aware of it, members of minority groups are. Employee selection and promotion studies continually
indicate bias, especially when those choices can be based on some factor
other than race.

SPECIAL ISSUES FOR PSYCHOTHERAPISTS OF COLOR

As a Latina psychotherapist, I am aware that many of my clients of color
choose to come to me because of my ethnic identity. At the same time,
people of color with internalized racism might choose to avoid seeing
someone like me. I am also aware that many of my White clients have to
go through some process of cognitive dissonance to assume my competency, because in this society, people from my ethnic background are not
assumed to be competent. So what happens when I have a White male
client who is angry at affirmative action policies and makes derogatory
statements about racial/ethnic minorities, perhaps even about members

of my ethnic group? A basic task for ethical practice is to remember the humanity of those with whom we work (Pope & Vasquez, 1998).

Comas-Diaz and Jacobsen (1995) address the interracial dyad involving a therapist of color and a White patient and provide a dynamic analysis of the contradictions, such as significance of power reversal and transferential and countertransferential reactions. They conceptualize this dyad as an opportunity for therapists of color to acquire a perspective from White patients and witness the reality experienced by their majority group patients. Alternatively, White patients can benefit from the contributions of the therapist of color, who has experience in overcoming the odds of achieving success. Both clients and therapists can thus heal and become more empowered.

Case Example 1

Let me provide an example of dealing with differences that evoke negative reactions in me. An older White male called by phone and asked an extensive number of questions about my background, training, years of experience, and approach to psychotherapy. He had a medical degree and a law degree. My automatic reaction was to deal with the anxiety he evoked by pathologizing him as paranoid and obsessive-compulsive; the healthier alternative was to compassionately acknowledge that this was the first time he had considered psychotherapy and that it was very difficult for him to be vulnerable and ask for help. I was able to conceptualize his "interrogation" as simply a strategy he used to feel relatively safer in embarking on a vulnerable endeavor with a person of color. These strategies can be explored in the psychotherapeutic process, and their relative merits and consequences can help the client be more thoughtful about their behaviors.

Most important, the Multicultural Guidelines encourage us to acknowledge differences and, even if they make us uncomfortable, to be respectful about the differences. We have all had experiences in which our critical negative judgments and perceptions were misplaced, inappropriate, and unfounded. We must be careful to determine when such a stance is legitimate in the psychotherapy room. When it is, I suggest that we must refer the client to a colleague.

INTERSECTION OF OPPRESSIVE FACTORS

According to the APA (2003) Multicultural Guidelines, it is helpful to recognize the intersection of racial and ethnic group membership with other dimensions of identity. Gender, age, sexual orientation, disability, religious/spiritual orientation, educational attainment and experiences, and socioeconomic factors are examples of other dimensions of identity that enhance or detract from one's identity and influence the way we relate to our clients.

Case Example 2

I had a call from a woman with a heavy Spanish accent. She asked whether I took Medicare clients and whether my office was accessible to wheelchairs. My anxiety increased for the following reasons. First, although a substantial portion of my clientele is Latina/o, I refer monolingual Spanish speakers to others; although I am a moderately fluent Spanish speaker, my vocabulary ebbs and flows, so I accept only Spanish-speaking clients who are bilingual enough to tolerate my lapses into English. Second, although I do accept Medicare clients, I limit the number, given the low reimbursement rates and the extra paperwork involved. Third, my office is intentionally accessible to wheelchairs, but the awkwardness of dealing with unknown disabilities raises anxieties for me. On the other hand, I know that such a client has only a limited number of bilingual, bicultural therapists in my community, and I am highly motivated to provide services for those who prefer a therapist such as myself. Thus, I went through the ambivalent process for a few minutes, accepted the client, and consulted and talked about my feelings with colleagues. The client and I met for several very productive sessions; the bonding occurred despite the challenges that I had to push through.

Many people of color have additional aspects of identity that intersect with their racial/ethnic identity to form "multiple oppressions." It behooves practitioners to be aware of how those out-group multiple dimensions of a person's identity affect them.

Reduction of Bias

The Multicultural Guidelines suggest a variety of strategies, gleaned from the social psychological literature, to reduce bias. The first and most critical is *awareness* of those attitudes (Gaertner & Dovidio, 2000). The second and third strategies are *effort* and *practice* in changing the automatically favorable perceptions of the in-group and negative perceptions of the out-group. How this change occurs has been the subject of many years of empirical effort, with varying degrees of support (Hewstone, Rubin, & Willis, 2002).

The social psychological literature further suggests that *increased contact* with other groups (Pettigrew, 1998) is helpful, particularly if the individuals are of equal status and the majority group person is able to take the other's perspective (Galinsky & Moskowitz, 2000) and has empathy for him or her (Finlay & Stephan, 2000). The psychotherapeutic situation can potentially be an ideal place for us to develop multicultural competence. Although the relationship is not equal and there is a power differential, it is a mutually engaging endeavor. The relationship is one based on respect and care, and the responsibility of the psychotherapist is to take the client's perspective with compassion and empathy. The combination of awareness of our attitudes and biases with effort and practice and contact with clients from diverse racial/ethnic groups will promote multicultural competence *if* we are willing to challenge our negative socialized biases.

Another strategy is to change the perception of "us versus them" to "we," or recategorizing the out-group as members of the in-group (Gaertner & Dovidio, 2000). This model has been shown to be effective, particularly under low-prejudice conditions and when the focus is on interpersonal communication (Hewstone et al., 2002). In addition, psychologists may want to actively increase their tolerance and trust of racial/ethnic groups (Kramer, 1999). The psychotherapeutic encounter can provide a way to recategorize the out-group individual as a member of one's in-group when one accepts a client into treatment. Continuous attention to one's reactions to clients is important. Attention should be paid, for example, to tendencies to not try as hard to begin on time, to delay seeing the client by making just one more phone call, and to fail to make sure that all is ready before the session (e.g., that notes are reviewed).

We all have clients who evoke respect in us, as well as clients who do not. Sometimes these reactions are to client personality variables, which are grist for the mill. At other times, our failure to feel respect for clients may be a result of biases, which a client must work hard to overcome. We are all subconsciously, automatically biased about a variety of differences. It is important to be aware of those reactions. The earlier review of the literature suggests some important constructive strategies: Assume the individual is worthy of membership in the in-group, tune in to the individual, hear the client's narratives and stories, and connect with the client as a human being. The goal of empathy requires suspending and managing our negative judgments, triggers, and reactions. If we do react to negative aspects of the client and judge those reactions to be legitimate and important therapeutic material (as opposed to bias), we must find ways to reflect that information in a way that allows clients to see their problematic behaviors.

ATTENDING TO THE CLIENT'S EXPERIENCE OF OPPRESSION IN THE PSYCHOTHERAPEUTIC PROCESS

Overlying the general problems presented by most racial/ethnic minority clients is a historical and/or personal experience of oppression and biases. Historical experiences of various populations differ and may be manifested in the expression of different belief systems and value sets among clients and across age cohorts. For example, therapists are strongly encouraged to be aware of the ways that enslavement has shaped the worldviews of African Americans (Cross, 1991). At the same time, the within-group differences among African Americans and others of African descent also suggest the importance of not assuming that all persons of African descent will share this perspective. Thus, knowledge about sociopolitical viewpoints and ethnic/racial identity literature is important and extremely helpful when working with individuals of racial/ethnic minority descent. Culturally centered practitioners assist clients in determining whether a problem stems from institutional or societal racism (or other prejudice) or individual bias in others so that the client does not inappropriately personalize problems. Consistent with the discussion in Multicultural Guideline 2, psychologists are urged to help clients recognize the cognitive and affective motivational processes involved in determining whether they are targets of prejudice.

IDENTIFYING AREAS OF STRENGTH AND RESILIENCE

I indicated earlier that one of the most important strategies in working with persons of color is to identify their strengths and resilience. Future research should shed light on the strengths and survivorship of various ethnic groups, despite various challenges (Vasquez & de las Fuentes, 2000). A 1992 report, for example, indicated that despite enduring poverty-level income, Latinos exhibit values and behaviors that included a strong belief in marriage and family, a vigorous work ethic, and a desire for education (Hayes-Bautista, 1992). California's fast-growing Hispanic population also had a historically low rate of welfare dependency, a high rate of participation in the labor force, good life expectancy rates, and a high percentage of healthy babies. In Texas, according to the Texas Department of Health's Bureau of Vital Statistics ("Hispanic Girls' Life Expectancy," 1996, p. B4), Hispanic baby girls born in 1995 will have the highest life expectancy of any racial or gender group; they are expected to live an average 80.3 years. Researchers hypothesized that because extended families provide emotional support, Hispanic women are less likely to live alone. They are also less likely to be smokers or drinkers, they may have a better diet, and their infant mortality rate is lower than other groups'.

Although we are encouraged to be aware of barriers, obstacles, and experiences of oppression among clients of color, it also is important to remain open to strengths and positive aspects of identity. For example, a study conducted by the Downing Street Group and the University of Michigan, reported in *Marketing to Women* ("Women's Level of Comfort," 2004), found that most women are relatively satisfied with their appearance. More than half (51%) of Caucasian women, 59% of African American women, and 60% of Hispanic women like the way they look! The expectation that women of color would use a White woman standard of beauty and report higher dissatisfaction than White women was certainly found to be erroneous in this study. We should thus be open to considering and exploring aspects of positive strengths in our clients of color.

UNIQUE ISSUES OF ASSESSMENT

Multiculturally sensitive practitioners are encouraged to be aware of the limitations of assessment practices, from intakes to the use of standardized assessment instruments (APA, 2002; Constantine, 1998). The APA Ethics Code (2002) urges psychologists to "use assessment instruments whose validity and reliability have been established for use with members of the population tested. When such validity or reliability has not been established, psychologists describe the strengths and limitations of test results and interpretation" (p. 1071). Psychologists assessing racially/ ethnically diverse clients are also urged to consider the individual's language preference.

In addition to the general issues that psychotherapists typically assess, culturally and sociopolitically relevant factors in a client's history may include relevant generational history (e.g., number of generations in the country, manner of coming to the country); citizenship or residency status (e.g., number of years in the country, parental history of migration, refugee flight, immigration); fluency in standard English or other language; extent of family support or disintegration of family; availability of community resources; level of education; change in social status as a result of coming to this country (for immigrant or refugee); work history; and level of stress related to acculturation (APA, 2003). Culturally centered practitioners are encouraged to take into account how these contextual factors may affect the client's worldview (behavior, thoughts, and feelings).

Another unique issue to assess is how the client has dealt with the experience of oppression. Some clients may be in denial (e.g., "I've never been discriminated against"). The risk for such a person is that when he or she does (inevitably) perceive discrimination, it can be devastating. Helms (1990) described the various stages of identity development for Blacks, Whites, and other persons of color. Denial is an initial stage in many of those models.

THE THERAPEUTIC SETTING

Psychologists are also encouraged to be aware of how their setting (neighborhood, building, and specific office) may appear to clients from diverse backgrounds. For example, bilingual phone service, receptionists, magazines in the waiting room, and other signage can demonstrate cultural and linguistic sensitivity (Arredondo, 1996). Some therapists choose to offer candies in bowls and coffee, tea, water, or other beverages to welcome clients. Theoretical orientation may inform this preference; from a dynamic viewpoint, a psychologist may not wish to promote the message that the psychologist's role is to give to and take care of one's clients. This approach is not wrong, it may simply not be the best fit. For those from cultures whose priority is to offer warmth and welcome, a friendly environment may provide more initial comfort.

MULTICULTURALLY SENSITIVE BOUNDARY ISSUES

Multiculturally sensitive practitioners are encouraged to develop skills and practices that are attuned to the unique worldview and cultural background of clients and to incorporate understanding of the client's ethnic, linguistic, racial, and cultural background into therapy. I would like to apply this principle to the area of professional boundaries.

Boundary setting has long been an important ethical responsibility for psychotherapists. It has evolved as an important strategy in applying the ethical proscription to "do no harm" to our clients. Because the needs of the psychotherapist may potentially obstruct therapy, the mental health professions have established guidelines, often referred to as boundaries, designed to minimize the opportunity for therapists to use their patients for their own needs and gratifications (Pope & Vasquez, 1998). It is the therapist's responsibility to know which behaviors harm and which help clients. Many clients have had family or other relationships in which psychological or physical boundaries or both have not been clear, and they are therefore unable to set appropriate boundaries for themselves. The therapist is especially responsible for distinguishing the therapeutic relationship from those previous harmful relationships; doing so is vital to the success of the therapeutic relationship, according to most psychotherapeutic models and theories.

Exceptions to Boundaries

Encounters outside of therapy, however, may be unavoidable when the lives of multicultural therapists overlap with those of the people they serve. Many gray areas exist in regard to behavior with clients, and it is in these areas that many seek rigid rules. Many multicultural (as well as feminist and humanistic) ethicists construe boundary maintenance in therapy as a continuous rather than a dichotomous issue. Therapists from these theoretical orientations tend to value being more authentic, genuine and/or transparent with their clients and more willing to delve into "gray areas" in their therapeutic relationships. The gray areas include multiple roles, attendance to client's life transitional events, self-disclosure, bartering, gift giving and receiving, and nonsexual touch and other expressions of care.

Exceptions to boundaries must be compatible with one's theoretical conceptualization. Multicultural Guideline 2, recognizing the importance of multicultural sensitivity, along with feminist/multicultural principles should inform therapists' decisions regarding when to make exceptions to boundaries. We must be sure that we can articulate the exception in our treatment process notes and that we recognize the importance of multicultural sensitivity/responsiveness involved in the decision.

Multiple Roles

The Ethics Code Standard 3.05 (APA, 2002) explicitly states that not every multiple relationship is necessarily unethical, as long as the multiple relationship would not reasonably be expected to cause impairment or risk exploitation or harm. This is an attempt to acknowledge those situations, communities, and groups in which multiple relationships are unavoidable or might benefit the client or both. The code is not designed to punish psychologists who engage in benign multiple relationships. It does not authorize therapists to engage in exploitive relationships, however. "A psychologist refrains from entering into a multiple relationship if the multiple relationship could reasonably be expected to impair the psychologist's objectivity, competence, or effectiveness in performing his or her functions as a psychologist, or otherwise risks exploitation or harm to the person with whom the professional relationship exists" (APA, 2002, p. 1065).

Life transitional events are situations that could be construed as creating a potential multiple role situation. These situations include client invitations to special events that, from a multicultural/feminist perspective, may be therapeutically meaningful, such as weddings, graduations, and performances. The important questions to ask include: Is my attendance symbolically or genuinely significant and productive for the client? How much is attendance for my own needs? Is there any risk of promoting dependency on the part of the client? Is there any risk of exploitation of the client? How might this impact others (clients, colleagues, community)?

Self-Disclosure

Feminist therapists were among the first to challenge the proscription against self-disclosure. The Feminist Therapy Institute (1990) code of ethics provides guidelines for therapist disclosure in the context of the power differential. With the well-being of clients as the overriding principle, the guidelines state, "A feminist therapist discloses information to the client which facilitates the therapeutic process. The therapist is responsible for using self-disclosure with purpose and discretion in the interest of the client" (p. 1). From a feminist perspective in general, the issue is to acknowledge the real and genuine aspects of the human interaction in psychotherapy. Psychodynamic approaches tend to focus more on the symbolic transaction, in which the therapist puts aside his or her feelings and contributions to the interaction and assumes that all issues that evolve in therapy are those of the client. In the feminist approach, it is also important to not deny various aspects of the symbolic transactions, including the power differential, because doing so is a failure to take responsibility for the roles that clients inevitably attribute to us by virtue of the therapist position. No matter how genuine and real aspects of the human part of the therapeutic interaction are, we still have responsibility to promote competent interventions that do no harm in our work with clients. Therefore, we must be careful that self-disclosures are in the service of the client and not designed to meet our own needs.

Self-disclosure, however, can be a powerful way to increase mutuality and connection with a client. Information is a form of power. Increased therapist visibility allows clients more power in the relationship than they would have with a less forthcoming therapist. Therapist self-disclosure also serves the function of allowing the client to reciprocate empathy, which can be an empowering experience especially for a racial/ethnic minority client. Analysis of each situation is important: What is therapeutically self-disclosing for one client may not be so for another.

When a client of color, for example, shares a horrific experience of failure, with shame and humiliation, it may be helpful for the therapist to share a similar experience. Doing say may convey that (1) the therapist understands the experience; (2) the therapist is with the person, not judging; and (3) one does survive such experiences.

Answering clients' questions is related to the issue of self-disclosure. In the psychoanalytic model, the goal is to not gratify the client and then process the anxiety from a dynamic perspective. If a Latina client asks, "Did you see the movie *Real Women Have Curves*?" and I answer with the question, "Why is that important to you?," the risk is that I will evoke shame and confusion in someone who is often shamed by virtue of her ethnicity and gender. One may easily answer the question so long as it is in an appropriate realm (nonprivate) and then process any significance. This is a subtle but potentially powerful difference: One approach fails to gratify the client and may elicit anxiety or shame, which can then be processed from a dynamic perspective; the other promotes connection, relating on a real, authentic, genuine level, and may also allow exploration of the need/anxiety/symbolic issue behind the question. The client and I can share perspectives of this Latina/o-focused movie, and then I may ask what it means to her that I saw it and that we shared perspectives about the experience. This approach allows for deeper and deeper recycling through issues in a relationship based on warmth, safety, mutuality, and respect.

Bartering

The APA's 1992 Ethics Code allowed for bartering as long as it was not exploitive or clinically contraindicated. It included the following sentence, however: "Psychologists ordinarily refrain from accepting goods, services, or other nonmonetary remuneration from patients or clients in return for psychological services because such arrangements create inherent potential for conflicts, exploitation, and distortion of the professional relationship" (p. 1602). Because it was perceived that this statement unnecessarily discouraged acceptable practices, the sentence was later eliminated. Psychologists must still refrain from bartering, however, if it is clinically contraindicated or if the resulting arrangement is exploitive. The position of the APA is an attempt to balance the practices in some rural and racial/ethnic minority communities in which bartering may be customary, with protection of the consumer from potential exploitation and problems created in the therapeutic relationship.

Giving and Receiving Gifts

The context of gift giving and receiving is crucial. Generally, gift giving is discouraged, because clients pay for services; receiving expensive gifts from clients can be a form of exploitation, as it may signify that the client does not feel worthy enough unless he or she gives continually. But it can simply be a healthy expression of care on the part of the client. It is important to understand the goals, motivations, and expectations when clients offer gifts.

On the other hand, when a Latina client who works near a restaurant brings me tacos because I squeezed her in during my lunch hour when she was in crisis, we don't need to spend half an hour processing the meaning of the tacos. We know that she felt appreciative, that it was a relatively easy, warm gesture, and that food is a common gift among Latinas. Sometimes a taco is just a taco!

Nonsexual Touch and Other Expressions of Care

Based on multicultural/feminist models, I believe that it is reasonable to assume that some clients may benefit from warm, caring, nonsexual hugs. Certain cultural groups, especially women from South American countries, tend to give hugs on a regular basis. Some African American men have special greetings and hand shakes that would be a special form of communication from an African American therapist. However, some clients feel violated at any touch. It is important for therapists to assess the meaning of nonsexual touch with clients. Factors to consider include the nature of the relationship, the client's personal history, the client's current mental status, the likelihood of adverse impact on the client, and clear theoretical rationale. What does a hug mean to this client in regard to power? Is it a communication of power over him or her? Or a communication of mutuality? It is important to assess whose need it is to hug—yours or the client's? It is important to remember that some clients have experienced numerous boundary violations and either are uncomfortable with touch or must control it to feel safe. What is the client's internal, personal phenomenological experience, and what have physical contacts meant to the client in his or her social context?

Summary of Boundary Issues

I do wish to acknowledge that boundary issues for women therapists are different from those for men therapists. Self-disclosure among men, especially of weakness and vulnerability, violates a gender norm, and touch is more dangerous for a male therapist in Western culture. When we discuss these issues, we must acknowledge the realities of the social construction of gender and the differential impact on women and men therapists, as well as on women and men clients. My challenge to the boundaries may be appropriate challenges for women therapists, but not necessarily for men therapists. Certain behaviors on the part of ethnic/racial minority therapists with their clients may not be appropriate for White therapists. But in general, I encourage the goal of recognizing the importance of multicultural sensitivity and responsiveness, knowledge, and understanding about ethnically and racially different individuals in the area of professional boundaries.

CONCLUSION

In applying our traditional models of practice, I encourage us all to practice sensitivity toward those from different cultures. We have to gain knowledge and experience about our racially/ethnically diverse clients and each individual client; we must listen to their narratives and avoid recreating shaming, oppressive experiences. In this chapter, I have applied the social psychological literature to the experience of the independent practitioner, especially in regard to the importance of recognizing and reducing one's biases and in understanding one's racial/ethnic minority and international clients. I have also suggested that traditional boundaries may have to be considered carefully when applying them to clients of color.

The "Guidelines for Providers of Psychological Services to Ethnic, Linguistic, and Culturally Diverse Populations" (APA, 1990) includes a definition of cultural mutuality. The definition describes, in part, the importance of relating to women, clients of color, and other oppressed groups in a respectful, connecting manner based on our knowledge of the clients' culture and also tuning in to aspects of the clients' needs that our therapeutic processes may help. Cultural mutuality is an important value for therapists who wish to be competent in working with persons of color and others who have historically been disenfranchised.

REFERENCES

Allport, G. W. (1954). *The nature of prejudice.* Cambridge, MA: Addison-Wesley.

American Psychological Association. (1990). *Guidelines for providers of psychological services to ethnic, linguistic, and culturally diverse populations.* Washington, DC: Author.

American Psychological Association. (2002). Ethical principles of psychologists and code of conduct. *American Psychologist, 57,* 1060–1073.

American Psychological Association. (2003). Guidelines on multicultural education, training, research, practice, and organizational change for psychologists. *American Psychologist, 58,* 377–402.

Arredondo, P. (1996). *Successful diversity management initiatives: A blueprint for planning and implementation.* Thousand Oaks, CA: Sage.

Comas-Diaz, L., & Jacobsen, F. M. (1995). The therapist of color and the White patient dyad: Contradictions and recognitions. *Cultural Diversity and Mental Health, 1,* 93–106.

Constantine, M. G. (1998). Developing competence in multicultural assessment: Implications for counseling psychology training and practice. *Counseling Psychologist, 26,* 922–929.

Cross, W. E., Jr. (1991). *Shades of Black: Diversity in African American identity.* Philadelphia: Temple University Press.

Dovidio, J. F., Gaertner, S. L., Kawakami, K., & Hodson, G. (2002). Why can't we just get along? Interpersonal biases and interracial distrust. *Cultural Diversity and Ethnic Minority Psychology, 8,* 88–102.

Feminist Therapy Institute. (1990). Feminist Therapy Institute Code of Ethics. In H. Lerman & N. Porter (Eds.), *Feminist ethics in psychotherapy* (pp. 38–40). New York: Springer.

Finlay, K. A., & Stephan, W. G. (2000). Improving intergroup relations: The effects of empathy on racial attitudes. *Journal of Applied Social Psychology, 30,* 1720–1737.

Fiske, S. T. (1998, 4th ed.). Stereotyping, prejudice and discrimination. In D. T. Gilbert, S. T. Fiske, & G. Lindzey (Eds.), *The handbook of social psychology* (Vol. 2, pp. 357–411). New York: McGraw-Hill.

Gaertner, S. L., & Dovidio, J. F. (2000). *Reducing intergroup bias: The common in group identity model.* Philadelphia: Brunner/Mazel.

Galinsky, A. D., & Moskovitz, G. B. (2000). Perspective-taking: Decreasing stereotype expression, stereotype accessibility, and in-group favoritism. *Journal of Personality and Social Psychology, 78,* 708–724.

Hayes-Bautista, D. (1992). *No longer a minority: Latinos and social policy in California.* Los Angeles: University of California, Chicano Studies Research Center.

Helms, J. E. (1990). *Black and White racial identity: Theory, research, and practice.* Westport, CT: Greenwood.

Hewstone, M., Rubin, M., & Willis, H. (2002). Intergroup bias. *Annual Review of Psychology, 57,* 575–604.

Hispanic girls' life expectancy longest. (1996, December 11). *Austin American Statesman,* B4–B5.

Kagan, S. (1977). Social motives and behaviors of Mexican-American and Anglo-American children. In J. L. Martinez Jr. (Ed.), *Chicano psychology.* New York: Academic Press.

Knight, G. P., Cota, M. K., & Bernal, M. E. (1993). The socialization of cooperative, competitive, and individualistic preferences among Mexican American children: The mediating role of ethnic identity. *Hispanic Journal of Behavioral Sciences, 15,* 291–309.

Kramer, R. M. (1999). Trust and distrust in organizations: Emerging perspectives, enduring questions. *Annual Review of Psychology, 50,* 569–598.

Opotow, S. (1990). Moral exclusion and injustice: An introduction. *Journal of Social Issues, 46,* 1–20.

Pedersen, P. B., Draguns, J. G., Lonner, W. J., & Trimble, J. E. (Eds.). (2002). *Counseling across cultures* (5th ed.). Thousand Oaks, CA: Sage.

Pettigrew, T. F. (1998). Applying social psychology to international social issues. *Journal of Social Issues, 54,* 663–675.

Pope, K. S., & Vasquez, M. J. T. (1998). *Ethics in psychotherapy and counseling: A practical guide.* San Francisco: Jossey-Bass.

U.S. Census Bureau. (2004). *U.S. Census 2000, Summary Files 1 and 2.* Retrieved August 29, 2004, from http://www.census.gov/main/www/cen2000.html.

U.S. Department of Health and Human Services. (2001). *Mental health: Culture, race, and ethnicity. A supplement to Mental Health: A report of the Surgeon General.* Rockville, MD: U.S. Department of Health and Human Services, Public Health Office, Office of the Surgeon General.

Vasquez, M. J. T., & de las Fuentes, C. (1999). American-Born, Asian, African, Latina, and American Indian adolescent girls: Challenges and strengths. In N. G. Johnson, M. C. Roberts, & J. Worell (Eds.), *Beyond appearance: A new look at adolescent girls.* Washington, DC: American Psychological Association.

Women's level of comfort with their appearance varies with race and income. (2004, July). *Marketing to Women: Trends, Research and Market Intelligence from EPM Communications, Inc., 1,* 6.

CHAPTER 7

Building Multicultural Competence around Indigenous Healing Practices

LINDA JAMES MYERS, EZEMENARI M. OBASI, MONICA JEFFERSON, MICHELLE ANDERSON, TAMARA GODFREY, AND JASON PURNELL

THE AMERICAN PSYCHOLOGICAL ASSOCIATION'S (APA) "Guidelines on Multicultural Education, Training, Research, Practice, and Organizational Change for Psychologists" (APA, 2003), henceforth referred to as the Multicultural Guidelines, provide clear direction in terms of building multicultural competence in mental health and educational settings. However, many challenges to implementing the Multicultural Guidelines are encountered as we consider working with those who function from a worldview very different from our own, such as people who value and practice indigenous healing methods. Indigenous healing is defined as helping beliefs and strategies originating from within a culture or society that are designed specifically for treating members of a given cultural group (Constantine, Myers, Kindaichi, & Moore, 2004; Lee, 1996; Sue & Sue, 1999). These beliefs and strategies are vital to the health and well-being of clients from particular cultural backgrounds. However, some mental health practitioners will have difficulty embracing the philosophical principles of worldview systems that are fundamentally different from their own, particularly with respect to some indigenous healing perspectives.

The purpose of this chapter is to present a strategy and model for implementing the Multicultural Guidelines as they relate to appreciating the role of indigenous healing practices. Specifically, we are proposing an interrogation of core beliefs (ICB) strategy, which can help ensure that the pitfalls of culturally incongruent and insensitive care are avoided and that encourages openness to indigenous healing practices. We discuss ways that our ICB strategy facilitates implementation of the Multicultural Guidelines to promote cultural competence around issues of indigenous healing practices in mental health and educational settings. In addition, we suggest how using a four-phase ICB strategy can address indigenous healing issues in a manner consistent with the Multicultural Guidelines. The four-phase strategy includes: (1) encouraging the identification and examination of one's own worldview assumptions given the dominant worldview of socialization in U.S. society; (2) examining the relationships between these assumptions and one's perceptions, thoughts, feelings, and experiences relative to indigenous healing practices; (3) comparing and contrasting the consequences of two worldviews that may be more optimal versus suboptimal in terms of moving toward cultural competence; and (4) learning to assess the shortcomings and strengths of all worldviews, including one's own, using a specific type of worldview analysis model. Case examples are used to illustrate how the ICB strategy can be implemented.

INDIGENOUS HEALING PRACTICES, CULTURAL COMPETENCE, AND THE INTERROGATION OF CORE BELIEFS STRATEGY

It is important for psychologists and educators to develop an appreciation for the inherent strengths of indigenous peoples' unique designs for living and patterns of interpreting reality, or worldviews. According to the Multicultural Guidelines (APA, 2003), "Knowing all there is to know about a person's ethnic or racial background is not sufficient to be effective unless psychologists are cognizant of their positions as individuals with a worldview and that this worldview is brought to bear on interactions they have with others" (p. 24). The first two Guidelines are interrelated:

> *Guideline 1:* Psychologists are encouraged to recognize that, as cultural beings, they may hold attitudes and beliefs that can detrimentally influence their perception of and interactions with individuals who are ethnically and racially different from themselves.

> *Guideline 2:* Psychologists are encouraged to recognize the importance of multicultural sensitivity/responsiveness, knowledge, and understanding about ethnically and racially different individuals.

To recognize that psychologists, as cultural beings, "may hold attitudes and beliefs that may detrimentally influence their perceptions of and interactions with individuals who are ethnically and racially different," it would be helpful to be able to identify the basis for those attitudes and beliefs in terms of cultural deep structure, worldview, and conceptual systems. In so doing, we develop greater "sensitivity/responsiveness, knowledge, and understanding" about those whose worldviews may differ from our own. The ICB strategy is offered as a means to accomplish these ends and an attempt to reduce detrimental biases in our thinking regarding others.

IDENTIFICATION AND EXAMINATION OF ASSUMPTIONS OF
ONE'S WORLDVIEW

The Multicultural Guidelines encourage psychologists to engage in the processes necessary to move toward multicultural competence and appreciation. However, they do not inform us of how to achieve movement in the desired direction at the deepest levels fueling our fears and discomfort: our worldview (Myers, 1998, 2003). Because the recommended first step in the ICB strategy is awareness, the identification and examination of assumptions of one's own worldview, let us apply this step in a general way to the concept of indigenous healing given the dominant worldview of socialization in the United States. In light of the definition of indigenous healing provided earlier, the helping beliefs and practices that originated in Western psychology may be considered indigenous healing primarily for the treatment of European Americans. Mainstream Western psychology, however, fails to define itself as such, thus leading to what are actually culture-specific social institutions, policies, and practices (mental health, educational, legal, religious) that function as if Western beliefs and customs are etic, or universal. Traditional healing practices are often associated with the African, Asian, Latin, and Native American communities of people of color and are treated as exotic departures from an ostensibly universal Western cultural norm.

The worldview of dominant socialization in the United States contributed to the legacy of monocultural hegemony characterizing non-Western beliefs and practices as artifacts of "primitive" people. This legacy prevails in Western academia and society to such an extent that certain beliefs are taken for granted as truth. Implementation of the first step of our ICB strategy requires bringing to conscious awareness the fact that all cultural frames of reference have value and consequences. For example, when the generalized worldviews of indigenous people versus colonizers are compared and contrasted, perceptions of worth will differ by virtue of the values, beliefs, experiences, and exposures of the perceiver, not some universally agreed upon arbitrary standard (Myers, 2003). Much work needs to be done to expand Western thinking and training to develop alternative assumptions appreciative of the strengths of diverse cultural worldviews. To facilitate this process the

ICB strategy recommends enlisting the assistance of a cultural informant who can aid in one's development by "telling it like it is" from his or her worldview. Self-knowledge requires deep thought and critical self-reflection; still, there will be aspects of ourselves that we cannot know without the support of the "other" because we are so close to our experiences and assumptions that gaps or biases in our knowledge may not be apparent to us.

It is these kinds of omissions in mainstream Western psychology and education that have led to the need for adoption of the Multicultural Guidelines by the APA (2003). Many practitioners are unfamiliar with the ways that socialization into the Western cultural worldview shapes their perception of other cultural perspectives. For example, it may be helpful, but painful, for members of the dominant culture to consider the socio-historical and political bases for the construct "indigenous" itself. The concept emerges as most meaningful in the context of colonization, the taking over of lands belonging to the original inhabitants or indigenous people and forcing them to accommodate to the cultural realities of the colonizing group.

Because humans are cultural beings influenced by the dominant worldview of their socialization, accepting that the superior/inferior or dominant/subordinate dynamic has been inherent in Western socialization from the beginning is important but may be difficult. Learning to appreciate indigenous or unfamiliar patterns of interpreting reality and designs for living is also extremely difficult. It requires careful examination and understanding of how one's own worldview impacts one's perceptions. Our first step suggests that such an examination can take place most effectively by engaging in dialogue with those who hold worldviews different from our own so that they can help us with our blind spots and vice versa.

Case Example 1

Dr. Smith is a European American professor in a psychology department. He currently teaches a course in psychopathology and research methods. Dr. Smith does not view himself as being a cultural or spiritual being. He is also wedded to the medical model to guide his work at the university. Dr. Smith believes that particles in the universe are independent from one another and can be objectively observed and studied. Furthermore, he firmly believes that Western science is the only method for ascertaining absolute truths. Given his worldview, Dr. Smith perceives indigenous healing practices as being rooted in baseless, primitive thought, thus having no place in scientific discussion. Dr. Smith does not believe that cultural phenomena should be discussed in his psychopathology and research methods course because there is little to no between-group human variation at the biological level of analysis. His classroom environment has been described as hostile to students who hold a different worldview orientation.

Dr. Smith is beginning to lose the enthusiasm that he once had for teaching and is seeking support from a special committee in his department set up to help faculty improve their teaching and deal with faculty development. Wisely, the administration has placed two members on the committee who are in a position to serve as compassionate, yet forthright cultural informants to support development toward multicultural competence.

The ICB strategy becomes the perfect vehicle to help Dr. Smith examine his worldview and begin to see why he is experiencing such difficulty. In implementing the first step of our strategy, we follow the kind of developmental sequence that allows for building on the strengths of Dr. Smith's perspective, as well as expanding and introducing competing paradigms as value added. Faculty or staff capable of being cultural informants to support Dr. Smith in this strategy for building cultural competence in an educational setting must be supported and can be trained to facilitate such a course of development. The payoff for such an endeavor is quite high: the improvement of Dr. Smith's teaching and mental health, greater student satisfaction, a more welcoming, inclusive learning environment, and increased multicultural competence in the educational setting.

RELATIONSHIPS BETWEEN ASSUMPTIONS, PERCEPTIONS, THOUGHTS, FEELINGS, BEHAVIORS, AND EXPERIENCES

Utilizing the ICB strategy to explore one's own worldview, with its values, notions of identity, and sense of self, enhances one's capacity to deliver quality mental health services to a variety of consumers. To be culturally sensitive and responsive, psychologists first need to recognize that many of the models with which Western psychologists work invalidate, dismiss, deny, or omit factors that many non-Western, indigenous healers and their respective cultures view as critical to understanding the human mind, body, and experience (Constantine et al., 2004). This includes conceptions of health, illness, healing, and treatment. Second, the Western system of treating illness and promoting health does not incorporate many of the techniques and interventions on which other cultures have relied throughout their histories.

The definition of terms such as *normality, abnormality, healthy, illness, adaptive,* and *maladaptive* are culture-bound and thus consistent with a particular worldview. Therefore, it is important for psychologists to identify what their definitions and boundaries are, why they exist, what their historical, social, political, economic, and spiritual significance is, and how these relate to or contrast with their client's conception of reality. This step is important because it will directly impact client conceptualization and treatment. Practitioner worldview determines to a large extent how problems are defined and which interventions are chosen to address them. However, the client's worldview may differ in important ways, and the lack of knowledge on the part of the practitioner can lead to confusion, unsuccessful interventions, premature termination, or serious psychological harm.

For example, notions of the multidimensional self, in which the individual is seen as inseparable from ancestors, future generations, nature, the community, and ultimately, the Creative Life Force (Grills & Ajei, 2002; Myers, 1999b, 2003; Myers & Haggins, 1998; Obasi, 2002), or other allocentric or interdependent views of the self in which individuals are often defined in connection to important others, are antithetical to Western, individualized notions of self. Because these two conceptions of self are rooted in two markedly different worldviews whose philosophical principles at the level of cultural deep structure form competing conceptual systems, we must learn how one worldview influences the capacity to appreciate the other. Indigenous people often have ample opportunity to learn, assess, and accommodate the dominant culture; the reverse tends not to be true.

Although conceptions of self as multidimensional may be prevalent outside of the United States and among the less assimilated in this society, most Western-trained psychologists and educators would find it problematic to try to incorporate such an understanding of self into their professional practice, much less rely on it to inform a treatment plan (Myers, 1999a). The challenge of understanding, valuing, and appreciating indigenous healing methods as part of multicultural competence requires that we go further than the cultural surface structure (systems of organization, dress, diet, language, rites, rituals, etc.) examinations to the next step of exploring and embracing differences in worldview.

The use of indigenous healing methods in a given community may vary according to issues such as worldview, age, gender, degree of acculturation, language proficiency, immigration, cultural values, symptoms, and cost of treatment (Applewhite, 1995; Macias & Morales, 2000; Myers, 1999a; Pourat, Lubben, Wallace, & Moon, 1999). The need to identify and incorporate indigenous forms of healing and helping when they are appropriate emerges when people are uncomfortable with the fundamental values and goals of Western-based counseling or psychotherapy. Awareness of the need for psychologists and other mental health professionals to learn to appreciate the worldview from which indigenous healing methods come, however difficult this may be, is implied in the third Guideline:

> *Guideline 3:* As educators, psychologists are encouraged to employ the constructs of multiculturalism and diversity in psychological education.

As the third Guideline implies, there is a well-developed literature (research, clinical, etc.) from which educators and trainers can draw their psychology curricula. However, carefully and consistently utilizing these resources requires an honest appraisal of the limitations of one's knowledge and experiences with respect to diverse worldviews. The ICB strategy is particularly suited to just such an appraisal around issues of multiculturalism and diversity as they pertain to indigenous healing methods, broadening the relative scope of thinking and depth of consideration regarding differences.

Using the ICB strategy, spirituality, alternative ways of knowing, and the psychological significance of historical, political, and social events and trauma are legitimate and necessary areas of study and discussion in the context of treating diverse clientele. When there is a commitment to understanding and appreciating the critical role played by such elements in the lives of clients, multicultural competence in education and training is advanced. In educational settings, this means that instructors and directors of training should be familiar with literature addressing nondominant groups from their cultural frames of reference and should integrate these sources into their training programs rather than marginalizing cultural groups and the literature relevant to them.

OPTIMAL VERSUS SUBOPTIMAL CONCEPTUAL SYSTEMS AND CULTURAL COMPETENCE

To build multicultural competence, the third step in the ICB strategy is to learn more about how clients' worldview either contributes to greater peace, well-being, and good health personally and collectively, or greater violence, insecurity, and compromised health. This step seeks a deeper understanding of how the conceptual systems (beliefs, values, philosophical assumptions, and principles) shaping consciousness serve to influence our perceptions, thoughts, feelings, behavior, and experience. This phase is difficult because it requires cultivating the ability to take the perspective of a worldview nondominant in the United States.

Emerging from Myers's (1988, 1992) earlier work examining the impact of cultural differences at the level of deep structure and worldview on the human capacity to value and appreciate difference, the ICB strategy provides a framework for examining one's attitudes and beliefs in the context of worldview. Theorizing that the philosophical assumptions and principles forming the core of one's worldview and conceptual system determine the likelihood of embracing or rejecting differences, the conceptual system characterizing each outcome has been identified (see Table 7.1). According to Myers, the conceptual system maximizing

Table 7.1

A Comparison of Optimal and Suboptimal Conceptual Systems

	Optimal	**Suboptimal**
Worldview	Holistic, integral, unity consciousness	Fragmented, disintegrative
Ontology	Spiritual/material, as one with extrasensory considerations	Material reality with spiritual aspect; dependent on five senses
Axiology	Interpersonal relationships Spirituality Communalism Harmony with nature	Acquiring objects Materialism Individualism Competition
Logic	Diunital reasoning emphasizing union of opposites (both/and)	Dichotomous reasoning emphasizing dualities (either/or)
Identity	Multidimensional self	Individual form
Self-worth	Intrinsic in being	Based on external characteristics
Epistemology	Self-knowledge gained through inductive synthesis and symbolist wisdom	External knowledge gained through counting and measuring

Adapted from *Understanding an Afrocentric Worldview: Introduction to Optimal Psychology*, by L. J. Myers, 1988, 1992. Dubuque, IA: Kendall/Hunt.

the potential for valuing and appreciating differences is holistic, comprehensive, cohesive, coherent, and integrative. Described as optimal, this conceptual system yields unity consciousness (Myers, 2003). The conceptual system maximizing the potential for discrimination, unwarranted detrimental bias, fear, and competition is fragmented, superficial, compartmentalizing, noncohesive, incoherent, and alienating. Described as suboptimal, this conceptual system yields racism, sexism, classism, homophobia, ageism, elitism, and so on.

Grounded in Myers's (1988, 1992, 2003) theory of optimal psychology (OP), the ICB strategy is also built on the premise that one's perceptions, thoughts, feelings, behaviors, and experiences are determined by the nature of the worldview and conceptual system one utilizes. Theory of OP focuses on intra-individual as well as intercultural differences in worldview, optimal versus suboptimal worldviews, and their implications for health, well-being, and the optimization of human consciousness. This phase of the ICB strategy is lifted from this broader theoretical framework to specifically focus on the processes of building multicultural competence through critical self-examination and reflection facilitated by juxtaposing of the two conceptual systems previously mentioned. Table 7.1 delineates two differing sets of assumptions. Interestingly, the two sets of assumptions mirror those that are often said to characterize indigenous and Western worldviews, although indigenous and nonindigenous people clearly utilize both. In addition, we see a convergence toward the optimal conceptual system at the higher stages of human development across cultural groups, from Western science and Eastern philosophies to African wisdom traditions (Alexander & Langer, 1990; Myers, 1999a, 2003).

Persons utilizing what Myers (1988, 1992, 1999a, 2003) characterizes as an optimal conceptual system experience unity consciousness. No longer is the most pressing question of identity "Who am I?" That question has been answered with a resounding "I am the individual and unique expression of an omnipotent, omniscient, omnipresent, Creative Life Force, whose nature is love, or the source of all good, Divine Spirit," as the Bogo of West Africa say, a "living sun." The new question is "How am I, and all else, Divine Spirit?" Knowing is experiential, based on reason illuminated by science or systematic observation, and inspiration, intuition, and insight are highly valued ways of knowing. The diunital logic characteristic of this conceptual system acknowledges the interrelatedness and interdependence of the optimal/suboptimal dichotomization of the continuum of consciousness, one serving to further inform the other with a focus on the greater good on intra-individual and inter-individual collective levels. In other words, the purpose of any negative in human experience is to provide the opportunity for growth and greater self-knowledge and self-mastery.

Optimal thinking helps overcome the bias and ignorance preventing legitimate assessment and treatment of clients from diverse backgrounds who embrace alternative worldviews and rely on indigenous healing methods. Not that all indigenous or nonindigenous people think any particular way, but now the practitioner is positioned to move beyond personal ego and other issues of socialization that might bias, alienate, fragment, and compromise health and well-being. The optimal mind-set fosters openness to and appreciation of the contributions of each individual and group in its own way, a pathway to culture-centeredness. The concern for and ability to move toward such culture-centeredness is addressed in the fourth Guideline, which speaks to research, and the fifth Guideline, which addresses culturally appropriate skills in clinical and other applied psychological practices:

Guideline 4: Culturally sensitive psychological researchers are encouraged to recognize the importance of conducting culture-centered and ethical psychological research among persons from ethnic, linguistic, and racial minority backgrounds.

Guideline 5: Psychologists strive to apply culturally appropriate skills in clinical and other applied psychological practices.

This third phase in the ICB strategy supports clear values for peace, justice, truth, reciprocity, order, harmony, and balance. As psychologists, we are mandated to adhere to APA's Ethical Principles of Psychologists and Code of Conduct (2002). One of the many challenges when working with indigenous interventions is the potential of axiological conflict. Given the fact that the APA document is based on a European American worldview and axiological system, higher value is often placed on ability to acquire material wealth and social status. The optimal/suboptimal framework provides a mechanism for exploring the extent to which one individual's worldview and a group's collective worldview will likely help foster greater appreciation for and valuing of differences or have a debilitating impact.

Training programs and other institutions seeking to make a commitment to revamping their research and clinical training agendas to respect indigenous healing practices and interventions can use the framework to assess themselves and the efforts of those working on related issues. This framework does not mean that individuals or groups cannot be challenged. It means that they should not be dismissed, denied, or ignored. It would then appear difficult to understand indigenous mental health in our current psychological framework without acknowledgment and appreciation of worldview differences like the one the optimal/suboptimal framework offers. It would also seem humanly impossible to learn the worldview of every cultural group, so the framework makes the process of building multicultural competence more manageable.

With these themes in mind, it is with extreme caution that the available conceptual and empirical information concerning indigenous healing should be reviewed. Using the ICB strategy can be helpful in that while the basic tenets put forth concerning cultural beliefs may be true, interpretation is best left to an individual willing to suspend the traditional Western philosophical assumptions as regards worldview and mental health. For example, Amazigo, Anago-Manze, and Okeibunor (1997) executed an epidemiological study regarding beliefs about the disease of urinary schistosmiasis in Nigeria. When they discovered what would appear to be unorthodox beliefs (e.g., the disease is a venereal disease or sign of maturity), the scholars did not immediately discount these beliefs as stupidity on the part of the people. Instead, the researchers examined these beliefs in a larger social/cultural context to facilitate more effective treatment. Further, Constantine et al. (2004) have identified several ways that counselors might integrate various forms of indigenous healing into their practices and maximize treatment compliance and effectiveness among people of color and immigrants.

Psychological education that does not utilize some strategy akin to the third phase of the ICB strategy to explore deep cultural assumptions at the level of worldview is incomplete at best. Essential to this enterprise is engagement of the multilayered processes of development. Understanding and identifying the source of one's own attitudes and beliefs should be treated as a necessary component in the training of competent psychologists. However, one must not only be knowledgeable about oneself as a cultural being with a specific worldview and how those assumptions support multiculturalism, but also have some exposure to and working knowledge of other worldviews.

ASSESSING THE SHORTCOMINGS AND STRENGTHS OF ALL WORLDVIEWS IN HEALING PRACTICES

The last of the Multicultural Guidelines holds particular relevance for indigenous healing practices, as the use of organizational change practices will be essential to supporting "culturally informed organizational (policy) development and practices" in their regard:

> *Guideline 6:* Psychologists are encouraged to use organizational change practices to support culturally informed organizational (policy) development and practices.

Cultural competence and responsiveness must become an essential part of organizational functioning; from hiring and admissions to training and ethics, all must be modified. Our ICB strategy can be very useful in aiding organizations and individuals in their critical self-examination processes, as well as with program implementation, as organizations seek to move beyond monoculturalism. Enhancing the diversity among various professionals (e.g., professors, students, clinicians, and staff) within the organization is a start to informing the system. But the diversity for which we are looking must be more than just at the superficial level of appearance; we must begin to think in terms of considering diverse worldviews. The mere presence of those who can assist with informing us of indigenous beliefs and practices will be rendered useless if we are not ready to listen, prepared to grow, and equipped to make change. Thus, in Phase 3, the ICB strategy provides experiential knowledge in terms of understanding and appreciating different worldviews by examining one's own thinking and juxtaposing it against an alternative worldview. The next phase of the ICB strategy, which incorporates a specific type of worldview analysis model, supplies a feasible method to help psychologists, researchers, and educators implement and achieve Guideline objectives by highlighting five specific philosophical constructs that shape the worldviews of various cultural groups. The fourth ICB step is best undertaken after the other plans of action have been explored, as the risks of projection and misinterpretation are far too great if the opportunity has not been taken to fully interrogate the parameters of one's own worldview before looking at the philosophical assumptions and principles of other cultural groups.

The components of the worldview analysis model that compose the fourth phase of the ICB strategy are known by the acronym CEOAT. The constructs to be examined within the CEOAT model are *cosmology* (beliefs regarding the nature of the universe), *epistemology* (beliefs regarding the nature of knowledge), *ontology* (beliefs regarding the nature of reality or being), *axiology* (beliefs regarding the nature of values), and *teleology* (beliefs regarding the nature of purpose). Table 7.2 provides an outline of the principles along with questions and potential answers that relate to each principle. When it comes to the consideration of indigenous healing practices in a culturally congruent fashion, either in terms of research or applied practice, anything short of addressing these fundamental principles will lead to misguided research or external cures at best, and invalid research or premature termination by the client at worst. The teleological thrust of the CEOAT model with regard to applied practice is to formulate a treatment plan that actualizes holistic healing in a way that is ontologically meaningful to the client. In terms of research, the CEOAT model provides the sound cultural grounding one needs to align the reality of the researcher with that of the subjects who hold a differing worldview.

A major asset of the fourth phase of the ICB strategy is that the CEOAT model provides an etic framework that can be used to guide emic psychotherapy. Should a client present with a worldview (cosmology, epistemology, ontology, axiology, teleology) that is consistent with European American middle-class culture, traditional psychological models would be applicable using the ICB strategy. However, should the client present with a different worldview, the CEOAT model from the ICB strategy will provide a robust system for identifying the differences and their implications for culturally congruent service delivery. Using the ICB strategy, implementation of culturally appropriate indigenous interventions can be pursued. Because emic interventions would probably optimize the holistic healing process, psychotherapists must be humble enough to recognize when their expertise has been surpassed and knowledgeable of specific referral resources.

Table 7.2
An Example of CEOAT Analysis of Worldview

Principle	Questions (Possible Answers)
Cosmology	1. How was the universe created? (Benevolent God, higher power, or spiritual source; Big Bang theory; mere chance) 2. How is it sustained? (Care and grace of God; spiritual animation; continuous series of physical and chemical reactions) 3. What entities form its major constituent parts? (Subatomic particles, bodies, masses; living and dead beings; God or gods) 4. What power(s) animate life and give it form? (Physical energy; DNA; spiritual power; God or gods)
Epistemology	1. What can be accepted as truth? (That which is perceived through senses; science; personally lived experience; spiritual discernment; cultural tradition) 2. What are the limits of human knowledge? (Current boundaries of scientific knowledge; individual perspective) 3. From whence does knowledge arise? (Critical study; personal experience; revelation; contemplation) 4. How is knowledge reliably transmitted from one individual to another? (Verifiable reports; oral tradition; familial transmission of culture) 5. How does one attain self-knowledge? (Psychotherapy; meditation; interpersonal relationships)
Ontology	1. What is the nature of reality? (All is chance and chaos; universe is intelligently designed and organized by benevolent Being or forces; material world is an illusory realm masking underlying spiritual dimension) 2. What exists? (Perceptible natural world; spiritual and material realms)
Axiology	1. What are the most important human strivings and the best ways to live life? (Loving service; personal achievement; maximized pleasure; search for wisdom and knowledge; unity with universe and divine) 2. How does one think about obligations to self and others? (Responsible for self and close others; responsible for all sentient beings)
Teleology	1. What is the purpose of any individual life? (None outside personal meaning; to be of use or help; achieving unity or enlightenment) 2. Why does one encounter the people and events in one's life? (Chance or coincidence; spiritual lessons or blessings)

DEVISING A CULTURALLY CONGRUENT
TREATMENT PLAN

To appreciate the level of complexity that will enter mental health facilities when indigenous beliefs are authentically honored, the reader is asked to define the notion of "self." For one community, the notion of self can be delineated as mental processes and personality characteristics that reside within the human body, or individual (West, 1997). For another community, the notion of self can be delineated as the harmonious interdependent interaction between the soul (spirit, character, personality, destiny, name, breath of life, etc.) and body (brain, heart, blood, emotions, intelligence, maternal lineage, paternal lineage, community, etc.), as a system that is interconnected to all things in the cosmos (Grills & Ajei, 2002; Obasi, 2002). For yet another community, the mere thought of defining the notion of self would cause disease and vulnerability because such a separate, permanent, and distinct construct does not exist for them (Daya, 2000). How, then, does a psychologist formulate a treatment plan when the target of therapeutic intervention is culture-bound? Prerequisites for thinking about and wielding indigenous interventions have been described using the three prior phases of the ICB strategy and the last phase implementing the CEOAT model. Once knowledge of self, one's worldview, and associated biases have been understood, the next step is to gain critical pieces of information that will be needed to provide a culturally congruent treatment plan.

Case Example 2

Kofi is a 25-year-old heterosexual Ghanaian male who is currently a graduate student in the school of medicine at a university in the United States. Kofi was born and raised in Ghana, West Africa, and most of his family lives in Kumasi, a traditional city in Ghana. While growing up, Kofi remembers the vast amount of cultural history and traditions he learned from his family and the community as a whole. He talked about learning rich information about his cultural traditions by watching the behaviors of others, while simultaneously receiving specific instruction from his grandparents and parents. On occasion, he learned specific rituals and customs from his peers. Kofi talked about his belief in consubstantiation, the principle that everything in the universe is interconnected and spiritual in nature. He disclosed several techniques (divination, meditation, etc.) that he was taught to gain knowledge and understanding about phenomena that failed to make sense at face value.

Kofi has been in the United States for 18 months and continues to long for his family and friends, misses activities he would participate in back home, is having difficulty communicating his feelings, and is having difficulty accepting American values, which he perceives as being drastically different from his own. Currently,

Kofi is experiencing "depressive and anxious-like" symptoms and is seeking psychotherapy for help as he no longer has access to traditional ways for dealing with such hardships.

The ICB strategy can be used to help guide potential psychological services that may be offered to Kofi. Based on this vignette, it is clear that Kofi's culture is very salient to him. He described vertical (e.g., grandparents and parents), horizontal (e.g., peers), and oblique (e.g., others) transmission of culture that was influenced by the processes of enculturation and socialization. Based on Kofi's cosmological beliefs, the therapist may want to facilitate a therapeutic relationship that is genuine and consistent with an interconnected and interdependent belief system.

The ICB strategy would suggest incorporating techniques such as divination and meditation into homework assignments aimed at gaining insight into his presenting concerns. Ultimately, Kofi is experiencing various symptoms associated with acculturative stress and could benefit from a treatment plan that can provide both a spiritual and a physical causal explanation for his presenting concerns. Kofi may also gain from specific referrals to local Ghanaian healers and/or communities, if available, that will have the capacity to address specific aspects of the healing process (rituals, rites, ceremonies, etc.) that may not be addressed in traditional psychotherapy.

CONCLUSION

In most traditional settings, traditional healers welcome the entire breadth of presenting concerns (cancer, spiritual cleansing, decision making, communal dilemmas, festivals, finding a lost object, protection from harm, marriage, nightmares, dizzy spells, broken bone, obtaining a job, fertility issues, etc.). It is not uncommon for traditional healers to provide services to as many as 100 individuals in one day. Compensation often is based on reciprocity, where donations are made for those services judged to have rendered acceptable results.

To provide such a broad spectrum and magnitude of services, the traditional healer must work within a larger support system. It is not uncommon for community members (spiritual and physical) to play specific roles (preparing medicine, obtaining material necessary to perform a specific ritual, etc.) in the healing process. Thus, the healer is not alone in the healing process. Additionally, such indigenous interventions require a level of knowledge and consciousness that is grounded in years of training and a lifetime of experience.

Although mental health professionals may ponder the possibility of administering indigenous interventions, they should be reminded that the practice of indigenous healing requires a compatible worldview and years of training and study. One way psychotherapists can benefit ethnic communities that present with a non-Western worldview is to interface with indigenous healers and resources in an attempt to provide a multidisciplinary treatment regime that will address the whole person in a way that is culturally meaningful. Continuing to support an imposed etic versus a derived emic approach to psychotherapy is unethical and leaves the burden squarely on the client's back when he or she is inappropriately assessed, diagnosed, and treated by an ontological system that fails to honor his or her cosmological, epistemological, ontological, axiological, and teleological way of viewing the world. The Multicultural Guidelines set the stage for building multicultural competence in mental health and educational settings. The four-phase ICB strategy goes a long way to delineate a means to implement the Multicultural Guidelines, particularly in the context of indigenous healing methods. Those of us most concerned about providing culture-centered and appropriate services to meet the mental health and educational needs of all people must continue to strive toward our vision. We now have the tools.

REFERENCES

Alexander, C. N., & Langer, E. J. (1990). *Higher stages of human development: Perspectives on adult growth.* New York: Oxford University Press.

Amazigo, U. O., Anago-Manze, C. I., & Okeibunor, J. C. (1997). Urinary schistosomiasis among school children in Nigeria: Consequences of indigenous beliefs and water contact activities. *Journal of Biosocial Science, 29,* 9–18.

American Psychological Association. (2002). *Ethical principles of psychologists and code of conduct.* Washington, DC: Author.

American Psychological Association. (2003). Guidelines on multicultural education, training, research, practice, and organizational change for psychologists. *American Psychologist, 38,* 377–402.

Applewhite, S. L. (1995). Curanderismo: Demystifying the health beliefs and practices of elderly Mexican Americans. *Health and Social Work, 20,* 247–253.

Constantine, M. G., Myers, L. J., Kindaichi, M., & Moore, J. L. (2004). Exploring indigenous mental health practices: The role of healers and helpers in promoting well-being in people of color. *Counseling and Values, 48,* 110–125.

Daya, R. (2000). Buddhist psychology, a theory of change processes: Implications for counselors. *International Journal for the Advancement of Counseling, 22*(4), 257–271.

Grills, C., & Ajei, M. (2002). African-centered conceptualizations of self and consciousness: The Akan model. In T. A. Parham (Ed.), *Counseling persons of African descent: Raising the bar of practitioner competence* (Vol. 18, pp. 75–99). Thousand Oaks, CA: Sage.

Lee, C. C. (1996). MCT theory and implications for indigenous healing. In D. W. Sue, A. E. Ivey, & P. B. Pedersen (Eds.), *A theory of multicultural counseling and therapy* (pp. 86–98). Pacific Grove, CA: Brooks/Cole.

Macias, E. P., & Morales, L. S. (2000). Utilization of health care services among adults attending a health fair in South Los Angeles county. *Journal of Community Health, 25,* 35–46.

Myers, L. J. (1988). *Understanding an Afrocentric worldview: Introduction to optimal psychology.* Dubuque, IA: Kendall/Hunt.

Myers, L. J. (1992). *Understanding an Afrocentric worldview: Introduction to optimal psychology* (2nd ed.). Dubuque, IA: Kendall/Hunt.

Myers, L. J. (1998). The deep structure of culture revisited. In J. D. Hamlet (Ed.), *Afrocentric visions: Studies in culture and communication* (pp. 3–14). Newbury Park, CA: Sage.

Myers, L. J. (1999a). Therapeutic processes for health and wholeness in the 21st century: Belief systems analysis and the paradigm shift. In R. L. Jones (Ed.), *Advances in African American psychology* (pp. 313–358). Hampton, VA: Cobb and Henry.

Myers, L. J. (1999b). Transforming psychology: An African American perspective. In R. L. Jones (Ed.), *Advances in African American psychology* (pp. 9–26). Hampton, VA: Cobb and Henry.

Myers, L. J. (2003). *Our health matters: Guide to an African (indigenous) American Psychology and cultural model for creating a climate and culture of optimal health.* Columbus, Ohio: Ohio Commission on Minority Health.

Myers, L. J., & Haggins, K. L. (1998). Optimal theory and identity development: Beyond the Cross model. In R. L. Jones (Ed.), *African American identity development* (pp. 255–274). Hampton, VA: Cobb and Henry.

Obasi, E. M. (2002). Reconceptualizing the notion of self from the African deep structure. In T. A. Parham (Ed.), *Counseling persons of African descent: Raising the bar of practitioner competence* (Vol. 18, pp. 52–74). Thousand Oaks, CA: Sage.

Pourat, N., Lubben, J., Wallace, S. P., & Moon, A. (1999). Predictors of use of traditional Korean healers among elderly Koreans in Los Angeles. *Gerontologist, 39,* 711–719.

Sue, D. W., & Sue, D. (1999). *Counseling the culturally different* (3rd ed.). New York: Wiley.

West, W. (1997). Integrating counseling, psychotherapy and healing: An inquiry into counselors and psychotherapists whose work includes healing. *British Journal of Guidance and Counseling, 25,* 291–311.

PART III

Applying the Multicultural Guidelines to Educational, Training, and Organizational Settings

CHAPTER 8

Academic Mental Health Training Settings and the Multicultural Guidelines

JEFFERY SCOTT MIO

> I don't think this was a very insightful article, and most of the
> items listed did not apply to me. For example, I can't arrange to
> be in the company of people only from my race, and I can't avoid
> spending time with those whom I mistrust and who have learned
> to mistrust my race.
>
> —40+ White heterosexual man

THE ABOVE STATEMENT is a paraphrase of what a man said in one of my multicultural courses in response to the influential McIntosh paper (1995; originally presented in 1986) on White privilege. In the many years I have been teaching this course, I have never had a student resist McIntosh's arguments, which she places in a context impossible for all but the *most* resistant to deny. Apparently, I had such a resistant student in this particular class. For those of you who are familiar with this seminal work, you know how difficult it is for White people to deny their own privilege after reading this piece. For those of you not familiar with this work, I highly recommend that you read it. The two responses that follow are much more typical reactions to McIntosh's chapter:

> Although I consider my upbringing to be relatively enlightened,
> my parents, who were leftists, never informed me of my white
> privilege. Evidently, for white '60s radicals, white privilege was
> unmentionable, unrecognized, an unspoken given. It would

129

have been good to have been schooled about it by my parents because certainly society wasn't going to teach me after I got out on my own.

. . . [Mcintosh's] 46 perks were eye-opening . . . not having to worry about whether or not the cop who stops me is stopping me because of my color . . . not having to worry about whether or not my color would cause the apartment manager to reject my application. A whole huge series of worries is eradicated from my life because of the light color of my skin and the straight and smooth texture of my hair.

—40+ White heterosexual woman

Last week my landlord informed my boyfriend . . . and myself that he was putting the condo where we live up on the market for sale. He did however, offer us the first bid, but we had to decline because of the lack of finances. Our place sold in three days and we now have . . . to move out. . . .

My neighbors, who are black, said, "Well, don't worry, although this may have been short notice, you guys could live anywhere you want because of the color of your skin; if you were black, it would be a different story." What she said had a profound effect on me, for I never considered my color as an issue or stressor in this troubling situation. . . .

This situation yet again made me think of Peggy McIntosh's article, "White Privilege, and Male Privilege." At that moment I came to see how "white privilege is indeed an invisible package of unearned assets," for the thought never occurred to me that I would have trouble finding a new place to live because of the color of my skin. My neighbor had also said, "Now, I would be a bit concerned with this short notice if you were black because your options would be severely limited." I came to see that this "color issue" was a daily reality for my neighbors and this made me realize how oblivious I was to my white privilege. I can be assured that my color will not stereotype me, deter me, or limit me in any way in finding a place, and this is my reality. I have to be cognizant that my color provides me with advantages that others may not receive simply because of the color of their skin.

—20+ White heterosexual woman

How do we get students to transition from the first individual's way of thinking to the second and third individuals' way of thinking? The adoption and publication of the "Guidelines on Multicultural Education,

Training, Research, Practice, and Organizational Change for Psychologists" (American Psychological Association [APA], 2003) is a major step in helping those of us who teach about multicultural issues in this process of transition.

THE ETHICS OF TEACHING MULTICULTURAL COMPETENCIES

The APA has been publishing and revising its ethical principles and codes of conduct for psychologists since 1953. The latest version was published in 2002. These principles clearly place service delivery for people with diverse backgrounds firmly into the very fabric of our training procedures:

2.01 Boundaries of Competence

(a) Psychologists provide services, teach, and conduct research with populations and in areas only within the boundaries of their competence, based on their education, training, supervised experience, consultation, study, or professional experience.

(b) Where scientific or professional knowledge in the discipline of psychology establishes that an understanding of factors associated with age, gender, gender identity, race, ethnicity, culture, national origin, religion, sexual orientation, disability, language, or socioeconomic status is essential for effective implementation of their services or research, psychologists have or obtain the training, experience, consultation, or supervision necessary to ensure the competence of their services, or they make appropriate referrals, except as provided in Standard 2.02, Providing Services in Emergencies. (pp. 1065–1066)

Such direct calls for sensitivity to issues of diversity have been in place at least since 1973 (see Bernal & Padilla, 1982; Mio & Awakuni, 2000). However, such calls have been resisted at both the individual and the institutional level (Mio & Awakuni, 2000; Sue et al., 1998). With the publication of the Multicultural Guidelines (APA, 2003), resistance to issues of diversity were further addressed. Although this resistance has not been completely eliminated, such formal procedures in organizations such as APA have taken away many of the arguments for resisting the issue. For example, as Sue et al. (1998) discussed, one of the arguments resisting multiculturalism came from quarters that asserted that standards in treating diverse populations did not exist. Obviously, such statements can no longer be made. However, another form of resistance suggests that it is difficult to translate the Multicultural Guidelines because they are too complex. This chapter translates some key elements of the Multicultural Guidelines into issues of teaching and training.

THE MULTICULTURAL GUIDELINES AND
ACADEMIC MENTAL HEALTH TRAINING

The Multicultural Guidelines were largely developed for mental health training, as the essence of these guidelines was based on the Sue et al. (1982) article in response to the directive by then-Division 17 President Allen Ivey. The six Multicultural Guidelines are designed to help psychologists understand how multicultural issues affect us in very profound ways when dealing with individuals who are different from ourselves. The main points of these Guidelines are (1) awareness of one's own attitudes and beliefs that may have been shaped by one's culture; (2) sensitivity to the worldviews of ethnically and racially different individuals; (3) the incorporation of multicultural perspectives in education; (4) cultural sensitivity when conducting research on ethnically, linguistically, and racially different individuals; (5) the application of culturally appropriate skills in conducting applied psychological practices; and (6) applying multicultural perspectives in organizational change processes. All of these Guidelines relate to mental health training, but Guidelines 1, 2, and 3 most directly relate to teaching about multicultural issues.

Guideline 1: Awareness of Our Own Attitudes and Beliefs

The more complete statement of this Guideline is as follows:

> *Guideline 1:* Psychologists are encouraged to recognize that, as cultural beings, they may hold attitudes and beliefs that can detrimentally influence their perceptions of and interactions with individuals who are ethnically and racially different from themselves. (APA, 2003, p. 382)

This Guideline provides the basis for all of the others. The McIntosh (1995) paper discussed earlier is an important piece to discuss early in an introductory multicultural course. It is an easy chapter to understand, and McIntosh writes in a clear fashion that cannot be resisted unless one is unreasonably entrenched in one's privilege. While the student who made the first statement opening this chapter was entrenched in his privilege, his statement opened up class discussion so that nearly all of his colleagues challenged his way of thinking (one or two students were fairly quiet and avoided conflict, so they did not contribute to class discussion, but they were clearly exasperated by his statement of resistance/privilege). To go beyond White privilege and apply this concept to all areas of unearned privilege, I discuss with students some examples from my own life of male privilege (included in the McIntosh paper) to give students a sense that even people who are aware of such issues can sometimes be blind to privilege unless their conceptions are evaluated carefully. In making myself vulnerable and open to self-inspection, I serve as a model for students to examine their own unearned privilege. I then ask students to discuss other areas of unearned privilege that apply to their lives. They typically come up with heterosexual, religious, and ability privileges. I point out forms of privilege that are not as readily accessible or that need a little more push for awareness, such as social class and language privileges.

The Continued Existence of Racism

Amazingly, some people still need to be made aware of the existence of racism. While White privilege is a form of subtle, covert racism, some of the more resistant students still seem to be unaware of some fairly overt racism that occurs in society and themselves. For example, a 20 plus-year-old White woman complained about reverse discrimination in one of my classes, and she also alienated some ethnic minority students outside of class by claiming that they got into our graduate program only because they were members of ethnic minority groups. In an earlier writing (Mio & Awakuni, 2000), I quoted a 30 plus-year-old White woman who stated, "Once again, I am feeling like because I am white, I am automatically privileged, prejudiced, you name it. I am truly sick of it!" (p. 96). To demonstrate the continuing existence of racism, I have found the film *The Color of Fear* (Lee, 1994) to be effective. This is a very powerful film about which most multicultural course professors know. It always leads to great class discussions and reactions from students. Students who continue to deny the existence of racism after watching this film may be beyond change.

Reaction Papers

Few students are as overtly resistant to the existence of racism as the two students in the previous paragraph, and I do not know how many students are silently as resistant, at least at the undergraduate level. However, in a graduate program, I get more of a sense of all students' levels of resistance through the use of what I have termed "reaction papers" (Mio & Barker-Hackett, 2003).[1] The reaction paper requires students to submit

---

[1] I use the reaction paper technique at the undergraduate level as well. However, because my undergraduate courses are so much larger than my graduate courses, it is more difficult to have everyone participate in class discussions. Thus, it is more difficult to monitor the connection between class discussions and the reaction papers. However, because of the more direct connection between my graduate students and their influence on potential ethnic minority clients, I monitor the class discussion much more closely and challenge students' positions more openly. Thus, I have a better sense of who the truly resistant students are and who are merely more quiet than their colleagues. Also, because there are many fewer students at the graduate level, all students have a chance to participate numerous times over the course of an entire term.

a weekly paper of one to two pages in reaction to something that occurred during the week related to any multicultural issue. This reaction may be to my lecture, to a film shown in class, to a class discussion, to an interaction with an individual outside of class, to a news item, or the like. Every week, I write a reaction back to the students' papers so that we may interact either didactically or confidentially, such as when a student needs an avenue to "vent" without appearing to be overtly racist to his or her classmates or to rail against a racist comment in class. I inform my students that I may use their reactions in professional writings, but I will protect their identities; however, if they do not want me to use their writings or if they want to exclude a specific paper from my professional writings, I honor their request. In the many years that I have been using this technique, no student has requested that I do not use any of his or her papers, and only one student indicated that a single paper was confidential because it contained identifying information about a friend. I periodically remind students of these parameters throughout the term.

Etic and Emic

Two important terms in the multicultural literature are "etic" and "emic" (Berry, 1969; Jahoda, 1982; Reynolds, 1999; Triandis, 1978). "Etic" refers to the process of trying to find universal behaviors, beliefs, and values across cultures. It is an attempt to build a theory of humanity by examining cultures from the outside and seeing the connections among cultures. "Emic" refers to an examination of behaviors and norms within a culture to determine what is important within the culture. Interpretations of terms, behaviors, and concepts may differ from culture to culture. For example, Triandis et al. (1993) discussed the difference in interpretation of the term "self-reliance" in the United States and Japan. Americans, living in an individualistic culture, interpret the term as related to the notion "I want to do my own thing," whereas in Japan it is related to the notion "I want to be responsible, and not be a burden on my collective" (p. 368). Such differences of interpretation make it difficult to compare cultures and determine universal understanding.

Berry (1969) cautioned against what he called "imposed etics," when those observing behaviors of other cultures impose their own values in their interpretations. Because most psychological research occurs in countries with a Western perspective, most cross-national studies have a Western (or dominant society) perspective, imposing Western or dominant values onto the behaviors exhibited by the cultures being observed. In one of my classes, I discussed this issue and gave an example of the famous Mischel (1958, 1961) studies on delay of gratification (Mio & Morris, 1990). Mischel's interpretation of the tendency of inner-city African

American children selecting smaller candy immediately instead of waiting until the next day for larger candy was that they did not know how to delay gratification. I discussed how this interpretation was an example of imposed etics, as Mischel was thinking that he was measuring delay of gratification, whereas the children he was studying may have had other things in mind, such as being hungrier than their counterparts in the White suburbs, not believing that the researcher was actually going to return the next day, or worrying that the candy may be stolen before they got it. In other words, the children were actually acting *adaptively* by taking the smaller amount of food immediately instead of waiting for the larger amount of food a day later. When I discussed this study in one of my classes, a student connected this with her own example of imposed etics. She said that when she was doing missionary work in Uganda in the late 1970s, it was upsetting to her that as soon as people got their monthly check they spent it all on food. By the end of the month, they began running out of food, so on some days they would go hungry. After a few months of observing this, she finally said, "Don't you realize how maladaptive your behavior is? All you have to do is save some of your money so that near the end of the month, you could buy more food." The response from the people was, "No, it is you who are suggesting a maladaptive behavior. We have hyperinflation here [it was something like 3,000% at that time], so our money buys much more food at the beginning of the month than it does at the end of the month." The student felt foolish that she had imposed her own values on their situation and was actually suggesting something that would have been much worse for those she was trying to help. Imposed etics is not necessarily venal in its intentions. However, it is a form of privilege in the same vein as McIntosh's discussion of White privilege.

Resistance among Colleagues

While much of the resistance to multiculturalism we encounter comes from students in our courses, some comes from our colleagues (see Mio & Awakuni, 2000). In my own experience, administrators are generally supportive of the broad concept of multiculturalism, although they may vary in the degree to which they dedicate resources to these issues. However, the real resistance has come from many faculty members who resist the new multicultural perspective. As I have written in the past (Mio & Awakuni, 2000), this was one of the major contributing factors that made me decide to give up a tenured position for an untenured position. At the time (1994), however, APA had not passed the Multural Guidelines, so APA's support for the general notion of multiculturalism was still vague and allowed many members of the association to resist its tenets. This allowed colleagues to make statements such as "We've done enough in this area" and "Multiculturalism is not important enough to support." As stated earlier, Sue et al. (1998) documented the history of much of the resistance to opening up the profession to accepting guidelines in dealing with multicultural issues, and many encounters I have had over the years have been along the lines about which Sue et al. have written.

With the publication of the Multicultural Guidelines, supporters of the multicultural movement have more leverage. Even before the Multicultural Guidelines were adopted by APA, I advocated in a number of public settings that faculty members who do not know much about multiculturalism should be required to take courses in this area. For example, at a meeting of state and provincial representatives at an APA convention, I related the following story. When I was a graduate student, one first-year professor was considered to have less than adequate statistical skills. The department's solution was to require him to take the statistics courses that the graduate students were taking. This shows real commitment to an important area of our profession. Can anyone imagine a department requiring professors to take multicultural courses? At this time, I cannot. This is mainly because those professors who are the most deficient in their multicultural understanding are those who were trained a generation or two before the present generation. I cannot imagine that those who are in power will require themselves to take remedial courses. As another example, when I was a graduate student, a professor who had established himself as one of the leading authorities in sensation and perception was hired by our department. Another professor whose specialty was in perception was motivated enough to take a seminar from this nationally recognized professor along with some of us graduate students. Again, I find it highly unlikely that an older professor who knows that his or her knowledge about multicultural psychology is lacking would be motivated enough to take a course from a prominent professor in multiculturalism, at least not at his or her own university. It is possible that professors might take sabbatical leaves to study with a prominent multicultural expert, but in so doing, the professor would not show the kind of vulnerability and humility that it sometimes takes to truly understand notions of privilege as it would to subject himself or herself to taking graduate courses with the very students that he or she will be teaching in other courses.

Success Stories of Awareness

Some of my most gratifying moments as a professor have come when students are demonstrably changed by my multicultural courses. The earlier quotations are examples of when students become aware of their privilege and work to understand how these issues are not only related to ethnic minority clients they might see in therapy later on but are related to their everyday interpersonal relationships and to their understanding of themselves. Such insights happen not only to White students but to ethnic minority students as well. For example, a Latina American was so impressed by the course that she asked me for a reading list of Latina/o issues that she could read on her own over the summer. Another Latina American, who had been resistant through much of the term because she thought she "knew it all" and did not feel that she should be required to take such a course, acknowledged that the course helped her to understand why she got some of the reactions she had from her Latino community regarding some of her own academic success. After reading the McIntosh piece on privilege, an Asian American woman excitedly talked about a game her husband and she now play, looking to see how many Asian men appear on television.[2] An African American man told me how sad my course made him feel that he did not know most of the material, despite the fact that he had lived it all of his life. This sadness, however, motivated him to learn more about the issues discussed in the course. Although I have not had the fortune of having any students who identified themselves as American Indian, a few who claim some American Indian heritage have been motivated to discover more about this part of their family history.

GUIDELINE 2: SENSITIVITY TO THE WORLDVIEWS OF ETHNICALLY AND RACIALLY DIFFERENT INDIVIDUALS

The more complete statement of this Guideline is as follows:

> Psychologists are encouraged to recognize the importance of multicultural sensitivity/responsiveness to, knowledge of, and understanding about ethnically and racially different individuals. (APA, 2003, p. 385)

Guideline 1 focuses on how individuals must understand their own biases that can be damaging if imposed on people of color and others who may have a different worldview; Guideline 2 focuses on how individuals must understand the worldviews of others. As Casas (1990) insisted, we

---

[2] In class, I particularly emphasize this point, as most Asians who are depicted on television are women who have a White boyfriend or husband. Unless one is viewing a martial arts program, Asian men are almost never seen, and if they are, they generally do not have any significant speaking parts. Asian men are almost never seen with White women or, interestingly, with Asian women.

should not only avoid doing harm but should actually attempt to help people. Mio and Iwamasa (1993) recounted Casas's presentation:

> [Casas] also pointed to the APA (1990) ethical principles, noting that a therapist or counselor should avoid personal issues that "are likely to lead to inadequate performance or harm to a client, colleague, student, or research participant" (p. 391). This stance of doing no harm says nothing about actually attempting to help an individual—we should simply not do any harm! He feels that the discipline has lost its heart, setting forth rules based on avoiding lawsuits as opposed to rules based on the altruistic roots on which our profession has been founded. This avoidance of lawsuits is in and of itself a White or Western concern, not a cross-cultural one. (p. 200)

With the publication of the Multicultural Guidelines, particularly Guideline 2, our profession has now taken the stance that we should understand others' worldviews for the purpose of helping them—quite a step from Casas's accusation over a decade ago.

Identity Development

As the Multicultural Guidelines suggest, one of the most important components of knowing the worldview of a client is an understanding of the identity development models. These models suggest that ethnic minority individuals go through a process of initially acting in ways that devalue or minimize the importance of their race or ethnicity in their daily interactions, then through a period of immersing themselves in their own race/ethnicity almost to the exclusion of people from other groups (particularly those in the majority), to an integration of their racial/ethnic identity into their sense of self. This allows them to have the security to interact with others and even show a preference for some beliefs, values, or behaviors from other cultures without threatening their own sense of racial/ethnic identity.

Students are typically not aware of these identity issues, nor do they initially understand that as therapists in training, they need to apply such identity development to themselves as well as their clients. Therapists who are persons of color must undergo the racial/ethnic identity development appropriate for their own racial/ethnic group. For White therapists, too, White/majority identity development models have been proposed (Helms, 1984, 1990, 1995). In these models, Whites may go through a period of naïvely believing that "people are people," that we are all the same. In this naïve view, issues of race and ethnicity are minimized or devalued, and the White majority perspective is imposed on everyone. This is an example of Berry's (1969) "imposed etics" on an individual level. As the individual begins to be exposed to the reality of racism and issues of White privilege (McIntosh, 1995), the individual begins to understand how his or her naïve perspective has fostered racism in its modern, disguised form. As the individual becomes more and more aware, he or she ultimately comes to a complete understanding of the problems of racism in society and works to eliminate it.

One of my favorite articles that combines issues of identity development with therapy issues is by Comas-Diaz and Jacobsen (1991). They discuss both intercultural and intracultural transference and countertransference issues that can arise in therapy. Comas-Díaz and Jacobsen point out that one needs to be aware of both the client's reactions and one's own reactions as they relate to ethnicity. Are the reactions due to true feelings, or are they based on a more general issue of ethnicity? For example, if an American Indian client is seeing a White therapist, resistance coming from the client may be based on general anger toward what Whites did to American Indians as opposed to what this particular therapist has said in therapy. Similarly, the therapist may be feeling that it is an interesting adventure to see an American Indian client in therapy, rather than dealing with the specific issues that the client came in to discuss. The resistant Latina whom I referred to earlier was particularly impressed with this article and found it to be useful in helping her to understand some of the reactions she had encountered.

Sue's (1978) Worldview Model

Another aspect of worldview not discussed in the Multicultural Competencies APA Guidelines is Sue's (1978) notion of the intersection between locus of control and locus of responsibility. This model suggests that people's worldviews can be described as a 2 × 2 matrix of internal locus of control (IC), external locus of control (EC), internal locus of responsibility (IR), and external locus of responsibility (ER). Thus, a worldview can be IC-IR, EC-IR, EC-ER, or IC-ER. The IC-IR cell is the dominant view in American society. It suggests that we have control over our own fate and that we are responsible for our own successes and failures. The EC-IR worldview suggests that we have little control over how other people view us, yet we are still responsible for their perceptions. The EC-ER worldview suggests that we have little control over our lives and we are not responsible for our condition. Finally, the IC-ER worldview suggests that we have the ability to perform well, but others are responsible for our lot in life. Sue (1978) and Sue and Sue (2003) suggest that the IC-IR view is the dominant one for White Americans, and the other three are potential worldviews of ethnic minorities. Placed in this context, those having the EC-IR worldview may feel that racism is preventing them from succeeding, yet it is their responsibility to succeed; thus, they feel alienated from society. Those having the EC-ER worldview may feel that there is nothing they can do about racism. Those having the IC-ER worldview may take a militant stance, feeling that they have the ability to succeed, but societal racism is keeping them from succeeding, so the only people they can trust are those in their own group.

One problem with the Sue (1978) model is that it seems to apply only to those who are not successful and are "victims" of racism. While this model may very well help us understand individuals who are in lower socioeconomic classes, it does not help us understand those who are in higher socioeconomic classes and those whose external locus of control is based on fate or forces larger than ourselves. For example, religious people may see personal choice as inconsequential in relation to "God's plan" or believe that behaviors are predetermined by the karma accrued from past lives. Thus, the very notion of locus of control may be a Western concept that does not translate well to other cultural perspectives. Again, however, this model may help us to understand those who are less successful than they believe they should be.

Individualism and Collectivism

The general perspectives of individualism and collectivism are forms of worldview. Moreover, as Triandis (1995) pointed out, individualism and collectivism should also be considered in relation to a horizontal versus vertical societal structure. These dimensions result in a horizontal individualistic perspective, where people feel that uniqueness is most important; a vertical individualistic perspective, where one's achievements are most important; a horizontal collectivistic perspective, where cooperation is most important; and a vertical collectivistic perspective, where being dutiful and knowing one's place is most important. The dominant Western view is that of individualism. Thus, students reared in this perspective may not understand the perspective of those reared in collectivist societies or in homes that emphasize collectivism. For example, after our class viewed a video on how American Indians are still being denied equal treatment in their ability to practice their religious beliefs, a 20+-year-old White man contended in our class discussion that these American Indians were being selfish in wanting to preserve the land for their religious beliefs. To even frame the contentions of the American Indian perspective in terms of selfishness was clearly an imposition of his own values and a misunderstanding of the American Indian position.

GUIDELINE 3: THE INCORPORATION OF MULTICULTURAL
PERSPECTIVES IN EDUCATION

The more complete statement of this Guideline is as follows:

As educators, psychologists are encouraged to employ the constructs of multiculturalism and diversity in psychological education. (APA, 2003, p. 390)

As I have written elsewhere (Mio, 2003), there are three general approaches to addressing multiculturalism in clinical training programs. One approach is to have a single course in multicultural psychology. This has been the traditional approach taken by most programs, where a professor who has particular expertise in the area introduces students to issues in the field. It is the easiest approach for a program to take, as it does not require that other professors have much knowledge about multicultural issues. A second approach is to have a cluster of courses that address multicultural issues from different perspectives. For example, one might have an introductory course in multicultural psychology, a testing course dedicated to multicultural issues, a research course dedicated to multicultural issues, and a clinical interventions course that discusses such issues. This approach requires a program to have more than one professor with multicultural expertise. A third approach is to have multicultural issues infused throughout the courses in the training program. Although this may be the ideal position to advocate, it might be unrealistic in programs where entrenched professors do not value multiculturalism. However, where this approach can be implemented, it offers the richest experience for students and will best prepare them for their future profession. Moreover, this approach can offer professors themselves the richest environment in which to explore multicultural issues and develop programmatic research to help push the field forward. In examining the history of psychology, one sees where departments that had a dedicated focus of attention among all of its faculty members were able to make important contributions to the field.

This last point is where I see much of the resistance in the field. Because many professors where trained in earlier models they do not want to give up, they have resisted training in new directions. For example, at a recent APA convention, I was attending a session on the importance of understanding multicultural issues when conducting therapy, and a gentleman in the audience actually said something to the effect of "I have been conducting therapy for years, and ethnicity doesn't matter. If students don't know how to work with ethnic minorities, I just keep assigning them such cases until they get it right." People in the audience were stunned at his ignorance. Not being one to hold my mouth, I replied, "I hope that you do not feel that it is okay for completely naïve therapists who do not know anything about multicultural issues to practice on ethnic minority clients, while you are insisting on them to be trained to deal with White clients *before* they see the White clients." I wonder how he might have reacted to the statement, "We do not have to train our students to conduct any therapy at all. All we have to do is throw them out into the world, and eventually they will learn to become therapists." The purpose of training programs is to train; multicultural training is an integral part of this training.

CONCLUSION

While many of us who have been working within a framework of multiculturalism have incorporated such issues in our teaching, therapy, and supervision, the publication of the Multicultural Guidelines has helped to standardize our efforts across the country. We still encounter individuals in our profession who are unaware of basic issues such as racial identity development and White privilege. The job of clinical training programs is to train students to be aware of these issues and to be effective therapists. However, some of our colleagues are also in need of training. To the extent that we can have an influence on our colleagues, many of whom may be tenured and senior to us, we must be continually vigilant for opportunities for teachable moments in multiculturalism. The Multicultural Guidelines establish the context; it is now up to us to continue the fight.

ACKNOWLEDGMENTS

Many students with whom I have worked over the years have inspired parts of this chapter, as indicated in some of the chapter's quotes. I greatly appreciate and acknowledge their contributions and inspiration.

REFERENCES

American Psychological Association. (1953). *Ethical standards of psychologists.* Washington, DC: Author.

American Psychological Association. (1990). Ethical principles of psychologists. *American Psychologist, 45,* 390–395.

American Psychological Association. (2002). Ethical principles of psychologists and code of conduct. *American Psychologist, 57,* 1060–1073.

American Psychological Association. (2003). Guidelines on multicultural education, training, research, practice, and organizational change for psychologists. *American Psychologist, 58,* 377–402.

Bernal, M. E., & Padilla, A. M. (1982). Status of minority curricula and training in clinical psychology. *American Psychologist, 37,* 780–787.

Berry, J. W. (1969). On cross-cultural comparability. *International Journal of Psychology, 4,* 119–128.

Casas, J. M. (1990, August). Ethical imperatives in multicultural counseling. In J. G. Ponterotto (Chair), *The White American researcher in multicultural counseling: Significance and challenges.* Symposium presented at the 98th Annual Convention of the American Psychological Association, Boston.

Comas-Diaz, L., & Jacobsen, F. M. (1991). Ethnocultural transference and countertransference in the therapeutic dyad. *American Journal of Orthopsychiatry, 61,* 392–402.

Helms, J. E. (1984). Toward a theoretical explanation of the effects of race on counseling: A Black and White model. *Counseling Psychologist, 12,* 153–165.

Helms, J. E. (Ed.). (1990). *Black and White racial identity: Theory, research, and practice.* Westport, CT: Greenwood.

Helms, J. E. (1995). An update of Helms's White and People of Color racial identity models. In J. G. Pontorotto, J. M. Casas, L. A. Suzuki, & C. M. Alexander (Eds.), *Handbook of multicultural counseling* (pp. 181–198). Thousand Oaks, CA: Sage.

Jahoda, G. (1982). *Psychology and anthropology: A psychological perspective.* London: Academic Press.

Lee, M. W. (Producer and Director). (1994). *The color of fear* [Motion picture]. (Available from Stir-Fry Productions, 1222 Preservation Park Way, Oakland, CA 94612)

McIntosh, P. (1986). *White privilege and male privilege: A personal account of coming to see correspondences through work in women's studies.* Paper presented at the Virginia Women's Studies Association Conference, Richmond, VA.

McIntosh, P. (1995). White privilege and male privilege: A personal account of coming to see correspondences through work in women's studies. In M. L. Andersen & P. H. Collins (Eds.), *Race, class, and gender: An anthology* (2nd ed., pp. 76–87). Belmont, CA: Wadsworth.

Mio, J. S. (2003). On teaching multiculturalism: History, models, and content. In G. Bernal, J. E. Trimble, A. K. Burlew, & F. T. L. Leong (Eds.), *Handbook of racial and ethnic minority psychology* (pp. 119–146). Thousand Oaks, CA: Sage.

Mio, J. S., & Awakuni, G. I. (2000). *Resistance to multiculturalism: Issues and interventions.* Philadelphia: Brunner/Mazel.

Mio, J. S., & Barker-Hackett, L. (2003). Reaction papers and journal writing as techniques for assessing resistance in multicultural courses. *Journal of Multicultural Counseling and Development, 31,* 12–19.

Mio, J. S., & Iwamasa, G. Y. (1993). To do, or not to do: That is the question for White cross-cultural researchers. *Counseling Psychologist, 21,* 197–212.

Mio, J. S., & Morris, D. R. (1990). Cross-cultural issues in psychology training programs: An invitation for discussion. *Professional Psychology: Research and Practice, 21,* 434–441.

Mischel, W. (1958). Preference for delayed reinforcement: An experimental study of a cultural observation. *Journal of Abnormal and Social Psychology, 56,* 57–61.

Mischel, W. (1961). Delay of gratification, need for achievement, and acquiescence in another culture. *Journal of Abnormal and Social Psychology, 62,* 543–552.

Reynolds, A. L. (1999). Etic/emic. In J. S. Mio, J. E. Trimble, P. Arredondo, H. E. Cheatham, & D. Sue (Eds.), *Key words in multicultural interventions: A dictionary* (pp. 115–116). Westport, CT: Greenwood.

Sue, D. W. (1978). Eliminating cultural oppression in counseling: Toward a general theory. *Journal of Counseling Psychology, 25,* 419–428.

Sue, D. W., Bernier, J., Durran, M., Feinberg, L., Pedersen, P., Smith, E., et al. (1982). Position paper: Cross-cultural counseling competencies. *Counseling Psychologist, 10,* 45–52.

Sue, D. W., Carter, R. T., Casas, J. M., Fouad, N. A., Ivey, A. E., Jensen, M., et al. (1998). *Multicultural counseling competencies: Individual and organizational development.* Thousand Oaks, CA: Sage.

Sue, D. W., & Sue, D. (2003). *Counseling the culturally diverse: Theory and practice* (4th ed.). New York: Wiley.

Triandis, H. C. (1978). Some universals of social behavior? *Personality and Social Psychology, 4,* 1–16.

Triandis, H. C. (1995). *Individualism and collectivism.* Boulder, CO: Westview.

Triandis, H. C., McCusker, C., Betancourt, H., Iwao, S., Yeung, K., Salazar, J. M., et al. (1993). An etic-emic analysis of individualism and collectivism. *Journal of Cross-Cultural Psychology, 24,* 366–383.

CHAPTER 9

Multicultural Competencies in Clinic and Hospital Settings

JAIRO FUERTES, ALEXA MISLOWACK, AND SHARON MINTZ

THIS CHAPTER IS organized into three sections. The first section discusses some of the mental health needs of minority populations in the United States documented in the literature. The second section examines the barriers to treatment that minority persons encounter, as documented in the literature. And the third section explores the relevance of the Multicultural Guidelines recently published by the American Psychological Association (APA, 2003) in addressing some of the needs and barriers to mental health services for racial and ethnic minority groups in the United States.

MENTAL HEALTH NEEDS OF MINORITY POPULATIONS

In 2001 (Department of Health and Human Services [DHHS], 2001c), the Surgeon General released a comprehensive and exhaustive report addressing the state of mental health for ethnic and racial minorities in the United States in which the disparity in the quality of mental health care for underserved minority patients was devastatingly exposed. No longer could mental health professionals and public health officers overlook the essential role that race and culture play in the experiences that these ever-growing multicultural populations face when seeking mental health treatment in various service settings, such as hospitals and community mental health clinics. The report revealed that for the four minority U.S. populations investigated (African Americans, American Indians and Alaskan Natives,

Asian Americans and Pacific Islanders, and Hispanic Americans), a multitude of mental health needs are being grossly insufficiently met due to a variety of social and interpersonal factors, including poverty, language and information barriers, and provider ignorance, racism, and overall culturally insensitive services. The report states that with respect to mental health services, racial and ethnic minority populations receive less care for mental health concerns, as well as less quality when they do get services (DHHS, 2001c).

The Surgeon General asserted very clearly and directly that based on the literature on patient needs and perceptions of medical and mental services, "*culture counts*," in that it influences the way people view, physically experience, and seek help for mental illness. He outlined several recommendations for service providers, professionals, and research scientists:

- Empirically investigate the efficacy of evidence-based treatments for minority members.
- Explore the ways different cultures experience mental illness, improving minority client access to care.
- Eliminate barriers to and enhance the quality of psychological services.
- Specifically, promote the advancement in evidence-based *multicultural competency training* for counselors, psychologists, psychiatrists, social workers, and other mental health professionals. (DHHS, 2001c)

The Surgeon General's report revealed that severe mental illnesses, such as Bipolar Disorder, Depression, and Schizophrenia, are found within every group in the United States and in the world, but barriers to mental health services exist in the United States on a disproportionate scale for racial and ethnic minority groups. The high cost of care, limited availability of services, and the social stigma of mental illness are common barriers that all patients face, but these factors are exacerbated for racial and ethnic minority group members (DHHS, 2001c). Racial and ethnic minority group members who have chronic mental illness have less access to treatment and experience poorer quality of treatment across community mental health centers and hospitals in the United States, even if they are insured and services are available in their communities. Diminished access and quality of care is exacerbated by factors such as provider and institutionally based racism and discrimination, language barriers between patients and doctors/agencies, patient mistrust of mental health treatment, and mismatch between patient and therapist expectations, among other reasons.

It is important to note that racial and ethnic minorities are more likely to represent vulnerable, "high-needs" populations, including those who are homeless, incarcerated, and institutionalized, which often have higher rates of mental disorders. Persons of low socioeconomic status (SES) are approximately two to three times more likely to experience mental illness, and socioeconomic factors influence the course of mental illnesses (World Health Organization, 2001). When factors such as SES are controlled for, community-dwelling minority patients have rates of mental illness comparable to that of Whites (DHHS, 2001b). The Surgeon General made it clear in his report that outcome disparities stem from minorities receiving less care and poorer quality of care, and not because their illnesses are more severe or prevalent in comparison to Whites living in similar communities (DHHS, 2001b).

The Community Mental Health Act of 1963 first revolutionized mental health care by providing mentally ill patients with outpatient, community-based care whose aim was to reintegrate those with psychological problems into the community. The trend for de-institutionalizing mental health patients reinforced the need for strong community bonds and supports (Alegria, Perez, & Williams, 2003). Community mental health centers (hereafter CMHCs) and hospital settings have traditionally served low-income, low-SES patients who lack mental health care insurance and often rely on federally funded psychological agencies. One may call these "the trenches of mental health care," where the poor experiencing psychological problems can receive first-line defense against their mental struggles. Racial and ethnic minority members are overrepresented in the low-SES strata in the United States, with American Indians and Alaskan Natives representing the poorest minority groups.

Ham (2003), reporting on a study conducted by Chow, Jaffe, and Snowden (2003), explained that minority clients living in low-poverty neighborhoods are more likely to receive psychological services through mental health professionals working in places such as CMHCs and hospitals rather than from professionals in private practice. Thus, it is important to understand the mental health needs of and barriers to treatment for minority patients within these settings and thereby possibly discover ways of improving access, availability, quality, and utilization of services. To best guide psychological treatment for specific minority patients, it is prudent to first assess the common mental health needs of minority populations within the service areas of CMHCs and hospitals. Although the mental health care needs of ethnic and racial minority groups are often difficult to ascertain due to differences in cultural beliefs and attitudes toward psychological problems, several studies have elucidated common mental health needs and issues found in minority communities.

Salient mental illnesses for minority group members include depression, alcoholism, Posttraumatic Stress Disorder (PTSD), and anxiety. American Indians and Alaskan Natives are five times more likely to die from alcohol-related problems than Whites and their suicide rate is 50% higher than the national average (DHHS, 2001c). Manson (2000) alerted counselors and other professionals to address the needs of Native American veterans, whose reported lifetime PTSD symptoms and alcohol dependency rates have been found to surpass veterans from other racial and ethnic groups. PTSD is also a fairly common diagnosis for immigrant patients from Southeast Asian countries (Chung & Bemak, 2002) and Hispanic veterans (DHHS, 2001c). Also, Hispanic Americans born in the United States have higher rates of mental illness than Hispanic immigrants from Mexico or Puerto Rico (DHHS, 2001c). Examination of the limited utilization of mental health services by ethnic and racial minority patients sheds light on some of their needs. For example, African Americans tend to delay seeking help until severe symptoms set in (DHHS, 2001b).

BARRIERS TO TREATMENT IN COMMUNITY CLINICS AND HOSPITALS

Treatment dropout rates for ethnic and racial minority patients are markedly higher than for White patients in CMHC and hospital settings (Klein, Stone, Hicks, & Pritchard, 2003; Sue, 1977; Walitzer, Dermen, & Connors, 1999). An examination of the multitude of barriers experienced by minority patients in hospitals and CMHCs may shed light on the dropout rate. The Surgeon General's supplementary report (DHHS, 2001b) identified the barriers that racial and ethnic minorities contend with in seeking treatment. These include:

- Language barriers.
- Stigma associated with mental illness and mental health care.
- Poverty, lack of insurance, cutbacks in funding.
- Institutional and individual racism and discrimination.

Differences in language between therapist and client pose one of the major barriers. It is interesting to note that according to the 1964 Civil Rights Act, mental health settings receiving federal funding must provide equal access to service for persons who do not speak English or have difficulties with the language (DHHS, 2001b); hospitals and CMHCs that comply with the law must provide translators. However, despite this legislation, language continues to be a major barrier to service. The diagnosis and treatment of mental illness is further compromised when communication of physical symptoms and emotional struggles is stymied. Takeuchi,

Bui, and Kim (1993) hypothesized that the limited number of bilingual professional staff deters recent immigrants, such as Hispanic immigrants, from seeking or properly using services at hospitals and CMHCs. In fact, it is estimated that approximately 50% of Asian American/Pacific Islander mental health patients cannot receive treatment because of the combination of their not understanding or speaking English and the lack of bilingual professionals (DHHS, 2001b).

Aside from patients not understanding the English language, Williams et al. (1995) identified barriers encountered by those with limited "functional health literacy," whereby the patient finds it difficult to understand his or her diagnosis and the provider's proposed or directed treatment plans. Additionally, people with chronic mental disease who go to CMHCs have been found to experience significant barriers to medical care, such as the coordination of their medical and mental health treatment by CMHC staff (Miller, Druss, Dombrowski, & Rosenheck, 2003). The stigma associated with mental illness and distrust in professional psychologists and psychiatrists appear to be significant obstacles to seeking and complying with treatment (DHHS, 2001b). Stigma and distrust stem from limited information about mental illness and mental health; these factors are likely fueled by cultural values that shame those who admit to mental problems to the extent that they would seek professional help. Distrust is also probably fueled by the depreciative treatment many minority patients experience when they do seek help. It should be noted that we do not currently understand how stigma arises and operates in cultural groups in the United States. The Institute of Medicine report published in 2001 concluded from a national study and exhaustive review of the evidence that racism and discrimination explain outcome disparities in medical treatment in the United States. For example, mental health professionals have been found to be less likely to use evidence-based care guidelines when treating African American and Hispanic American patients in comparison to White patients (DHHS, 2001b).

A mismatch in client-provider expectations has been presented as an additional hurdle to care because minority group members may be unfamiliar with the goals or nature of counseling/mental health services or with the standard roles by which clients and therapists are expected to abide (DHHS, 2001b). Providers and patients often hold incongruent values and beliefs surrounding the identification and treatment of mental illness. For example, somatic symptoms may be more likely than emotional or psychological complaints for Asian American minority patients seeking treatment (Yen, Robins, & Lin, 2000). Professionally trained mental health providers are often unaware of or disinterested in knowing patients' interpretations of their problems and rarely seek to negotiate with their patients how they may approach their problems. "Clinical environments that do not respect, or are incompatible with, the cultures of the people they serve may deter minorities from using services and receiving appropriate care" (DHHS, 2001a, Chapter 2: Culture counts, para. 2, fifth bullet).

The minimal availability of services is another barrier for treatment because "safety net providers," such as CMHCs and hospital emergency rooms, which disproportionably serve minority patients, have experienced financial cutbacks (Hudson, 1990). States increasingly depend on benefits from Medicaid, and many have cut their levels of funding to hospitals and CMHCs. Compounding the problem is ethnic and racial minorities' limited access to mental health insurance. In comparison to the 14% of uninsured White Americans, it is estimated that 25% of African American patients, 20% of American Indian/Alaskan Native, 21% of Asian American/Pacific Islander, and 37% of Hispanic patients are uninsured in the United States (DHHS, 2001b). However, even those individuals fortunate enough to have insurance encounter difficulties in utilizing the mental health service and insurance systems (e.g., American Indians, Manson, 2000), for example, in having access to and coverage for qualified bilingual providers or access to medicines and specialists (Alegria et al., 2001).

Limited continuity of care within the managed care system challenges minority patients' ability to easily access services. Garfield (1994) encouraged CMHCs and hospitals to carefully examine the clinical environment. Client and provider characteristics such as race and ethnicity and provider multicultural competence should be examined when evaluating the utilization of mental health services, because these factors underlie patients' experiences and decisions to continue with treatment and the attitudes of staff toward their patients and their jobs.

Finally, due to CMHCs' reliance on funding sources such as Medicare and Medicaid, they must comply with budgetary and other government restrictions. Over the past 20 years, CMHCs have experienced large cutbacks in funding. At the same time, counselors and other mental health professionals have been pressured to meet productivity standards, which has been cited as a major contributor to counselors' and social workers' dissatisfaction with their professions (Lorber & Satow, 1975). Lorber and Satow hypothesized that high minority client dropout rates at CMHCs were really a result of counselor dissatisfaction rather than client dissatisfaction with treatment. We did not find studies testing this hypothesis, but found this observation interesting and worth pursuing in research.

Because racism, discrimination, and cultural differences have been cited as barriers to utilization in these settings, some have argued for the possible effectiveness of ethnic, racial, or class matching in CMHCs (Rieff & Riessman, 1965). For example, Gamst, Dana, Der-Karabetian, and Kramer (2001) provided evidence for the success of racial/ethnic matching in preventing dropout in a CMHC for Asian American patients. However, the lack of available mental health professionals from ethnic and racial minorities who could serve as counseling dyad counterparts presents a significant challenge for adopting this approach in CMHCs and hospitals. According to the Surgeon General's report, ethnic and racial minority mental health professionals are truly the minority in the field of professional applied psychology. For example, Holzer, Goldsmith, and Ciarlo (1998), as cited in DHHS (2001c), found that only 2% of psychiatrists, 2% of psychologists, and 4% of social workers in the United States are African American (DHHS, 2001c), thereby severely limiting the feasibility of the ethnic matching solution.

MULTICULTURAL GUIDELINES

In this section we review the Multicultural Guidelines published by the APA in 2003 and speculate as to how these Multicultural Guidelines may address some of the needs and barriers discussed earlier. The APA Multicultural Guidelines are valuable to the current topic in that they were based on a review of data similar to those we uncovered on racial and ethnic minority populations' needs and barriers with respect to mental health. The APA Multicultural Guidelines are intended to address important issues of service delivery, training/education, and research with respect to mental health and racial and cultural minority groups in the United States (by using the term "cultural," the APA implies that the Multicultural Guidelines may be relevant to more than just racial and ethnic minority groups, such as gay/lesbian/bisexual populations, the physically disabled, and low-SES groups of any race). For our purposes, we maintain a focus on racial and ethnic minority populations with special attention to immigrant populations in the United States. We encourage the reader to review in depth the Multicultural Guidelines published by the APA, as we present only general observations about each area in the Multicultural Guideline report and focus on tying the guidelines to the needs and barriers presented earlier.

The Multicultural Guidelines emphasize the importance of multicultural competence at the individual level, particularly with respect to provider self-awareness, knowledge of specific cultures and needs of clients, and sophisticated use of skills that are tailored to the beliefs, needs, and unique circumstances of clients. The APA Multicultural Guidelines also emphasize education, research, and training activities that may further the establishment of competence across mental health settings and population needs.

The first Guideline addresses issues of therapist and agency bias, racism, discrimination, and other cognitive errors that affect access to health care and the quality of care for minority patients. This is a reality that is unequivocal and must be embraced by mental health professionals interested in providing better, equitable care to minority patients. *Racism is alive and well in mental health care and it must be actively addressed.* Guideline 1 states, "Psychologists are encouraged to recognize that, as cultural beings, they may hold attitudes and beliefs that can detrimentally influence their perceptions of and interactions with individuals who are ethnically and racially different from themselves" (APA, 2003, p. 382). The old adage "Counselor, know thyself" has never been truer. Providers must realize that they are vulnerable to cognitive errors in perception and judgment, that these errors are often fueled by biases, stereotypes, or lack of information about their patients, and that these errors can affect their approach and care of their clients (Abreu, 2001). These errors can also affect providers' interpersonal style with their patients and may very well affect the questions they ask (or do not ask), the information they elicit from patients, their interpretation of patients' reports, their decision making with respect to diagnosis and treatment plan, and their ability to partner with and foster trust in their patients. Mental health providers must also be aware of physician and nurse bias and actively promote the equitable treatment of racial, ethnic, and minority clients. Beyond good medicine and ethical and professional psychological practice, this guideline may keep individuals and hospitals from becoming embroiled in legal or political problems due to physician/provider bias or malpractice.

The next Multicultural Guideline encourages psychologists "to recognize the importance of multicultural sensitivity/responsiveness to" and knowledge of ethnic and racial minority individuals (APA, 2003, p. 385). This Guideline emphasizes the central role of culture in clients' experiences, perceptions, and values, particularly in relation to mental health and problems in living. APA "recognizes the broad scope of dimensions of race, ethnicity, language, sexual orientation, gender, age, disability, class status, education, religious/spiritual orientation, and other cultural dimensions" (2003, p. 380).

It is important for mental health professionals to have not only a medical or psychiatric/psychological understanding of the client's problems, but an understanding of the *person* experiencing those problems. Berlin and Fowkes (1983) provided a simple but useful model for effectively engaging in a cross-cultural encounter in medical settings. Providers are encouraged to adapt the L-E-A-R-N model of intervention:

1. Listen with empathy and understanding to the patient's perception of the problem.
2. Explain your understanding and perception of the problem.
3. Acknowledge and discuss differences and similarities in the perception of the problem.
4. Recommend treatment.
5. Negotiate an agreement on treatment and follow-up.

As the Surgeon General concluded, "culture counts" in mental health services, and the patient's culture-based beliefs and perspectives have to be at least acknowledged or negotiated in order to engage the patient in the treatment of the problem. This level of communication is crucial in helping the client understand how the problem will be treated and to win his or her consent and commitment. Kleinman (1981) provided a set of questions that can elicit health beliefs in clinical encounters. These questions are useful in engaging clients in communication and in participating in their treatment and in conveying provider interest and respect in the client's perception of the problem and in his or her input in resolving or treating the problem. Kleinman's questions are the following:

- What do you call your problem? What name does it have?
- What do you think caused your problem?
- Why do you think it started when it did?
- What does the problem do to you?
- How severe is it? Will it have a short or long course?
- What do you fear the most about this problem?
- What are some of the chief problems it has caused you?
- What kind of treatment do you think you should receive?
- What are the results that you hope to obtain from treatment?

The first two APA Multicultural Guidelines just reviewed address some of the more human and interpersonal barriers and needs, such as patient mistrust, the stigma of mental health illness, mismatch of expectations between patients and providers, and possibly language or communication difficulties. It behooves providers to appreciate the very real nature of patient ambivalence about mental health treatment and diagnosis as well patients' ambivalence about accepting help (Arredondo & Toporek, 1996). This issue is particularly relevant and important when examined from the perspective of adherence to treatment. Adherence to treatment is important in human terms, as measured by diminished suffering, improved quality of life, and even making the difference between life and death. However, adherence is also important in financial terms, as measured by lost productivity, unused or misused resources, and the potential need for more expensive and invasive procedures such as hospitalization.

The third APA Multicultural Guideline refers to psychologists as educators: "As educators, psychologists are encouraged to employ the constructs of multiculturalism and diversity in psychological education" (2003, p. 386). There is preliminary evidence that multicultural education and training for mental health professionals is effective in promoting their multicultural awareness and sensitivity (e.g., Brown, Parham, & Yonker, 1996). Typically, multicultural education strategies are anchored in the first two Guidelines outlined in the APA report: understanding one's own cultural lenses and biases and being aware of others' cultural beliefs, backgrounds, biases, and formative influences. Training, according to the APA, is the utilization of psychological education for advancing practical and research expertise. Indeed, this third Guideline may also stimulate continuing education practices in workshops, conferences, and readings in professional journals on effective multicultural service delivery. Education becomes important in the long run in diminishing racism and discrimination. Education can also increase the number of mental health providers who are members of racial and ethnic minority groups in the United States and who speak languages other than English. Lack of culturally sensitive services, of providers who are minority group members, and of providers who are fluent in second languages is implicated in decreased access and quality of mental health services to racial and ethnic minority populations in hospitals and CMHCs.

To keep practitioners current with the latest innovations and culturally sensitive interventions, Guideline 4 recommends involvement with research: "Culturally sensitive psychological researchers are encouraged to recognize the importance of conducting culture-centered and ethical psychological research among persons from ethnic, linguistic, and racial minority backgrounds" (APA, 2003, p. 388). This Guideline addresses the importance of examining needs, barriers, and effective interventions through research. The vast amount of clinical research in applied psychology has historically been conducted with predominantly European American populations, although new initiatives and incentives are in place to encourage research with minority, underserved populations (Goode & Harrison, 2000). For example, the National Institute of Mental Health and other National Institutes of Health agencies now require gender and minority inclusion estimates on all projects prior to approving or releasing funding. The Surgeon General's report (DHHS, 2001c) specifically outlined the lack of evidence and knowledge base for established treatments and effective interventions with racial and ethnic minority populations. This type of research may inform some of the issues raised in the fifth Guideline of the APA report, regarding culturally sensitive psychological practices. These issues include *best practices* and *optimal conditions* for effective mental health treatment to the burgeoning minority and ethnic subgroups and communities in the United States. Research is needed to better address the types of needs among these communities and to identify the way members and families in these communities experience and manifest problems and mental illness. This type of continued research effort is important because these communities and individuals continue to grow, develop, and react to the changing social, financial, and cultural pressures and realities that surround them. Continued research efforts are also in order so that we can better plan and execute outreach practices and develop organizational strategies that may effectively reach and be accepted by racial, ethnic, and immigrant communities.

The sixth and last Guideline states: "Psychologists are encouraged to use organizational change processes to support culturally informed organizational (policy) development and practices" (APA, 2003, p. 392). This Guideline encourages psychologists to take on the role of advocate. For instance, psychologists working in an environment with minimal organizational change in response to the changing racial and ethnic demographics in our society are encouraged to advocate for changes that incorporate cultural sensitivity and diversity. According to the National Center for Cultural Competence (NCCC; n.d.) and the Office of Minority Health of the Department of Health and Human Services, cultural competence must be systematically incorporated at every level of a health organization, for example, by having a written strategic plan that outlines goals, policy, and operational plans, by maintaining proper patient health information, and by maintaining participatory and collaborative partnerships with their respective communities. The NCCC recommends that clinicians make sure the organization they are representing has the following: (1) continuing multicultural competency training for all staff members, (2) financial backing to enhance cultural competence in all levels of the organization, (3) an ongoing evaluation process to assess current population needs, (4) means of attaining translation and interpretation assistance, and (5) guidelines that promote community outreach.

This Guideline is the most crucial in making changes happen. Without advocacy, organizational policies will remain the same, leaving minority clients at a disadvantage. By promoting minority clients' needs, mental health professionals can assist in overcoming many barriers to better care and overall client satisfaction. Organizations must realize that they cannot wait for the forces of gradualism to reach them. Concerned mental health professionals and administrators must individually take responsibility for initiating and implementing change (Howard-Hamilton, 2000).

These changes include hiring and retaining personnel who are racial/ minority group members, hiring and retaining personnel who speak languages other than English, properly training all personnel in ethical multicultural service delivery and outreach, and working collaboratively with schools, universities, and religious and spiritual leaders, including inviting them to take influential positions within the system. For example, hospitals and CMHCs can have community leaders as active members on their boards of directors, with the goals of maintaining connections with the communities they serve and of continually improving their services to meet the needs of their constituents. Hospitals and CMHCs should also develop and promote programs that are preventive in nature and focus on helping racial, minority, and immigrant/refugee families and individuals adapt and grow in the United States. These issues may not rise to the level of diagnosis or medical/mental distress, but are considerable in complexity and emotional effect. These issues include coping with social difficulties such as not speaking English, coping with the loss of relatives and support networks in the country of origin, dealing with racism and oppression (e.g., at work, in finding appropriate housing), and coping with family difficulties that arise, such as when children learn the language and absorb cultural influences much faster than their parents. In other words, mental health planning and outreach should include primary as well as secondary and tertiary interventions.

CONCLUSION

This chapter has addressed many of the current problems in providing mental health services to racial, minority, and immigrant clients, as well as provided some suggestions for addressing these issues. We reviewed the recent report published by the Surgeon General of the United States (DHHS, 2001c) and the Multicultural Guidelines published by the APA (2003) and provided recommendations to address some of the needs of the fast-growing racial, ethnic, and immigrant populations in the United States. Given the current (and also projected) demographic changes taking place in this country, and given the indisputable evidence on treatment outcome disparities for minority patients, it is absolutely essential that health care organizations and mental health professionals begin immediately to implement organizational, clinical, and training changes that address the needs and problems of this segment of our society. It is also important for researchers and funding agencies to engage in and promote research that explains and predicts the phenomenon of outcome disparities, that examines the most effective treatment interventions for racial and ethnic minority groups, and that examines the role of provider multicultural competence in addressing the health care needs of these patient populations.

REFERENCES

Abreu, J. M. (2001). Theory and research on stereotypes and perceptual bias: A didactic resource for multicultural counseling trainers. *Counseling Psychologist, 29,* 487–512.

Alegria, M., McGuire, T., Vera, M., Canino, G., Matias, L., & Claderon, J. (2001). Changes in access to mental health care among the poor and nonpoor. *American Journal of Public Health, 91,* 1431–1434.

Alegria, M., Perez, D. J., & Williams, S. (2003). The role of public policies in reducing mental health status disparities for people of color. *Health Affairs, 22,* 51–64.

American Psychological Association. (2003). Guidelines on multicultural education, training, research, practice, and organizational change for psychologists. *American Psychologist, 58,* 377–402.

Arredondo, P., & Toporek, R. (1996). Operationalization of the multicultural counseling competencies. *Journal of Multicultural Counseling and Development, 24,* 42–78.

Berlin, E., & Fowkes, W. A. (1983). Teaching framework for cross-cultural health care. *Western Journal of Medicine, 139,* 934–938.

Brown, S. P., Parham, T. A., & Yonker, R. A. (1996). Influence of a cross-cultural training course on racial identity attitudes of White women and men: Preliminary perspective. *Journal of Counseling and Development, 74,* 510–516.

Chow, J. C., Jaffe, K., & Snowden, L. (2003). Racial/ethnic disparities in the use of mental health services in poverty areas. *American Journal of Public Health, 93,* 792–797.

Chung, R. C., & Bemak, F. (2002). Revisiting the California Southeast Asian mental health needs assessment data: An examination of refugee ethnic and gender differences. *Journal of Counseling and Development, 80,* 111–119.

Department of Health and Human Services. (2001a). Chapter summaries and conclusions. In *Mental health: Culture, race, and ethnicity: A supplement to mental health: A report of the Surgeon General* (chap. 2 of Executive summary). Retrieved January 29, 2004, from http://www.mentalhealth.org/cre/execsummary-6.asp.

Department of Health and Human Services. (2001b). Executive summary. In *Mental health: Culture, race, and ethnicity: A supplement to mental health: A report of the Surgeon General.* Retrieved January 29, 2004, from http://www.surgeongeneral.gov/library/mentalhealth/cre/execsummary-1.html.

Department of Health and Human Services. (2001c). *Mental health: Culture, race, and ethnicity: A supplement to mental health: A report of the Surgeon General.* Retrieved January 18, 2004, from http://www.mentalhealth.samhsa.gov/cre/toc.asp.

Gamst, G., Dana, R. H., Der-Karabetian, & Kramer, T. (2001). Asian American mental health clients: Effects of ethnic match and age on global assessment and visitation. *Journal of Mental Health Counseling, 23,* 57–71.

Garfield, S. L. (1994). Research on client variables in psychotherapy. In A. E. Bergin & S. L. Garfield (Eds.), *Handbook of psychotherapy and behavior change* (4th ed., pp. 190–228). New York: Wiley.

Goode, T. D., & Harrison, S. (2000). *Cultural competence in primary health care: Partnerships for a research agenda.* Retrieved December 18, 2003, from Georgetown University, Center for Child and Human Development, National Center for Cultural Competence web site: http://www.georgetown.edu/research/gucdc/nccc/ncccpolicy3.html.

Ham, B. (2003, May 22). Minorities get different mental health care in rich neighborhoods. *Health Behavior News Service.* Retrieved January 18, 2004, from http://www.eurekalert.org/pub_releases/2003–05/cfta-mgd052203.php.

Holzer, C. E., Goldsmith, H. F., & Ciarlo, J. A. (1998). Effects of rural-urban county type on the availability of health and mental health care providers. In R. W. Manderscheid & M. J. Henderson (Eds.), *Mental health, United States.* Rockville, MD: Center for Mental Health Services.

Howard-Hamilton, M. (2000). Programming for multicultural competencies. *New Directions for Student Services, 90,* 67–78.

Hudson, C. G. (1990). The performance of state community mental health systems: A path model. *Social Service Review, 64,* 94–120.

Institute of Medicine. (2001). Social risk factors. In *Health and behavior: The interplay of biological, behavioral, and societal influences* (chap. 4). Retrieved March 1, 2004, from http://www.nap.edu/books/0309070309/html.

Klein, E. B., Stone, W. N., Hicks, M. W., & Pritchard, I. L. (2003). Understanding dropouts. *Journal of Mental Health Counseling, 25,* 89–100.

Kleinman, A. (1981). *Patients and healers in the context of culture.* Berkeley, CA: University of California Press.

Lorber, J., & Satow, R. (1975). Dropout rates in mental health centers. *Social Work, 20,* 308–312.

Manson, S. M. (2000). Mental health services for American Indians and Alaska Natives: Need, use, and barriers to effective care. *Canadian Journal of Psychiatry, 45,* 617–626.

Miller, C. L., Druss, B. G., Dombrowski, E. A., & Rosenheck, R. A. (2003). Barriers to primary medical care among patients at a community mental health center. *Psychiatric Services, 54,* 1158–1160.

National Center for Cultural Competence: Conceptual frameworks/models, guiding values and principles. (n.d.). Retrieved February 27, 2004, from Georgetown University, Center for Child and Human Development, National Center for Cultural Competence web site: http://gucchd.georgetown.edu//nccc/framework.html.

Rieff, R., & Riessman, F. (1965). The indigenous nonprofessional: A strategy of change in community mental health programs [Monograph]. *Community Mental Health Journal 1,* 3–32. New York: Behavioral Press.

Sue, S. (1977). Community mental health services to minority groups: Some optimism, some pessimism. *American Psychologist, 32,* 616–624.

Takeuchi, D. T., Bui, K. T., & Kim, L. (1993). The referral of minority adolescents to community mental health centers. *Journal of Health and Social Behavior, 34,* 153–164.

Takeuchi, D. T., & Cheung, M. (1998). Coercive and voluntary referrals: How ethnic minority adults get into mental health treatment. *Ethnicity and Health, 3,* 149–158.

Walitzer, K. S., Dermen, K. H., & Connors, G. J. (1999). Strategies for preparing clients for treatment. *Behavior Modification, 23,* 129–151.

Williams, M. V., Parker, R. M., Baker, D. W., Parikh, N. S., Pitkin, K., Coates, W. C., et al. (1995). Inadequate functional health literacy among patients at two public hospitals. *Journal of the American Medical Association, 274,* 1677–1682.

World Health Organization. (2001). *The world health report: Mental health—new understanding, new hope.* Retrieved March 14, 2004, from www.who.int/whr2001/2001/main/en/pdf/whr2001.en.pdf.

Yen, S., Robins, C. J., & Lin, N. (2000). A cross-cultural comparison of depressive symptom manifestation: China and the United States. *Journal of Consulting and Clinical Psychology, 68,* 993–999.

CHAPTER 10

Using the Multicultural Guidelines in College Counseling Centers

Ruperto M. Perez, Mary A. Fukuyama, and Nancy C. Coleman

Colleges and universities parallel U.S. society at large by echoing the critical issues that are present in the country. As the United States has increasingly become a more pluralistic society with the population growth of various racial and ethnic groups, institutions of higher education have also mirrored this trend (U.S. Census Bureau, 2001). The changing scene of college and university campuses is marked by an ever increasing diversity of students representing various racial and ethnic groups (Carnevale & Fry, 2000; *Chronicle of Higher Education*, 2003). As campuses continue to reflect a growing diversity of students of color, colleges and universities are faced with the challenge of establishing services to meet the academic and personal needs of these students. Predominantly White institutions may be particularly challenged by difficulties in understanding and effectively serving the needs of their students of color. These difficulties may be due, in part, to complexities in assessing the needs of racial and ethnic minority students, lack of institutional leadership and financial support in establishing adequate services, or aspects of institutional racism (either covert or overt) that hinder or prevent services for racially

The authors gratefully acknowledge the helpful assistance of the members of the Counseling Center Multicultural Services Committee at the University of Florida (Jamie Funderburk, Carlos Hernandez, Lauren Roscoe, Kevin Stanley) for their feedback and helpful comments on an earlier version of this chapter.

160

and ethnically diverse students. Yet, the importance of counseling centers in providing support services to ethnically and racially diverse students is paramount for these students' academic success, retention, and quality of life (Archer & Cooper, 1998).

University and college counseling centers play a distinct role in assisting students from racially and ethnically diverse backgrounds by providing support for their academic and personal success. Students of color may not initially seek counseling on their own or may not view counseling as a means to address interpersonal difficulties or more serious concerns (Archer & Cooper, 1998; Oliver, Reed, Katz, & Haugh, 1999). Given that current demographic trends indicate a growing diversity in the student population in institutions of higher education (Carnevale & Fry, 2000; *Chronicle of Higher Education*, 2003), it becomes extremely important for counseling centers to become multiculturally competent in all areas of service to students and to their campus communities. Specifically, counseling centers provide key services in the areas of counseling and therapy, training of predoctoral interns and graduate practicum students, and outreach and consultation. Multicultural competence is crucial to a counseling center's ability to successfully provide for the needs of and promote diversity within an increasingly pluralistic college and university community.

A number of authors (Archer & Cooper, 1998; Fukuyama & Delgado-Romero, 2003; Reynolds & Pope, 2003) have written on the importance and implementation in counseling centers of multicultural competencies developed by the Association of Multicultural Counseling and Development (AMCD; Arredondo et al., 1996) and the American Psychological Association's (APA) "Guidelines for Providers of Psychological Services to Ethnic, Linguistic, and Culturally Diverse Populations" (APA Office of Ethnic Minority Affairs, 1993). In 2002, APA adopted as policy the "Guidelines on Multicultural Education, Training, Research, Practice, and Organizational Change for Psychologists" (APA, 2003) that serves as an aspirational document for psychologists in integrating and infusing multicultural issues related to race and ethnicity in all key aspects of the practice of psychology. The purpose of this chapter is to explore how these Multicultural Guidelines may be implemented in college and university counseling centers. Specifically, we examine implementation of the Multicultural Guidelines in the areas of direct service (counseling and therapy), training (internship and practicum), and organizational change and recommend systematic ways in which the Multicultural Guidelines may be incorporated and integrated in the various counseling center services. In our examination, we affirm the multifaceted nature of human existence, the richness of a culturally diverse society, and the overarching guiding principles and philosophy of the Multicultural Guidelines that all persons exist in a world of similarities and differences and that client experience and behavior are shaped by their cultural contexts. Although the primary focus of the Multicultural Guidelines is racial/ethnic diversity, we also acknowledge that cultural diversity may encompass a variety of sociopolitical dimensions, including disabilities, class, sexual orientation, and religion. We also affirm the need and importance of all psychologists to examine their own biases that may influence therapy with clients and to affirm a commitment to their own self-awareness and a celebration of the diversity and richness of human culture.

COUNSELING AND THERAPY

"Guideline 5: Psychologists are encouraged to apply culturally appropriate skills in clinical and other applied psychologist practices" (APA, 2003, p. 390). Culturally competent therapy is ethical therapy. Developing cultural competence in counseling and therapy is a three-point process involving (1) the therapist's cultural awareness of self, (2) the therapist's cultural awareness of clients, and (3) implementation of culturally appropriate interventions. Given the increasing racial and ethnic diversity at institutions of higher education, counseling centers are in a prime position to assist students of color to face the challenges of academia and adulthood. As such, it is important that counseling centers recognize this growing student diversity and reflect a commitment to multiculturalism at the heart of their service and mission to students and the campus community. This section outlines a three-point process of providing culturally competent therapy in counseling centers and describes strategies for implementation of the Multicultural Guidelines in therapy.

THERAPIST'S CULTURAL AWARENESS OF SELF

Culturally competent counseling and therapy begins with therapists' examination and awareness of their own cultural contexts and the existence and sources of personal biases that may hinder effective and culturally competent therapy with clients. The importance of therapist awareness of personal, cultural biases is a foundation for effective and competent multicultural counseling specified by the Multicultural Guidelines. For counseling center psychologists, awareness of their own cultural prejudices is the first key step in practicing culturally competent therapy.

Several authors have emphasized the importance of therapist self-awareness of cultural biases and the impact of these biases on providing culturally competent therapy to students (Jenkins, 1999; Reynolds, 1995, 1999; Reynolds & Pope, 2003). For counseling center psychologists, awareness of personal cultural biases is a prerequisite for providing culturally competent therapy for students. Awareness of cultural biases allows therapists insight into their own cultural blind spots when working with ethnically and racially diverse clients and serves as a guide for continued learning and professional development. On the other hand, a lack of awareness of cultural bias may have a significant impact on the therapeutic relationship and working alliance with clients of color such that therapeutic efficacy is hindered (Atkinson & Lowe, 1995; Thompson & Jenal, 1994). Therapists' unexplored hidden biases (Greenwald & Banaji, 1995) may unintentionally affect the therapeutic relationship regardless of how affirming a therapist may be regarding issues of diversity. Therapists should be encouraged to engage in experiential learning, peer consultation, and professional development training to further develop their own awareness and multicultural counseling competencies.

THERAPIST'S CULTURAL AWARENESS OF CLIENTS

The second step in culturally competent counseling is the therapist's cultural awareness of clients. Based on the underlying philosophy and principles of the Multicultural Guidelines, it is important that therapists gain cultural awareness and understanding of their clients' experiences and the way presenting concerns or difficulties may be influenced by racial and ethnic variables as well as the intersection of those variables with issues of racism or other forms of societal oppression that exists on college and university campuses. The importance of understanding the client's cultural history and issues regarding race and culture has been at the heart of previous scholarship in the area of multicultural counseling and models of providing multicultural counseling (e.g., Carter & Helms, 1992; Helms & Cook, 1999; Sue et al., 1998). For counseling center psychologists, tapping into the cultural worldview of the client is critical to establishing a healthy and meaningful therapeutic alliance. Counseling center psychologists should endeavor to develop insight into the impact of the sociocultural context of their clients' experiences. For example, a client's racial, ethnic, and cultural identity issues explored during an intake session can be valuable information for the therapist in attempting to fully understand the cultural context of the client's concerns.

IMPLEMENTING CULTURALLY APPROPRIATE INTERVENTIONS

Integrating self-awareness and client understanding are the key elements to providing culturally appropriate therapy for racially and ethnically diverse counseling center clients. Culturally competent therapy is the result of the therapist's awareness of self and awareness and appreciation of clients' sociocultural context of history and experience. Culturally competent therapy recognizes the broad spectrum of therapeutic work with clients, including individual, group, and assessment. The culturally competent therapist is able to acquire and draw on therapeutic skills and techniques that are culturally affirming and helpful to the client. In what Atkinson and Lowe (1995) refer to as "culturally responsive therapy," the hallmark of effective counseling with ethnically and racially diverse clients is that "culturally responsive counseling results in greater client willingness to return to counseling, satisfaction with counseling, and depth of self-disclosure" (p. 403).

STRATEGIES FOR IMPLEMENTATION

A number of models describe ways to implement multiculturally effective interventions (e.g., Helms & Cook, 1999; Roysircar, Sandhu, & Bibbins, 2003; Sue, 2001; Sue et al., 1998). For counseling centers, a number of strategies exist to implement the Multicultural Guidelines in direct service. In their comprehensive review, Reynolds and Pope (2003) described how college and university counseling centers can integrate multicultural competencies in a number of areas, including therapy, assessment, outreach and consultation, and training. The Multicultural Guidelines give counseling centers a clear direction in which to guide services to culturally diverse clients and students. The challenge for counseling centers is how to fully integrate the Multicultural Guidelines into the complexities and variety of student needs and concerns. As the severity of student concerns has increased over the years (Benton, Robertson, Tseng, Newton, & Benton, 2003), counseling centers are challenged to meet the growing need for services. With students of color seeking therapy, counseling centers are faced with how to implement strategies that facilitate therapist self-awareness and skills which leads to greater understanding of the sociocultural context of their clients that facilitates for culturally competent therapy.

Fukuyama and Delgado-Romero (2003) describe ways in which multicultural competencies can be integrated and infused in a counseling center agency. Among these recommendations, the need for continuous and regular staff development regarding multicultural issues is at the heart of providing culturally competent therapy. As an example, the "teams model" of clinical services can be effective in implementing the Multicultural Guidelines in clinical service. The clinical teams model allows for integration of therapist knowledge and awareness of cultural competencies, an exploration of salient cultural issues for clients, and an examination of therapist and trainee bias.

Using the clinical teams model, senior staff and trainees at the Counseling Center at the University of Florida are involved in one of four clinical teams. Each team is composed of senior staff, counseling associates, and trainees (i.e., interns, practicum students). The teams review intakes of new clients and assign clients to an appropriate counselor. Overall, teams serve the function of managing the demands for counseling services in assigning clients to team members and serve as a resource regarding referrals and for peer consultation of ongoing clients. It is in the context of the clinical teams that the Multicultural Guidelines may be fully integrated. For example, in reviewing intakes of new clients, team members are encouraged to integrate cultural aspects of clients in their presentation to team members, thus gaining an understanding and awareness of clients' cultural history and context. The team then considers client needs based on factors related to culture and the intersection of racial and ethnic diversity as these impact clients' presenting concerns. Senior staff and trainees discuss how to best meet clients' presenting concerns while affirming their culture and demonstrating culturally competent and culturally responsive therapy. Clients are then matched and assigned to senior staff or trainees who may best serve their therapy needs.

Within the clinical teams, members also are offered an opportunity to examine their cultural biases and blind spots. Members are invited to engage in "difficult dialogues" to explore biases and gain the awareness and skills needed to provide culturally competent therapy. Senior staff share with trainees their own challenges and struggles in facing their biases and ways to attend to them in therapy. Trainees receive mentoring from senior staff in how to examine their internal biases, ways to attend to them in counseling, and techniques and resources for developing culturally competent therapy. This openness to dialogue and group consultation in an exploration of biases and an affirmation of the importance of diversity is possible only in a counseling center that explicitly espouses, as one of its primary values, the importance of cultural diversity. All in all, a team's model can prove useful in integrating the various aspects of the Multicultural Guidelines to provide culturally competent therapy to students.

In sum, implementation of the Multicultural Guidelines in university and college counseling centers is a three-step integrative approach involving therapist self-awareness, cultural awareness of clients, and culturally appropriate interventions. While a number of strategies exist that allow counseling centers to integrate this three-step approach; the teams model of clinical service is one such strategy that is effective and efficient. In the context of a center that values diversity and multiculturalism, the teams model allows staff and trainees to engage in an ongoing examination of cultural biases and to share experiences that lead to culturally competent and affirming therapy with racially and ethnically diverse students.

TRAINING AND EDUCATION

"Guideline 3: As educators, psychologists are encouraged to employ the constructs of multiculturalism and diversity in psychological education" (APA, 2003, p. 386). A large number of college and university counseling centers have a long tradition of training and educating graduate practicum students and predoctoral interns. The culturally diverse client population in counseling centers provides them with rich opportunities to explore issues related to multiculturalism and diversity through clinical work and supervision.

A number of factors can help to promote multiculturalism and diversity in counseling center training programs. For example, an institutional mission statement that embraces multicultural sensitivity and awareness in education can lend support to the training program's emphasis on multicultural training. In addition, graduate students in psychology programs are becoming increasingly diverse and multiculturally sophisticated (Pope-Davis, Liu, Toporek, & Brittan-Powell, 2001). These factors combine to create a fertile environment for exploration of multicultural issues in counseling center training programs. This section explores ways to incorporate and operationalize the Multicultural Guidelines into a counseling center training program. Attention is paid to the importance of developing a multicultural philosophy of training and the role of intern seminars, supervision, and professional development in developing multicultural competence.

MULTICULTURALISM: A PHILOSOPHY OF TRAINING

Training interns and practicum students to become multiculturally competent in their work with clients is a necessary, core element in any psychology training curriculum. For predoctoral internship programs accredited by APA, diversity and multiculturalism are an essential area of training (*Guidelines and Principles for Accreditation of Programs in Professional Psychology;* APA Committee on Accreditation, 2002). The key to a program's success in training interns and practicum students in multicultural competence is the dedication and commitment of the program to issues of diversity. The adoption of a multicultural mission statement by the training program demonstrates a commitment to provide practicum students and interns with competent and appropriate experience and mentoring in addressing multicultural issues in therapy. Moreover, a training program's multicultural mission statement provides an overarching philosophy of training that mirrors the center's multicultural commitment and sets the professional standard of behavior for the counseling center system (Appendix A, p. 174). Incorporating and clearly articulating a multicultural mission statement that expresses the value of multicultural sensitivity, knowledge, and awareness within the training program, allows for specific training strategies and experiences to be designed and implemented. As a result, the curriculum for the training program can be grounded in and articulated from a multicultural philosophy of training that is consistent with the program's and center's valuing of diversity.

INTERN SEMINARS

Many training programs in college and university counseling centers include multicultural training through targeted multicultural seminars (Sevig & Etzkorn, 2001). Intern seminars that provide both didactic and experiential components of learning can be effective in facilitating interns' knowledge regarding multicultural competencies and skills as well as facilitating interns' personal awareness of internalized cultural biases. As such, multicultural seminars are an important component of the predoctoral internship curriculum. At the internship level, the focus of multicultural training needs to be on integration of multicultural identities with professional identity development. Intern seminars that target trainees' self-awareness through experiential learning and application of knowledge to clinical work can be helpful to interns in integrating their awareness and knowledge of ethnic and racial identity issues and implementing culturally competent therapeutic strategies and interventions. At the same time, it is imperative that training occur not only in targeted seminars but that multicultural sensitivity and awareness be addressed in all training activities, including intern selection, orientation, individual and group supervision, seminars, and evaluation. Further, it is strongly recommended that all evaluation processes and written evaluation materials incorporate multicultural competencies that are directly related to the training program's multicultural goals and objectives (e.g., Appendix B, p. 175). Often, practicum students and interns of color are given feedback about the integration of their cultural and professional identities as part of the evaluation experience. Less often, White European American counseling center trainees receive such feedback about the integration of their cultural and professional identities (Parker & Schwartz, 2002; Sandhu & Looby, 2003).

INTERN SUPERVISION

Individual and group supervision in practicum and intern training provides a tremendous opportunity for the implementation of this Guideline. Counseling center internships may include a training component in which doctoral interns provide supervision to practicum students. In addition, "supervision of supervision" may be provided both in individual supervision and group supervision of supervision. As a result of the increasing diversity among training cohorts, opportunities exist for rich exploration of multicultural issues within supervisory dyads. For example, in one semester of group supervision of supervision at the University of Florida Counseling Center, all five of the predoctoral intern-practicum student supervisory dyads represented cross-cultural supervision relationships.

In addition to the racial and ethnic diversity among the dyads, there is also diversity in terms of sexual orientation and religious affiliation. Trainee attitudes and beliefs that may affect their work with clients are explored in supervision, within supervisory dyads that are often cross-cultural themselves. In addition, the individual and group supervision of supervision provided to the interns is multicultural. As a result, the complexity of the multicultural fabric is woven deeply into the tapestry of supervision in the counseling center training experience.

Fostering Intern Professional Development

Although the increased diversity and complexity in training cohorts provides rich opportunity for exploration of attitudes and beliefs, it also brings with it increased needs for safety in the training group. When interns or practicum students are culturally and racially different from one another, training staff and the counseling center environment must be equipped to foster safe environments for trainees to engage in challenging and sometimes difficult interactions with one another. Providing a sense of safety allows interns to take risks in crossing boundaries of racial/cultural self-exploration and self-disclosure. It is important to attend to ethical considerations regarding trainee self-disclosure consistent with the 2002 APA Ethics Code (APA, 2002, pp. 1068–1069) to afford interns a safe and confidential environment (Code 7.04, 7.05). One example of how to foster cultural exploration among interns is to offer them access to their own support group independent of the counseling center's operations. This arrangement can provide interns with a therapeutic space to explore their own racial/cultural issues, the developmental tasks and stages of the internship, and their relationships with one another.

All in all, a counseling center training program's commitment to multiculturalism is only as good as the degree to which training in multicultural competencies is evident in the training curriculum. Taken together, successful integration of multicultural competencies in an intern training program involves a commitment by the center to provide multicultural training, a knowledgeable and diverse training staff, and the resources to provide interns with experiences to foster their own personal exploration of race and ethnicity. Multicultural competencies must be reflected and incorporated across the training curriculum, including intern seminars, supervision, and direct client experiences. More important, integrating multicultural competencies in a training program requires a counseling center that articulates a philosophy and commitment to multicultural training and puts awareness into action.

COUNSELING CENTER ORGANIZATIONAL CHANGE

"Guideline 6: Psychologists are encouraged to use organizational change processes to support culturally informed organizational (policy) development and practices" (APA, 2003, p. 392). Incorporating multiculturalism into any organization is like remodeling a building. There are varying degrees of change that can be implemented, and as change happens, one can anticipate the unexpected to happen. There are also varying degrees of commitment of time and resources. For instance, does one bring in an architect, a contractor, and an interior designer, or go to the local building supply store for a do-it-yourself venture? Implementing multicultural competencies at the organizational level is essential for making long-lasting change. To do otherwise, that is, to not address the foundational components of the organization, would be like splashing a new coat of paint on an old, established building—a gesture toward change, but only touching the surface. In this section, we summarize the key elements of applying the Multicultural Guidelines to organizational and systemic change in counseling centers. We also draw from contributions in the multicultural counseling literature and provide examples of applications. We are optimistic and realistic about the tasks of becoming a multicultural organization: It can be done (Fukuyama & Delgado-Romero, 2003; Van Loon, 2001).

BUILDING A MULTICULTURAL COUNSELING CENTER

Sue et al. (1998) have described the characteristics of a multiculturally competent organization: "(1) values diversity, (2) possesses the capacity for self-assessment or cultural auditing, (3) clarifies its visions, (4) understands dynamics of difference, (5) institutionalizes cultural knowledge, (6) adapts to diversity" (p. 107). They suggest that before organizational change can take place, an initial assessment be conducted that identifies both resources and barriers to change. Several steps are enumerated to integrate multicultural competencies: (1) Cultivate support for changes, (2) develop diverse leadership, (3) develop multicultural policies (including input from consumers), and (4) implement competencies (awareness, knowledge, and skills).

Ponterotto and Alexander (1995) developed a multicultural competency checklist for counseling training programs that is applicable to counseling center functions. Their checklist provides a quick outline by which one can assess agency priorities. Included are the following points: (1) minority representation among faculty, staff, and students; (2) curriculum issues; (3) counseling practice and supervision; (4) research considerations; (5) student and faculty competency evaluation; and (6) physical environment. For example, they suggest that an organization will become truly multicultural only when at least 30% of its faculty and staff are from visible minority backgrounds. This figure applies to student trainees, support staff, and client contacts as well, presuming that there are diverse populations from which to draw. Given that in some states, "minorities" are becoming the "majority" demographically speaking, this criterion can easily be met. It is easier to make organizational change when at least a third of the staff are committed to multiculturalism.

Research by Sue et al. (1998) and Ponterotto and Alexander (1995) raises the question who initiates and carries out organizational change toward becoming multiculturally competent? In some systems, individuals or committees are designated to be the "experts" to integrate multicultural competencies. Although it is beneficial to have designated leadership in this area, our experience has shown us that this is a "both/and" situation, of using specialists *and* involving all members of the whole system. That is, to make structural and policy changes it is necessary to have specified expertise (e.g., a multicultural services committee), endorsement from the top levels of administration, and cooperation and input from all staff. Thus, it is helpful to look at organizational change from a broad perspective.

Morris (1995) examined employee reactions to change in the context of businesses becoming more international in scope. She suggested that change works best when workers feel empowered and participate in the change process, from the ground up, so to speak. When people are invited to give input into the change process they feel more in control. Employee input can be facilitated through training initiatives that focus on multicultural competencies. Thus, a top-down balanced with a bottom-up approach works best.

Grieger (1996) has outlined a "template" for a multicultural counseling center: (1) Discuss and define the term "multicultural" to reflect an inclusive and broad definition; (2) write a multicultural mission statement; (3) cultivate leadership and support from the top in terms of administration; (4) review all policies to determine impact on diverse populations served; (5) recruit and retain diverse staff; (6) train all staff in multicultural competencies; (7) encourage and reward scholarly activities in this area; (8) expect multicultural competence in all programs; (9) set a multicultural tone in the physical environment; and (10) conduct assessment and program evaluation to ensure quality of service and accountability for implementing the Multicultural Guidelines.

Arredondo (1996) also has delineated a systematic approach to multicultural organizational development with an emphasis on "planning and managing diversity initiatives." Although her initial work was designed for the business sector, the steps to implement multiculturalism apply equally well in higher education (Arredondo, 2003). Her blueprint includes the following: (1) preparing for an initiative, (2) clarifying the motivating factors, (3) articulating a vision, (4) conducting a self-study/gathering data, (5) organizing the strategic plan (goals and objectives), (6) implementing tactics, and (7) measuring for impact, recognizing and rewarding progress.

Engaging in multiculturalism includes several dynamic processes: understanding and celebrating cultural similarities and differences, understanding and clarifying dimensions of power and privilege (e.g., hierarchies), and understanding how those in power define "difference" and establish cultural norms. To challenge the status quo in counseling and psychology is to call into question the assumptions on which counseling centers traditionally function. Such questions are not simply answered. To facilitate dialogue people need to feel safe to explore issues such as cultural bias, prejudice, and oppression. One can expect resistance for a variety of reasons, but a positive view of resistance is that change is indeed happening. However, there are pitfalls to the change process, ranging from defensiveness about social "-ism's" to reluctance to giving up power and privilege.

In sum, a number of scholars have examined how counseling centers may establish ways to infuse and integrate multiculturalism and diversity within the foundation of their agencies. Templates of change, blueprints for organizational development, and steps for building a multicultural foundation are only as effective as the total commitment of a counseling center and its staff to truly become multicultural in all aspects.

MULTICULTURAL COMPETENCIES AND COUNSELING CENTER ORGANIZATIONAL CHANGE

It is obvious from these suggestions that multicultural organizational change is a major undertaking, like remodeling a home, which requires changing structures and functions. It is an ongoing process that requires a long-term commitment. Thus, multiculturalism cannot be integrated into systems by having one workshop or bringing in a speaker. We have witnessed the infusion and integration of multiculturalism in the University of Florida Counseling Center over a period of 40 years (since the social revolution movements that began in the 1960s). A more detailed description of implementing multicultural counseling competencies at the University of Florida Counseling Center has been described elsewhere (see Fukuyama & Delgado-Romero, 2003). What follows are some examples that illustrate the suggestions enumerated above.

The Counseling Center at the University of Florida has established a Multicultural Services Committee which functions on a par with clinical services and training committees, the two major functions of the Counseling Center. Consistent with the Center's multicultural mission statement (Appendix C, p. 176), the purpose of this committee is to provide leadership for innovative diversity programming and to evaluate ways to promote multiculturalism at the Center and on campus. All interns rotate through the committee during their predoctoral internship year. It is important that the Multicultural Committee has credibility to implement new ideas. Because the University of Florida is a predominantly White campus, specific programs have been developed to focus on retention of students of color (Jackson, Delgado-Romero, Bryant, & Carroll, 2002).

In addition, a brown-bag lunch series invites campus staff and students to engage in relevant diversity-themed topics, such as "Understanding Islam," "Exploring Invisible Identities," and "Gender-Bending." The Multicultural Services Committee also provides leadership for an annual multicultural retreat that includes all Center permanent staff. This provides an opportunity for staff to engage in dialogue, to improve relations among staff over time, and to incorporate new staff into a diversity ethic.

Establishing a committee to oversee and provide leadership in infusing and incorporating multicultural issues in a counseling center agency can be a beneficial and productive way of promoting diversity and ensuring culturally competent practices. Periodic evaluations of how multiculturalism is being incorporated are necessary.

Having a multicultural services committee can be helpful, but it is not a panacea. There is a danger of some staff assuming that only the "experts" will address multicultural issues or will work with students of color, or that only the faculty of color will take responsibility for infusing multiculturalism. This sort of tokenism can be avoided by involving everyone in the process of self-study (both as individuals and as a system), evaluation, and discussion of organizational change. This can be facilitated by bringing in an organizational consultant and focusing time and energy on this process, and/or designating a work group or task force to implement policy changes. For example, such task groups may be used to review various aspects of a center's operations, such as reviewing intake forms, intern evaluation forms, brochures, and Web site to ensure that a multicultural perspective is reflected and integrated.

Bringing in a consultant can be a significant decision for a counseling center interested in incorporating outside opinion and expertise as another way to implement policy changes. The advantages of bringing in a consultant are many. In addition to a consultant's expertise on multiculturalism and organizational development, staff members benefit from the objectivity of an outside person. However, consultants who are not prepared adequately for group needs may step into potentially sensitive issues. Even asking a simple question such as "What's going on?" may feel threatening to group power dynamics.

On the other hand, a consultant who provides self-study assessment materials and negotiates a clear agenda with staff input will likely be facilitative in the long run. Such a consultation engages the staff where they are and provides guidance and direction for further development. Staff can read materials, complete assessments, develop a common vocabulary, and share on a personal level. Inviting staff to contribute to the consultation process versus staff feeling forced to implement change is key to promoting investment in and dedication to multicultural competence and promoting successful organization change. In the final analysis, these programs would not be effective if the faculty and staff were not invested in making the counseling center truly multicultural. Taking the time for faculty to engage in dialogue with each other, develop trust and understanding, deal with issues in peer supervision, and address multicultural themes in professional continuing education workshops can help keep the topic of multiculturalism alive and dynamic.

In addition to changes at the agency level, the broader institutional structures and student affairs priorities must be considered. Staff psychologists and interns have the potential to be internal consultants to effect change in various areas on campus. As examples, consultation projects by the University of Florida Counseling Center interns have included such initiatives as setting up peer counseling at the Institute for Hispanic Cultures, developing outreach workshops for international students' spouses, training campus ministers in diversity issues, and helping to establish a lesbian/gay /bisexual "Friends and Allies Program," to name a few.

One might wonder how long it may take a system to incorporate the new Multicultural Guidelines. From our perspective, integrating the Multicultural Guidelines is a journey to be traveled rather than a finish line to be crossed. It requires a continuous and combined effort and commitment from all counseling center faculty and staff. Because the environment and the person-in-context are ever evolving and ever changing, it is important that counseling centers also evolve and change to ensure that their services are culturally competent and reflect the diversity of their clients.

CONCLUSION

Culturally competent therapy is ethical therapy. Trends toward greater demographic diversity in the United States and international relations add relevant additional pressures and challenges for higher education and counseling centers in today's world.

The APA "Guidelines on Multicultural Education, Training, Research, Practice, and Organizational Change for Psychologists" provide counseling center psychologists with a direction for integrating and infusing culturally competent practice in the areas of counseling and therapy, training, and organizational change. The goals to which the Multicultural Guidelines aspire are aimed at the role of the counselor as social change agent and as an advocate in affirming cultural diversity. For counseling center professionals, these goals are not accomplished by individual action alone, but by collective action of the entire agency. Providing culturally competent services and initiating and maintaining an organization that values diversity is a shared commitment and value. We urge counseling center staff to work on both individual and systemic levels to incorporate the Multicultural Guidelines and to work toward promoting and enhancing diversity initiatives on their campuses.

APPENDIX A

SAMPLE MULTICULTURAL TRAINING MISSION STATEMENT

The infusion of multiculturalism into the training program occurs in several ways. Interns receive individual supervision for their work with diverse clients. They also may consult with faculty who have expertise in working with clients from different cultural backgrounds. In supervision, interns are encouraged to talk about their professional identity development, which includes the integration of their personal, cultural and professional identities. In terms of the formal structure of the training program the interns participate in a 6-week Multicultural Seminar and in a 6-week Gender Roles Seminar, both of which directly address cultural and individual differences and diversity. In addition, for 6 to 8 weeks of the Fall semester, the interns' group supervision focuses on multicultural issues and interns present culturally diverse clients in a case conference format.

Interns' competence in working with cultural and individual differences is evaluated in writing as part of the Supervisor's Evaluation of Intern Competencies form, which is completed each semester. Evaluation is made by supervisor's review of tapes, group supervision's observations in multicultural case conference, multicultural seminar leader's observations of interns' participation in seminar, and through feedback offered by any other faculty who have opportunities to observe or evaluate interns' work in this area (University of Florida Counseling Center Self-Study Report, 2000, © University of Florida Counseling Center).

APPENDIX B

Sample Multicultural Training Goals, Objectives, and Evaluation

Training Goals and Objectives

Awareness and Appreciation of Diversity	GOALS	OBJECTIVES	EVALUATION
To develop competency in understanding the influence of culture, race, gender, sexual orientation, ethnicity, religion and able-bodiedness in the delivery of professional services.	1. Interns maintain diversity on caseloads. 2. Interns present outreach workshops to university community on diversity related topics. 3. Participate in multicultural seminar. 4. Additional didactic and experiential seminars. 5. Readings related to diversity issues. 6. Present multicultural issues in multicultural group supervision for half of the fall semester. 7. Participate on multicultural services committee. 8. Participate in campus activities, such as the assemblies for various groups represented on our multicultural campus.	1. Observations of multicultural sensitivity and awareness by individual supervisors, group supervisors, seminar facilitators and training staff. 2. Review of video tapes and audio tapes. 3. Narrative and objective feedback at midterm and final evaluations. 4. Individual supervisors and training staff members on clinical team monitor intern caseloads to assure diversity.	1. Supervisors and training staff have evaluated interns positively regarding awareness and appreciation of diversity. 2. Interns have presented a variety of outreach programs related to diversity in residence halls, the Counseling Center's Diversity lunch series, and in the university community. 3. Eleven out of fifteen interns over the past three years have completed on-going consultation projects directly related to diversity issues.

Source: University of Florida Counseling Center Self Study Report, September 2000. © University of Florida Counseling Center.

APPENDIX B (Continued)

Evaluation of Multicultural Training Goals and Objectives

Evaluation Rating Scale

5   = Performs this activity with outstanding ability, initiative and adaptability. Comparable to a competent independent practitioner.

4   = Performs this activity independently and with more than acceptable quality.

3   = Performs this activity well, usually without assistance and/or direct supervision. The accepted and typical level of performance.

2   = Can perform this activity, but requires direct supervision and assistance. Below the expected level of competence at this level of training.

1   = Not able to perform this activity satisfactorily. Functioning below the expected level, and remedial work recommended.

N/A = Not Applicable

Awareness and Appreciation of Human Diversity

- Demonstrates sensitivity to the needs of diverse populations. ☐
- Articulates knowledge of appropriate campus/community resources. ☐
- Demonstrates awareness of own attitudes and values and how these affect the counseling process. ☐
- Demonstrates theoretical knowledge of multicultural counseling and effectively uses theory to guide intervention. ☐
- Shows awareness of impact of power, oppression and privilege on human and client welfare. ☐
- Displays ability to interact with colleagues from diverse backgrounds. ☐
- Demonstrates well integrated personal cultural identity and professional identity. ☐
- Understands dynamics of racism, sexism, heterosexism, able-ism and other social issues which impact interpersonal, intergroup and counseling relationships. ☐

Source: Excerpted from "Self Study Report," by the University of Florida Counseling Center, Evaluation of Intern Competencies Form, 2004, available from the Counseling Center, University of Florida, P301 Peabody Hall, P.O. Box 114100, University of Florida, Gainsville, FL 32611-4100. © University of Florida Counseling Center.

APPENDIX C

Sample Multicultural Mission Statement

The promotion of human welfare is the primary principle guiding the professional activity of the counseling psychologist and the counseling psychological service unit. Consistent with this principle, we believe that each person has worth and should be treated with dignity and respect. We value acceptance and appreciation for all differences among people, including those of race, gender, sexual orientation, ethnicity, functional ability, socioeconomic status, age, and religious affiliations. We believe that valuing cultural diversity facilitates human growth and development, and enhances the quality of life in our community and on our campus. Therefore, we deplore acts of bigotry, discrimination and social injustices. Because of these beliefs, we are committed to enhancing our awareness and understanding of cultural diversity on our campus at all levels. Our mission is to actively incorporate this philosophy into our professional activities. These activities include: clinical services, training, outreach and consultation, written materials, staff selection and development, policies and procedures, administrative support services, paraprofessional services, research, teaching and scholarly activity (University of Florida Counseling Center, 2003, p. 2. © University of Florida Counseling Center).

REFERENCES

American Psychological Association. (2002). Ethical principles of psychologists and code of conduct. *American Psychologist, 57,* 1060–1073.

American Psychological Association. (2003). Guidelines on multicultural education, training, research, practice, and organizational change for psychologists. *American Psychologist, 58,* 377–402.

American Psychological Association, Committee on Accreditation. (2002). *Guidelines and principles for accreditation of programs in professional psychology.* Retrieved November 1, 2004, from http://www.apa.org/ed/accreditation.

American Psychological Association, Office of Ethnic Minority Affairs. (1993). Guidelines for providers of psychological services to ethnic, linguistic, and culturally diverse populations. *American Psychologist, 48,* 45–48.

Archer, J., & Cooper, S. (1998). *Counseling and mental health services on campus: A handbook of contemporary practices and challenges.* San Francisco: Jossey-Bass.

Arredondo, P. (1996). *Successful diversity management initiatives: A blueprint for planning and implementation.* Thousand Oaks, CA: Sage.

Arredondo, P. (2003). Applying multicultural competencies in predominantly white institutions of higher education. In G. Roysircar, D. S. Sandhu, & V. E. Bibbins (Eds.), *Multicultural competencies: A guidebook of practices* (pp. 229–242). Alexandria, VA: American Counseling Association.

Arredondo, P., Toporek, R., Brown, S. P., Jones, J., Locke, D. C., Sanchez, J., et al. (1996). Operationalization of the multicultural counseling competencies. *Journal of Multicultural Counseling and Development, 24,* 42–78.

Atkinson, D. R., & Lowe, S. M. (1995). The role of ethnicity, cultural knowledge, and conventional techniques in counseling and psychotherapy. In J. G. Ponterotto, J. M. Casas, L. A. Suzuki, & C. M. Alexander (Eds.), *Handbook of multicultural counseling* (pp. 387–414). Thousand Oaks, CA: Sage.

Benton, S. A., Robertson, J. M., Tseng, W., Newton, F. B., & Benton, S. L. (2003). Changes in counseling center client problems across 13 years. *Professional Psychology: Research and Practice, 34,* 66–72.

Carnevale, A., & Fry, R. A. (2000). *Crossing the great divide: Can we achieve equity when Generation Y goes to college?* Princeton, NJ: Educational Testing Service.

Carter, R. T., & Helms, J. E. (1992). The counseling process as defined by relationship types: A test of Helms' interactional model. *Journal of Multicultural Counseling and Development, 20,* 181–201.

Chronicle of Higher Education. (2003). The 2003–2004 Almanac. Retrieved March 1, 2004, from http://chronicle.com/prm/weekly/almanac/2003/nation/0101503.htm.

Fukuyama, M. A., & Delgado-Romero, E. A. (2003). Against the odds: Successfully implementing multicultural counseling competencies in a counseling center on a predominately White campus. In G. Roysircar, D. S. Sandhu, & V. E. Bibbins (Eds.), *Multicultural competencies: A guidebook of practices* (pp. 205–216). Alexandria, VA: American Counseling Association.

Greenwald, A. G., & Banaji, M. R. (1995). Implicit social cognition: Attitudes, self-esteem, and stereotypes. *Psychological Review, 102,* 4–27.

Grieger, I. (1996). A multicultural organizational development checklist for student affairs. *Journal of College Student Development, 37,* 561–573.

Helms, J. E., & Cook, D. A. (1999). *Using race and culture in counseling and psychotherapy: Theory and process.* Boston: Allyn & Bacon.

Jackson, L., Delgado-Romero, E. A., Bryant, T., & Carroll, C. (2002, September). *ASPIRE: A counseling center approach to address the needs of African-American college students at predominantly White institutions.* Paper presented at the Dennis H. May Conference on Diversity Issues and the Role of Counseling Centers, Urbana, IL.

Jenkins, Y. M. (1999). Salient themes and directives for college helping professionals. In Y. M. Jenkins (Ed.), *Diversity in college settings: Directives for helping professionals* (pp. 217–238). New York: Routledge Kegan Paul.

Morris, L. (1995). Why don't we change? *Training & Development, 49,* 59–62.

Oliver, J. M., Reed, K. S., Katz, B. M., & Haugh, J. A. (1999). Students' self-reports of help-seeking: The impact of psychological problems, stress, and demographic variables on utilization of formal and informal support. *Social Behavior and Personality, 27,* 109–128.

Parker, W. M., & Schwartz, R. C. (2002). On the experience of shame in multicultural counseling: Implications for white counselors-in-training. *British Journal of Guidance and Counselling, 30,* 311–318.

Ponterotto, J. G., & Alexander, C. M. (1995). A multicultural competency checklist for counseling training programs. *Journal of Multicultural Counseling and Development, 23,* 1–21.

Pope-Davis, D. B., Liu, W. M., Toporek, R. L., & Brittan-Powell, C. S. (2001). What's missing from multicultural competency research: Review, introspection, and recommendations. *Cultural Diversity and Ethnic Minority Psychology, 7,* 115–138.

Reynolds, A. L. (1995). Multiculturalism in counseling and advising. In J. Fried (Ed.), *Shifting paradigms in student affairs: Culture, context, teaching, and learning* (pp. 155–170). Lanham, MD: University Press of America.

Reynolds, A. L. (1999). Working with children and adolescents in the schools: Multicultural counseling implications. In R. H. Sheets & E. R. Hollins (Eds.), *Aspects of human development: Racial and ethnic identity in school practices* (pp. 213–230). Mahwah, NJ: Erlbaum.

Reynolds, A. L., & Pope, R. L. (2003). Multicultural competence in counseling centers. In D. B. Pope-Davis, H. L. K. Coleman, W. M. Liu, & R. L. Toporek (Eds.), *Handbook of multicultural competencies in counseling and psychology* (pp. 365–382). Thousand Oaks, CA: Sage.

Roysircar, G., Sandhu, D. S., & Bibbins, V. E. (2003). *Multicultural competencies: A guidebook of practices.* Alexandria, VA: Association for Multicultural Counseling and Development.

Sandhu, D. S., & Looby, E. J. (2003). Multicultural competency interventions for building positive racial identity in white counselor trainees. In G. Roysircar, D. S. Sandhu, & V. E. Bibbins (Eds.), *Multicultural competencies: A guidebook of practices* (pp. 17–28). Alexandria, VA: Association for Multicultural Counseling and Development.

Sevig, T. D., & Etzkorn, J. (2001). Transformative training: A year-long multicultural counseling seminar for graduate students. *Journal of Multicultural Counseling and Development, 29,* 57–72.

Sue, D. W. (2001). Multidimensional facets of cultural competence. *Counseling Psychologist, 29,* 790–821.

Sue, D. W., Carter, R. T., Casas, J. M., Fouad, N. A., Ivey, A. E., Jensen, M., et al. (1998). *Multicultural counseling competencies: Individual and organizational development.* Thousand Oaks, CA: Sage.

Thompson, C. E., & Jenal, S. T. (1994). Interracial and intraracial quasi counseling interactions when counselors avoid discussing race. *Journal of Counseling Psychology, 41,* 484–491.

University of Florida Counseling Center. (2000). Self-study report. (Available from the Counseling Center, University of Florida, P301 Peabody Hall, P. O. Box 114100, University of Florida, Gainesville, FL 32611–4100)

University of Florida Counseling Center. (2003, September). *Policy and procedures manual.* (Available from the Counseling Center, University of Florida, P301 Peabody Hall, P. O. Box 114100, University of Florida, Gainesville, FL 32611–4100)

University of Florida Counseling Center. (2004). Evaluation of Intern Competencies Form. (Available from the Counseling Center, University of Florida, P301 Peabody Hall, P. O. Box 114100, University of Florida, Gainesville, FL 32611–4100)

U.S. Census Bureau. (2001). U.S. Census 2000, Census Briefs 1 and 2. Retrieved February 25, 2004, from http://www.census.gov/population/www/cen2000/briefs.html.

Van Loon, R. (2001). Organizational change: A case study. *Innovative Higher Education, 25,* 285–302.

CHAPTER 11

Application of the Multicultural Guidelines to Psychologists Working in Elementary and Secondary Schools

MAI M. KINDAICHI AND MADONNA G. CONSTANTINE

ELEMENTARY AND SECONDARY SCHOOL SETTINGS

IN THE 2001–2002 academic year, over 47 million students were educated in 91,380 public elementary and secondary schools throughout the United States (National Center for Education Statistics [NCES], 2003). This figure reflects an increase of over 11% in the past decade (NCES, 2003). Nearly 40% of these students were students of color, the majority of whom live in metropolitan areas (NCES, 2003). In comparison to estimates of the national population (U.S. Census Bureau, 2003), the population of school-age children and adolescents exhibits greater racial and ethnic diversity than the larger U.S. population. Additionally, the number of immigrant school-age children has been increasing steadily (Kopala, Esquivel, & Baptiste, 1994). Projections indicate that students of color will constitute the majority of school-age children attending public schools by the year 2020 (Campbell, 1994). In response to the increasing cultural pluralism in elementary and secondary educational environments, it is urgent that psychologists and other mental health professionals working in school systems demonstrate cultural responsiveness and sensitivity in their practice and service (Lopez & Rogers, 2001; Rogers & Lopez, 2002).

Demographic shifts in the representation of students of color in elementary, middle, and secondary school provide a general rationale for psychologists who work in school systems to develop and exhibit cultural responsiveness. These psychologists are responsible for fostering an appreciation for and sensitivity to multicultural issues in educational communities and for identifying intrapersonal, interpersonal, and systemic factors that affect the development and learning processes of culturally diverse students. Although attention to multicultural issues seems to be increasing in many training programs that focus on school-age children, such issues are not infused consistently throughout these programs (Rogers, Hoffman, & Wade, 1998; Rogers, Ponterotto, Conoley, & Wiese, 1992). As a result, psychologists in the schools may not feel prepared to address the mental health and academic needs of students from diverse cultural backgrounds (Constantine, 2002; Rogers & Lopez, 2002).

The American Psychological Association's (APA) *Guidelines on Multicultural Education, Training, Practice, and Organizational Change for Psychologists* (2003), herein referred to as the APA Multicultural Guidelines, suggest best practices in applying multicultural knowledge, sensitivity, and skills for psychologists and other mental health professionals. The Multicultural Guidelines provide a framework for identifying salient issues in the development of multicultural competence in school settings and delineate present and future directions in mental heath intervention, training, and research in school settings. This chapter discusses ways in which the Multicultural Guidelines may be applied in elementary and secondary schools.

MULTICULTURAL COUNSELING COMPETENCE AND THE APA MULTICULTURAL GUIDELINES IN SCHOOLS

Over the past 2 decades, the tripartite model of multicultural counseling competence (Arredondo et al., 1996; D. W. Sue, Arredondo, & McDavis, 1992; D. W. Sue et al., 1998) has represented a vital conceptual framework to illustrate how psychologists may best understand and work with individuals from diverse cultural backgrounds. According to this model, multicultural counseling competence includes awareness of personal assumptions, values, and biases related to race, ethnicity, and culture (i.e., *awareness*); understanding the worldviews of culturally diverse clients and having knowledge of historical and current cultural dynamics in society (i.e., *knowledge*); and developing abilities to create and implement culturally appropriate interventions (i.e., *skills*).

The APA Multicultural Guidelines (APA, 2003) offer six broad recommendations that underscore the importance of professional psychology's response to social, demographic, and cultural changes in the United States.

This document represents a response to calls in the profession (e.g., D. W. Sue, Bingham, Porche-Burke, & Vasquez, 1999) for inclusion and appreciation of mental health issues relevant to people of color in the larger psychological community. The Multicultural Guidelines are presented next, and their relevance to psychologists working in elementary and secondary school systems is discussed at some length.

> *Guideline 1:* Psychologists are encouraged to recognize that, as cultural beings, they may hold attitudes and beliefs that can detrimentally influence their perceptions of and interactions with individuals who are ethnically and racially different from themselves. (APA, 2003, p. 382)

The APA Multicultural Guidelines assert that all people are multicultural beings, all interpersonal interactions are cross-cultural, and our experiences are understood through and nested in cultural worldviews (APA, 2003; Arredondo et al., 1996). Thus, culturally responsive psychologists working in schools need to be cognizant of cultural stereotypes and assumptions that may be operative in their interactions with and regarding diverse student groups. These psychologists are encouraged to reflect on how their cultural values and experiences of privilege and discrimination have shaped their perspectives as cultural beings (Lee, 2001). More specifically, their potential color-blind attitudes to issues related to race and ethnicity (e.g., Neville, Worthington, & Spanierman, 2001) may promote inequitable treatment and inattention to specific needs of students of color. Psychologists working in the schools might unknowingly operate from racial and ethnic stereotypes, which could occlude their sensitivity to and identification of students' mental health concerns, particularly the concerns of students of color.

Through active and continuous self-exploration, psychologists' cultural self-awareness can guide their recognition of the ways that others (e.g., students, teachers, and school staff) might deal with cultural differences, and they can use that recognition to develop interpersonal and systemic interventions in the schools (Rogers, 2000). Psychologists can pursue several methods of working toward greater cultural self-awareness. For example, because prior multicultural training has been shown to be positively predictive of both self-reported and demonstrated multicultural counseling competence (e.g., Constantine, 2002; Constantine & Gushue, 2003; Pope-Davis, Reynolds, Dings, & Nelson, 1995), psychologists should participate in ongoing training and professional development activities (e.g., conferences) related to multicultural competence. Moreover, multicultural training experiences focusing specifically on cultural self-awareness may promote psychologists' consciousness of themselves as racial beings and, in turn, foster greater effectiveness in various professional capacities (Constantine, 2002). In addition, psychologists are encouraged to participate in experiential exercises wherein they work to develop cultural empathy, reflect on their experiences of difference, and identify their reactions to various cross-cultural issues (Arnold, 1993).

> *Guideline 2:* Psychologists are encouraged to recognize the importance of multicultural sensitivity/responsiveness to, knowledge of, and understanding about ethnically and racially different individuals. (APA, 2003, p. 385)

Research has indicated that increased knowledge of and contact with culturally diverse people is positively associated with less reliance on stereotypes and the endorsement of culturally biased beliefs (see APA, 2003, for review). Thus, the development of cultural self-awareness may be fostered alongside expanding knowledge of cultural values and sociopolitical histories of culturally diverse groups. For example, psychologists working in schools should possess a thorough understanding of various racial and ethnic identity development models as applied to specific cultural populations in order to understand and appreciate the heterogeneity of racial and ethnic attitudes and experiences within cultural groups (e.g., Cross, 1971; Parham & Helms, 1981; Sodowsky, Kwan, & Pannu, 1995; S. Sue & Sue, 1971). Such models may, for example, inform psychologists about how students of color might be developing their identities as racial and ethnic beings in the context of a dominant White society and/or school system.

Psychologists working in elementary and secondary school systems also should possess awareness and knowledge about the experiences of immigrant students, particularly with regard to the migration, acculturation, linguistic, interpersonal and social, and academic challenges that these populations face (Constantine & Gushue, 2003; Kopala et al., 1994; Maital, 2000; Williams & Butler, 2003). For example, some recently immigrated students are challenged by second-language acquisition and might experience value conflicts between the norms and practices of their countries of origin and those of the United States; such difficulties could result in the development of cultural adjustment concerns (Ho, 1992; Williams & Butler, 2003). Furthermore, some immigrant students might experience both formal (e.g., on school applications or school records) and informal (e.g., social and interpersonal relationships) racial categorizations for the first time in their lives in the context of U.S. culture, and they might fear exposure to racial or ethnic discrimination and cultural stereotyping in these situations. Thus, psychologists working in school settings could assist immigrant students by normalizing many of their cultural adjustment reactions, encouraging them to use culturally congruent strategies to deal with their adjustment stressors (e.g., using a social support network consisting of same-ethnic or same-racial peers), and working to change school environments or settings that may consciously or unconsciously perpetuate prejudicial attitudes and discriminatory behavior toward these students.

Guideline 3: As educators, psychologists are encouraged to employ the constructs of multiculturalism and diversity in psychological education. (APA, 2003, p. 386)

Psychologists who work in school settings are uniquely positioned to promote the multicultural competence of other members of the school community. For example, psychologists could conduct programs for teachers, administrators, and other school personnel that provide information relevant to the development, adjustment, and academic success of school-age children from racially, ethnically, and linguistically diverse backgrounds (Rogers et al., 1999). In particular, in-service training programs could focus on identifying how teaching objectives and strategies might be modified and implemented in various ways to suit the learning styles and needs of culturally diverse students. Additionally, psychologists could build relationships with families and communities to cocreate learning environments in which parents, community members, and school staff may learn about cultural values, traditions, and norms relevant to diverse children's educational experiences (Brown, 1997).

The role of consultation in school systems allows psychologists to infuse and draw greater attention to multicultural issues in teaching methods and school climates (Ingraham, 2000). For example, psychologists may be employed as consultants to these systems to inform teaching staff about specific curricular and instructional needs of culturally and linguistically diverse students. For instance, students who are members of cultural groups that tend to endorse highly collectivistic values (i.e., valuing and prioritizing close interpersonal relationships over independence and self-reliance; Markus & Kitayama, 1991) might respond more effectively to group assignments in class rather than individual assignments. In response to the diversifying American classroom, psychologists also could serve as consultants to teachers to educate them about salient cultural differences in students' expressions of psychological distress or other emotional concerns that could affect or compromise their learning or academic experiences.

Guideline 4: Culturally sensitive psychological researchers are encouraged to recognize the importance of conducting culture-centered and ethical psychological research among persons from ethnic, linguistic, and racial minority backgrounds. (APA, 2003, p. 388)

The APA Multicultural Guidelines encourage psychological researchers to be grounded and attentive to ways that race, ethnicity, and culture may relate to psychological phenomena, variables, and constructs, as well as to generate and design culturally relevant and ethical research projects (APA, 2003). In the past, psychological research conducted in school settings has minimally attended to culture-related variables (e.g., Constantine, 2002; Ingraham, 2000; Lopez & Rogers, 2001; Meyers, 1995; Rogers et al., 1999). Recently, researchers in education and psychology (e.g., Ingraham, 2000; Meyers, 1995) have called for greater use of qualitative and naturalistic methodologies in school consultation and practice-based nquiry that attends to multicultural issues in schools (Rogers, 2000). Ingraham summarized the extant empirical research on multicultural consultation and found that the majority of the studies were analogue in nature and the inclusion of race-related content determined ratings of consultant effectiveness and cultural sensitivity. Although the majority of research related to multicultural consultation in the schools has focused on cultural diversity among parents as consultees (e.g., Brown, 1997) or students as clients, increased attention to issues of diversity and multiculturalism across all parties involved in school systems (e.g., teachers and staff) is needed (Ingraham, 2000).

Another area of research that may be critical to psychologists working in school systems is outcome evaluations of prevention and intervention programs geared toward racially, ethnically, and linguistically diverse student populations and families on interpersonal and systemic levels (Walsh, Galassi, Murphy, & Park-Taylor, 2002). Leong (1996) underscored the importance of implementing *emic* or culturally relativistic approaches, in which interventions are developed in consideration of clients' worldviews, cultural values, and perspectives; this contrasts with *etic* or universalistic approaches, in which the philosophical assumptions that frame interventions are assumed to be applicable across cultural and racial backgrounds. The "cultural accommodation" approach (Leong, 1996) allows culture-specific values, beliefs, and practices to be identified and integrated into existing theories and frameworks in psychology, thereby challenging Eurocentric biases in psychology. Examples of cultural accommodation approaches include *Cuento* therapy among Latino children (Constantino, Malgady, & Rogler, 1986) and Network therapy among Native Americans (LaFromboise, Trimble, & Mohatt, 1990). In the context of school systems, psychologists can conduct efficacy studies on the utility of cultural accommodation approaches with regard to academic outcomes and measures of psychosocial adjustment among students of color.

> *Guideline 5:* Psychologists are encouraged to apply culturally appropriate skills in clinical and other applied psychological practices. (APA, 2003, p. 390)

Culturally competent practice in elementary and secondary schools encompasses the ability to utilize appropriate individual and group counseling interventions, familial consultation, and advocacy. Pinto (1981) suggested a model of multicultural consultation wherein consultants are aware of their cultural biases, exhibit cultural empathy, match the goals of consultation to the values of the consultees (e.g., families) and clients (students), and modify their mechanisms of consultation to be culturally appropriate for consultees. Tarver Behring and Ingraham (1998) reported that educational consultation that is conducted in the absence of a multicultural framework may compromise holistic attention to students' needs, perpetuate teachers' unawareness of culturally relevant information, and neglect opportunities to modify academic environments and build relationships with families and communities. Consultation with culturally diverse families entails an appreciation of the multiple definitions and structures of families, including extended family units and fictive kinship relationships, grandparents who serve as primary parenting figures, and single-parent households.

Psychologists working in elementary and secondary school systems also are in a position to offer unique prevention programs informed by traditional counseling expertise in individual and group counseling and consultation (Kenny, Waldo, Warter, & Barton, 2002). For example, prevention programs specifically targeted at fostering cultural diversity and countering students' prejudices have been shown to positively influence teachers' perceptions of students' cooperative social skills (Salzman & D'Andrea, 2001). Moreover, psychologists who work in school systems could consider collaborating with community leaders and professionals to design and implement mental health programs directed toward students and their parents. The development of collaborative relationships in counseling and consultation in schools necessitates an awareness and adeptness in identifying differences in communication styles and cultural values and an ability to form effective working alliances across cultural differences (Rogers & Lopez, 2002; Rogers et al., 1999).

Psychologists in the schools also must attend to the potential limitations of assessment instruments and diagnostic methods in relation to students of color (Constantine, 1998). To promote fairness and equity in testing (American Educational Research Association [AERA], APA, & National Council on Measurement in Education, 1999; Suzuki, Ponterotto, & Meller, 2001), psychologists are strongly encouraged to evaluate the applicability of psychological tests (i.e., with regard to reliability and validity, construct equivalence, and language bias) to populations that are distinguished by race, gender, ethnicity, language, or other classifications. The use of standardized instruments on populations for which normative data have not been made available may compromise the accuracy of test or evaluation results (AERA et al., 1999). Culturally competent psychologists have knowledge about the characteristics of the normative populations on which tests were validated, as well as the limitations of these tests on other populations (APA, 2003). Psychologists also are required to offer testing in students' native languages if standardized and normed translations of the tools are available (Rogers et al., 1999). They also are encouraged to assess the degree to which such translations reflect linguistic, functional, and conceptual equivalence of the construct(s) in question (Rogler, 1999).

> *Guideline 6*: Psychologists are encouraged to use organizational change processes to support culturally informed organizational (policy) development and practices. (APA, 2003, p. 392)

Above and beyond intrapersonal and interpersonal interventions, psychologists working in school settings can indirectly foster the academic and psychological development of students of color through necessary organizational changes. For instance, research has indicated that students of color report higher levels of academic efficacy and success in educational environments that are supportive of cultural pluralism and reflect cultural values synchronous to those of their group membership (Adan & Felner, 1995). Thus, as an example of instituting structural or organizational change to promote multicultural diversity, psychologists might encourage school systems to increase their representation of teachers of color and people of color in administrative positions. Moreover, through collaborations with parents and community leaders, psychologists could foster opportunities for parents and important others to be involved more deliberately in educational decision making with regard to their children in the school system (Rogers et al., 1999).

CONCLUSION

Because of the increasing presence of racially, ethnically, and linguistically diverse students in U.S. school systems (NCES, 2003; U.S. Census Bureau, 2003), many psychologists working in the schools are positioned to contribute to the positive academic and psychosocial experiences of students of color. The APA Multicultural Guidelines provide a framework for psychologists to become more responsive to the diverse needs of students of color in individual and group counseling, assessment, consultation, and organizational change. Psychologists' cultural self-awareness and their personal recognition of challenges that students of color may encounter in school systems can guide their search for greater cultural knowledge and implementation of culturally responsive intervention skills. It seems clear that many psychologists' personal and professional commitment to multicultural competence will have a profound impact on students' educational, vocational, and psychological adjustment and well-being in school systems.

REFERENCES

Adan, A. M., & Felner, R. D. (1995). Ecological congruence and adaptation of minority youth during the transition to college. *Journal of Community Psychology, 23,* 256–269.

American Educational Research Association, American Psychological Association, & National Council on Measurement in Education. (1999). *Standards for educational and psychological testing.* Washington, DC: American Educational Research Association.

American Psychological Association. (2003). Guidelines on multicultural education, training, research, practice, and organizational change for psychologists. *American Psychologist, 58,* 377–402.

Arnold, M. S. (1993). Ethnicity and training marital and family therapist. *Counselor Education and Supervision, 33,* 139–147.

Arredondo, P., Toporek, R., Brown, S. P., Jones, J., Locke, D. C., Sanchez, J., et al. (1996). Operationalization of the multicultural counseling competencies. *Journal of Multicultural Counseling and Development, 24,* 42–78.

Brown, D. (1997). Implications of cultural values for cross-cultural consultation with families. *Journal of Counseling and Development, 76,* 29–35.

Campbell, P. R. (1994). *Population projections for states, by age, race, sex: 1993 to 2020: Current population reports, P25–P1111.* Washington, DC: U.S. Bureau of the Census.

Constantine, M. G. (1998). Developing competence in multicultural assessment: Implications for counseling psychology training and practice. *Counseling Psychologist, 6,* 922–929.

Constantine, M. G. (2002). Racism attitudes, White racial identity attitudes, and multicultural counseling competence in school counselor trainees. *Counselor Education and Supervision, 41,* 162–174.

Constantine, M. G., & Gushue, G. V. (2003). School counselors' ethnic tolerance attitudes and racism attitudes as predictors of their multicultural case conceptualization of an immigrant student. *Journal of Counseling and Development, 81,* 185–190.

Constantino, G., Malgady, R. G., & Rogler, L. H. (1986). Cuento therapy: A culturally sensitive modality for Puerto Rican children. *Journal of Consulting and Clinical Psychology, 54,* 639–645.

Cross, W. E. (1971). The Negro-to-Black conversion experience: Toward a psychology of Black liberation. *Black World, 20,* 13–27.

Ho, M. K. (1992). *Minority children and adolescents in therapy.* Newbury Park, CA: Sage.

Ingraham, C. L. (2000). Consultation through a multicultural lens: Multicultural and cross-cultural consultation in schools. *School Psychology Review, 29,* 320–343.

Kenny, M. E., Waldo, M., Warter, E. H., & Barton, C. (2002). School-linked prevention: Theory, science, and practice for enhancing the lives of children and youth. *Counseling Psychologist, 30,* 726–748.

Kopala, M., Esquivel, G., & Baptiste, L. (1994). Counseling approaches for immigrant children: Facilitating the acculturative process. *The School Counselor, 41,* 352–359.

LaFromboise, T. D., Trimble, J. E., & Mohatt, G. V. (1990). Counseling intervention and American Indian tradition: An integrative approach. *Counseling Psychologist, 18,* 628–654.

Lee, C. C. (2001). Culturally responsive school counselors and programs: Addressing the needs of all students. *Professional School Counseling, 4,* 257–261.

Leong, F. T. L. (1996). Toward an integrative model for cross-cultural counseling and psychotherapy. *Applied and Preventive Psychology, 5* 189–209.

Lopez, E. C., & Rogers, M. R. (2001). Conceptualizing cross-cultural school psychology competencies. *School Psychology Quarterly, 16,* 270–302.

Maital, S. L. (2000). Reciprocal distancing: A systems model of interpersonal processes in cross-cultural consultation. *School Psychology Review, 29,* 389–400.

Markus, H. R., & Kitayama, S. (1991). Culture and the self: Implications for cognition, emotion, and motivation. *Psychological Review, 98,* 224–253.

Meyers, J. (1995). A consultation model for school psychology services: Twenty years later. *Journal of Educational and Psychological Consultation, 6,* 73–81.

National Center of Educational Statistics. (2003). *Overview of public elementary and secondary schools and districts: School year 2001–2: Statistical analysis report.* U.S. Department of Education. Publication number: NCES 20034111. Retrieved April 2, 2004, from http://www.nces.gov.

Neville, H. A., Worthington, R. L., & Spanierman, L. B. (2001). Race, power, and multicultural counseling psychology: Understanding White privilege and color-blind racial attitudes. In J. G. Ponterotto, J. M. Casas, L. A. Suzuki, &

C. M. Alexander (Eds.), *Handbook of multicultural counseling* (2nd ed., pp. 257–288). Thousand Oaks, CA: Sage.

Parham, T. A., & Helms, J. E. (1981). The influence of black students' racial attitudes on preferences for counselor's race. *Journal of Counseling Psychology, 28,* 250–257.

Pinto, R. F. (1981). Consultant orientations and client system perceptions: Styles of cross-cultural consultation. In R. Lippitt & G. Lippitt (Eds.), *A resource for organizational diagnosis and intervention* (pp. 57–74). Washington, DC: International Consultants Foundation.

Pope-Davis, D. B., Reynolds, A. L., Dings, J. G., & Nielson, D. (1995). Examining multicultural counseling competencies of graduate students in psychology. *Professional Psychology: Research and Practice, 26,* 322–329.

Rogers, M. R. (2000). Examining the cultural context of consultation. *School Psychology Review, 29,* 414–418.

Rogers, M. R., Hoffman, M. A., & Wade, J. (1998). Notable multicultural training in APA-approved counseling psychology and school psychology programs. *Cultural Diversity and Ethnic Minority Psychology, 4,* 212–226.

Rogers, M. R., Ingraham, C. L., Bursztyn, A., Caligas-Segredo, N., Esquivel, G., Hess, R., et al. (1999). Providing psychological services to racially, ethnically, culturally, and linguistically diverse individuals in the schools: Recommendations for practice. *School Psychology International, 20,* 243–264.

Rogers, M. R., & Lopez, E. C. (2002). Identifying critical cross-cultural school psychology competencies. *Journal of School Psychology, 40,* 115–141.

Rogers, M. R., Ponterotto, J. G., Conoley, J. C., & Wiese, M. J. (1992). Multicultural training in school psychology: A national survey. *School Psychology Review, 21,* 603–616.

Rogler, L. H. (1999). Methodological sources of cultural insensitivity in mental health research. *American Psychologist, 54,* 424–433.

Salzman, M., & D'Andrea, M. (2001). Assessing the impact of a prejudice prevention project. *Journal of Counseling and Development, 79,* 341–346.

Sodowsky, G. R., Kwan, K. K., & Pannu, R. (1995). Ethnic identity of Asians in the United States. In J. G. Ponterotto, J. M. Casas, L. A. Suzuki, & C. M. Alexander (Eds.), *Handbook of multicultural counseling* (pp. 123–154). Thousand Oaks, CA: Sage.

Sue, D. W., Arredondo, P., & McDavis, R. J. (1992). Multicultural counseling competencies and standards: A call to the profession. *Journal of Multicultural Counseling and Development, 20,* 64–88.

Sue, D. W., Bingham, R. P., Porche-Burke, L., & Vasquez, M. (1999). The diversification of psychology: A multicultural revolution. *American Psychologist, 54,* 1061–1069.

Sue, D. W., Carter, R. T., Casas, J. M., Fouad, N. A., Ivey, A. E., Jensen, M., et al. (1998). *Multicultural counseling competencies: Individual and organizational development.* Thousand Oaks, CA: Sage.

Sue, S., & Sue, D. W. (1971). Chinese-American personality and mental health: *Amerasia Journal, 1,* 36–49.

Suzuki, L. A., Ponterotto, J. G., & Meller, P. J. (Eds.). (2001). *Handbook of multicultural assessment: Clinical, psychological, and educational applications* (2nd ed.). New York: Jossey Bass.

Tarver Behring, S., & Ingraham, C. L. (1998). Culture as a central component of consultation: A call to the field. *Journal of Educational and Psychological Consultation, 9,* 57–72.

United States Census Bureau. (2003). National population estimates: Characteristics. Retrieved June 28th, 2003 from http://eire.census.gov/popest/data /national/tables/asro/NAEST2002-ASRO-04.php.

Walsh, M. E., Galassi, J. P., Murphy, J. A., Park-Taylor, J. (2002). A conceptual framework for counseling psychologists in schools. *Counseling Psychologist, 30,* 682–704.

Williams, F. C., & Butler, S. K. (2003). Concerns of newly arrived immigrant students: Implications for school counselors. *Professional School Counseling, 7,* 9–14.

CHAPTER 12

Building Multicultural Competence in Clinical Supervision

MARIE L. MIVILLE, DINELIA ROSA, AND
MADONNA G. CONSTANTINE

THE RECENT APPROVAL as policy of the "Guidelines on Multicultural Education, Training, Research, Practice, and Organizational Change for Psychologists" by the American Psychological Association (APA, 2003) highlights the need for psychologists to better meet the mental health needs of various racial and cultural groups in the United States. The Multicultural Guidelines provide clear impetus and opportunities for mental health training administrators to evaluate and revise their programs to ensure that graduates can effectively work with clients from culturally diverse backgrounds. These Multicultural Guidelines can be applied across a variety of pedagogical contexts, ranging from the overall curriculum (in both academic and applied settings) to the individual professional relationships established as part of the training curriculum. This chapter reviews Multicultural Guidelines relevant to a core set of professional relationships that likely influence trainees for the entirety of their respective programs, clinical supervision. Without a doubt, the supervisory relationship presents many opportunities and challenges in which the Multicultural Guidelines can serve as a framework to enhance and deepen awareness, knowledge, and skills. We briefly present theoretical approaches and empirical findings relevant to applying these Multicultural Guidelines to supervision, followed by case examples that help illustrate conceptualization of and interventions with trainees in supervision contexts.

KEY MULTICULTURAL GUIDELINES

Although all of the APA Multicultural Guidelines arguably apply to clinical supervision contexts, we highlight Guidelines 1, 2, and 5 as being important to supervision specifically, and Guideline 6 as critical for guiding the creation of a training context in which multicultural competence serves as a central and guiding aspect of clinical supervision. Guideline 1 is especially relevant as it refers specifically to psychologists: "Psychologists are encouraged to recognize that, as cultural beings, they may hold attitudes and beliefs that can detrimentally influence their perceptions of and interactions with individuals who are ethnically and racially different from themselves" (APA, 2003, p. 382). Thus, multicultural competence begins with mental health professionals developing awareness regarding biases, stereotypes, and misinformation regarding culturally different people. Guideline 1 strongly urges avoidance of the color-blind approach, instead promoting the development of more complex social attitudes and worldviews that incorporate the multiple identities that people (including supervisors, supervisees, and their clients) may adopt. Developing awareness regarding multicultural issues falls in line with the general goals of supervision, regardless of theoretical approach, which usually includes developing and heightening supervisee self-awareness that subsequently can aid a client's growth and development (e.g., Bernard & Goodyear, 1998; Gonzalez, 1997). Thus, Guideline 1 may be viewed as an essential or parallel process with the overall goals of supervision of promoting the personal development of supervisees.

Guideline 1 must be understood in light of supervisors as well; that is, it is difficult, even impossible, to facilitate and promote awareness of multicultural competence in supervisees if supervisors have not experienced similar development (Constantine, 1997, 2003; Norton & Coleman, 2003). Indeed, several scholars (Ancis & Ladany, 2001; Helms & Cook, 1999) have proposed interaction models predicting that effective supervision will be based on both supervisor and supervisee awareness regarding multicultural issues.

Guideline 2 proposes: "Psychologists are encouraged to recognize the importance of multicultural sensitivity/responsiveness to, knowledge of, and understanding about ethnically and racially different individuals" (APA, 2003, p. 385). In addition to awareness of attitudes and biases, psychologists thus must develop an adequate racial-cultural knowledge base regarding their clients, including historical influences, sociopolitical pressures and precedents, legal and policy issues, language concerns, values, customs, beliefs, acceptable behaviors (both verbal and nonverbal), and social competencies, along with important psychological processes, such as acculturation and racial and ethnic identity development. As with Guideline 1, Guideline 2 promotes the view that multicultural competence necessarily includes obtaining accurate knowledge, a goal also in line with general goals of supervision (Bernard & Goodyear, 1998; Gonzalez, 1997). Again, an adequate knowledge base by supervisors is essential to providing effective supervision regarding multicultural competence.

Finally, Guideline 5 states: "Psychologists are encouraged to apply culturally appropriate skills in clinical and other applied psychological practices" (APA, 2003, p. 390). This guideline applies in at least two general ways to culturally different clients. The first refers to learning to use basic counseling skills in culturally appropriate and sensitive ways (Ivey & Ivey, 2002). As Helms and Cook (1999) note, "One of the goals of racially and culturally responsive supervision is to 'allow race [and culture] to enter the room'" (p. 282). Thus, one focus of supervision with respect to Guideline 5 is to promote the use of general counseling skills (e.g., attending, focusing, reframing) that invite dialogue about issues of racism, oppression, and discrimination. It is essential that persons in the more powerful or privileged position (e.g., counselor, supervisor) initiate this dialogue given its sociopolitical and emotionally evocative nature (Ancis & Ladany, 2001; Fukuyama, Miville, & Funderberk, 2005; Helms & Cook, 1999). Along with promoting the use of basic counseling skills, supervisors must provide a "holding" environment that promotes the dialogue about multicultural issues. Jarmon (1990) emphasizes holding as an important function of supervisors. A task of supervisors is to create an environment in which supervisees feel safe to describe the details of their therapeutic experiences, including biases, stereotypes, fears, and transference and countertransference. This environment should involve the expression of feelings around racial and cultural issues. For supervisors to provide a holding environment for supervisees, they must be aware of the potential feelings that may arise and must feel comfortable allowing them in the room.

A second way to apply Guideline 5 to supervision is in the instruction of culturally appropriate techniques for specific racial and ethnic groups (e.g., NTU therapy) as well as indigenous healing methods (e.g., sweat lodge ceremonies). These may be taught in several ways and should be complemented, even preceded, by courses focusing on these topics. Culturally specific techniques are particularly important to teach in training settings that serve racially and culturally different clients, such as Behavioral Health Agencies in the Indian Health Service (for Native Americans). Learning these techniques involves becoming familiar with indigenous forms of healing, as well as bridging with indigenous healers in the local community (Sue & Sue, 2003). Another way of approaching supervision within Guideline 5 is to provide training on intervention strategies for specific topics (e.g., domestic violence, sexual education, HIV counseling) that target racial and cultural groups. For example, working with supervisees to develop and provide psychoeducational interventions for African American women (who today are the primary racial and gender group at risk of contracting AIDS in the United States) will likely lead to training in intervention strategies at individual, group, and community levels. As always, the competence of supervisors in these areas is essential to their effectiveness. In addition to knowledge and skill level, competence is also reflected in supervisors' capacity to be flexible in teaching students the application of therapeutic models that will be adapted to the specific multicultural needs of clients. As with Guidelines 1 and 2, therefore, training either before or simultaneously with supervisees must occur for supervisors (Ancis & Ladany, 2001).

Together, Guidelines 1, 2, and 5 represent guides to acquiring the requisite attitudes, knowledge, and skills, respectively, of multiculturally competent practice in professional psychology (Sue & Sue, 2003). Clinical supervision is clearly a context in which the applications of these Multicultural Guidelines for training can either be effectively promoted or diminished. The following section reviews theoretical approaches and empirical findings that further help to create supervision contexts that enable multicultural competence for both supervisors and supervisees.

Guideline 6 describes larger systemic issues affecting clinical supervision: "Psychologists are encouraged to use organizational change processes to support culturally informed organizational (policy) development and practices" (APA, 2003, p. 392). Supervision does not occur in a vacuum. Indeed, supervision that is provided in a larger training context that emphasizes multicultural competence in *all* aspects of training (e.g., program goals; faculty, administrators, and staff psychologists; courses and training seminars; research; and the surrounding environment; Ponterotto, 1997; Sue et al., 1998) will be more effective than supervision in which this does not occur. One theoretical approach we present in the following section emphasizes an ecological framework to training and supervision (Rosa, Miville, & Farber, 2004). This approach purports that supervision necessarily exists in context, and that supervisors' behaviors become part of the context in which supervisees learn. Subsequently, therapy provided by supervisees to their clients becomes the context in which the clients survive and thrive (or fail to do so).

RELEVANT THEORETICAL APPROACHES
AND EMPIRICAL FINDINGS

Two primary findings regarding supervision research with a multicultural focus are its sparseness relative to other areas of supervision research (Ancis & Ladany, 2001; Bernard & Goodyear, 1998) and the critical importance of supervisor competence (Constantine, 1997, 2003; Norton & Coleman, 2003). The good news regarding existing research in this area indicates that when supervision is multiculturally focused, supervisees come to perceive themselves as possessing greater multicultural counseling competence as a result (e.g., Constantine, 2001; Ladany, Inman, Constantine, & Hofheinz, 1997; Pope-Davis, Reynolds, Dings, & Nielson, 1995). That is, focusing on multicultural issues in supervision leads to positive outcomes in supervisees' self-efficacy regarding their multicultural competence.

Unfortunately, a primary factor interfering with a multicultural focus in supervision is the competence of supervisors themselves (Constantine, 2003). Typically, in most supervision contexts, supervisors' authority or ability to influence stems from a self-perception of expertise and knowledge of theory and technique that goes beyond that of their students. Unfortunately, lack of multicultural training coupled with a position of power on the part of supervisors is often a recipe for neglect and potential harm to supervisees and their clients (Fukuyama et al., 2005). In the supervisory relationship, supervisors' authority derives from their capacity to participate in, reflect on, and process enactments and to interpret relational themes that arise in the therapeutic or supervisory dyad (Frawley-O'Dea & Sarnat, 2001). From within this relationship, supervisors can positively influence their supervisees with respect to multicultural competence (and lack of formal training therein) by having "honest and meaningful explorations of their own personal values, cultural experiences, and cultural biases and stereotypes [providing] supervisees with excellent models in discussing their own personal and professional challenges" (Constantine, 2003, p. 385). Supervisors must allow for the discussion of issues related to race and culture between supervisor and supervisee. In the supervisory relational context, supervisors actively invite supervisees to articulate their experience of the supervisory relationship. This experience will serve as a model for supervisees to bring up race- and culture-related issues and allow the experience of feelings associated with these issues, thus helping to decrease the anxiety about a similar focus in the therapy relationship with the client. For this process to be effective, supervisors must be willing to share their own experiences dealing with anxieties around racial and cultural biases. Thus, with respect to the

Multicultural Guidelines, an important adage for supervisors to be cognizant of is Counselor, train thyself!

Other research regarding multicultural issues in supervision has focused on the dynamics of the supervision relationship, investigating variables that influence the effectiveness of same-race/culture-versus different-race/culture dyads in supervision. Variables that have been studied include critical incidents (Fukuyama, 1994), racial identity (Ladany, Britten-Powell, & Pannu, 1997; Ladany, Inman, et al., 1997), and styles of expression (Helms, 1982; Helms & Cook, 1999), including avoidance of multicultural issues by either supervisor or supervisee (e.g., Constantine, 1997; Fong & Lease, 1997). These findings have been summarized in other sources (e.g., Constantine, 2003; Norton & Coleman, 2003); here, it is sufficient to note the following for the purposes of this chapter: (1) Findings are mixed regarding the significance of racial identity in supervision, though the dynamics of different versus same identity statuses or themes (i.e., parallel, progressive, and regressive) appears to affect the supervision relationship; (2) qualities and skills of the supervisor affect supervisees both positively (providing support, being involved in multicultural activities) and negatively (lack of supervisor awareness, negative evaluation for culturally competent practice by the supervisee); and (3) both supervisors and supervisees may respond avoidantly or aggressively to multicultural issues in supervision in which there is anxiety or discomfort.

Implications of these findings for supervision practice yield the following suggestions:

- Supervisors need to assess racial and cultural identity attitudes of both themselves and their supervisees. Of critical importance is identifying from the outset of the supervisory relationship the areas of convergence and divergence supervisors share with their supervisees regarding racial and cultural issues. Supervisors need to be aware of and acknowledge their areas of tensions or bias and prepare how to negotiate with each supervisee the unique resolutions of these tensions or biases. At the same time, supervisors must be able to identify areas of anxiety or bias in their supervisees and strategize helping them to develop awareness and skills to confront these, both in supervision and in therapy. That there might be significant areas of convergence (i.e., no overt tensions to resolve between supervisor and supervisee based on racial or cultural issues) does not necessarily indicate that there is no need to focus on race and culture in supervision. Indeed, recognizing this potential convergence can act as an important source of support to the supervisee, as well as maintain openness to discussing these issues as they arise.

- Relatedly, supervisors need to assess the knowledge base and identify strengths and weaknesses of both themselves and their supervisees. Anxiety in multicultural supervision may stem not only from biases but also from lack of knowledge about and experience in working with culturally different people. Targeting the racial-cultural knowledge base for dealing with the specific client load of the supervisee (or of the agency in which the supervision takes place) is an excellent place to begin.

- Supervisors greatly affect the quality of multicultural supervision both by what they do and by what they do not do. Developing awareness about the racial and cultural issues that are "push buttons" for the supervisor, and subsequently the supervisee, will enable the focus of supervision to target avoidant or aggressive responses to racial and cultural issues. Activities beyond the supervision dyad also increase the supportive context in which multicultural supervision occurs. Being involved as a multicultural or social justice leader in local and national settings (e.g., advising a racial/ethnic or other student group focused on oppression, organizing marches, serving in leadership roles of organizations promoting these values) provides a clear message to supervisees about the importance of being multiculturally competent.

A number of theoretical and conceptual frameworks have been proposed to describe and incorporate multicultural issues in supervision. These include both approaches specifically developed with multicultural issues in mind (e.g., Ancis & Ladany, 2001; Brown & Landrum-Brown, 1995; Norton & Coleman, 2003) and approaches adopting existing models to incorporate multicultural issues (e.g., Gonzalez, 1997; Martinez & Holloway, 1997; Rosa et al., 2004). As with empirical findings, these models and approaches have been nicely summarized in other sources (e.g., Constantine, 2003; Norton & Coleman, 2003). Indeed, although there currently are not a large number of approaches to draw on, there are several supervision models from which to choose that seem potentially effective. Unfortunately, most of these approaches have little empirical support, but from a heuristic level, they provide some excellent ways to conceptualize clinical supervision focused on multicultural outcomes with respect to awareness, knowledge, and skills described in Guidelines 1, 2, and 5. We encourage the reader to seek the original sources to learn more specifically about these approaches and models. Following are brief descriptions of supervision models and approaches that we believe will facilitate supervision focused on developing multicultural competence based on the Multicultural Guidelines.

RACIAL AND ETHNIC IDENTITY AND INTERACTION MODELS

Without a doubt, racial and ethnic identity development has drawn much attention to research and theory of multicultural issues in mental health and education, and supervision is no exception. Helms and Cook (1999) reviewed how supervision dyads can be affected by differing or conflicting and parallel identity statuses (e.g., parallel, progressive, regressive). The authors also provided two aspects of a here-and-now approach that build on the interaction model: experiencing and illuminating. *Experiencing* refers to "the ways in which the participants in the parallel dyads perceive each other, feel toward each other, and relate to each other . . . feelings and events as they occur in the supervisory relationship become foci of the work in supervision" (p. 285). The approach involves the supervisor asking the supervisee to recall reactions to verbal and nonverbal behaviors that occured in therapy and supervision. By incorporating a consistent here-and-now focus on racial/ethnic issues, the supervisee will likely experience *illumination*, where "the supervisee has acquired a cognitive framework that permits her or him to generalize from present circumstances to subsequent interactions. . . . This framework may influence the supervisees' diagnosis and conceptualization of the client's problem, the therapist's expectations for the therapy process, the dynamics of the therapy relationship, and/or the therapy outcome" (p. 286).

Norton and Coleman (2003) have recently proposed that in addition to the interaction model, supervisors must also examine the working alliance that is developed as part of the supervision relationship. The supervisory working alliance involves three aspects: "(1) mutual agreements and understandings regarding the goals sought in the change process; (2) the tasks of each of the partners; [and] (3) the bonds between the partners necessary to sustain the enterprise" (Bordin, 1993, as cited in Norton & Coleman, 2003, p. 127). Norton and Coleman contend that although the racial identity interaction model is useful in explaining attitude change, it does not focus on how or why these attitudes affect supervision processes. The authors believe the working alliance helps with this task by focusing on the shared bonds and tasks of supervision: "The working alliance is the oil in the engine of supervision" (p. 127).

Ancis and Ladany (2001) recently proposed a supervision model specifically targeting the supervisors' and supervisees' identities and social interactions, the heuristic model of nonoppressive interpersonal development. The model expands the focus of identity development to the multiple identities, both oppressed and privileged, that each person has. Ancis and Ladany assert that for any given demographic variable (e.g., race, gender, sexual orientation), an individual can be a member of one of two groups, a socially oppressed group (SOG) or a socially privileged group (SPG). Thus, for each demographic variable, individuals progress through phases called means of interpersonal functioning (MIF), that refer to thoughts, feelings, and behaviors people have about their SOGs and SPGs. Ancis and Ladany propose that there are four stages of development of awareness about oppression and privilege based on these group memberships. The stages range from apathy and complacency to acceptance and awareness of social oppression, coupled with behavioral proficiency: Adaptation, Incongruence, Exploration, and Integration. It might be interesting to examine how the MIF model parallels or influences more general supervision models focusing on overall developmental issues, such as the integrated developmental model (IDM) of supervision (Stoltenberg, McNeill, & Delworth, 1998).

EXISTING SUPERVISION THEORIES AND MODELS

A number of scholars have suggested that multicultural issues can simply be incorporated into existing supervision theories and approaches, such as the discrimination model, IDM, or approaches based on personality theories (Bernard & Goodyear, 1998). A potential pitfall with this suggestion, particularly for those models based on traditional personality theories, is that these approaches have little to no emphasis on the cultural dynamics of individuals and the supervisory relationship (Ancis & Ladany, 2001; Constantine, 2003). However, a number of intriguing adaptations of these models have recently been made. For example, Gonzalez (1997) discusses his use of both interpersonal process recall (IPR) and the discrimination model in multiculturally focused supervision. With respect to IPR, Gonzalez emphasizes that the approach/avoidance dynamics (based on two opposed states: the need for and fear of people) of any relationship can help articulate issues that occur between culturally different people (e.g., therapist/client, supervisor/supervisee). Another aspect of IPR allows clients and supervisees to voice their own personal constructions of reality, including clinical and supervisory realities. Gonzalez also has adapted the discrimination model (Bernard, 1981, as cited in Gonzalez, 1997), which describes a series of roles supervisors may adopt (teacher, counselor, consultant) in supervision to include a new role, *supervisor-as-partial-learner*. Gonzalez distills three meanings about this role: (1) It facilitates collaboration between "mutual experts" versus a more hierarchical approach in traditional roles, (2) it allows for incorporation of a wealth of knowledge that supervisees can be invited to review and include in their professional work, and (3) supervisors "can genuinely learn from . . . supervisees without pretending power differentials do not exist" (p. 368). This new role can help bridge supervisors and supervisees in those areas in which neither is proficient, but still recognizes and maintains the authoritative and evaluative role of the supervisor.

Another supervision approach that may be incorporated into multiculturally focused supervision is the systems approach to supervision (SAS; Martinez & Holloway, 1997). The SAS model clearly articulates assumptions governing supervision: Supervision is an opportunity to learn that must occur in the context of a professional relationship, actively involve supervisees, focus on both content and process, and involve knowledge and skills acquisition. Seven factors are delineated in the SAS model: the core factor (supervision relationship), contextual factors (institution, supervisor, supervisee, and client), and the tasks and function (or roles and skills and knowledge base) of supervision. An intriguing focus of supervision in SAS that helps build multicultural competence is focusing on *knowing how* to interact with culturally different clients (versus simply *knowing what* differences may exist). The SAS is one of the few overarching supervision models that encompasses from entry to outcome specific learning objectives and interventions of supervision; racial-cultural issues can be directly incorporated into these learning strategies.

Finally, a systems or ecological approach has been proposed by Rosa et al. (2004), who assert that the supervision relationship must be conceptualized from an ecological framework (see Figure 12.1). Thus, although much attention has been placed on supervisees and supervisors, the training context in which supervision occurs is necessarily influential as well. From the ecological perspective, individuals' psychic life is viewed not entirely as an internal process; individuals are influenced by their contexts, which they influence as well. Supervisees' systems are composed of many and various components, all interrelated with and influencing one another. When therapists work with clients within a system, therapists' behaviors become part of their clients' context. Applying this model to the supervisor-supervisee relationship, we suggest that the work of both supervisors and supervisees is influenced by the context. If the supervision relationship is the only or even the first point of training in which multicultural competence is the focus, the effectiveness of this focus will be more limited than if supervision were complementing multicultural training from other aspects of the program.

Supervision in an ecological conceptualization requires the promotion of an open system among all parts involved because each part is interrelated. A systems approach can promote and facilitate the open discussion

Figure 12.1

Ecological model of competence training. Adapted from *The Ecology of Human Development: Experiments by Nature and Design,* by U. Bronfenbrenner, 1979, Cambridge, MA: Harvard University Press.

of multicultural issues between supervisees and supervisors as well as other constituents, allow for the open assessment of how much supervisors are incorporating the discussion of multicultural issues in supervision, and facilitate the incorporation of evaluation tools to assess the supervisory relationship from the multicultural perspective. The main challenge to address in taking an ecological perspective in multicultural supervision is the need to integrate the work of supervisors into the ecology of training settings in a way that will be meaningful and of greater impact at all levels.

SUPERVISION INTERVENTIONS FOR BUILDING MULTICULTURAL COMPETENCE

Supervision interventions that facilitate multicultural competence based on Guidelines 1, 2, and 5 can range from traditional interventions (challenging/confronting, processing transference/countertransference) to specific skills aimed at building these competencies. Constantine (1997) also has provided a series of specific questions that supervisors and supervisees need to ask from the outset of their relationship. These include:

1a. What are the main demographic variables (e.g., race/ethnicity, gender, sexual orientation, age, socioeconomic status) that make up my cultural identity?

1b. What worldviews (e.g., assumptions, biases, values) do I bring to the supervision relationship based on these cultural identities?

2a. What values systems, based on my demographic identities, are inherent in my approach to supervision?

2b. What values systems, based on my demographic identities, underlie the strategies and techniques I use in supervision?

3a. What knowledge do I possess about the worldviews of supervisors/supervisees whose cultural identities differ from mine?

3b. What skills do I possess for working with supervisors/supervisees whose cultural identities differ from mine?

4a. What are some of my struggles and challenges in working with supervisors/supervisees who are culturally different from me?

4b. How do I address or resolve these issues?

 5. In what ways would I like to improve my abilities in working with culturally diverse supervisors/supervisees?

Additionally, the choice of supervision model or approach for building multicultural competence aids in choice of interventions. Some approaches (e.g., IPR, SAS) are quite specific in types of available interventions. Other models provide guidance (e.g., Ancis & Ladany, 2001) as to which interventions might be more effective during a particular phase or stage of supervision. Effectiveness of these interventions also will depend on openness and awareness of both supervisor and supervisee.

We believe the key to effective multicultural supervision is to be clear, planful, and proactive regarding supervision approaches that are adopted to develop a focus for building multicultural competence in supervision. This process must involve identifying appropriate goals related to the chosen approach (which may be collaboratively developed with the supervisee), along with specification of relevant outcomes and interventions to achieve these outcomes (see Ancis & Ladany, 2001, for specific supervision competencies). Finally, it is critical to assess the effectiveness of the approaches and interventions that have been adopted by evaluating the outcomes with respect to attitudes, knowledge, and skills specified through the model. Following are case examples that illustrate how multicultural competence can be developed in a variety of supervision relationships.

Case Example 1

Dr. Imelda Acosta, Latina (Cuban American) supervisor, 45, born and raised in the United States and highly acculturated to both Latina/o and mainstream cultures, supervises Dahlia, a 25-year-old Latina graduate student born in Puerto Rico, who came to the United States as an undergraduate to earn a doctoral degree in counseling psychology. The supervisee presents a client, Carolina, a 26-year-old Latina born in Costa Rica and raised in New York City from the age of 6. The main presenting problem of the client is around issues of juggling the family roles of wife and mother of a 4-year-old child with a career as an administrator in a successful advertising agency. The client strongly believes that her husband, Joaquin, who also is Latino and was raised in Costa Rica, should collaborate more with her in the family chores. Joaquin disagrees, insisting that as a woman, she should be the primary person taking care of the child and the home. The client feels trapped, is starting to experience some symptoms of depression, and is debating whether to quit her job.

In supervision, Dahlia expresses her feelings that the client is being selfish and not considering her family role. Dr. Acosta suggests another perspective, stating that Carolina is probably struggling with potential conflicts associated with family traditional roles versus independence/autonomy in a marital relationship. Dr. Acosta adds that the client may be dealing with issues of acculturation associated with gender roles. Dahlia becomes defensive regarding this conceptualization and the potential differences between her and the client around the presenting problem. Dahlia feels disappointed that her Latina supervisor does not agree with her, though she does not express this directly to Dr. Acosta. Dahlia feels that she did not receive the support she expected in supervision and is beginning to question Dr. Acosta as a "good Latina supervisor."

Key Multicultural Supervision Issues and Competencies

In terms of racial and ethnic similarities and differences of supervisor, supervisee, and client, there were similar (Latina) though different racial/ethnic heritages (Cuban, Puerto Rican, and Costa Rican) across Dr. Acosta, Dahlia, and Carolina. There also were different acculturation processes that occurred for each due to differing lengths of time in and association with the United States. As a result, divergent values, customs, and social norms were expressed both in the supervision process and in stated goals and expected outcomes of therapy. Multicultural supervision competencies here relate to developing awareness of differing impacts of race (Latino/a) and ethnicity (Costa Rican, Puerto Rican) and acculturative processes among persons of presumably same or similar race and ethnicities.

The presumed racial-cultural match of supervisor and supervisee led the supervisee to expect the supervisor's support regarding her assessment of the client. Multicultural supervision competencies relate to developing awareness regarding these expectations and strategizing how to build on this match as well as how to negotiate differences within the dyad that may arise, as based on other important dimensions, such as ethnicity, socioeconomic status, and sexual orientation.

The impact of acculturation plays a role in racial and cultural issues intersecting with gender role expectations for both supervisee and supervisor, given differing gender role expectations that exist between predominant Latino/a cultures and mainstream society in the United States. The supervisee likely was not aware of the impact of acculturation on her own identity and how this affected her reactions to the client as well as the supervisor. Dr. Acosta seemed to have greater awareness of the interaction of race and gender reactions and countertransference, though she, too, may need to examine her own expectations regarding the interplay of race, ethnicity, and gender. Multicultural supervision competencies here relate to developing awareness regarding the racial-cultural basis of one's gender role expectations and how these are in conflict within oneself, subsequently affecting the therapeutic and supervisory relationship.

KEY MULTICULTURAL SUPERVISION STRATEGIES

At the outset of supervision, before the discussion of any client, the supervisor can use Constantine's (1997) questions regarding worldview, values systems, knowledge, and skills to set the stage for a multicultural focus in supervision and to identify areas of convergence and divergence regarding these topics. Assessment of racial-cultural identities as well as values and acculturation level of supervisor and supervisee also help clarify expectations regarding the focus of supervision and identify potential areas of tension and conflict.

Upon presentation of the client, Dr. Acosta might utilize the processes of experiencing and illumination to help Dahlia develop awareness regarding her thoughts and feelings about Carolina and articulate her own values and expectations regarding gender roles in the context of culture. Such an open dialogue will allow Dahlia to better understand and intervene with Carolina, rather than spending the therapy time "fighting" her own gender role and culture conflicts.

Follow-up to discussion of the case in subsequent sessions may involve processing Dahlia's reaction to supervision. This involves observation by Dr. Acosta of verbal and nonverbal interactions (e.g., possible silences or disengagement from supervision by Dahlia) and acknowledging these changes in a nonevaluative manner. The supervisee expected unconditional agreement and support based on presumed racial-cultural similarity of supervisor and supervisee. The development of a more complex understanding of race and culture necessarily incorporates intragroup differences, along with the evocation of relevant thoughts and feelings that can lead to a deeper understanding about how race and culture specifically are affecting the case in question. Additionally, a follow-up dialogue will further strengthen the working alliance between the supervisor and supervisee.

Case Example 2

Dr. Cathy Jackson is a 52-year-old White female who is supervising Mike, a 32-year-old White male graduate student, for an initial intake of a potential case for psychotherapy. Presenting the case, the student relates that Mary, a 35-year-old Native American client, lost her mother to a chronic illness approximately 2 years ago. Although she presented with symptoms of depression during that time, these symptoms currently appeared to be in remission. Mary came to therapy because she is having problems with her 15-year-old daughter. Nevertheless, Mike expressed concerns regarding some symptoms that have no clear etiology but appeared somewhat unusual. According to him, the client "speaks" to her mother at least once a week and feels she is always accompanying the client. Mary gets many "signs" of her mother's presence, sometimes being visited in dreams, and at times has found herself talking to her mother about various issues, including the presenting problem with her daughter. The family does not seem to be concerned, nor did Mary describe this as a problem. She did report some difficulty sleeping, but this did not appear related to the presenting symptoms. Mike expressed concerns about the constellation of symptoms and feels that Mary would benefit from a psychiatric evaluation to rule out possible Major Depression with psychotic features.

Dr. Jackson validates Mike for his concerns, although she notes that the client comes from a different racial-cultural background than either of them. As a result, Dr. Jackson recommends that before moving ahead with the psychiatric recommendation, it may be worth consulting a Native American colleague and healer with whom the agency has previously worked. The purpose of the consultation is to explore how acceptable these client behaviors might be from the client's racial-cultural perspective, particularly after having a significant loss like the one experienced by the client. Dr. Jackson also explains that this will add to both the supervisor's and supervisee's knowledge about Native Americans because she recognized herself not to be well versed in the area. The student feels validated, appreciates the supervisor's honesty, and agrees to the consultation.

Key Multicultural Supervision Issues/Competencies

In cases of same-race-versus-different-race dyads, there is the risk of missing important cultural information without sufficient knowledge about racial-cultural differences. This risk is of particular concern in situations like that of Case Example 2, involving majority group members (e.g., being White) in authoritative roles, such as supervisor and therapist. The case highlights that when someone has majority or privileged social status, there are important racial-cultural issues relevant to supervision (multicultural competence refers not only to issues of minority status); issues relevant to privileged status also must be a focus in supervision, as in Mike's initial presumption that the client's symptoms indicated psychopathology rather than a normative grieving process. The multicultural competency here is developing an awareness of how privileged status may inhibit one's ability to perceive possible racial or cultural issues.

The primary multicultural supervision issue is accurate assessment of psychological functioning versus illness of clients. The supervisee expressed concern regarding client symptoms, and the supervisor responded by first acknowledging (and modeling awareness of) potential racial-cultural differences between the client and the therapist and supervisor. Most important, rather than pathologize the client's presenting symptoms, the supervisor acknowledged that she was unsure about the nature of these symptoms and suggested consultation. The supervisor in this case took on the role of supervisor-as-partial-learner. The key multicultural supervision competency here for both supervisors and supervisees is to be aware of their limits of racial-cultural knowledge and competence and assess what further knowledge and skills might be needed.

Key Multicultural Supervision Strategies

As with Case Example 1, the use of multicultural questions and assessment of racial and cultural identity, values, and acculturation at the outset helps create the expectation that supervision will have a multicultural focus, including for supervisor/supervisee dyads of similar and majority-privileged status. Such a focus enables discussion on issues of oppression and privilege as well as culturally based responses to traumatic events, such as the loss of a loved one.

During the discussion of the case, Dr. Jackson acknowledged the limits of her competence and provided an appropriate suggestion for consultation (rather than simply asking the client) regarding grief reactions among Native American people. Part of consultation was to gain further knowledge and skills in recognizing the grief reactions of the client.

The above examples poignantly illustrate how focusing on multicultural competence in the course of clinical supervision is essential to providing effective interventions that minimize potential harm that can emanate from biases or lack of knowledge or skills. To be sure, these examples may be interpreted from a variety of theories and supervision interventions. The key for each supervisor is to conceptualize and strategize interventions for building multicultural competence from the outset of supervision, rather than simply waiting for these issues to come forth, or worse, ignoring or denying them. As noted previously, direct focus on multicultural competence in supervision results in increased supervisee self-efficacy to deal with racial-cultural issues in therapy. Guidelines 1, 2, and 5 provide the necessary framework for assessing the attitudes, knowledge, and skills necessary for these competencies.

CONCLUSION

The increasing racial and cultural diversity of society in the United States, along with various civil rights movements in the twentieth century, created a sociopolitical context driving the adaptation of the "Multicultural Guidelines on Education, Research, Practice, and Organizational Change for Psychologists" by the American Psychological Association (2003). These Multicultural Guidelines are critical for assessing current training programs with respect to preparing psychologists to effectively work with a racially and culturally diverse clientele. The past 2 decades have produced some excellent research and theoretical models for building multicultural competence through clinical supervision. This chapter has highlighted important empirical findings and theories relevant to building multicultural competence in supervision. However, although a number of theoretical approaches have been proposed, much research is needed to validate these approaches and their purported outcomes.

Despite the current lack of research, we assert that theory must guide supervision, including facilitating multicultural competence. We believe that theory necessarily directs supervision by providing a framework for its focus, process, interventions, and outcomes; this framework may be adopted either overtly or covertly by supervisors. We contend that it is essential to consistently incorporate theoretical approaches or models for supervision that specifically facilitate multicultural competence development (i.e., awareness, knowledge, skills).

We further believe that multicultural supervision necessarily must incorporate the intersection of various identities. In addition to the Multicultural Guidelines, APA has recently adopted guidelines relevant to building competence based on sexual orientation and age, and is discussing adopting similar guidelines regarding gender (for further information regarding these guidelines, please consult the APA website, apa.org). To be more effective in building multicultural competence, supervisors must be aware of and knowledgeable about the various group memberships that affect themselves, their supervisees, and the clients they serve. The case examples presented here serve as reminders of how these various identities affect each other, often providing areas of tension and conflict as well as meaning and sources for change (e.g., gender as nested in race and culture). Far from diluting the emphasis on race or culture, we propose that a multidimensional focus can only enhance multicultural competence in supervision contexts.

REFERENCES

American Psychological Association. (2003). Guidelines on multicultural education, training, research, practice, and organizational change for psychologists. *American Psychologist, 58,* 377–402.

Ancis, J. R., & Ladany, N. (2001). A multicultural framework for counselor supervision. In L. J. Bradley & N. Ladany (Eds.), *Counselor supervision: Principles, process, and practice* (pp. 63–90). Philadelphia: Brunner-Routledge.

Bernard, J. M., & Goodyear, R. K. (1998). *Fundamentals of clinical supervision.* Boston: Allyn & Bacon.

Bronfenbrenner, U. (1979). *The ecology of human development: Experiments by nature and design.* Cambridge, MA: Harvard University Press.

Brown, M. T., & Landrum-Brown, J. (1995). Counselor supervision: Cross-cultural perspectives. In J. G. Ponterotto, J. M. Casas, L. A. Suzuki, & C. M. Alexander (Eds.), *Handbook of multicultural counseling* (pp. 263–286). Thousand Oaks, CA: Sage.

Carney, C. G., & Kahn, K. B. (1984). Building competencies for effective cross-cultural counseling: A developmental view. *Counseling Psychologist, 12,* 111–119.

Constantine, M. G. (1997). Facilitating multicultural competency in counseling supervision. In D. B. Pope-Davis & H. L. K. Coleman (Eds.), *Multicultural counseling competencies: Assessment, education and training, and supervision* (pp. 310–324). Thousand Oaks, CA: Sage.

Constantine, M. G. (2001). Multiculturally-focused counseling supervision: Its relationship to trainees' multicultural counseling self-efficacy. *The Clinical Supervisor, 20,* 87–98.

Constantine, M. G. (2003). Multicultural competence in supervision: Issues, processes, and outcomes. In D. B. Pope-Davis, H. L. K. Coleman, W. M. Liu, & R. L. Toporek (Eds.), *Handbook of multicultural competencies in counseling and psychology* (pp. 383–391). Thousand Oaks, CA: Sage.

Fong, M. L., & Lease, S. H. (1997). Cross-cultural supervision: Issues for the White supervisor. In D. B. Pope-Davis & H. L. K. Coleman (Eds.), *Multicultural counseling competencies: Assessment, education and training* (pp. 387–405). Thousand Oaks, CA: Sage.

Frawley-O'Dea, M. G., & Sarnat, J. E. (2001). *The supervisory relationship: A contemporary psychodynamic approach.* New York: Guilford Press.

Fukuyama, M. A. (1994). Critical incidents in multicultural counseling supervision: A phenomenological approach to supervision research. *Counselor Education and Supervision, 43,* 142–151.

Fukuyama, M. A., Miville, M. L., & Funderburk, J. R. (2005). Personal narratives about heterosexism in counseling psychology: How the "Closet" still exists today. In J. M. Croteau, J. S. Lark, M. A. Lidderdale, & B. Chung (Eds.), *Deconstructing heterosexism in the counseling professions: Multicultural narrative voices* (pp. 137–157). Thousand Oaks, CA: Sage.

Gonzalez, R. C. (1997). Postmodern supervision: A multicultural perspective. In D. B. Pope-Davis & H. L. K. Coleman (Eds.), *Multicultural counseling competencies: Assessment, education and training, and supervision* (pp. 350–386). Thousand Oaks, CA: Sage.

Helms, J. E. (1982). *Differential evaluations of minority and majority counseling trainees' practicum performance.* Unpublished manuscript, Southern Illinois University, Carbondale.

Helms, J. E., & Cook, D. A. (1999). *Using race and culture in counseling and psychotherapy: Theory and process.* Boston: Allyn & Bacon.

Ivey, A. E., & Ivey, M. G. (2002). *Intentional interviewing and counseling with Infotrac: Facilitating client development in a multicultural society.* Pacific Grove, CA: Brooks/Cole.

Jarmon, H. (1990). The supervisory experience: An object relation perspective. *Psychotherapy, 22*(2), 195–201.

Ladany, N., Brittan-Powell, C. S., & Pannu, R. K. (1997). The influence of supervisory racial identity interaction and racial matching on the supervisory working alliance and supervisee multicultural competence. *Counselor Education and Supervision, 36,* 284–304.

Ladany, N., Inman, A. G., Constantine, M. G., & Hofheinz, E. W. (1997). Supervisee multicultural case conceptualization ability and self-reported multicultural competence as functions of supervisee racial identity and supervisor focus. *Journal of Counseling Psychology, 44*(3), 284–293.

Martinez, R. P., & Holloway, E. L. (1997). The supervision relationship in multicultural training. In D. B. Pope-Davis & H. L. K. Coleman (Eds.), *Multicultural counseling competencies: Assessment, education and training, and supervision* (pp. 325–349). Thousand Oaks, CA: Sage.

Norton, R. A., & Coleman, H. L. K. (2003). Multicultural supervision: The influence of race-related issues in supervision process and outcome. In D. B. Pope-Davis, H. L. K. Colman, W. M. Liu, & R. L. Toporek (Eds.), *Handbook of multicultural competencies in counseling and psychology* (pp. 114–134). Thousand Oaks, CA: Sage.

Ponterotto, J. (1997). Multicultural counseling training: A competency model and national survey. In D. B. Pope-Davis & H. L. K. Coleman (Eds.), *Multicultural counseling competencies: Assessment, education and training, and supervision* (pp. 111–130). Thousand Oaks, CA: Sage.

Pope-Davis, D. B., Reynolds, A. L., Dings, J. G., & Nielson, D. (1995). Examining multicultural competencies of graduate students in psychology. *Professional Psychology: Research and Practice, 26,* 322–329.

Rosa, D., Miville, M. L., & Farber, B. (February, 2004). *A culturally competent training clinic: Challenges and strategies implementing the APA guidelines in a training setting.* Paper presentation at the annual Cross-Cultural Winter Roundtable, Teachers College, Columbia University, New York, New York.

Stoltenberg, C., McNeill, B., & Delworth, U. (1998). *IDM supervision: An integrated developmental model for supervision model for counselors and therapists.* San Francisco: Jossey-Bass.

Sue, D. W., Carter, R. T., Casas, J. M., Fouad, N. A., Ivey, A. E., Jensen, M., et al. (1998). *Multicultural counseling competencies: Individual and organizational development.* Thousand Oaks, CA: Sage.

Sue, D. W., & Sue, D. (2003). *Counseling the culturally diverse: Theory and practice (4th ed.).* New York: Wiley.

CHAPTER 13

Effective Multicultural Consultation and Organizational Development

DERALD WING SUE AND MADONNA G. CONSTANTINE

STUDENTS IN GRADUATE schools of psychology, social work, and other helping professions generally receive minimal preparation for consultation and organizational principles and practices (Atkinson, Thompson, & Grant, 1993; Sue, 1995). Although their training has placed high priority on developing counseling or clinical skills and helping them to devise effective intervention strategies (Constantine, 2001), less importance has been placed on teaching trainees how organizational dynamics affect their own roles and those of their "consumers" (e.g., clients, students, employees). As a result, trainees may become effective direct service providers in terms of individual counseling, but may be unable to act in a consulting capacity with their clients or affect client systems in meaningful ways (Harrison, 2004).

These deficiencies are even more glaring when issues of diversity in an organizational context are the focus of change (Pedersen & Carey, 2003). Not only must service providers be culturally competent, they also need to understand how diversity affects institutions. It is becoming increasingly clear, for example, that many educational institutions and mental health delivery systems continue to take an ethnocentric view of the world and need to be awakened to the realities facing them today and tomorrow (Sue, Carter, et al., 1998). Although the United States is the most culturally diverse nation in the world (excepting perhaps Canada), the mental health professions continue to be parochial and monocultural

212

(Sue, Parham, & Santiago, 1998). Incorporating diversity and multicultural principles into organizational consultation and development represents a major challenge to our training institutions (Lipsky, Seeber, & Fincher, 2003).

The importance of multicultural organizational development was strongly reinforced when the Council of Representatives of the American Psychological Association (APA) in 2002 took a historic step by passing the "Guidelines on Multicultural Education, Training, Practice, and Organizational Change for Psychologists" (2003). One of these Multicultural Guidelines as related to organizational change and development forms the backbone of this chapter: "Psychologists are encouraged to use organizational change processes to support culturally informed organizational (policy) development and practices" (p. 392). To accomplish this goal means engaging in roles other than providing individual counseling or therapy (Constantine, Kindaichi, Arorash, Donnelly, & Jung, 2002). As indicated in the APA Multicultural Guidelines, psychologists must (1) be prepared to facilitate culturally informed organizational development of policies and practices; (2) play various roles, such as change agent, advocate, and consultant; and (3) understand the principles and practices of multiculturalism.

The diversification of the United States has had a tremendous impact on our economic, social, legal, political, educational, and cultural systems (Sue, Parham, et al., 1998). Organizational entities that fail to successfully implement diversity into the very structures of their operations will fail to be relevant to their clients or consumers. In the mental health field, clinics and providers must begin to alter the nature of their service delivery systems to recognize cultural diversity. The development of culturally appropriate mental health delivery systems for a diverse population may require major changes in the very structure of the organization (e.g., clinic, mental health center, medical institution). Likewise, educational institutions are undergoing major turmoil in the movement toward multicultural education. Yet, few educators possess the knowledge or expertise to help move them from a monocultural to a multicultural educational institution as reflected in the curriculum, teaching and learning styles, campus climate, and support systems (Banks & Banks, 2004). Business and industry also must recognize that the workforce and their customer base are changing radically (Morrison & Von Glinow, 1990). Unless they begin to incorporate diversity into the workforce and recognize that the consumers of their goods and services increasingly will be people of color, they soon may go out of business.

Taken together, it is clear that health care systems, school systems, justice systems, and other organizations may create problems for culturally diverse populations because they operate from an ethnocentric perspective. Such an assertion also can apply to professional mental health organizations such as the APA and the American Counseling Association. Both of these associations currently function under monocultural standards of professional practice and ethics (Sue, 2001). How do organizations move toward a more multicultural stance?

SYSTEMS-FOCUS VERSUS PERSON-FOCUS IMPLICATIONS

The helping professions have too long suffered from tunnel vision and accepted an extremely narrow definition of counseling and clinical work. It does little good to be culturally competent in clinical work when the very organizations that employ counselors are not receptive to multicultural practice or directly punish counselors when they choose to exercise alternative types of helping skills. When it is organizational policies, practices, and structures that prevent clients from receiving culturally relevant services and act oppressively toward service providers, a failure to understand systemic dynamics and to intervene on behalf of diverse populations can prevent equal access and opportunities for clients (James & Gilliland, 2001). Further, systems forces can be oppressive and cause problems encountered by our clients. Let us use a case example to illustrate how a person focus as opposed to a system or organizational focus can lead to mistaken diagnosis and treatment.

Case Example

Malachi Rolls (a pseudonym) is a 12-year-old African American student attending a predominantly White grade school in Santa Barbara, California. He has been referred consistently for counseling by his teachers because of "constant fighting" with students on the school grounds. In addition, his teachers noted that Malachi was doing poorly in class and was inattentive, argumentative toward authority figures, and disrespectful. The most recent incident, an especially violent one, required the assistant principal to physically pull Malachi away from seriously injuring a fellow student. He then was suspended from school for 3 days and subsequently referred to the school psychologist. Malachi was diagnosed with a conduct disorder, and the psychologist recommended immediate counseling to prevent the untreated disorder from leading to more serious "antisocial behavior." The recommended course of treatment consisted of medication and therapy aimed at eliminating Malachi's aggressive behaviors and "controlling his underlying hostility and anger."

Malachi's parents, however, objected strenuously to the school psychologist's diagnosis and treatment recommendations. They described their son as feeling isolated, having few friends, being rejected by classmates, feeling invalidated by teachers, and feeling "removed" from the content of his classes. They noted that all of the fights were generally instigated by "baiting" and "name calling" by his White classmates, that the school climate was hostile toward their son, that the curriculum was very Eurocentric and failed to include African American perspectives, and that school personnel and teachers seemed naïve about racial and multicultural issues. They hinted strongly that racism was at work in the school district and enlisted the aid of the only Black counselor in the school, Ms. Jones. Although Ms. Jones seemed to be understanding and empathic toward Malachi's plight, she was reluctant to intercede on behalf of the parents. Being a recent graduate from the local college, Ms. Jones feared being ostracized by other school personnel.

The concerns of Malachi's parents were quickly dismissed by school officials as having little validity. These officials contended that Malachi needed to be more accommodating, to reach out and make friends rather than isolating himself, and to take a more active interest in his schoolwork. Further, they asserted that it was not the school climate that was hostile, but that Malachi needed to "learn to fit in." "We treat everyone the same, regardless of race. This school doesn't discriminate," stated the school officials.

To more thoroughly understand this case from an organizational perspective, several principles are outlined next.

Principle 1: A failure to develop a balanced perspective between person focus and system focus can result in false attribution of the problem. It is apparent that school officials have attributed the locus of the problem to Malachi and are convinced that he is impulsive, angry, inattentive, unmotivated, disrespectful, and a poor student. He is labeled as having a conduct disorder with potential antisocial traits. Diagnosis of the problem is internal; that is, it resides in Malachi. Unfortunately, the psychologist and teachers fail to entertain another perspective: that Malachi may not be the problem, and that the organizational climate and culture of the school could be a major cause of his problematic behaviors. For example, suppose Malachi gets into fights because he is teased mercilessly by fellow students who use racial slurs (e.g., "nigger," "juggle bunny," "burr head")? Suppose he is the only Black student on the campus and feels isolated? Suppose the educational curriculum does not present the contributions of African Americans and represents Blacks in demeaning ways? In other words, suppose there is good reason for why this 12-year-old feels isolated, rejected, devalued, and misunderstood at school?

Principle 2: A failure to develop a balanced perspective between person focus and system focus can result in an ineffective and inaccurate treatment plan potentially harmful to the client. In this case, how one defines the problem affects the treatment focus and plan. If Malachi's problems are due to internal and intrapsychic dynamics, then it makes sense that the cure be directed toward changing the person. Malachi's fighting behavior is perceived as dysfunctional and should be eliminated by having him learn to control his anger or through medication that might correct his internal biological state. But what if the problem is external? Will having Malachi stop his fighting behavior result in the elimination of teasing from White classmates? Will it make him more connected to the campus? Will it make him feel more valued and accepted? Will he relate more to the content of courses that denigrate the contributions of African Americans? We contend that treating the "symptoms" or eliminating fighting behavior actually may make Malachi more vulnerable to racism.

Principle 3: When the client is the organization and not an individual, it requires a major paradigm shift to attain a true understanding of problem and solution identification. Let us assume that Malachi is getting into fights because of the hostile school climate and the invalidating nature of his educational experience. Given this assumption, we ask the question Who is the client? Is it Malachi or the school? In his analysis of schizophrenia, R. D. Laing, an existential psychiatrist, once asked the following question: "Is schizophrenia a sick response to a healthy situation, or is it a healthy response to a sick situation?" In other words, if it is the school system that is dysfunctional ("sick") and not the individual client, do we or should we adjust that person to a sick situation? If we view the fighting behavior as a learned response to a sick situation, then eliminating the unhealthy situation (e.g., teasing, insensitive administrators and teachers, monocultural curriculum) should receive top priority.

Principle 4: Organizations are microcosms of the wider society from which they originate. As a result, they are likely to be reflections of the monocultural values and practices of the larger culture. In this case, it is not far-fetched to assume that White students, teachers, and administrators may have inherited the racial biases of their forebears. Further, multicultural education specialists have decried the biased nature of traditional educational curricula. Although education is supposed to convey truth and knowledge, it often has been the culprit in perpetuating false stereotypes and misinformation about various groups in our society. It has done this, perhaps not intentionally, but through omission, fabrication, distortion, or selection of information designed to emphasize the contributions of certain groups over others. The result is that institutions of learning become sites that perpetuate myths and inaccuracies of certain groups in society, which can have devastating consequences for students of color. Further, policies and practices that "treat everyone the same" may themselves be culturally biased. If this is the institutional context from which Malachi is receiving his education, little wonder that he exhibits so-called problem behaviors.

Principle 5: Organizations are powerful entities that inevitably resist change and possess in their arsenal many ways to force compliance among workers. To go against the policies, practices, and procedures of an institution can bring about major punitive actions. Let us look at the situation of Malachi's counselor, Ms. Jones. There are indications in this case that she understands that Malachi may be the victim of racism and a monocultural educational system that invalidates him. If she is aware of this factor, why is she so reluctant to act on behalf of Malachi and his parents? First, it is highly probable that, even if she is aware of the true problem, she lacks the knowledge and skill to intervene on a systemic level. Second, there are many avenues open to institutions to demand compliance on the part of employees. Voicing an alternative opinion, especially against the prevailing beliefs, can result in ostracism by fellow workers, a poor job performance rating, denial of a promotion, even firing. Thus, even the most enlightened helping professionals might find their good intentions thwarted by their lack of systems intervention skills and fear of punitive actions.

Principle 6: When multicultural organizational development is required, alternative helping roles that emphasize systems intervention must be part of the role repertoire of the helping professional. Because traditional counseling and therapy roles focus on a one-to-one or small group relationships, interventions in these modalities may not be productive when dealing with larger ecological and systemic issues. Competence in changing policies, practices, procedures, and structures within organizations requires a different set of knowledge and skills. Among them, consultation becomes crucial in helping institutions move from a monocultural to a multicultural institution. Malachi's school and the school district need a thorough cultural audit, institutional change in the campus climate, sensitivity training for all school personnel, increased racial and ethnic personnel at all levels of the school system, and a revamping of the curriculum to be more multicultural. These are major tasks that require multicultural awareness, knowledge, and skills on the part of organizational consultants.

ATTRIBUTES OF EFFECTIVE MULTICULTURAL ORGANIZATIONAL CONSULTATION

As we noted earlier, becoming culturally competent requires not only changes at an individual practice level, but also changes associated with how we define helping roles (Constantine et al., 2002). The roles of a multicultural organizational consultant are significantly different from those of a conventional counselor or therapist. Helping professionals with minimal understanding of consultation possess only individual change skills rather than systemic change skills. Thus, they may be unable to help organizations move toward becoming entities that allow for equal access and opportunity for a diversity of groups (Sue, Carter, et al., 1998). Effective multicultural organizational consultants must possess four broad and all-encompassing characteristics: (1) an understanding of their own worldview in relationship to other diverse worldviews, (2) knowledge and expertise in systems and organizational principles and development, (3) the ability to play a variety of roles in the consultation process, and (4) a clear vision of multicultural organizational development and how it contrasts with monocultural organizational structures (Sue & Sue, 2003). Looking closely at the APA Multicultural Guidelines suggests several goals for the development of culturally competent consultants and multicultural organizations.

WORLDVIEW AWARENESS

Culturally competent consultants are aware of their cultural values, biases, and assumptions about human behavior. They realize that they are products of their cultural conditioning and have developed a worldview that influences their perceptions of problem definition, problem-solving strategies, and communication and interpersonal styles (e.g., consultation style, clinical style, managerial style, teaching style). Worldview awareness is most likely to be displayed when consultants are able to compare and contrast their worldview with those of their culturally different clients, students, coworkers, or consumers.

Being able to see their own worldview clearly and acknowledge that it is one of many allows organizational consultants to see others' worldviews as equally valid and legitimate. If the worldview of consultants is similar to that of the organization they wish to change, they can use that awareness to identify potential problematic areas. For example, a consultant who values individualism, personal achievement, and competition may have experience in how his or her worldview might create difficulties with individuals who value a collectivistic and cooperative approach to interpersonal relationships and problem solving. Organizations with performance appraisal systems that are imbued with the value of individualism may unwittingly deny promotion to an Asian American employee who does not appear to be competitive or aggressive. Not only is the lack of promotion unfair, but the company has lost a valuable opportunity to promote an employee who may have benefited the company. Some superiors may not realize that many Asians and Asian Americans define leadership as working behind the scenes, building group consensus, and forming collaborative-cooperative relationships.

Awareness of one's own worldview also relates to understanding oneself as a racial-cultural being (Rothenberg, 2002). What does it mean, for example, to be a White American? What does it mean to be a person of color? Answers to these questions have been addressed by racial and cultural identity development theories formulated by many multicultural psychologists (Hardiman, 1982; Helms, 1990; Ponterotto, 1988; Sue & Sue, 2003). In most cases, it is important for the consultant to realize that institutions are situated in such a manner as to pave the way for Whites, while creating obstacles to people of color. This is perhaps one of the most difficult aspects of organizational dynamics for White consultants to understand. It deals with what has been called "White privilege," which is defined as the unearned benefits and privileges awarded to White Americans by virtue of their skin color. It has two components: It advantages Whites by allowing easier access and greater opportunities to the rewards of the society, and it disadvantages people of color by placing obstacles to success in their path. Personal beliefs such as "The cream of the crop will rise to the top," "I made it on my own," and "If you work hard enough, you can succeed" reinforce the myth of meritocracy. These beliefs unfairly punish people of color for their "lack of ability to succeed," while rewarding Whites for the superior positions they occupy. Space limitations do not allow us to elaborate on this important concept, but the following statement may help drive home the point. Molly Ivins, a syndicated columnist, once said of George W. Bush during his run for president of the United States, "George Bush was born on third base and believes he hit a triple."

MULTICULTURAL ORGANIZATIONAL DEVELOPMENT AND SYSTEMS EXPERTISE

Few mental health professionals possess knowledge and expertise in systems theory, organizational development, and organizational change. Although traditional organizational development work shares similarities with multicultural organizational development, it differs along several important dimensions. First and foremost, it views organizational change from a social justice perspective and assumes that institutions engage in unintentional discrimination and oppression. Second, it assumes that inequities in organizations are not due solely to poor communication, lack of knowledge, poor management or person-organization fit, but also to monopolies of power. Third, it views conflict as inevitable in the change process and not necessarily unhealthy. These assumptions are also based not only on an understanding of basic change principles, but on a realization that multicultural organizational development is also a sociopolitical act.

We made reference earlier to how culturally competent consultants are aware of themselves as racial and cultural beings and would benefit from understanding the various stages or characteristics of identity development. Likewise, effective consultants must be able to identify how organizations vary in their awareness of how racial, cultural, ethnic, sexual orientation, and gender issues affect the experiences of their clients or workers. In the case of Malachi's school district, we might characterize it as being a thoroughly monocultural educational institution. If institutions are to be truly multicultural, provide culturally relevant services to their clients of color, and provide for equal access and opportunity in the hiring, retention, and promotion of people of color, they must move from being a monocultural to a multicultural entity (Bowser, Auletta, & Jones, 1993). The first step is to understand characteristics of organizations that impede cultural diversity. The second step involves intervening to make organizational change. Sue (1995, pp. 483–485) summarized various models in the field (e.g., Barr & Strong, 1987; Cross, Bazron, Dennis, & Isaacs, 1989; D'Andrea, Daniels, & Heck, 1991; Foster, Jackson, Cross, Jackson, & Hardiman, 1988; Highlen, 1994; Katz & Miller, 1988; Sue, 1991) to describe a developmental stage process by which organizations move from a primarily monocultural orientation to a more multicultural one:

1. *Monocultural organizations:* At the one extreme are organizations that are primarily Eurocentric and ethnocentric. They believe in the following premises and practices:
   - There is an implicit or explicit exclusion of people of color, women, and other societally oppressed groups.
   - Many organizations are rigged to advantage the dominant White majority. In these cases, Whites are privileged.
   - There is only one best way to deliver health care, manage, teach, or administrate.
   - Culture does not affect management, mental health, or education.
   - Clients, workers, or students should assimilate.
   - Culture-specific ways of doing things are neither recognized nor valued. Everyone should be treated the same.
   - An organization should represent a "melting pot" of cultures instead of focusing on identifying distinct cultural groups.
2. *Nondiscriminatory organizations:* As organizations become more culturally aware and enlightened, they enter another stage, often referred

to as "nondiscriminatory." The following premises and practices characterize these organizations:

- The organization has inconsistent policies and practices regarding multicultural issues. Certain departments (or mental health practitioners or managers or teachers) are becoming sensitive to cultural issues, but it is not an organizational priority.
- Leadership may recognize the need for some action, but there is no systematic program or policy to address issues of prejudice and bias.
- There is an attempt to make the organizational climate or services less hostile or "different," but these changes are superficial and often without conviction. They are more for public relations purposes or perceptions.
- Equal employment opportunity and affirmative action policies and the numerical symmetry of people of color and women are implemented grudgingly.

3. *Multicultural organizations:* As organizations become progressively more multicultural, they begin to value diversity and evidence continuing attempts to accommodate ongoing cultural change. In essence, these organizations:

- Are in the process of working on a vision that reflects multiculturalism.
- Reflect the contributions of diverse cultural and social groups in their missions, operations, products, and services.
- Value diversity and view it as an asset.
- Actively engage in visioning, planning, and problem-solving activities that allow for equal access and opportunities.
- Realize that equal access and opportunities do not mean equal treatment.
- Value diversity (not just tolerate it) and work to diversify their environment.

Knowing these characteristics and how they function in an organization allows multicultural organizational development consultants to (1) conduct an accurate assessment of where an institution is situated with respect to diversity, (2) foresee possible obstacles to organizational change, (3) identify where systems intervention is required, and (4) develop a strategic plan to implement needed changes.

EXPANDED ROLE DEFINITIONS

If helping professionals are to be effective multicultural organizational development consultants, they must adopt roles and engage in activities that have not been traditionally considered "professional" or "ethical" in nature. In the field of mental health practice, for example, certain traditional therapeutic taboos operate: (1) Therapists do not give advice and suggestions, (2) therapists do not serve in multiple roles within helping relationships, (3) therapists do not disclose their own personal thoughts and feelings, (4) therapists do not accept gifts, and (5) therapists do not barter services (Sue & Sue, 2003). Not only has it been shown that these behaviors have therapeutic benefit to many clients of color, but consultation often requires engaging in some of these behaviors (e.g., giving advice and suggestions and self-disclosure). Work with populations of color suggests that out-of-office sites and activities (client homes, churches, volunteer organizations, etc.) and alternative helping roles (ombudspersons, advocates, consultants, organizational change agents, facilitator of indigenous healing systems, etc.) may prove to be more therapeutic and are viewed as effective interventions in the field of consultation. We refer you to the excellent description of alternative helping roles and the conceptual framework presented by Atkinson et al. (1993) for a fuller presentation.

We need to recognize that sociocultural factors (e.g., inadequate or biased education, poor socialization practices, biased values, and discriminatory institutional policies) in some institutions create many of the difficulties encountered by individuals. As helping professionals, we frequently are placed in the position of treating clients who represent the aftermath of failed and oppressive policies and practices. Although treating troubled clients (remediation) is a necessity, our task would be an endless and losing venture unless the true sources of the problem (e.g., discrimination and oppression) are changed. It certainly makes more sense to take a proactive and preventive approach to helping by attacking the cultural and institutional bases of the problem. Having helping professionals increase their skills in effective systems intervention demands knowledge of multicultural organizational development. The effective multicultural organizational development consultant must be able to help organizations develop new rules, regulations, policies, practices, and structures that enhance multiculturalism and allow for equal access and opportunity. Thus, taking on alternative roles beyond the traditional clinical one is a necessity.

CLEAR VISION OF MULTICULTURAL DEVELOPMENT

What is a multicultural organization, and what does it look like? What characteristics and conditions need to exist for an institution to move from being monocultural to multicultural? We have already outlined a multicultural organizational development model that gives us clues to the creation of equal access and opportunity. It means reviewing policies, practices, and organizational structures to remove potential barriers that disadvantage people on the basis of race, gender, or sexual orientation (Robinson & Howard-Hamilton, 2000). It means creating new policies, practices, and internal structures that will support and advance cultural diversity. To truly value diversity, however, means altering the power relations in organizations to minimize structural discrimination. This may mean including people of color in decision-making positions and sharing power with them and constructing diversity programs and practices with the same economic and maintenance priorities as other valued aspects of the company.

Although being a truly multicultural organization remains an ideal, successful work in the field of multicultural organizational development requires one to have a clear vision of multiculturalism and a multicultural organization. These are aspirational goals that consultants in the field must strive to attain. *We define a multicultural organization as committed (action as well as words) to diverse representation throughout all levels, sensitive to maintaining an open, supportive, and responsive environment, working toward and purposefully including elements of diverse cultures in its ongoing operations, carefully monitoring organizational policies and practices for the goals of equal access and opportunity, and authentic in responding to changing policies and practices that block cultural diversity.*

To achieve these goals, work on multicultural organizational development reveals important conditions that must exist in organizations that hope to become more multicultural in outlook:

- Multicultural commitment must come from the very top levels. It is clear that diversity implementation is most effective when strong leadership is exerted on behalf of multiculturalism. For higher education, it may be the provost, chancellor, president, dean, or chair. For mental health delivery systems, it may be the director or program supervisors. For public schools, it may be the board of education, superintendent, or principal. For business and industry, it may be the chief executive officer, board of directors, or upper management. In any case, reaching these key individuals is critical.
- Each organization should have a written policy, mission statement, or vision statement that frames the concepts of multiculturalism and diversity into a meaningful operational definition. It should not be a cosmetic statement, but must be stated in such a manner as to infuse the concepts throughout its operations, structures, and policies.

- The organization should have a multicultural and diversity action plan with clear objectives and time lines. This plan encourages accountability.
- Multicultural accountability must be built into the system. Certain divisions, departments, and individuals must be held responsible for achieving the goals of diversity and multiculturalism.
- The organization should create a superordinate or oversight team that is empowered to assess, develop, and monitor the organization's development with respect to the goals of multiculturalism. This group must have the ability to influence, formulate, and implement multicultural initiatives.
- Organizations must be unafraid to actively solicit feedback from employees related to issues of race, culture, gender, ethnicity, and sexual orientation. Feedback from employee groups provides a rich source of information related to work climate issues, policies and practices, and more.
- Multicultural competence should be infused into evaluation criteria and used for hiring and promotion of employees. By incorporating multicultural expertise into performance evaluations, the issues of race and gender would be minimized because Euro-Americans with multicultural expertise would also be evaluated positively.
- Culturally sensitive organizations recognize that mentoring and support networks for employees of color are vital for their success and that the presence of an "old boys' network" might adversely affect these individuals.
- Active coalition building and networking among minorities and women, for example, should be valued. Multicultural organizations recognize that being a client or employee of color can deplete energy and result in feelings of alienation.
- The organization must be committed to a systematic and long-term plan to educate the entire workforce concerning diversity issues.

Producing these conditions and changes is fundamental to meeting the challenge of cultural diversity. Again, multicultural organizational development consultants are most effective if they are aware of their own worldviews, possess expertise in systems change, can play a variety of change agent roles, and have a clear multicultural vision.

REFERENCES

American Psychological Association. (2003). Guidelines on multicultural education, training, research, practice, and organizational change for psychologists. *American Psychologist, 38*, 377–402.

Atkinson, D. R., Thompson, C. E., & Grant, S. K. (1993). A three-dimensional model for counseling racial ethnic minorities. *Counseling Psychologist, 21,* 257–277.

Banks, J. A., & Banks, C. A. M. (2004). *Handbook of research on multicultural education.* San Francisco: Jossey-Bass.

Barr, D. J., & Strong, L. J. (1987, May). Embracing multiculturalism: The existing contradictions. *ACU-I Bulletin, 20–23.*

Bowser, B. P., Auletta, G. S., & Jones, T. (1993). *Confronting diversity issues on campus.* Newbury Park, CA: Sage.

Constantine, M. G. (2001). Predictors of observer ratings of multicultural counseling competence in Black, Latino, and White American trainees. *Journal of Counseling Psychology, 48,* 456–462.

Constantine, M. G., Kindaichi, M., Arorash, T. J., Donnelly, P. C., & Jung, K.-S. K. (2002). Clients' perceptions of multicultural counseling competence: Current status and future directions. *Counseling Psychologist, 30,* 407–416.

Cross, T., Bazron, B. J., Dennis, K. W., & Isaacs, M. R. (1989). *Toward a culturally competent system of care.* Washington, DC: Child and Adolescent Service System Program Technical Assistance Center.

D'Andrea, M., Daniels, J., & Heck, R. (1991). Evaluating the impact of multicultural training. *Journal of Counseling and Development, 70,* 143–150.

Foster, B. G., Jackson, G., Cross, W. E., Jackson, B., & Hardiman, R. (1988). *Workforce diversity and business.* Alexandria, VA: American Society for Training and Development.

Hardiman, R. (1982). *White identity development: A process-oriented model for describing the racial consciousness of White Americans.* Unpublished doctoral dissertation, University of Massachusetts, Amherst.

Harrison, T. C. (2004). *Consultation for contemporary helping professionals.* Boston: Pearson.

Helms, J. E. (Ed.). (1990). *Black and white racial identity: Theory, research and practice.* New York: Greenwood.

Highlen, P. S. (1994). Racial ethnic diversity in doctoral programs of psychology: Challenges for the twenty-first century. *Applied and Preventive Psychology, 3,* 91–107.

James, R. K., & Gilliland, B. E. (2001). *Crisis intervention strategies.* Belmont, CA: Brooks/Cole.

Katz, J. H., & Miller, E. A. (1988). Between monoculturalism and multiculturalism: Traps awaiting the organization. *O. D. Practitioner, 20,* 1–5.

Lipsky, D. B., Seeber, R. L., & Fincher, R. D. (2003). *Emerging systems for managing workplace conflict.* San Francisco: Jossey-Bass.

Morrison, A. M., & Von Glinow, M. A. (1990). Women and minorities in management. *American Psychologist, 45,* 200–208.

Pedersen, P. B., & Carey, J. C. (2003). *Multicultural counseling in schools.* Boston: Allyn & Bacon.

Ponterotto, J. G. (1988). Racial consciousness development among White counselor trainees: A stage model. *Journal of Multicultural Counseling and Development, 16,* 145–156.

Robinson, T. L., & Howard-Hamilton, M. F. (2000). *The convergence of race, ethnicity, and gender.* Columbus, OH: Merrill.

Rothenberg, P. S. (2002). *White privilege.* New York: Worth.

Sue, D. W. (1991). A model for cultural diversity training. *Journal of Counseling and Development, 70,* 99–105.

Sue, D. W. (1995). Multicultural organizational development: Implications for the counseling profession. In J. G. Ponterotto, J. M. Casas, L. A. Suzuki, & C. M. Alexander (Eds.), *Handbook of multicultural counseling* (pp. 474–492). Thousand Oaks, CA: Sage.

Sue, D. W. (2001). Multidimensional facets of cultural competence. *Counseling Psychologist, 21,* 790–821.

Sue, D. W., Carter, R. T., Casas, J. M., Fouad, N. A., Ivey, A. E., Jensen, M., et al. (1998). *Multicultural counseling competencies: Individual and organizational development.* Thousand Oaks, CA: Sage.

Sue, D. W., Parham, T. A., & Santiago, G. B. (1998). The changing face of work in the United States: Implications for individual, institutional, and societal survival. *Cultural Diversity and Mental Health, 4,* 153–164.

Sue, D. W., & Sue, D. (2003). *Counseling the culturally diverse: Theory and practice* (4th ed.). New York: Wiley.

PART IV

The Multicultural Guidelines and Culturally Sensitive Research

CHAPTER 14

Culturally Sensitive Research: Where Have We Gone Wrong and What Do We Need to Do Now?

JANET CHANG AND STANLEY SUE

THE IMPORTANCE OF culture is increasingly being recognized in mental health initiatives, public policy, research programs, and experimental studies. One of the major themes of the Surgeon General's Report (U.S. Department of Health and Human Services, 2001) was that culture "counts." Culture counts, not only in the understanding of individuals that we observe, but also in determining the methodologies, theories, and conclusions employed by the observer. The impetus to advance multicultural research, though limited in practice, is evident to some extent. Specifically, the American Psychological Association (APA) established the "Guidelines on Multicultural Education, Training, Research, Practice, and Organizational Change for Psychologists" (APA, 2003), reinforcing the importance of taking into account diversity and culture.

In this chapter, we address several issues with respect to the importance and implementation of multicultural research, empirical and conceptual issues relevant to multicultural research, and applications and strategies for multicultural research based on the Multicultural Guidelines (APA, 2003). First, we discuss empirical research and conceptual information pertinent to multicultural research—namely, the idea that mainstream scientific practices and challenges inherent in conducting ethnic minority and cultural research have essentially hindered multicultural research. Second, we present important elements of the Multicultural Guidelines relevant to multicultural research and provide examples in which these Multicultural Guidelines may be applied. Finally, we propose several strategies that will help researchers and mental health professionals develop their multicultural competence.

MAINSTREAM SCIENTIFIC PRACTICES AND CHALLENGES INHERENT IN MULTICULTURAL RESEARCH

How have the practices of science hindered multicultural research? Raising this question makes a bold claim about the limitations, or rather, weaknesses, of certain scientific practices, which in turn point to a number of issues concerning multicultural research. For example, why do we see a paucity of multicultural research? Why is consensus on the quality of such research often lacking? Why is funding for multicultural research relatively sparse? The facts are that there are fewer researchers in the field, researchers may lack interest in multicultural issues or lack appropriate training in such research, and an adequate baseline of knowledge on ethnic minority or cultural groups may be lacking. Furthermore, the field is relatively new and underdeveloped, and this type of research involves small and difficult to study populations. But why are there few researchers, why is interest low, what accounts for the lack of appropriate training, and why is the baseline of knowledge so inadequate? Ultimately, we believe that there is a selective enforcement of scientific principles that negatively affects the quantity and quality of ethnic research (S. Sue, 1999). This bias is subtle and systemic in psychological science. Moreover, it contributes to the conceptual and methodological problems encountered when conducting multicultural research.

Adherence to claims to the truth, to neutrality and objectivity, to the Western conception of the self-contained individual, to the Western narrative of progress, to a universal standard for scientific investigations, and to modernist ideology characterizes current practices in scientific inquiry. However, several shortcomings can be found in the traditional positivist empiricist approach to science and psychology. Mainstream psychology privileges a traditional research paradigm, operates with a Western bias, provides inadequate measurements of the context, and emphasizes significance testing while overlooking effect size and pattern differences (Van de Vijver & Leung, 2000). Furthermore, social scientists make choices that are valued over others—that tend to favor certain values, certain social groups, and certain kinds of social activities (Gergen, 1978).

As a method of inquiry, the scientific method involves the systematic collection of data through controlled observations and testing of hypotheses. In psychological science, the primary goal of research is to describe, understand, predict, and control phenomena. Central to all of science is the need to determine cause-and-effect relationships. This desire to draw causal conclusions is reflected in the importance placed on experimental studies. Because of the uncertainty in determining cause and effect, observational and correlational designs are often considered inadequate, and experimental designs are usually preferred (Aronson, Wilson, & Brewer, 1998). Aronson, Wilson, and Brewer highlighted the advantages of the experimental method: (1) the ability to control variation, (2) random assignment to conditions, and (3) more confidence in specifying the causal relationship between independent and dependent variables.

Discovering causal relationships is established by conducting research with internal and external validity. Internal validity refers to the extent to which conclusions can be drawn about the causal effects of one variable on another (e.g., manipulating the independent variable and observing the consequences on the dependent variable). Researchers are concerned with threats to internal validity, which can undermine causal conclusions and inferences made from empirical results. This research focus reflects the idea that internal validity is "the sine qua non of good experimental research" (Aronson, Wilson, & Brewer, 1998, p. 129). On the other hand, external validity—the extent to which one can generalize the results of research to populations and settings of interest—is usually not considered first and foremost in the research enterprise. The test for generality usually requires the use of different populations or settings. If external validity is low, one may question the robustness of a psychological phenomenon and, consequently, the psychological reality of that phenomenon (Aronson, Wilson, & Brewer, 1998).

Given that internal and external validity are so integral to experimental design, is it possible to maximize them both? Aronson, Wilson, and Brewer (1998) suggested that experiments are unlikely to be equally high in internal and external validity. Thus, psychologists are confronted with a formidable undertaking: "designing a study that is well-controlled (high in internal validity), has independent and dependent variables that are good reflections of the conceptual variables of interest (high in construct validity), and is generalizable to other settings and people (high in external validity)" (p. 131). Unfortunately, maximizing both internal and external validity is a fundamental problem in psychology.

The problem is that, in reality, the scientific principles of internal and external validity are not equal partners in the research endeavor. In practice, researchers pay much attention to internal validity, whereas external validity is often not subjected to investigation. Researchers often publish papers that describe elaborate and rigorous experiments with sound internal validity. With respect to external validity, these papers may simply include a few sentences that acknowledge that the findings may be limited or encourage other researchers to study the generality of the findings. At worst, these papers may assume that the findings are universally applicable. The assumption of the generality of findings and the dominance of internal over external validity are evident in much of the psychological research being conducted.

Several practices in psychological science demonstrate the relative lack of concern over external validity and disinterest in multicultural research (S. Sue, 1999). First, as noted by Sears (1986), psychological research has been conducted primarily on college students. Many theories of human beings have been derived from the study of that population (studies that often reveal a great deal of rigor and ingenuity in research designs to enhance internal validity). Use of this narrow data base has led researchers to conclude that individuals tend to be compliant and yielding to social influences, that attitudes are poor predictors of actual behavior, and that self-perceptions are based on external cues rather than introspection (Sears, 1986). These inferences have shaped psychology's portrayal of human beings, for individuals are viewed as being egocentric and possessing a weak sense of self. Yet, college students hardly constitute a representative sample of the American population in terms of educational attainments, age, ethnicity, social class, attitudes, values, and other key variables. To the extent that college students are unlike other members of the population and contrived testing situations are unlike natural settings, psychology's depiction of human behavior is distorted. In other words, there are limits to the generalizability of research findings based on the use of a nonrepresentative sample.

Second, we must consider the fact that most of the psychological research in the world is conducted by American researchers. Participants in research are largely Americans. That is, Americans study Americans and then generate general theories of human beings. The assumption is that research findings are universally generalizable. However, Americans represent only about 5% of the world's population (Population Reference Bureau, 2003). This statistic means that theories and findings evolve primarily from the studies of one country representing only a small proportion of the world's population. Using this limited population base is neither good practice nor good science. It violates established principles of sampling and generalization and points to the lack of interest in external validity.

Internal validity is more valued in basic research, in which investigators are interested in understanding the underlying psychological mechanisms. Researchers in mainstream psychology appear to be guided by process-oriented research; they first examine the fundamental mechanisms underlying cognition, emotion, motivation, and other psychological phenomena, and only then will they attempt to relate psychological constructs to problems or situations in the real world (Aronson, Wilson, & Brewer, 1998).

These researchers are primarily motivated to understand causal relationships. In contrast, cultural researchers have tended to focus more on the exploration of, rather than the explanation of, cross-cultural differences (Van de Vijver & Leung, 1997). As a result, these differences are left open to various interpretations, and causal inferences may not be justified.

Korchin (1980) argued that the generality of findings is questioned only when research involves ethnic minority populations. He and his colleague conducted research on why some African American youths had made extraordinary achievements. Findings from their research were submitted to a journal for publication. Korchin's paper was rejected, and one reviewer thought that the research was grievously flawed because it lacked a White control or comparison group. Korchin raised two important questions: Why was a White control group necessary if the interest was in African Americans? Why do we not require studies of Whites to have an African American control group? The inherent bias is that it seems that research on ethnic minority populations must show its relevance to other groups or more general phenomena, but research on White American populations need not show its relevance to other groups. Instead, research on ethnic minorities and other cultures has been criticized on several fronts.

Discrepancies between internal and external validity are also quite apparent in single-subject experiments. In single-subject experiments (e.g., using an ABAB time-series design), extraneous variables such as maturation, reactivity, and other factors can be controlled. Individuals also serve as their own control, thereby requiring a smaller sample of participants to detect a statistically significant effect. Internal validity is strong, and alternative explanations for causal relationships can be eliminated. However, generality of findings from such a design is limited.

Another example of the tendency to assume generality is revealed in our attempts to identify effective mental health treatments. The APA Division 12 Task Force on Psychological Interventions was given the charge of determining which psychotherapeutic interventions had met rigorous criteria (including replication) for being designated as an empirically validated (or supported) treatment. A number of treatments had met the criteria for designation. Yet, no rigorous study had ever been conducted on the effectiveness of treatment for members of ethnic minority groups (Chambless et al., 1996). How, then, can treatments be designated as validated, where validity is attributed to the properties of the treatment itself, when cross-cultural validity has never been established? That is, treatments are considered valid even though they have not been tested with different ethnic populations. Should not one of the criteria for validation be the treatment's effectiveness with different populations? If this is not a criterion, then treatment validity should be designated as valid only for the population studied. The consequences of not establishing the cross-cultural validity of mental health treatments are undoubtedly severe (Bernal & Scharron-del-Rio, 2001).

The dominance of internal over external validity is also apparent in the mental health field. In mental health research, a distinction is made between efficacy (which has been considered the gold standard for outcome research) and effectiveness research. Efficacy studies examine the outcomes of mental health interventions often using experimental methods, control over the influence of extraneous variables, and laboratory-like settings. Such procedures greatly enhance internal validity. On the other hand, effectiveness research examines the outcome of mental health interventions in a naturalistic setting (e.g., a mental health clinic), where internal validity can often be problematic. Random assignment of clients, clear-cut experimental manipulations, matched experimental and control groups, and other features that promote internal validity may not be possible in such settings.

Whereas efficacy research may employ strict exclusion criteria in the selection of clients to study, this is frequently not the case in effectiveness research. For example, in an efficacy study of a treatment for schizophrenia, exclusionary criteria might include comorbidity, current use of psychotropic medication, and a non-White population. That is, clients who have more than one disorder, who are using psychotropic medication, and who are members of an ethnic minority group may be excluded from the study to exert greater control over possible extraneous variables. However, this practice would limit the applicability or generality of the findings—an external validity problem. On the other hand, effectiveness research examines treatment outcomes in more real-life situations, where patients may have multiple disorders, may be taking medication, and may be members of various racial groups.

On the whole, these examples demonstrate how the selective reinforcement of certain scientific principles actually undermines scientific inquiry and research. Assuming the generality of theories, measures, findings, and treatments leads to a gross neglect of possible cultural or ethnic variations in psychological phenomena. In essence, external validity is a casualty in the researchers' crusade to generate causal inferences from their findings. Consequently, the study of culture and tests of generality are secondary, and research on culture and ethnic groups inevitably falls short of the standard.

Difficulties involved in conducting research on ethnic minorities and other cultures (e.g., using conceptually equivalent measures, funding, and problems for interpretation) pose a challenging obstacle to meeting the demands of rigorous experimental designs. Although the basic experimental paradigm in psychology is certainly not without its flaws, weaknesses in conceptual, theoretical, and methodological aspects of multicultural research hinder the ability to meet rigorous standards of high internal validity.

A number of researchers have pointed out the limitations of the global, dimensional approach to studying cultures (Bond, 2002; Fiske, 2002; Kitayama, 2002; Matsumoto, 1999; Miller, 2002; Oyserman, Coon, & Kemmelmeier, 2002a, 2002b). In particular, the individualism-collectivism model of culture poorly captures or accounts for cultural differences. The constructs employed are broad and abstract—poorly measured or simply assumed to hold true. In his critique of Markus and Kitayama's (1991) theory of independent and interdependent self-construals, Matsumoto (1999) argued that the assumptions underlying this theory are based on cultural stereotypes pitting the East against the West and that culture is operationalized at the country or national level. Operationalizing culture in terms of responses to a scale or measure also fails to demonstrate how culture influences cognition, emotion, and motivation. Cross-cultural differences may be attributed to measurement artifacts (Van de Vijver & Leung, 2000).

Problems of cross-cultural conceptual equivalence make measurement of cultural differences in values and behaviors difficult. Validity problems inherent in employing rating or ranking methods to compare values across cultures are unavoidable, for the meaning of certain values is culturally constructed, based on social comparison processes or a sense of deprivation (Peng, Nisbett, & Wong, 1997). Hence, these rating methods demonstrate low criterion validity; self-reported value judgments are inconsistent with actual behaviors (Peng et al., 1997). Likewise, cross-cultural value comparisons are confounded by the reference-group effect (i.e., individuals from different cultures compare themselves with different referent groups in self-report questionnaires; Heine, Lehman, Peng, & Greenholtz, 2002). In addition, cross-cultural differences pose a problem for interpretation because differences in mean scores are not restricted to a single interpretation (Van de Vijver & Leung, 2000).

Although some researchers study non-Western populations, these researchers tend to approach the study of other cultures or ethnic groups within a traditional psychological paradigm. That is, cross-cultural psychologists test the universality of psychological theories and findings. Even though the aim of cross-cultural research is to make cross-cultural comparisons, cultural differences are actually interpreted in light of cross-cultural similarities (Poortinga, 1998). For example, the need for positive self-esteem is generally considered to be a universal phenomenon.

Arguments suggesting that this psychological tendency is relegated to Western culture are countered by the idea that cultural differences in self-esteem are due to impression management and self-presentational concerns (i.e., cultural rules of public display). In contrast, cultural psychologists view the self as completely contextualized within a culture and, therefore, expect cultural variations in psychological processes (e.g., Shweder, 1991).

When non-White populations are studied, there is a tendency to aggregate individuals based on a homogeneous group identity to obtain adequate sample sizes. For instance, samples of Asian and Pacific Islander Americans are typically used, but they represent a multitude of diverse, separate Asian and Pacific Islander ethnic populations rather than a single shared identity (S. Sue, Kurasaki, & Srinivasan, 1999). Research on an aggregate would be most appropriate when members that form the aggregate share similar characteristics other than their racial or cultural identity (S. Sue et al., 1999).

Together, mainstream scientific practices and the challenges inherent in multicultural research highlight the need to encourage the awareness and adoption of the Multicultural Guidelines (APA, 2003). Given the changes and developments in the history of psychology that have accompanied a growing and diverse population, the focus on multiculturalism in the education, research, training, and practice of psychology should not be characterized as a mere trend. The issues confronting multicultural researchers are many and far from being resolved. Consequently, the Multicultural Guidelines for multicultural research and competence serve a valuable purpose in addressing these issues and highlighting the role of culture and diversity.

GUIDELINES FOR MULTICULTURAL RESEARCH AND COMPETENCE

Reflecting growing knowledge and emerging data about the influence of context on behavior and the importance of culture and diversity issues, the "Guidelines on Multicultural Education, Training, Research, Practice, and Organizational Change for Psychologists" (APA, 2003) emphasize cultural awareness and knowledge of self and others as well as the application of multiculturalism in the education, training, research, and practice of psychology. These Multicultural Guidelines address a number of issues facing psychologists today (Hall, in press).

The emergence of cultural critiques of psychology, growing recognition of the importance of cultural competence in therapy, and an ever increasing ethnically and culturally diverse population provided the rationale for the first two APA Multicultural Guidelines. According to the first guideline, psychologists must commit to the idea that cultural awareness and knowledge of self and others are integral to an understanding of others in research, training, and practice. As members of a particular culture, psychologists are encouraged to identify their own inherent biases that affect how they perceive and interact with others who belong to a different culture (APA, 2003). With respect to the second guideline, psychologists are expected to acknowledge and incorporate the importance of multicultural perspectives in understanding and responding to those individuals who are ethnically and racially different. These recommendations for psychologists have several important implications for multicultural research, including the type of framework they may adopt (e.g., individualism-collectivism framework [Markus & Kitayama, 1991] and considerations regarding stereotyping in perceptions [Greenwald & Banaji, 1995]).

As researchers and mentors, psychologists also serve simultaneous roles as educators. Working with other psychologists, graduate students, and other individuals, psychologists are encouraged to utilize multiculturalism and diversity constructs in psychology education and training (APA, 2003; D. W. Sue & Sue, 2003). Incorporating multicultural and culture-specific education in the teaching of psychology to undergraduate and graduate students, in clinical and research settings, in mentoring relationships, and in postgraduate education has the effect of increasing the understanding of ethnic and diversity issues and ultimately producing a greater number of competent and effective multicultural researchers, educators, and practitioners.

In terms of research, psychological researchers are expected to be culturally sensitive by appreciating the importance of culture and ethics in conducting research with ethnically, linguistically, and racially diverse individuals (APA, 2003). Employing a culture-centered perspective would benefit multicultural research to the extent that it would improve research generation and design, assessment, analysis, and interpretation.

In clinical and applied settings, psychologists are expected to apply awareness and knowledge of culturally appropriate skills and practices (APA, 2003). Accordingly, psychologists are encouraged to view clients within their cultural context, employ culturally and linguistically appropriate assessment instruments and procedures, and use culturally appropriate interventions as well as a broad range of interventions. This guideline is also important for improving multicultural research in that education, research, training, and practice are all intimately interconnected. Developing and incorporating cultural sensitivity in training and practice is just as integral as advancing multicultural education and research.

Finally, psychologists can act as agents of change and as policymakers. Psychologists are positioned to support culturally informed organizational (policy) development and practices by interacting with government agencies, community organizations, and other sectors of society (APA, 2003). Informed by their own experiences and knowledge of multicultural research, psychologists can be proactive in facilitating organizational change processes. Psychologists' efforts are not limited to the clinical or therapeutic domain; rather, psychologists have been and will continue to serve as health care administrators, corporate and government consultants, expert witnesses, and in other roles.

In short, the Multicultural Guidelines outlined by APA (2003) not only reflect and address changing demographics in the population and developments in psychology, but also provide recommendations to increase the multicultural knowledge and skills of psychologists. These Multicultural Guidelines prioritize cultural and diversity issues that are often overlooked in mainstream psychology. However, the nature and purpose of culturally sensitive research is still questioned and subject to debate, despite movements toward considering and incorporating culture in research, practice, and training. One major challenge to conducting culturally sensitive research is the number and complexity of considerations (e.g., methodological and conceptual) involved. To address these challenges and issues, it may be beneficial to consider the ways the APA Multicultural Guidelines may be applied.

APPLICATIONS OF THE MULTICULTURAL GUIDELINES

The Multicultural Guidelines (APA, 2003) provide insight into relevant issues that psychologists face. Case examples are presented and discussed to demonstrate how the Multicultural Guidelines may be applied to multicultural research.

Psychological researchers are encouraged to develop studies that reflect empirical and conceptual information about culture and its influence on research traditions and skills as well as the sample and variables under examination (APA, 2003). Central to this aim, researchers must be aware of their own biases and cultural assumptions made by their research questions. Awareness of biased or stereotypic attitudes and values may lead to effort and practice to change these automatic associations (APA, 2003). Although researchers may be encouraged to be aware of and to change these biases, some researchers may continue to undervalue the importance of culture and diversity issues. In situations in which ethnicity is simply considered a categorical variable and there is no interest in ethnic or cultural differences, researchers should still acquire more information about specific characteristics of their sample (e.g., immigration status and level of acculturation). Obtaining this information may provide insight into explaining unexpected findings or significant effects that can be accounted for by these factors.

In other situations, researchers may value multicultural research but lack training in conducting this type of research. Like other research endeavors, psychologists can be informed by theory and past research prior to formulating hypotheses and designing a study. Furthermore, using cultural informants may be an indispensable resource to researchers who are unfamiliar with certain cultural values, norms, and issues. These cultural consultants can assist researchers in different aspects of the research process, including developing hypotheses, designing studies, and interpreting findings. These researchers may also benefit from consultations with more established multicultural researchers.

Like psychological researchers who undervalue culture and diversity issues, both inexperienced and more experienced researchers who value multicultural issues may still demonstrate biases and stereotypic attitudes. In situations in which ethnic or cultural differences are the primary focus, researchers need to be careful about the generalizations and conclusions they make. Theoretical and practical implications are dependent on not only the findings, but also the sample. For example, one major challenge confronting researchers using samples of Asian Americans or other "broad" ethnic groups involves the tendency to aggregate individuals on the basis of general group identity (e.g., S. Sue et al., 1999). Researchers striving to be multiculturally competent must be particularly sensitive to characteristics of their sample.

Psychological researchers would benefit from utilizing culturally sensitive techniques, such as sophisticated large-scale sampling techniques. As we discussed earlier, adequate sampling of certain ethnic minority populations is rather difficult. To address this issue, psychological researchers must define their target research group and employ sampling procedures appropriate for the research question. For example, in the Chinese American Psychiatric Epidemiological Study in Los Angeles County (Takeuchi et al., 1998), researchers employed a multistage sampling design to randomly select Chinese Americans for participation in a study about lifetime and 1-year prevalence rates of depression and dysthymia. Over 1,700 adults, 18 to 65 years of age, who lived in Los Angeles County and spoke English, Cantonese, or Mandarin composed the sample. Researchers could then examine the heterogeneity within a single Asian American ethnic group. Although this type of study requires generous funding, researchers interested in a particular ethnic minority population can employ smaller-scale, convenient sampling methods but also attend to specific characteristics of their sample.

In addition to sampling more distinct groups, psychological researchers must address the increasingly diverse nature of their samples. Participants or respondents may differ with respect to various social and demographic characteristics (e.g., socioeconomic status and language proficiency) that may confound ethnic comparisons (Okazaki & Sue, 1995). Moreover, these individuals may vary in their level of acculturation and may be monocultural, bicultural, or multicultural. Specifically, individuals may adopt different cultural paradigms in different situations (Lehman, Chiu, & Schaller, 2004). For instance, bicultural or multicultural individuals may identify with a single culture or multiple cultures in a given context. These issues concerning cultural frame switching and cultural identification are particularly important to research design and to interpretations of findings. Researchers need to be sensitive to these issues, which are highly relevant to attaining multicultural competence.

Similar to difficulties related to sampling, gaining cooperation from research participants can be challenging. Issues relating to the influence of cultural norms, privacy and confidentiality, power relations, and the like affect the relationship between the researcher and the participant or respondent. Rapport is essential to establishing a dialogue between researchers and participants. More important, an understanding of participants' cultural background and worldviews on the part of psychologists is critical to the research process. In developing an evaluation of African American community leadership, community psychologist James Kelly (1999) familiarized himself with African American history, sought guidance from African American colleagues, and engaged in dialogues with important community leaders. He discovered that the church and the pastor played significant roles in this community. He also realized that music was highly valued in the community. Both Kelly and the executive director of the host organization shared a love of jazz, thereby allowing a common ground to be established and trust to form. Kelly and his research team could work alongside community members to evaluate the organization's efforts of recruiting and training community residents as advocates for their improved welfare. This example demonstrates how the dynamics between researchers and participants can affect the research process.

The extent to which the Multicultural Guidelines (APA, 2003) can be applied to multicultural research is certainly not limited to these case examples or vignettes. The Multicultural Guidelines can apply to different aspects of multicultural research in various ways. Implementing the

Multicultural Guidelines involves recognizing the importance of multicultural research and developing strategies for multicultural competence.

STRATEGIES FOR DEVELOPING MULTICULTURAL COMPETENCE

Two main problems have essentially hindered the development of multicultural research and multicultural competence: (1) practices in psychological science (e.g., valuing internal validity, traditional positivist empiricist approach) and (2) methodological and conceptual difficulties in conducting multicultural research. These problems are further exacerbated by the fact that a number of psychologists who are not engaged in multicultural research are not entirely convinced of the value of culture and diversity issues in research. Consequently, the behaviors and beliefs of psychologists conducting multicultural research are not necessarily normative in mainstream psychology. However, these problems can be addressed by developing strategies that psychologists and mental health professionals can use to develop their multicultural competence in research and by promoting and conducting multicultural research. Multicultural researchers and mental health professionals alike would benefit by addressing issues relevant to multicultural research, issues outlined earlier in this chapter. Strategies to develop multicultural competence as related to multicultural research center on fundamental scientific practices.

Although obstacles or problems related to conducting multicultural research appear daunting, mental health professionals must not shy away from addressing these issues. At all levels of scientific inquiry, psychologists must address issues of hypothesis formation, sampling, research design, data analysis, and data interpretation within a multicultural framework. In other words, psychologists as researchers must be informed, aware, and educated about multicultural issues before embarking on any research endeavor. Psychologists can also help develop their multicultural competence by seeking out other multicultural researchers for support, guidance, and resources and by being open to alternative methods of inquiry.

Challenges to the dominant research paradigm in psychology should not be avoided or ignored. Questioning the generality of theories, existing methodological considerations, and certain scientific principles promotes scientific progress and invites alternative approaches to the study of psychological phenomena. For example, qualitative methods may be more culturally sensitive than quantitative methods because culture-specific approaches may be utilized. Likewise, unconventional approaches to psychological inquiry may appear to undermine mainstream psychology but, in fact, enhance and improve the ways psychologists undertake and interpret research. Although the postmodernist critique of scientific inquiry challenges the prevailing Zeitgeist and fundamental assumptions in which scientific inquiry is rooted, the relationship between constructionism and psychological science is not necessarily antagonistic (Gergen, 1973, 1997).

Social constructionism "invites one to challenge the objective basis of conventional knowledge" (Gergen, 1985, p. 267). Knowledge is not objective, individualistic, or historic, but actually derived from communal interchange (Gergen, 1985). Moreover, constructionism can improve psychological inquiry in various ways (Gergen, 1997). First, the democratic and reflective nature of constructionism lends itself to multiple voices being heard, an interchange between the discipline and the public, and various interpretations. Second, constructionism challenges the status quo, revives marginal discourse, and fosters societal value of psychological theory. Finally, constructionism's orientation toward social reconstruction promotes the reconceptualization of the self and recognizes individuals as cultural and relational beings. In particular, constructionism encourages multiple approaches to psychological inquiry, such as qualitative research, ethnographic approaches, and cultural psychology. With respect to multicultural research, multiple approaches to the study of culture and ethnic groups should be employed and improvements to current multicultural research should be pursued.

Although past cross-cultural studies have focused on the exploration of cultural differences, more recent studies have moved away from simple exploration to the explanation of cultural differences. In the example given earlier, cross-cultural studies on self-enhancement and self-criticism addressed the question of whether the need for positive self-esteem is universal or culture-specific. Finding through anecdotal accounts, historical facts, and empirical evidence that this psychological tendency is specific to North American culture, Heine, Kitayama, and others have argued that culture (i.e., independent and interdependent self-construals) moderates this tendency. More recently, Heine et al. (2001) have proposed that Japanese self-criticism and accompanying self-improvement motivations are rooted in an incremental theory of self. This shift from exploration to explanation nurtures attention to theoretical and methodological issues and improvements.

Overreliance on the individualism-collectivism model of culture has revealed the limited value of this framework. Similar to the idea that internal validity is "the sine qua non of good experimental research," use of individualism and collectivism scales has become the sine qua non of good cross-cultural research (Aronson, Wilson, & Brewer, 1998, p. 129; Kitayama, 2002). However, the operationalization of culture in terms of nation-level individualism and collectivism defines culture in static and dichotomized terms. Culture needs to be studied as a process rather than as an index or a variable (Greenfield, 1997). Because meanings, practices, and psychological processes constitute culture, adopting a system view instead of an entity view of culture captures its dynamic and online nature (Kitayama, 2002). Therefore, researchers should not be limited to using self-report attitudinal measures. Alternative options include the use of participant observation and the study of systems of kinship, religion, taboos, and other institutions and practices (Fiske, 2002), the study of cultural meaning (Greenfield, 1997; Miller, 2002), the use of scenario methods (Peng et al., 1997), and the assessment of online responses (Kitayama, 2002). Perhaps the development of multimethod and cross-domain methods, incorporating extra-individual factors (e.g., demographic, economic) and self-report measures, behaviors, and observations, will also facilitate multicultural research (Matsumoto, 1999). Ultimately, solutions to conceptual and methodological problems in multicultural research and to poor scientific practices involve both theoretical and practical considerations.

First, cultural considerations are critical in all phases of research. In an effort to recognize the importance of multicultural issues, researchers should proceed with specific cultural hypotheses to test or with cultural issues in mind. Consequently, the training of researchers with expertise in ethnic minority and cross-cultural research is important. Graduate and postdoctoral training programs should offer opportunities to learn about methodological and conceptual problems in multicultural research and the means to conduct rigorous multicultural research. Emerging and current psychologists can learn about and adopt multicultural perspectives to inform their research and practices. Second, the importance of ethnic and cross-cultural research in validating the universality or applicability of theories, methodologies, and measures should be emphasized. In fact, all theories as well as measures should be rated as to their cross-cultural adequacy. For example, if Theory A is grounded in research on only one population, it should be considered a local (emic) theory until tested and validated with other populations. On the other hand, Theory B, which has been tested and validated with many different populations, should be viewed as being more robust, rigorous, and stringent in meeting research criteria and more applicable than Theory A to human beings in general. It is indeed impressive for a researcher to not only create theories and measures, but also demonstrate their meaningfulness for a variety of populations. In effect, researchers must test the cross-cultural generalizability of theories, methodologies, and measures or limit the application of the findings to the population that was studied. On a related note, researchers need to expand psychological studies involving underrepresented or overlooked populations (e.g., Southeast Asian immigrants). Fostering multicultural competence entails developing a range of research endeavors representative of the diversity in the real world. Finally, the inclusion of participants or cultural informants in aspects of multicultural research would allow psychologists to be privy to alternative and nonacademic perspectives. Although the inclusion of participants is not typical in psychological research, it would allow psychologists to achieve greater multicultural authenticity.

Increasing the demand for external validity and addressing conceptual and methodological issues inherent in multicultural research will improve research on ethnic minorities and other cultures. These objectives can be greatly facilitated by practical efforts—namely, increasing and encouraging publications regarding multicultural issues not only in topic-specific or division journals, but also in mainstream psychology journals and books. Discussion and examination of the bias in science and the consequences of the selective enforcement of scientific principles should also serve to expand the possibilities of scientific inquiry. Moreover, developing strategies to improve and develop multicultural competence as related to multicultural research will aid psychologists and mental health professionals. At the same time, psychologists and mental health professionals must continually educate themselves and others about multicultural issues. Reevaluating the prevailing Zeitgeist and improving on existing research paradigms should lead to continued scientific progress in terms of increased multicultural research and competence.

REFERENCES

American Psychological Association. (2003). Guidelines on multicultural education, training, research, practice, and organizational change for psychologists. *American Psychologist, 58,* 377–402.

Aronson, E., Wilson, T. D., & Brewer, M. B. (1998). Experimentation in social psychology. In D. T. Gilbert, S. T. Fiske, & G. Lindzey (Eds.), *The handbook of social psychology* (4th ed., Vol. 1, pp. 99–142). Boston: McGraw-Hill.

Bernal, G., & Scharron-del-Rio, M. R. (2001). Are empirically supported treatments valid for ethnic minorities? Toward an alternative approach for treatment research. *Cultural Diversity and Ethnic Minority Psychology, 7,* 328–342.

Bond, M. H. (2002). Reclaiming the individual from Hofstede's ecological analysis—A 20-year odyssey: Comment on Oyserman et al. (2002). *Psychological Bulletin, 128,* 73–77.

Chambless, D. L., Sanderson, W. C., Shoham, V., Bennett-Johnson, S., Pope, K. S., Crits-Christoph, P., et al. (1996). An update on empirically validated therapies. *The Clinical Psychologist, 49,* 5–18.

Fiske, A. P. (2002). Using individualism and collectivism to compare cultures—A critique of the validity and measurement of the constructs: Comment on Oyserman et al. (2002). *Psychological Bulletin, 128,* 78–88.

Gergen, K. J. (1973). Social psychology as history. *Journal of Personality and Social Psychology, 26,* 309–320.

Gergen, K. J. (1978). Toward generative theory. *Journal of Personality and Social Psychology, 36,* 1344–1360.

Gergen, K. J. (1985). The social constructionist movement in modern psychology. *American Psychologist, 40,* 266–275.

Gergen, K. J. (1997). The place of the psyche in a constructed world. *Theory and Psychology, 7,* 723–746.

Greenfield, P. M. (1997). Culture as process: Empirical methods for cultural psychology. In J. W. Berry, Y. H. Poortinga, & J. Pandey (Eds.), *Handbook of cross-cultural psychology: Vol. 1. Theory and method* (2nd ed., pp. 301–346). Boston: Allyn & Bacon.

Greenwald, A. G., & Banaji, M. R. (1995). Implicit social cognition: Attitudes, self-esteem, and stereotypes. *Psychological Review, 102,* 2–27.

Hall, G. N. (in press). Cultural competence in clinical psychology research. *Clinical Psychologist.*

Heine, S. J., Kitayama, S., Lehman, D. R., Takata, T., Ide, E., Leung, C., et al. (2001). Divergent consequences of success and failure in Japan and North America: An investigation of self-improving motivations and malleable selves. *Journal of Personality and Social Psychology, 81,* 599–615.

Heine, S. J., Lehman, D. R., Peng, K., & Greenholtz, J. (2002). What's wrong with cross-cultural comparisons of subjective Likert scales? The reference-group effect. *Journal of Personality and Social Psychology, 82,* 903–918.

Kelly, J. G. (1999). Contexts and community leadership: Inquiry as an ecological expedition. *American Psychologist, 54,* 953–961.

Kitayama, S. (2002). Culture and basic psychological processes—Toward a system view of culture: Comment on Oyserman et al. (2002). *Psychological Bulletin, 128,* 89–96.

Korchin, S. J. (1980). Clinical psychology and minority problems. *American Psychologist, 35,* 262–269.

Lehman, D. R., Chiu, C.-Y., & Schaller, M. (2004). Psychology and culture. *Annual Review of Psychology, 55,* 689–714.

Markus, H. R., & Kitayama, S. (1991). Culture and the self: Implications for cognition, emotion, and motivation. *Psychological Review, 98,* 224–253.

Matsumoto, D. (1999). Culture and self: An empirical assessment of Markus and Kitayama's theory of independent and interdependent self-construal. *Asian Journal of Social Psychology, 2,* 289–310.

Miller, J. G. (2002). Bringing culture to basic psychological theory—Beyond individualism and collectivism: Comment on Oyserman et al. (2002). *Psychological Bulletin, 128,* 97–109.

Okazaki, S., & Sue, S. (1995). Methodological issues in assessment research with ethnic minorities. *Psychological Assessment, 7,* 367–375.

Oyserman, D., Coon, H. M., & Kemmelmeier, M. (2002a). Cultural psychology, a new look: Reply to Bond (2002), Fiske (2002), Kitayama (2002), and Miller (2002). *Psychological Bulletin, 128,* 110–117.

Oyserman, D., Coon, H. M., & Kemmelmeier, M. (2002b). Rethinking individualism and collectivism: Evaluation of theoretical assumptions and meta-analyses. *Psychological Bulletin, 128,* 3–72.

Peng, K., Nisbett, R. E., & Wong, N. Y. C. (1997). Validity problems comparing values across cultures and possible solutions. *Psychological Methods, 2,* 329–344.

Poortinga, Y. H. (1998). Cultural diversity and psychological invariance: Methodological and theoretical dilemmas of cross-cultural psychology. In J. G. Adair, D. Belanger, & K. L. Dion (Eds.), *Advances in psychological science: Vol. 1. Social, personal, and cultural aspects* (pp. 229–245). Hove, England: Psychology Press.

Population Reference Bureau. (2003). Population of United States compared to world population in mid-2003. Retrieved June 22, 2004, from http://www.prb .org//datafind/datafinder.htm.

Sears, D. O. (1986). College sophomores in the laboratory: Influences of a narrow data base on social psychology's view of human nature. *Journal of Personality and Social Psychology, 51,* 515–530.

Shweder, R. A. (1991). *Thinking through cultures: Expeditions in cultural psychology.* Cambridge, MA: Harvard University Press.

Sue, D. W., & Sue, D. (2003). *Counseling the culturally diverse: Theory and practice* (4th ed.). New York: Wiley.

Sue, S. (1999). Science, ethnicity, and bias: Where have we gone wrong? *American Psychologist, 54,* 1070–1077.

Sue, S., Kurasaki, K. S., & Srinivasan, S. (1999). Ethnicity, gender, and cross-cultural issues in clinical research. In P. C. Kendall, J. N. Butcher, & G. N. Holmbeck (Eds.), *Handbook of research methods in clinical psychology* (pp. 54–71). New York: Wiley.

Takeuchi, D. T., Chung, R., Lin, K., Shen, H., Kurasaki, K., Chun, C., et al. (1998). Lifetime and twelve-month prevalence rates of major depressive episodes and dysthymia among Chinese Americans in Los Angeles. *American Journal of Psychiatry, 155,* 1407–1414.

U.S. Department of Health and Human Services. (2001). *Mental health: Culture, race, and ethnicity—A supplement to mental health: A Report of the Surgeon General.* Rockville, MD: U.S. Department of Health and Human Services, Substance Abuse and Mental Health Services Administration, Center for Mental Health Services.

Van de Vijver, F. J. R., & Leung, K. (1997). *Methods and data analysis for cross-cultural research.* Thousand Oaks, CA: Sage.

Van de Vijver, F. J. R., & Leung, K. (2000). Methodological issues in psychological research on culture. *Journal of Cross-Cultural Psychology, 31,* 33–51.

CHAPTER 15

Conducting Quantitative Research in a Cultural Context: Practical Applications for Research with Ethnic Minority Populations

SHAWN O. UTSEY, RHEEDA L. WALKER, AND
NAA OYO A. KWATE

QUANTITATIVE RESEARCH METHODS are thoroughly enmeshed in a Western epistemological framework and, therefore, are inherently limited in their application across racial, ethnic, cultural, and linguistic participant populations (Akbar, 1991; Gergen, Gulerce, Lock, & Misra, 1996). Relying on positivist philosophical assumptions (i.e., reality is objective and independent of those who observe it; unbiased observation of this reality constitutes scientific knowledge), the quantitative researcher attempts to construct the physical, social, and psychological reality of participants in a selected sample and then applies this reality to a larger (target) population. Although objectivity is the clarion call of the quantitative researcher, the truth of the matter is that scientific knowledge is culturally encapsulated, and the quantitative (i.e., purportedly objective) methods that generate this knowledge are not free from bias (Scarr, 1985). In an effort to check the cultural hegemony of Western science on the provision of psychology services to persons from diverse racial, ethnic, cultural, and linguistic groups living in the United States, the American Psychological

Association (APA, 2003) has prescribed a set of Guidelines for multicultural education, training, research, practice, and organizational change.

The "Guidelines on Multicultural Education, Training, Research, Practice, and Organizational Change for Psychologists" were developed by a joint task force of Divisions 17 and 45 of the APA (2003) and provide a praxis model for the provision of culturally responsible and relevant psychological services to individuals from diverse racial, ethnic, cultural, and linguistic backgrounds. Acknowledging that all individuals exist in a social, political, and economic context, the Multicultural Guidelines recognize the specific needs of historically marginalized and disenfranchised racial, ethnic, and cultural groups as they relate to providing mental health services. Moreover, the Multicultural Guidelines delineate the specific knowledge, skills, and awareness needed for all psychologists and mental health practitioners to function competently amid the rapid and dramatic demographic changes occurring in the United States.

The Multicultural Guidelines also provide specific goals for psychologists to develop their repertoire of multicultural competencies. According to the APA (2003), the aims of the Multicultural Guidelines are as follows: (1) to provide a rationale for addressing issues of diversity in education, training, research, practice, and organizational change; (2) to develop a literature base that includes the current technologies available for developing multicultural competencies and empirical research findings that support the proposed Guidelines; (3) to encourage the development of enhanced education, training, research, practice, and organizational change methodologies; and (4) to introduce paradigms that broaden the scope of psychology as a discipline. The Multicultural Guidelines are a timely and welcome initiative that provides psychologists with a framework for the provision of culturally appropriate services in an increasingly diverse society.

The current chapter discusses issues related to conducting quantitative research in a cultural context. In so doing, we relate our arguments to those Multicultural Guidelines that are relevant to conducting quantitative research. Our discussion of conceptual issues includes an examination of the distinction between positivist and postpositivist research philosophies, emic and etic worldviews, individualistic versus collectivistic orientations, and issues of conceptual equivalence across cultures. The chapter also outlines the complexities of various research designs (e.g., survey research, experimental designs) and sampling issues unique to diverse racial, ethnic, cultural, and linguistic populations. Last, but certainly not least, we address the ethical issues relevant to conducting responsible research with multicultural populations.

WHAT IS MULTICULTURAL RESEARCH?

A logical starting point in thinking about multicultural research is to simply interrogate the terms "research" and "culture." McMillan and Schumacher (2001) define research as "a systematic process of collecting and logically analyzing information (data) for some purpose" (p. 9). According to Matsumoto (1994), "Research is the primary way by which psychologists uncover 'truths' about the world" (p. 1). Culture might be defined as "common sense, communication with others . . . routine rhythms and rituals of life that are taken for granted . . . [and] the patterning downward of social relations by shared symbolic apparatuses—language, aesthetic sensibility, and core value orientations conveyed by master metaphors" (Kleinman, 1996, p. 16). Similarly, Geertz (1973) posits that "[culture] denotes an historically transmitted pattern of meanings embodied in symbols, a system of inherited conceptions expressed in symbolic forms by means of which men communicate, perpetuate, and develop their knowledge about and attitudes toward life" (p. 89).

Multicultural research, then, is the empirical examination of, or inquiry into, the experiences of individuals from diverse cultural backgrounds (Brislin, 1976; Matsumoto, 1994) and the systematic inclusion of culture when dissecting psychological phenomena. One aim of multicultural inquiry is to test the limitations of scientific knowledge by studying people from diverse cultural backgrounds to determine the extent to which universal truths can be established or refuted (Matsumoto, 1994). Testing the limits of scientific knowledge through multicultural research is achieved by uncovering predictable differences and similarities in the behavior of individuals. An important caveat to this definition is that the differences (or similarities) between the cultural groups must be theoretically meaningful. Another aim of multicultural research, according to the APA (2003), is to increase psychologists' understanding of how social, political, historical, and economic factors influence the behavior of individuals from different cultural backgrounds.

The methodological goals of multicultural research are not altogether different from those of "traditional" psychological inquiry. For example, issues of credibility, design validity (i.e., internal and external validity), and the ethical treatment of human research participants are equally germane to the multicultural researcher as to traditional researchers. Moreover, some theoretical concepts developed in traditional psychology are amenable to multicultural inquiry. For example, self-esteem is a concept characteristic of the ideas and values emanating from individualistic societies where individuals are motivated to feel good about themselves and to strive for attainment of personal goals and personal happiness

(Triandis, 1995). In contrast, Luhtanen and Crocker (1992) developed the Collective Self-Esteem Scale to assess the phenomenon of self-esteem in collectivistic cultures.

The Multicultural Guidelines reiterate what many psychologists have long argued: Researchers must systematically consider culture in design, implementation, and interpretation of data. White (1972) argued that "it is difficult if not impossible to understand the lifestyles of Black people using traditional psychological theories, developed by White psychologists to explain White behavior." White's statement is applicable across underrepresented racial/ethnic groups in the United States and poignantly expresses the sentiment of the Multicultural Guidelines. The Multicultural Guidelines assert that individuals cannot be understood apart from their cultural context. An authentic and inclusive understanding of human behavior requires consideration of cultural, economic, and social contexts when providing clinical services *and* conducting research. With regard to quantitative research, the Multicultural Guidelines delineate three key areas to address: (1) research generation and design, (2) assessment, and (3) analysis and interpretation. We discuss these in turn.

RESEARCH GENERATION AND DESIGN

The Multicultural Guidelines note that competent research generation and design begins with appropriate research questions. Williams and Mitchell (1991) and Hilliard (1994) suggested that the basic research question changes based on the cultural perspective. That is, researchers' culturally biased presuppositions influence which research questions are generated. As an example, Williams and Hilliard have argued the illegitimacy of intellectual testing among certain underrepresented groups. For example, characteristics that are deemed relevant to assessment of intelligence among White, middle-class families may be considered inconsequential among first-generation Latino families. The question "What intellectual skills are necessary to successfully navigate a novel cultural environment?" speaks to a different set of needs from "What intellectual skills are necessary to be successful in college?" Multicultural research should include theoretical approaches that are sensitive to and complement the population of interest. In another example, acculturation is said to be important to assess well-being among immigrant groups in the United States as it is linked to ethnic and cultural identity. Thus, acculturation, ethnic identification, or the intersection of these phenomena should be routinely considered in multicultural research. Zane and Mak

(2003) noted that "acculturation is one of the most significant psychological processes of psychosocial adaptation for many ethnic minority individuals" (p. 58). A thorough understanding of help-seeking behavior and other mental health issues among people of color hinges on some consideration of acculturation and degree of acceptance of mainstream culture in the United States.

Guideline 3 encourages psychologists to employ multiculturalism in psychological education. This is obviously the first step in training investigators to design culturally competent research. However, the degree to which psychology has been successful in this regard is dubious. It has long been the case that the majority of multicultural research has been conducted by researchers of color. One study found this to be the case for 58% of the most prolific authors in the ethnic minority literature (Hall & Maramba, 2001). The numbers of psychologists of color in academia remain small, but these relatively few conduct most of the research in multicultural issues. Merely increasing the numbers of researchers of color will not in and of itself ameliorate the marginalization of culture in psychology. Change must be implemented more directly in the education of future psychologists of all racial and ethnic backgrounds. The APA (2002) accreditation guidelines require training programs to provide students with the opportunity to acquire and demonstrate substantive knowledge of cultural and individual diversity. However, the reality is that most training programs do not include substantive attention to such topics. Only 10 years ago, 74% of programs did not require even one course related to working with diverse populations (Bernal & Castro, 1994). Today, more programs require such a course, but it is rare that the requirement exceeds one course. In addition, multicultural issues are not well integrated into the rest of the department curricula. Again, even if the numbers of psychologists of color increase, the majority of research will be designed and conducted by European Americans who have not received adequate training in cultural issues. This is not to imply that psychologists of color are off the hook with regard to cultural training. Merely coming from an ethnic minority background does not automatically equip researchers to conduct culturally appropriate work, particularly because their formal training may have been bereft of instruction in this area. At best, without purposeful attendance to these issues, researchers may find themselves contributing to the status quo in psychological science. At worst, they may perpetuate the legacy of scientific racism endemic in the discipline by overpathologizing populations or by attributing individual differences to distal variables such as genetics rather than more proximal factors such as historical circumstance and social class (Zuckerman, 2003).

ASSESSMENT

Assessment is another key area for competent social science research, as outlined by the Multicultural Guidelines. Instrumentation that is valid and reliable across groups is necessary (Matsumoto, 1994). Further, constructs that encompass the reality of all populations should be the rule rather than the exception. The measures used to operationalize independent and dependent variables also require careful selection. Although few measures that are widely used have been validated with diverse populations, the data that they produce are accepted without caveats and interpreted as objective. For example, a PsycINFO search for the Beck Depression Inventory (Beck, Steer, & Garbin, 1988) yields 4,906 abstracts, not including dissertations; adding "African American" to the search reduces the total to 28. Similarly, abstracts containing the NEO-FFI (a measure assessing the Five-Factor Model of personality; Costa & McCrae, 1992) are reduced from 83 to 0. When measures are not tested in multicultural populations, researchers have no means by which to evaluate whether a particular scale will yield results similar to that found in European American samples. Indeed, research does show that some scales elicit response bias in diverse samples (e.g., Azocar, Arean, Miranda, & Munoz, 2001; Cole, Kawachi, Maller, & Berkman, 2000; Iwata, Turner, & Lloyd, 2002).

Yet, despite the fact that sociocultural background weighs heavily on how individuals view the world, express themselves, and respond to inquiry—including in the form of structured paper-and-pencil questionnaires—most psychological scales were originally developed with European American samples and are assumed to be universally applicable to all groups. This practice reflects Malgady's (1996) contention that the prevailing view representing the status quo leads to the formulation of a null hypothesis that assessment is uniform across ethnic groups. This hypothesis prevails unless sufficient empirical force enables its nullification or rejection. If sufficient evidence to refute it is not obtained, clinicians do not reject the null and operate from a universalist, color-blind stance. In this paradigm, if a Type I error is committed (incorrectly rejecting the null), assessment and diagnostic procedures are judged to be culturally biased when they are not, resulting in the unnecessary development of culture-specific interventions. Thus, the mental health system shoulders the burden of misspent resources. However, if a Type II error is committed (incorrectly failing to reject the null), people of color will be misdiagnosed or unfairly evaluated.

If cultural bias were to be specified as the null hypothesis (as Malgady contends it should), the two types of errors would be reversed, and client-centered rather than system-centered errors would be more grievous.

Thus, we would presume bias on the part of mainstream assessment procedures unless proven innocent (Malgady, 1996). This is the stance researchers must take to conduct the most culturally sensitive and, thus, scientifically rigorous assessments possible. With regard to measures, then, this means that researchers will need to determine whether the measures they seek to use have been validated for the population of interest, and if not, should do some initial pilot-testing of the measure before beginning the study. It may also be necessary to modify items based on relevant information drawn from the literature on cultural psychology.

The literature on symptom presentation in cross-cultural contexts is instructive here. Kleinman and Good (1985) noted that the salient features of depression differ in both meaning and form in different cultures. For example, Chinese Americans, socialized in a collectivist perspective where interpersonal relations are highly regarded, are said to relate depression to alienation and marginalization (Kleinman & Kleinman, 1985), neither of which is listed among *DSM-IV* criteria for Depression. Further differences in the expression of depressive symptomatology (i.e., somatic rather than cognitive symptoms) omit key constructs in the investigation and assessment of target variables. Similarly, African American response profiles for certain scales on the Minnesota Multiphasic Personality Inventory-II are known to be elevated and, thus, overpathologized on this measure (Gynther & Green, 1980). In sum, widely used measures and key psychiatric diagnoses often ignore or understudy the reality of people of color in the United States. Given that researchers have already identified weaknesses and gaps in the literature with regard to underrepresented persons, future research should first seek to address known methodological flaws and limitations and avoid replicating past mistakes.

The introductory comments to the Multicultural Guidelines refer to the absence of reciprocity in research studies. Reciprocity refers to the provision of resources (e.g., skills building or guidance for change and intervention) to ethnically diverse communities who have participated in research studies. Assessment provides an excellent opportunity for researchers to provide group results and suggestions for change in the community. For example, Black church settings provide opportunities for conducting research with relatively large numbers of African American people. Studies in these settings are conducive to provision of group results and follow-up workshops. Thus, possible social change is informed by empirical data, and follow-up investigations provide opportunities for applied research and evaluation. As an example, clinicians may provide psychoeducation and communication skills training to alleviate poor health practices and medical noncompliance among African American elderly who are leery of health care practitioners.

ANALYSIS AND INTERPRETATION

Analysis and interpretation is the third element in conducting competent research outlined by the Multicultural Guidelines. Matsumoto (1994) makes the case that researchers should have an equal understanding of fundamental multicultural issues as well as basic methodological design. When interpreting data, researchers should state explicitly that the findings may not hold for ethnic groups who are not well represented in the sample. Ideally, a study of intelligence among European American children would be analogous to the experience of African American children. However, Kwate (2001) shows the ways in which the Wechsler Intelligence Scale for Children III, a widely used intelligence test for children, is undergirded by a Eurocentric perspective to the exclusion of any other point of view. Thus, when interpreting such data, researchers must consider more than the psychometric properties of the instrument, including the cultural biases within which it may be steeped.

CONCEPTUAL CONSIDERATIONS IN MULTICULTURAL RESEARCH

Epistemology is the branch of philosophy that studies the nature of knowledge and the process by which knowledge is acquired and validated (Gall, Borg, & Gall, 1996; Veroff & Goldberger, 1995). A researcher's epistemological position plays a fundamental role in the way his or her research is conducted. Researchers who subscribe to a positivist epistemology make the assumption of an objective reality (Gall et al., 1996; Maxim, 1999; McMillian & Schumacher, 2001). They believe that physical and social reality is independent of those who observe it, and that observations of this reality, if unbiased, constitute scientific knowledge. In contrast, researchers who subscribe to postpositivist epistemology believe that the study of individuals' interpretations of social reality must occur at the local, immediate level (Maxim, 1999). For example, a positivist researcher who sought to investigate anxiety levels experienced by adults who grew up in an abusive parental environment would first define the population and then administer a measure of anxiety to as many members of the population as he or she could find. The researcher, working from the standpoint that anxiety is a linear, quantifiable reality, would then calculate an anxiety score to be used in inferential statistical analysis. The positivist would then make statements about the immediate sample that would be applied to individuals with similar characteristics. In contrast, the postpositivist researcher would select particular adults (local) rather than survivors in general (distant). The postpositivist would be interested in understanding what anxiety is, how it is measured, how it is situated in social context, the likelihood of objectivity, and how the researcher affects the construction of knowledge.

The distinction between emic and etic conceptual (and operational) frameworks is fundamental to contemporary thinking about multicultural psychological research. According to Pike's (1967) original proposal, "The etic viewpoint studies behavior as from outside a particular system, and as an essential initial approach to an alien system. The emic viewpoint results from studying behavior as from inside the system" (p. 37; as cited in Berry, 1989). Essentially, the etic approach to multicultural research seeks to uncover universal truths that can be generalized across cultures, whereas the emic approach offers an understanding of how individuals from a particular culture construct their own reality (Berry, 1989; Matsumoto, 1994). Both approaches have value in creating new knowledge. There are, however, several distinct advantages to an emic approach for conducting multicultural research. First, it provides a glimpse into how language and culture are constructed by indigenous persons. Second, it provides an understanding of the indigenous person's daily life and how attitudes, motives, interest, and personality are formed. Last, it adds legitimacy to the study of human behavior as a predictive science (Berry, 1989).

It is important to note that the emic-etic distinction is not a dichotomy, but simply reflects two separate perspectives on understanding data (i.e., behavioral observations). The choice of orientation (i.e., emic vs. etic), however, will inevitably influence an investigator's theoretical formulation and method of inquiry, as well as the behavioral phenomena selected for study (Berry, 1989). Although the emic and etic approaches differ in their associated theories, methods, and phenomena of interest, they converge in relation to a final goal of multicultural research. Using a comparative framework, multicultural researchers seek to formulate generalizations across cultural groups (Berry, 1989; Brislin, 1983). In other words, they uncover the complexities of a psychological phenomenon in one culture, compare that understanding to the same phenomenon in a different culture, and then make generalizations about the phenomenon across cultures. When using a comparative framework for multicultural research care must be taken to ensure that the behaviors of interest are functionally equivalent (i.e., represent the same phenomenon in each culture). This task is most challenging when comparing behavioral phenomena in two or more cultural milieus that have diametrically opposing worldviews.

One of the most popular and widely researched cultural milieus is the individualism-collectivism social orientation (Triandis, 1990). In individualist cultures, people are motivated to feel good about themselves, strive for attainment of personal goals, pursue material wealth, and become independent of others by developing personal qualities that serve to distinguish them from others (Suh, Diener, Oishi, & Triandis, 1998). In contrast, individuals from collectivistic cultures view themselves in the context of their family, community, or social group (Arrindell et al., 1997). Harrison, Wilson, Pine, Chan, and Buriel (1995) use the term "ancestral worldview" to connote a collectivistic social orientation in which there is a fluidity of boundaries between the self and other entities, both physical and nonphysical (i.e., spiritual). Given the conceptual and operational distinctions between individualistic and collectivistic worldviews, it is essential that investigators formulate both emic (culture-specific) and etic (universal) definitions of the psychological construct being examined.

It is important to note that for the purpose of conducting multicultural research, the individualism-collectivism cultural orientations are not necessarily polar opposites. Moreover, neither orientation is assumed to be superior to the other. A major purpose of the individualism-collectivism distinction is to characterize the influence of cultural worldviews on individuals' perceptions of self (Triandis, 1995). This information can be essential for formulating appropriate research questions, identifying conceptually equivalent measures of the constructs being studied, gaining access to the population of interest, and correctly interpreting the study's findings. Consequently, multicultural researchers must be cognizant of the worldviews indigenous to the populations they are studying and seek to incorporate them into their conceptual formulations, methodology, and statistical analysis.

The current technology available for conducting multicultural research is limited. For the most part, paper-and-pencil self-report measures are the order of the day. Researchers have noted the inherent difficulty with this simplified approach to measuring psychological constructs across cultures (Keith, Heal, & Schalock, 1996; Kuyken, Orley, Hudelson, & Sartorius, 1994). To successfully transport psychological constructs across cultures, investigators must establish conceptual, semantic, item, and scalar equivalence between the host culture and the target culture (Kuyken et al., 1994).

Conceptual Equivalence

Conceptual equivalence relates to the existence of a given concept in both the host culture and the target culture. To achieve conceptual equivalence, not only must the concept exist in both cultures, its expression must also be identical in each culture. Establishing conceptual equivalence is of considerable importance in determining whether a measure is valid for use in both the host culture and the target culture.

SEMANTIC EQUIVALENCE

Semantic equivalence in multicultural assessment is determined by the denotative and connotative uniformity of words (Kuyken et al., 1994). The denotative meaning of a word refers to its symbolic representation and is primarily determined by its dictionary meaning. The primary mode of evaluating the denotative meaning of a word is through linguistic analysis. Connotative equivalence, on the other hand, is the meaning implied by a word. For example, words associated with happiness (e.g., satisfied, gratified, fulfilled) in Western culture may evoke different associations in Asian or African cultures (e.g., harmony, balance, spiritness; Matsumoto, 1994). For multicultural assessment to be effectively carried out, both denotative and connotative equivalence must exist.

ITEM EQUIVALENCE

Multicultural assessment requires the contextual equivalence of the items belonging to the measure being used to evaluate the construct of interest (Kuyken et al., 1994). Without contextual equivalence, the validity of the evaluative process will be compromised. For example, if researchers want to measure the effects of depression on quality of life across cultures, they must first establish that depression occurs in the same context across cultures and that the items intended to measure depression have the same ability to do so in each culture.

SCALAR EQUIVALENCE

Scalar equivalence refers to the degree to which the measurement scale of a given instrument has equivalent value in cultures where it will be employed (Kuyken et al., 1994). For example, measures of psychological constructs that use a Likert scale with a range of, say, 1 to 7, where 1 = "a little" and 7 = "a lot," assumes that the construct of interest can be quantified in a linear fashion in both the host and the target culture. Likert scales have been found to be ineffective in cultures where adhering to the social norm is desirable (Mertens, 1998). In such cases, respondents are likely to choose a response typifying the tendency to select a value close to the middle of the scale so as not to appear different from the group.

DESIGN ISSUES IN MULTICULTURAL RESEARCH

Quandaries in the design of quantitative research with populations of color are long-standing. Operationalization of constructs, survey use, and sampling are among the particular issues that require a shift in thinking among researchers. Ongoing concerns can be addressed given a concerted effort to step outside of research designs that may be culturally biased. Here we discuss particular problems with certain constructs and other preliminary errors that undermine culturally competent research.

Survey research, a popular data-gathering strategy, is in need of strict parameters for maximum proficiency. Survey questionnaires tend to be based on a monolithic point of view and include a single cultural perspective. Such data-gathering strategies profoundly limit the investigator's ability to consider alternative (culture-bound) hypotheses. Popper's (1935/1959) notion of "falsification" insisted that scientists arrive at a conclusion by ruling out *all* alternative hypotheses. When culture is not considered, the process of scientific inquiry is compromised. A strong research plan would develop a database of measures that are known to be psychometrically sound across cultures. Further, validity studies should be conducted for other measures that are frequently used but not yet validated in populations of color. Word (1992) noted that just as U.S. standardized measures are translated in other countries, similar efforts should be made to ensure the utility of these measures among African Americans.

Design flaws can undermine the success of a culturally competent research methodology. Parham, White, and Ajamu (2000) noted that quantitative measures limit our understanding of complex human behavior, particularly those of culturally diverse populations. They note that a *combination* of quantitative and qualitative tools would allow for a more comprehensive and informed assessment in many cultures. Parham et al. noted that when sampling populations, some researchers assume within-group homogeneity; for example, Mexicans in Mexico, first-generation Puerto Ricans in East Harlem, and third-generation Cubans in Miami may simply be lumped together as "Latinos."

Ideally, the suggestions listed in this chapter will be implemented in undergraduate and graduate education so that institutions begin to systematically produce culturally competent quantitative investigators. Systematic training in culture increases the likelihood that new investigators will recognize the importance of research design that is culture-sensitive. However, research is necessarily a collaborative process, and this is particularly true for multicultural research. Investigators who do not have expertise with the culture of interest should collaborate with someone who is knowledgeable about the culture. Sinha (1984) referred to this process as horizontal collaboration. Researchers should compose investigative teams of scholars from diverse backgrounds, particularly those that match the target population. This is not to suggest that every individual of color will be able to lend insight to all cultural factors of interest simply by virtue of sharing similar background. Moreover, the danger of tokenism on a research team is real. However, it is equally problematic for investigators to create research teams that are entirely European American to work in communities of color, particularly if a substantive knowledge base regarding critical cultural issues is lacking. In addition, depending on the research question, obtained data may be strongly related to the characteristics of the research team. For example, research has shown that African Americans are less likely to report that an incident was caused by discrimination if these judgments had to be made aloud in the presence of a nonstigmatized group member (Stangor, Swim, Van Allen, & Sechrist, 2002). Many African Americans also hold significant distrust of the research enterprise, particularly in a medical context (Corbie-Smith, Thomas, & St. George, 2002; Corbie-Smith, Thomas, Williams, & Moody-Ayers, 1999). Although a more diverse research staff is likely to go a long way toward building interest and interpersonal trust, it also remains true that all investigators must gain substantial knowledge about the community from which they hope to recruit participants. Pilot studies are useful as first steps, whereby participant feedback can be shared with expert collaborators before making adjustments (Matsumoto, 1994).

METHODOLOGICAL ISSUES IN MULTICULTURAL RESEARCH

From a methodological perspective, there are several strategies researchers should employ to conduct multiculturally centered work. It may appear to be stating the obvious to argue that study samples should be composed of individuals from several racial/ethnic backgrounds. Nevertheless, a quick perusal of published research reveals that study samples continue to be overwhelmingly European American, a trend that has existed for the past several decades (Graham, 1992). Rather than attempting to match national demographics, local representation is much more appropriate. Researchers attempting to create a diverse participant sample in Salt Lake City are faced with the real constraint that Utah has a population that is 0.8% African American, 1.7% Asian, and 9.5% Latino. If, however, the researcher is conducting the study in Los Angeles, there is no excuse for a sample that is 90% European American—situations we have seen at recent (winter 2004) conference presentations. In other instances, studies may include negligible proportions of multicultural populations to meet National Institutes of Health guidelines, which require the inclusion of minorities. In this case, it is extremely unlikely that the researchers will be able to draw any conclusions about the question of interest as it applies to this small subsample, if statistical analyses can be conducted at all.

It is also critical for researchers to consider how sociocultural factors might inform intervention studies. Most often, researchers create an intervention to test question X using methodology Y with population Z, and after its completion, they comment in the discussion sections of published reports on the ways this research might be extended to other populations, including individuals of color. In other words, these factors are treated as an aside related to external validity. What happens much less frequently is for researchers to consider whether question X is informed by an appropriate conceptual framework; whether methodology Y takes into account culturally appropriate procedures; and whether population Z should have been the study focus from the outset.

Multicultural Guideline 2 posits that psychologists should recognize the importance of gaining knowledge about ethnically and racially different individuals. This includes not only psychological theories from a multicultural perspective, but also knowledge regarding historical and sociological experiences of major cultural groups. At present, however, psychology remains very much apart from other social sciences and humanities that study these issues. This is particularly true for interdisciplinary work in ethnic studies departments.

Departments such as American studies, African American studies, Asian American or East Asian studies, and Latin American or Chicano studies retain faculty who hold degrees and teach in a variety of social science and humanities disciplines, such as sociology, history, anthropology, and economics. Psychology faculty, however, tend to be few and far between in these multidisciplinary departments. We can see this trend if we examine doctoral universities classified in the Top 50 by the 2003 *U.S. News and World Report* ("America's Best Colleges, 2003," 2003). For example, while there are 36 African American studies departments at these institutions, only three of them retain psychology faculty. Of 30 Asian American studies departments, only five retain psychology faculty, and of 34 Latin American studies departments, only three retain psychologists. Moreover, for almost all of these departments, a lone psychologist represents the discipline.

Many of the universities in the top 50 represent the "old guard" of psychology, those who established laboratories in the founding years of the discipline (Benjamin, 2001; Rice, 2000) and have a long history in the field. These universities are also represented in other rankings of excellence, such as levels of federal research-and-development expenditures, library research holdings ("Top Institutions in Federal Research and Development Expenditures 2001," 2003), and membership in the Association of American Universities. Thus, psychology departments at these universities likely set trends for the discipline as a whole. The unfortunate trend being set here is for psychologists to steer clear of departments that focus on race and culture. It would appear, then, that breadth of knowledge regarding ethnicity and culture encouraged by Guideline 2 could be impeded by institutional structures. Psychology's relative isolation from interdisciplinary sociocultural study reflects the minimization of culture in psychological science and will continue to hamper multicultural research as long as the isolation persists.

ETHICAL ISSUES IN CONDUCTING MULTICULTURAL RESEARCH

This final section appears last not because it is least important; on the contrary, its significance requires closing the chapter with attention to these issues. There is a long and dubious history of unethical and exploitive research practices perpetrated against communities of color. This is especially true as it relates to research with Black populations in the United States (e.g., see Guthrie, 1998; Thomas & Sillen, 1972). The atrocities committed by a number of unethical investigators have occurred in spite of federal and state protections against such practices. In some cases, the abuses have been blatant and committed with reckless disregard, but the majority of ethical violations are more subtle.

The now infamous Tuskegee study is but one example. This U.S. government-sponsored experiment began in 1934; 400 Black men suffering from syphilis were allowed to go untreated so as to trace the natural course of the disease. The study continued and its participants remained untreated until 1974, well after it was discovered that penicillin was an effective cure for syphilis (Jones, 1993). Moreover, the men in the Tuskegee study were never asked to give their informed consent to participate in the research. Despite the fact that these egregious violations of human protection occurred decades ago, the U.S. government (under the presidency of Bill Clinton) acknowledged only recently the heinous nature of the Tuskegee study and issued a public apology.

As recently as 1997, research has been conducted that engendered public outcry. Breggin (1998) discussed psychiatric research conducted among African American and Latino children in New York City and described it as "medical racism." Breggin noted the use of a previously banned experimental drug, a "trend to mislead parents about the dangers of psychiatric drugs," and invasion of privacy in a drug study that was said to have "no potential benefit to the children."

These are just a few examples of the more extreme historical and contemporary abuses that have been perpetrated on people of color by the research community. Given the history of unethical and exploitive research practices with Blacks and other ethnic minority groups, it is not surprising that these populations continue to be underrepresented in the majority of medical and psychological research studies. This phenomenon, no doubt, is in large part the result of the distrust of persons of color toward the larger research community. In fact, a study by Shavers, Lynch, and Burmeister (2000) found that a sample of Black adults surveyed in Detroit in 1998 and 1999 indicated that their awareness of the Tuskegee study had a negative impact on their willingness to participate in research studies. This study clearly demonstrates the need for major efforts aimed at rehabilitating (or habilitating) the reputation of the research community in the eyes of communities of color.

Research ethics and institutional review boards safeguard vulnerable populations (e.g., mentally ill or disabled persons, minorities, prisoners) against exploitation and abuse by members of the research community. Their origins are in the world's response to the atrocities committed by Nazi researchers in German concentration camps (Keith-Spiegel & Koocher, 1985). In 1948, several German physicians were criminally prosecuted for their role in conducting sadistic medical experiments on concentration camp prisoners without their consent. Following a number of high-profile criminal proceedings, the Nuremberg Code was established as a first in the protection of vulnerable populations against unethical research practices. The Nuremberg Code stated that participation in research should be voluntary, that participants should give their consent, and that the benefits of the research must outweigh its risks (Keith-Spiegel & Koocher, 1985). The Declaration of Helsinki, established in 1964 by the World Medical Association, reinforced the provisions of the Nuremberg Code safeguarding research participants against abuse. This document went further by proposing that research with humans should be based on laboratory and animal experimentation, that research protocols be reviewed by independent committees, and that research be conducted by individuals who are scientifically qualified (Breggin, 1998).

In 1974, and as a result of the negative publicity from the Tuskegee study, the National Research Act was passed in the United States. This legislation created the National Commission for the Protection of Human Subjects of Biomedical and Behavioral Research, whose aim was to identify the basic ethical principles that should govern biomedical and behavioral research involving human subjects (Breggin, 1998). In carrying out its mission, the Commission prepared the Belmont Report, which summarized the basic ethical principles identified by the group during their working session. The three basic ethical principles identified by the Commission were (1) respect for persons via informed consent, (2) beneficence via a risks-benefits assessment, and (3) justice based on equitable selection procedures for research participants. In addition to the federal legislation for the ethical conduct of biomedical and behavioral research, a number of disciplines have developed their own code of ethics for conducting research. For example, the APA (2002) developed specific standards for psychologists conducting research with both animal and human participants in their Ethical Principles of Psychologists and Code of Conduct. The APA's professional code of conduct governing research with human subjects is an important safeguard aimed at protecting vulnerable persons from exploitation and abuse. However, it falls short in providing guidance in the unique complexities of conducting multicultural research.

Specific ethical guidelines for conducting multicultural research with human participants have been proposed by a number of scholars (e.g., Fisher et al., 2002; Marshall & Batten, 2003). These efforts are primarily in response to the recent increase in attention to addressing health disparities in relation to ethnic minority mental health issues. In July 2001, the Science and Public Policy Directorates of the APA, the Child and Adolescent Consortium of the National Institute of Mental Health, and the Fordham University Center for Ethics Education convened a meeting of national leaders in bioethics, multicultural research, and minority mental health issues (Fisher et al., 2002). The goal of this meeting was to develop guidelines for ethical decision making in conducting mental health research involving ethnic minority children and adolescents. These guidelines are too lengthy to review here, but are available in a report published in the 2002 *American Psychologist, 57* (pp. 1024–1040). The major prescriptions of this document are as follows: (1) The risks and benefits of research should be evaluated according in the cultural context of the target population, (2) informed consent procedures should be respectful to the cultural reality of the study's participants, (3) confidentiality and disclosure parameters should be congruent with the cultural values of the study's participants, and (4) researchers should seek community and participant input into the study's design, implementation, and interpretation of findings. These guidelines are by no means exhaustive but are intended as a supplement to federal, state, and professional (APA) ethical codes for conducting research with human participants.

Marshall and Batten (2003) are among the scholars who have responded to the need for an ethical code of conduct for conducting multicultural research. They acknowledge the contribution of existing ethical codes to the protection of vulnerable persons, but assert that they do not go far enough in addressing the complexities of research conducted in a cultural context. According to Marshall and Batten, some essential components to conducting ethical multicultural research include ensuring a representation of multiple voices, enhancing moral discernment, promoting social change, and facilitating a reciprocal collaboration between the researchers and the participants. Again, the prescriptions recommended by these authors are too lengthy to review given the space constraints of this chapter. However, we will summarize the main points. First, it is essential that researchers incorporate the values and worldview of the cultural group being studied into the conceptualization, design, and implementation of the research plan. Researchers should be cognizant of the degree to which their worldview differs from that of the study's participants and should respect those differences. Informed consent, entry into the field, and participant roles are all issues that must be redefined in relation to the cultural values and belief systems of the target population. Furthermore, the community in which the study is being conducted should have control over the research agenda being advanced. Community control should include the study's purpose, methodology, composition of the research team, and budget. Last, issues related to data collection, writing, and the dissemination of findings should reflect a culturally sensitive framework and include community involvement. Participatory action research has been recommended as an appropriate framework for conducting multicultural research that relies on the participants and community members to define the social reality of the target population (Marshall & Batten, 2003).

Ethical codes are guidelines that provide researchers with a decision-making paradigm for conducting and disseminating research in a way that is not harmful to the participant or community. Recognizing the limitations of these codes in relation to conducting research across cultures, several scholars have begun the process of delineating the complexities of ethical conduct in the context of communities of color. What we have now is a foundation on which to establish sound ethical practices for conducting research with racial and ethnic minority populations.

CONCLUSION

In this chapter, we have attempted to guide quantitative researchers in the intricacies of culturally sensitive, culturally competent research design and interpretation. Given the increasingly diverse demographics of the U.S. population, such work is critical in theoretically and methodologically sound psychological science. We discussed conceptual issues in multicultural research, design, and methodological concerns, and ethical issues relevant to conducting culturally competent research. In sum, we assert that researchers should generate questions that consider alternative possibilities, namely, those that are culture-specific. Consideration of valid testing and assessment tools and interpretation of results that assist rather than harm the cultural group of interest are also important. We assert that there is an ethical imperative in conducting culturally appropriate research. A diligent commitment to multicultural research that is strategic and purposeful will contribute to an emerging field of research that is effective and useful in understanding the complex array of human behavior.

REFERENCES

Akbar, N. (1991). Paradigms of African American research. In R. Jones (Ed.), *Black psychology* (3rd ed., pp. 709–725). Berkeley, CA: Cobbs and Henry.

American Psychological Association. (2002). Ethical principles of psychologists and code of conduct. *American Psychologist, 57,* 1060–1073.

American Psychological Association. (2003). Guidelines on multicultural education, training, research, practice, and organizational change for psychologist. *American Psychologist, 58,* 377–402.

America's best colleges, 2003. (2003). *U.S. News & World Report.* Retrieved July 15, 2003, from http://www.usnews.com/usnews/edu/college/rankings/brief/natudoc/tier1/t1natudoc_brief.php.

Arrindell, W. A., Hatzichristou, C., Wensink, J., Rosenberg, E., Twillert, B., Stedema, J., et al. (1997). Dimensions of national culture as predictors of cross-national differences in subjective well-being. *Personality and Individual Differences, 23,* 37–53.

Azocar, F., Arean, P., Miranda, J., & Munoz, R. F. (2001). Differential item functioning in a Spanish translation of the Beck Depression Inventory. *Journal of Clinical Psychology, 57,* 355–365.

Beck, A. T., Steer, R., & Garbin, M. (1988). Psychometric properties of the Beck Depression Inventory: Twenty-five years of evaluation. *Clinical Psychology Review, 8,* 77–100.

Benjamin, L. T. (2001). American psychology's struggles with its curriculum: Should a thousand flowers bloom? *American Psychologist, 56,* 735–742.

Bernal, M. E., & Castro, F. G. (1994). Are clinical psychologists prepared for service and research with ethnic minorities? *American Psychologist, 49,* 797–805.

Berry, J. W. (1989). Imposed etics-emics-derived etics: The operationalization of a compelling idea. *International Journal of Psychology, 24,* 721–735.

Berry, J. W., Irvine, S. H., & Hunt, E. G. (1987). *Indigenous cognition: Functioning in cultural context.* Dordrecht: Nijhoff.

Breggin, P. R. (1998). Recent FDA decision highlights ethical issues in drug research on children, 1998. Retrieved July 2, 2004, from http://breggin.com/overview.

Brislin, R. W. (1976). Comparative research methodology: Cross-cultural studies. *International Journal of Psychology, 11,* 215–229.

Brislin, R. W. (1983). Cross-cultural research in psychology. *Annual Review of Psychology, 34*, 363–400.

Cole, S. R., Kawachi, I., Maller, S. J., & Berkman, L. F. (2000). Test of item-response bias in the CES-D scale: Experience from the New Haven EPESE study. *Journal of Clinical Epidemiology, 53*, 285–289.

Corbie-Smith, G., Thomas, S. B., & St. George, D. M. (2002). Distrust, race and research. *Archives of Internal Medicine, 162*, 2458–2463.

Corbie-Smith, G., Thomas, S. B., Williams, M. V., & Moody-Ayers, S. (1999). Attitudes and beliefs of African Americans toward participation in medical research. *Journal of General Internal Medicine, 14*, 537–546.

Costa, P. T., & McCrae, R. R. (1992). *Revised NEO Personality Inventory and NEO Five-Factor Inventory professional manual.* Lutz, FL: Psychological Assessment Resources.

Fisher, C. B., Hoagwood, K., Boyce, C., Duster, T., Frank, D. A., Grisso, T., et al. (2002). Research ethics for mental health science involving ethnic minority children and youths. *American Psychologist, 57*, 1024–1040.

Gall, M. D., Borg, W. R., & Gall, J. P. (1999). *Educational Research: An Introduction.* White Plains, NY: Longman.

Geertz, C. (1973). Thick description toward an interpretive theory of culture. *The interpretation of cultures.* New York: Basic Books.

Gergen, M. M., Gulerce, A., Lock, A., & Misra, G. (1996). Psychological science in cultural context. *American Psychologist, 51*, 496–503.

Graham, S. (1992). "Most of the subjects were White and middle class": Trends in published research on African Americans in selected APA journals, 1970–1989. *American Psychologist, 47*, 629–639.

Guthrie, R. V. (1998). *Even the Rat Was White* (2nd ed.). Boston: Allyn & Bacon.

Gynther, M., & Green, S. (1980). Accuracy may make a difference, but does a difference make for accuracy? A response to Pritchard and Rosenblatt. *Journal of Counseling and Clinical Psychology, 48*, 268–272.

Hall, G. C. N., & Maramba, G. G. (2001). In search of cultural diversity: Recent literature in cross-cultural and ethnic minority psychology. *Cultural Diversity and Ethnic Minority Psychology, 7*, 12–26.

Harrison, A. O., Wilson, M. N., Pine, C. J., Chan, S. Q., & Buriel, R. (1995). Family ecologies of ethnic minority children. In N. R. Goldberger & J. B. Veroff (Eds.), *The culture and psychology reader.* New York: New York University Press.

Hilliard, A. G. (1994). What good is this thing called intelligence? *Journal of Black Psychology, 20*, 430–443.

Iwata, N., Turner, R. J., & Lloyd, D. A. (2002). Race/ethnicity and depressive symptoms in community-dwelling young adults: A differential item functioning analysis. *Psychiatry Research, 110*, 281–289.

Jones, J. H. (1993). *Bad Blood: The Tuskegee Syphilis Experiment.* New York: Free Press.

Keith, K., Heal, L., & Schalock, R. (1996). Cross-cultural measurement of critical quality of life concepts. *Journal of Intellectual and Developmental Disability, 21*, 273–293.

Keith-Spiegel, P., & Koocher, G. P. (1985). *Ethics in psychology: Professional standards and cases.* New York: McGraw-Hill.

Kleinman, A. (1996). How is culture important for *DSM-IV?* In J. E. Mezzich, A. Kleinman, H. Fabrega, & D. L. Parron (Eds.), *Culture and psychiatric diagnosis: A DSM-IV perspective.* Washington, DC: American Psychiatric Press.

Kleinman, A., & Good, B. (1985). Introduction: Culture and depression. In A. Kleinman & B. Good (Eds.), *Culture and depression: Studies in the anthropology and cross-cultural psychiatry of affect and disorder* (pp. 1–33). Berkeley and Los Angeles: University of California Press.

Kleinman, A., & Kleinman, J. (1985). Somatization: The interconnectedness in Chinese society among culture, depressive experiences, and the meanings of pain. In A. Kleinman & B. Good (Eds.), *Culture and depression: Studies in the anthropology and cross-cultural psychiatry of affect and disorder* (pp. 1–33). Berkeley and Los Angeles: University of California Press.

Kuyken, W., Orley, J., Hudelson, P., & Sartorius, N. (1994). Quality of life assessment across cultures. *International Journal of Mental Health, 23,* 5–27.

Kwate, N. O. A. (2001). Intelligence or Misorientation?: Eurocentrism in the WISC-III. *Journal of Black Psychology, 27,* 221–238.

Luhtanen, R., & Crocker, J. (1992). A collective self-esteem scale: Self-evaluation of one's social identity. *Personality and Social Psychology Bulletin, 18,* 302–318.

Malgady, R. G. (1996). The question of cultural bias in assessment and diagnosis of ethnic minority clients: Let's reject the null hypothesis. *Professional Psychology: Research and Practice, 27,* 73–77.

Marshall, A., & Batten, S. (2003). Ethical issues in cross-cultural research. *Connections, 3,* 139–151.

Matsumoto, D. (1994). *Cultural influences on research methods and statistics.* Prospect Heights, IL: Waveland Press.

Maxim, P. S. (1999). *Quantitative research methods in the social sciences.* New York: Oxford University Press.

McMillan, J. H., & Schumacher, S. (2001). *Research in education.* New York: Longman.

Mertens, D. M. (1998). *Research methods in education and psychology: Integrating diversity with quantitative and qualitative approaches.* Thousand Oaks, CA: Sage.

Parham, T. A., White, J. L., & Ajamu, A. (2000). *The psychology of Blacks: An African centered perspective.* Upper Saddle River, NJ: Prentice-Hall.

Popper, K. R. (1959). *The logic of scientific discovery.* New York: Basic Books. (Original work published 1935)

Rice, C. E. (2000). Uncertain genesis: The academic institutionalization of American psychology in 1900. *American Psychologist, 55,* 488–491.

Scarr, S. (1985). Constructing psychology: Making facts and fables for our times. *American Psychologist, 40,* 499–512.

Shavers, R., Lynch, C. F., & Burmeister, L. F. (2000). Knowledge of the Tuskegee Study and its impact on the willingness to participate in medical research studies. *Journal of the National Medical Association, 92,* 563–572.

Sinha, J. (1984). Toward partnership for relevant research to the Third world. *Indian Journal of Psychology, 19,* 1–2.

Stangor, C., Swim, J. K., Van Allen, K. L., & Sechrist, G. B. (2002). Reporting discrimination in public and private contexts. *Journal of Personality and Social Psychology, 82,* 69–74.

Suh, E., Diener, E., Oishi, S., & Triandis, H. C. (1998). The shifting basis of life satisfaction judgments across cultures: Emotions versus norms. *Journal of Personality and Social Psychology, 74,* 482–493.

Thomas, A., & Sillen, S. (1972). *Racism and psychiatry.* New York: Carol Publishing.

Top institutions in federal research and development expenditures 2001. (2003). *The Chronicle of Higher Education,* p. A26. Retrieved May 16, 2003 from http://chronicle.com/prm/weekly/v49/i36/36a02601.htm.

Triandis, H. C. (1990). Cross-cultural studies of individualism and collectivism. In J. Berman (Ed.), *Nebraska symposium on motivation, 1989* (pp. 41–133). Lincoln: University of Nebraska Press.

Triandis, H. C. (1995). The self and social behavior in differing cultural contexts. In N. R. Goldberger & J. B. Veroff (Eds.), *The culture and psychology reader.* New York: New York University Press.

Veroff, J. B., & Goldberger, N. R. (1995). What's in a name? The case for "Intercultural" psychology. In N. R. Goldberger & J. B. Veroff (Eds.), *The culture and psychology reader.* New York: New York University Press.

White, J. L. (1972). Toward a Black psychology. In R. L. Jones (Ed.), *Black psychology.* New York: Harper & Row.

Williams, R. L., & Mitchell, H. (1991). The testing game. In J. Jones (Ed.), *Black Psychology.* Berkeley, CA: Cobb and Henry Publishers.

Word, C. O. (1992). Cross-cultural methods for survey research in Black urban areas. In K. A. Burlew, W. C. Banks, H. P. McAdoo, & D. A. Azibo (Eds.), *African American psychology* (pp. 28–42). Newbury Park, CA: Sage.

Zane, N., & Mak, W. (2003). Major approaches to the measurement of acculturation among ethnic minority populations: A content analysis and an alternative empirical strategy. In K. Chun, P. Organista, & G. Marin (Eds.), *Acculturation: Advances in theory, measurement, and applied research.* Washington, DC: American Psychological Association.

Zuckerman, M. (2003). Are there racial and ethnic differences in psychopathic personality? A critique of Lynn's (2002). Racial and ethnic differences in psychopathic personality. *Personality and Individual Differences, 35,* 1463–1469.

CHAPTER 16

Conducting Culturally
Sensitive Qualitative Research

DEVIKA DIBYA CHOUDHURI

THE MULTICULTURAL GUIDELINES

One of the key elements of the American Psychological Association's (APA, 2003) "Guidelines on Multicultural Education, Training, Research, Practice, and Organizational Change for Psychologists" is the notion of a cultural lens. The Multicultural Guidelines define culture as an embodiment of worldview, a complex of systems of values, beliefs, and resultant practices that shape the way individuals make meaning of the world. Using a visual metaphor, a cultural lens is then simply the field of vision that incorporates the landscape of culture. The Multicultural Guidelines invite psychologists to use a cultural lens, acknowledging the ways in which culture shapes their own lens, the multiple meanings that individuals may make about themselves and their contexts, and ways to be responsive and sensitive to such understandings of the world. Specifically, in terms of conducting research, Guideline 4 asks investigators to appreciate the importance of conducting culture-centered research and be sensitive to cultural issues regarding research focus, design, and methods.

A cultural lens, by definition, is rooted in the subjective, the internal worldview view of a particular person from his or her particular location in the world. This subjectivity of internally constructed meaning, as opposed to a presumed externally objective reality true for all persons in all times and contexts, is the socially constructed position of qualitative research.

OVERVIEW OF QUALITATIVE RESEARCH

The practice of qualitative inquiry covers a variety of research methods and approaches that operate from an interpretive paradigm, developing portrayals of a complex and dynamic reality (Glesne & Peshkin, 1992). Symbolic interactionism (Blumer, 1969), feminist inquiry (Olesen, 1994), grounded theory (Strauss & Corbin, 1990) action research, case studies, and ethnographies are examples of the plethora of approaches constituting qualitative inquiry (Bogdan & Biklen, 1992).

Qualitative research strives to understand the epistemological nature of phenomena through the subjective experiences of the persons who are concerned with such phenomena. Essentially, it is the process of finding out what people think and feel impressionistically and narratively rather than quantifiably. As such, this methodology lends itself particularly well to understanding the experiences and worldviews of diverse persons. For instance, Gibson (2002) looked at the experience of African American grandmothers who were caregivers to grandchildren whose parents were not able to provide them with adequate care. This phenomenon of kinship care, culturally congruent in the African American community, needed a qualitative approach to explore a complex, sensitive, and contextually rich situation and capture the lived experience of this clinically significant group.

Qualitative approaches are becoming increasingly popular as a methodology for conducting research in psychology (Ponterotto, 2002). Unlike many of the social sciences that have viewed humans as social beings, psychology typically considered humans as individuated selves in isolation (McLeod, 1996) and tended to link itself more closely with the natural sciences. Quantitative methods dominated the field, the gold standard of empiricism being the randomized control-trial experiment (Walsh-Bowers, 2002). Qualitative research methods were used primarily in clinical case studies to generate further understanding, and such research was usually presented in ways that implied objectivity and authoritative expertise on the part of the researcher. Walsh-Bowers (2002) used the qualitative approach of interviewing to investigate the experiences of psychology researchers with qualitative methods and found that a strong theme was the perceived difficulty of qualitative research being accepted within the canon of psychology, as well as the lack of adequate training in qualitative research. Despite these obstacles, over the past few decades, there has been an increasing realization that qualitative methods might be useful in answering particular kinds of questions (Rennie, 1996). The place of qualitative research may well be to generate discovery of phenomena rather than verification, because when there is little known about a field, qualitative inquiry is useful for generating themes that may be operationalized by later quantitative research (Heppner, Kivlighan, & Wampold, 1992).

One way of comparing these methodologies and seeing the resultant gain is to examine two approaches to a single topic. Bracey, Bámaca, and

Umaña-Taylor (2004) explored the relationship between self-esteem and ethnic identity development among biracial and monoracial adolescents through administering different measures to a large group of adolescents. They found that biracial adolescents had significantly lower self-esteem than Black adolescents but significantly higher than Asian adolescents. Biracial adolescents reported higher levels of ethnic identity than White adolescents, though lower than Black and Asian adolescents. The authors also found a significant positive relationship between self-esteem and ethnic identity.

In a qualitative approach to the topic of biracial identity, Gillem, Cohn, and Throne (2001) used a case study method following two biracial youth to describe their identity development. Rather than deriving statistical significance from their findings, this approach allowed the generation of narrative examples of the complex process of racial identity development. Although each participant identified as Black, the paths they took were very different and had different meanings and consequences. Embracing Blackness for one individual meant feeling betrayed by White physical traits and experiencing rejection from other Blacks, resulting in his low self-esteem; for the other, it meant finally achieving high self-esteem and a refusal to reject any part of herself, including her positive relationship with her White parent.

Both quantitative and qualitative approaches, therefore, generate useful information that is derived differently and can be applied differently. Whereas the first allows for generalizability, the second allows for deeper understanding of an issue in terms of context and complexity.

Hill, Thompson, and Williams (1997) described a step-by-step process of conducting consensual qualitative research, a method of action research well-suited for studying complex clinical phenomena in counseling. Beyond coding therapist and client behaviors or creating scales to determine the strength of the working alliance, qualitative research can focus on the meanings such experiences hold for the client and the therapist as they naturally occur, discovering inductively what may guide the process. By focusing on the meaning of experience, qualitative research can be helpful in generating more ideas about what clients find helpful, useful, nonoppressive, and empowering, while taking into account the diversity of clients and the context of their interactions with counselors. The following set of studies demonstrates the building of a strong foundational basis through qualitative research.

Thompson, Worthington, and Atkinson (1994) investigated how African American women college students responded in simulated client sessions to African American and European American counselors who either made a point of raising racial issues or avoided the topic. Sessions were videotaped and the interactions qualitatively analyzed. One of the findings that emerged was that the pseudo-clients self-disclosed more intimately when asked directly about their experiences as Black women on a majority White campus. Extending that study, Thompson and Jenal (1994) focused on the pseudo-clients and further analyzed their interactions with their race-avoidant or universalistic counselors. They found that the pseudo-clients who raised issues of race were likely to either concede to their counselor's universalistic responses or to disengage from their counselor. Frequently, when the pseudo-clients were met with race-neutralizing responses on presenting their racial issues, they would become exasperated. In essence, the clients needed to negotiate their counselor's posture on race. Continuing to build on this theme from the perspective of the therapists, Knox, Burkard, Johnson, Suzuki, and Ponterotto (2003) used consensual qualitative research to look at how African American and European American psychologists experienced and responded to race issues in cross-racial therapy dyads. The data from structured interviewing of the psychologists suggested that although participants reported similar training experiences, rates of preparatory, supervisory, and continuing education experiences that related to race and multicultural issues were much higher for the African American therapists. Not surprisingly, therefore, European American therapists reported greater discomfort about addressing race in cross-racial therapy dyads.

As well as investigate therapist self-perceptions and experiences about addressing race, qualitative approaches can give us information about multicultural development and supervision (Fukuyama, 1994), inform us about identity development as multicultural practitioners (Constantine, 1999), and illuminate processes of racism (Robinson & Ginter, 1999). Ponterotto (1998) commented that qualitative approaches were also particularly well-suited for multicultural training research because of the need for in-depth and highly descriptive studies that came out of the grounded theory tradition. While theory-driven or deductive approaches flourish, there is a need to balance them with theory-developing or inductive approaches.

CULTURAL SENSITIVITY IN CONDUCTING QUALITATIVE RESEARCH

There are two different levels of cultural sensitivity to be accounted for in this research paradigm. On the first level is the foundational understanding that all qualitative research is informed by culture. Because all individuals, including the researcher, are cultural beings, the impetus, focus, and methods of the research will be shaped by the researcher's worldview. Given this position, it is impossible to conduct culturally neutral qualitative research. Thus, all strategies are developed to identify, articulate, and manage subjectivity rather than to eliminate it. There are several important aspects of highlighting the cultural lens and participant perspectives which will be discussed in the following sections.

BRACKETING

The task of the researcher is to interrogate the cultural lens he or she brings to the research, explaining it to the reader so as to provide the reader with a direction from which to judge the research. This reflexivity (McLeod, 1996) in qualitative research defines the trustworthiness of the researcher. It also allows researchers to *bracket* their own subjectivities to allow participant voices and meanings to be more clearly heard.

For example, when a European Canadian woman seeks to do research with women of color (Gerrard, 1995), it is critical to articulate why she chose to engage in such research as well as describe the conflicting tensions that her participants felt and her own positions on these issues. With less soul searching, but as much attention to detail, the authors of a study on African American and European American therapists' experiences of addressing race in psychotherapy (Knox et al., 2003) described themselves in terms of their identities, positions, and experiences with multiculturalism. Obviously, this is very different from the quantitative research position, where the investigators are separate from their research and are subjects who report but are not scrutinized in turn. In qualitative research, the question is one of exploring and clarifying the boundaries of subjectivity rather than seeking to banish it. On a related note, Nevid and Sta Maria (1999) point out that it is important when working with participants from ethnic minority groups that have a long history of oppression to acknowledge cultural mistrust. A researcher needs to both account and prepare for the potentially mistrustful and hostile reactions and responses she or he may encounter and strategize means of building trust.

A helpful technique to use to sensitize the researcher to cultural issues is the use of the bracketing interview (Fontana & Frey, 2000). Prior to entering the field to collect data, the researcher is thoroughly interviewed by a colleague. The focus of the interview is on the researcher's subjectivity and background. One particular strategy to delineate this is to ask the researcher questions similar to those the researcher proposes to ask participants. Because qualitative researchers often bring identities as well as intrinsic experiences and perspectives to their research, this process allows those phenomenological assumptions to be articulated and then set aside so as to sensitize the researcher to what may emerge from the participants.

Sensitizing Research Questions

Once the researcher has developed a coherent statement that explains his or her cultural location, it is time to apply a cultural lens to the research itself. Several areas are germane here that are peculiar to qualitative inquiry. On the one hand, qualitative research can be explicitly designed to be action research, focused on sociopolitical and historical problems of domination, alienation, and social struggle. For instance, Gerrard (1991) explored the intersections of racism and sexism in three stories of women of color experiencing counseling. Constantine (1999) analyzed the themes arising in 17 autobiographical narratives of racism generated by counselors. On the other hand, a research method that strives to capture the richness and complexity of experience may also be extremely intrusive and potentially harmful. It is necessary to tread cautiously when the focus of research is on areas of vulnerability, with the concurrent potential for impeding and doing harm to clients (McLeod, 1996). There are a number of resources available to researchers to sensitize them to the issues relevant to the population of interest. For instance, Stubben (2001) details some of the particular issues around American Indian and Alaskan Native family values and environments that a researcher must be sensitive to in conducting research with such populations.

Examining areas of social identity such as race, gender, sexual orientation, or socioeconomic class, where the researcher is treading on sensitive ground mined by the experiences of oppression and discrimination, requires sensitivity. As an example, if the researcher wishes to study the experiences of Latinas, the questions designed to explore this issue will need to be asked only after building a trusting relationship. It will be important for the researcher to develop a coherent explanation of who is meant by the identity label "Latina." Are participants approached on the basis of self-identification, identification based on appearance, familial heritage, identified culture of origin, or perhaps familiarity with Spanish? This is where work done prior to entering the field is crucial so that the researcher is not caught completely off-guard by complexities about which he or she is unaware. Imagine the potential harm done by a naïve researcher, unaware of the implications, who expresses surprise that the Latina participant does not speak Spanish. The Latina participant needs to understand the researcher's interest, believe that the experience of sharing will have ultimate positive value, and feel safe when she chooses to disclose. The consequences of the process undertaken by the researcher impact not only the participant's safety but also the quality of the data. After all, a participant who is distrustful will either refuse to participate or will give shallow or misleading responses. The complexity and richness of her experience will be lost to the study.

PROTECTING PARTICIPANTS

Beyond asking unsafe or potentially hurtful questions, ethical issues arise because anonymity is difficult to maintain in intimate samples where stories told are saturated with unique markers and changing too many such markers will drastically change the landscape of the narrative. Given the exploratory nature of the inquiry, risks are harder to determine in advance. Finally, the close contact between researcher and participant blurs traditional boundaries that separate researcher and subject (Grafanaki, 1996). Researchers must give careful attention to the protection of their participants. Beyond the requirements for the protection of human subjects, researchers must also consider the particular threats that can arise when someone speaks out about issues of culture or oppression. For instance, if a researcher is exploring the organizational system of a school, is it possible to sufficiently disguise the voices of the two African American teachers while retaining the integrity of their experience? If there are few people of color in the setting, simply changing the specific ethnic group identification will not create anonymity. Is there a possibility that members of the setting who read the research can not only identify the participants but also negatively target them for speaking out about racial matters?

Researchers can use several strategies to protect their participants. Careful explanation to participants about the risks of participation encourages participants to give informed consent, as well as demonstrating respect for the participant's ability to weigh risks and choose with deliberation. Developing multiple ways to protect anonymity, including inviting participants to choose pseudonyms, changing identifying details of location, and conducting interviews in neutral sites, is also helpful. Often, presenting participants with completed research reports allows them the option to comment, critique, and perhaps withdraw participation if the risks are too great. In presenting research, developing blended narratives that exemplify the emerging themes also reduces the presence of unique identifying markers.

TRIANGULATION

Triangulation is the combination of various methodologies in the study of the same phenomena (Patton, 1990). Taken from the term used in land surveying, it implies that taking bearings in two or more directions allows one to locate oneself more accurately at the intersection. Triangulation can take place in (1) data collection, using a variety of data sources; (2) investigators, using multiple investigators or evaluators; or (3) theories, by applying multiple perspectives to a single problem.

As pointed out by Halbrook and Ginsberg (1997), ethnographic transference and countertransference become significant issues to explore in conducting qualitative research. As foundational elements of analytic theories of psychotherapy, transference and countertransference originally referred to the client's displacement of feelings and attitudes applicable to significant figures onto the analyst and vice versa (Reber, 1995). In the context of qualitative research, it refers to the displacement of such feelings and attitudes between the researcher and the participant. For instance, when a counselor begins interviewing participants who had been clients in counseling, many may respond to the investigator as a counselor rather than a researcher (Choudhuri, 2003). In turn, the boundaries of how the researcher responds to these participants may begin to blur as to whether a response is therapeutic or investigative. It is important that researchers explore and address these issues in multiple ways.

As mentioned earlier, bracketing is important to articulate why the research became the focus of the researcher's attention so as to be able to catch and filter the prevailing reactivities that may lead to ethnographic countertransference. During the course of the research, investigators may use multiple interviewers to gather data from different sorts of interview relationships. Therefore, the ways in which Vietnamese American participants are responding specifically to a Vietnamese American interviewer may be highlighted by the different content of the participant's responses to African American and European American interviewers. Stephenson, Wolfe, Coughlan, and Koehn (1999) conducted two sets of qualitative interviews with older adults, changing the gender of the interviewer/participant pairing to have both cross-gender and same-gender interviews to assess the differences. They found that both the male and female participants focused on very different topics and content based on the interviewer's gender. Having multiple interviewers allowed for this effect to be discovered and discussed. Another method of exploring these issues is the safety of multiple staggered interviews with the same participant, where the researcher can explore the content of previous interviews and remain alert to transferential phenomena, as well as bring it up to be explored with the participants. Sharing transcripts of interviews with participants for them to expand on, correct, or modify is another way of addressing these issues. The act of bringing the research *to* participants rather than simply getting it *from* them invites participants to become partners in the research, and often they will address the issues of authority and identity spontaneously.

One of the advantages of qualitative research is the flexibility and creativity that can be used. For instance, Kim, Brenner, Liang, and Asay (2003), in their study of 1.5-generation Asian Americans, decided to use electronic mail as a way to safeguard their participants from shame and possible loss of face as they described sensitive adaptation experiences. Given traditional Asian cultural values of restraint, the investigators believed that a face-to-face interview format would reduce forthright and comprehensive self-disclosure. On the other hand, Hendrix (1998), in researching college students' perceptions of professor credibility by race, deliberately chose to be open with her identity as a Black woman researcher investigating student perceptions. Rather than having White confederates assist in interviewing White students, she chose to present to the reader her rationale for not doing so and then explore how both Black and White student interviewees responded to her.

SENSITIVE DATA ANALYSIS

The point when the researcher leaves the field and begins making sense of the data is sometimes referred to as "data mining," with a very real sense that the researcher is entering the overwhelming, claustrophobic, and dimly illuminated code mines (Glesne & Peshkin, 1992). This is the part of the journey where the researcher begins to make sense of the data and de facto applies a particular cultural lens to the material. The data, too, often consist of an intersubjective dialectical experience (Crossley, 1996): the record of conversations between researcher and participants, the record of observations by the researcher, or memos by the researcher articulating responses, reactions, and experiences in the fieldwork. Even texts and historical materials that may be part of the data have been purposefully selected. On this material, the researcher strives to impose some order and meaning. Methods to maintain cultural sensitivity and highlight multiple representations are necessary.

Strategies include using inductive analysis, so that codes, categories, and themes come out of the data rather than being imposed. Starting with indigenous concepts and typologies (Patton, 1990), that is, verbal categories that were used by participants rather than asked by researchers, helps this process. For instance, if the researcher was studying children in a diverse sixth-grade classroom, starting to code by applying words used by the children and teachers rather than by the theoretical literature may open more possibilities of capturing the meaning of the diversity experience from the perspective of the participants.

Triangulation is again important in data verification and validation. Many studies use teams of researchers to examine the data and code separately, before coming together to share their coding systems. In some cases, the primary researcher will code the data and then ask an external reader to review the codes assigned. Alternatively, a helpful set of participants may review preliminary findings and give feedback and critique of the data analysis. This testimonial validity, where the interpretation is judged by those whose experience is being represented is an important strategy (Chwalisz, Wiersma, & Stark-Wroblewski, 1996). Another method is to search for negative cases, the instances that do not fit the identified pattern. Such contradictions may be the exception that proves the rule, or they may cause modifications in the rule or even cast doubt on the rules generated.

Epochè (Douglass & Moustakas, 1984) is the point in phenomenological qualitative analysis where the researcher requires a suspension of judgment so as to be able to appreciate the phenomena without imposing meaning too soon. One way to strive to meet this challenge is to test out rival explanations to generate alternative explanations.

RHETORIC AND REPRESENTATION

One of the most significant tests of qualitative research comes in the aftermath. The data are gathered and the analysis is complete; leaving the final task of writing. This is often the most difficult as well as the most potentially problematic part of the method. The researcher must represent the phenomena as accurately as possible while striving to be intellectually honest regarding the representational fiction. The postmodernist stance claims that all representations, because they *are* representations, are embedded in the language, culture, institutions, and political environment of the representer (Said, 1979). Thus, all representations are to some extent fictional, or storytelling, because the representer is forming this fiction from the raw material of the participants as described. In conducting multicultural research, the researcher who represents the phenomena of his or her participants must be aware that there are sociocultural and political dimensions and must make such awareness an explicit part of the story (Dumont, 1978). The power relations involved in any project where human beings are the subject of knowledge must be contended with. The art of using rhetoric becomes a tricky business. It is important that representations of the research use culturally congruent metaphors, develop thoughtful explanations of lived experience, and are sensitive to the danger of reducing complexity to stereotypes in the service of minimalism. For instance, in representing the family issues of youth classified as delinquent, Madden-Derdich, Leonard, and Gunnell (2002) stated that they wanted to both validate experiences verified in previous research as well as offer voices that were underrepresented in the literature. They noticed and highlighted the divergence in perceptions between youths and parents about problem areas in the family. Whereas the parents were focused, as is much of the current literature, on altering the children's behavior, the children wanted to alter interactions and communications within the family. Rather than reaching for a blaming explanation, the authors argued that perhaps these parents placed responsibility for change on their children due to a cumulative perception of their own powerlessness.

ROLE OF THE READER

On the converse side is that cultural sensitivity and dealing with these contradictions of who represents whom, how and with what purpose, and in which context with what consequence is as much a task of the reader as it is of the writer. One of the accepted givens of quantitative psychological research is that research and representation are the responsibility of the researcher. The consumers of research are relatively passive. However, in qualitative research, the reader has as many responsibilities to make meaning of the representation. The reader is the final test of the credibility and legitimacy of the research. Does it have face validity? Does the researcher articulate his or her position and subjectivity adequately? Is there sufficient thick description for the reader to judge whether the themes are legitimate? Does it seem real? Can the study provide a new understanding or perception of phenomena? These are all questions the reader must struggle with in reading any qualitative research. If investigation of phenomena, analysis, and representation are sociocultural acts, than so is reading an active endeavor of applying cultural sensitivity and critique.

CONCLUSION

One of the virtues of qualitative research is its inclusionary nature and ability to give voice to marginalized people through both the research process itself as well as the narrative. The importance of this kind of research cannot be overemphasized, particularly when dealing with issues of cultural sensitivity. Qualitative research has the potential to contribute to dramatic paradigm changes and offer psychologists and other mental health workers an opportunity to address the Multicultural Guidelines from both primary perspectives. In addition, as Hoshmand (1997) commented, instead of simply conceptualizing research through the methodology used, it can be conceptualized as located in particular contexts within particular subcultures of practice. Instead of just using research to inform us about cultural practice, we can also turn our gaze to the embodied research itself as a form of cultural practice.

To engage in research that is a transaction across cultures, the researcher must first explore and articulate knowledge of self and social identities and then, in the act of encountering and engaging in the research, develop an understanding of multiple cultural contexts, experiences, and identities (APA, 2003).

REFERENCES

American Psychological Association. (2003). Guidelines on multicultural education, training, research, practice, and organizational change for psychologists. *American Psychologist, 58*, 377–402.

Blumer, H. (1969). *Symbolic interactionism: Perspective and method.* Englewood Cliffs, NJ: Prentice-Hall.

Bogdan, R. C., & Biklen, S. K. (1992). *Qualitative research for education* (2nd ed.). Boston: Allyn & Bacon.

Bracey, J. R., Bámaca, M. Y., & Umaña-Taylor, A. J. (2004). Examining ethnic identity and self-esteem among biracial and monoracial adolescents. *Journal of Youth and Adolescence, 33*, 123–32.

Choudhuri, D. D. (2003). Qualitative research and multicultural competency: An argument for inclusion. In D. Pope-Davis, H. Coleman, W. Liu, & R. Toporek (Eds.), *The handbook of multicultural counseling competencies.* Thousand Oaks, CA: Sage.

Chwalisz, K., Wiersma, N., Stark-Wroblewski, K. (1996). A quasi-qualitative investigation of strategies used in qualitative categorization. *Journal of Counseling Psychology, 43*, 502–509.

Constantine, M. G. (1999). Racism's impact on counselors' personal and professional lives: A response to the personal narratives on racism. *Journal of Counseling and Development, 77*, 68–72.

Crossley, N. (1996). *Intersubjectivity: The fabric of social becoming.* London: Sage.

Douglass, B., & Moustakas, C. (1984). *Heuristic inquiry: The internal search to know.* Detroit: Center for Humanistic Studies.

Dumont, J. (1978). *The headman and I: Ambiguity and ambivalence in the fieldworking experience.* Austin: University of Texas Press.

Fontana, A., & Frey, J. H. (2000). The interview: From structured questions to negotiated text. In N. K. Denzin & Y. S. Lincoln (Eds.), *Handbook of qualitative research* (2nd ed.). Thousand Oaks, CA: Sage.

Fukuyama, M. A. (1994). Critical incidents in multicultural counseling supervision: A phenomenological approach to supervision research. *Counselor Education and Supervision, 34*, 142–151.

Gerrard, N. (1991). Racism and sexism, together, in counseling: Three women of color tell their stories. *Canadian Journal of Counseling, 25*, 555–566.

Gerrard, N. (1995). Some painful experiences of a white feminist therapist doing research with women of color. In J. Adleman & G. Enguidanos (Eds.), *Racism in the lives of women: Testimony, theory, and guides to antiracist practice.* Binghamton, NY: Harrington Park Press.

Gibson, P. A. (2002). Caregiving role affects family relationships of African American grandmothers as new mothers again: A phenomenological perspective. *Journal of Marital and Family Therapy, 28*, 341–353.

Gillem, A. R., Cohn, L. R., & Throne, C. (2001). Black identity in biracial Black/White people: A comparison of Jacqueline who refuses to be exclusively Black and Adolphus who wishes he were. *Cultural diversity and Ethnic Minority Psychology, 7,* 182–196.

Glesne, C., & Peshkin, A. (1992). Becoming qualitative researchers: An introduction. White Plains, NY: Longman.

Grafanaki, S. (1996). How research can change the researcher: The need for sensitivity, flexibility, and ethical boundaries in conducting qualitative research in counselling/psychotherapy. *British Journal of Guidance and counseling, 24,* 329–338.

Halbrook, B., & Ginsberg, R. (1997). Ethnographic countertransference in qualitative research: Implications for mental health counseling. *Journal of Mental Health Counseling, 19,* 87–93.

Hendrix, K. G. (1998). Student perceptions of the influence of race on professor credibility. *Journal of Black Studies, 28,* 738–763.

Heppner, P. P., Kivlighan, D. M., & Wampold, B. E. (1992). *Research design in counseling.* Pacific Grove, CA: Brooks/Cole.

Hill, C. E., Thompson, B. J., & Williams, E. N. (1997). A guide to conducting consensual qualitative research. *Counseling Psychologist, 25,* 517–572.

Hoshmand, L. T. (1997). The normative context of research practice. *Counseling Psychologist, 25,* 599–605.

Kim, B. S., Brenner, B. R., Liang, C. T., & Asay, P. A. (2003). A qualitative study of adaptation experiences of 1.5 Generation Asian Americans. *Cultural Diversity and Ethnic Minority Psychology, 9,* 156–170.

Knox, S., Burkard, A. W., Johnson, A. J., Suzuki, L. A., & Ponterotto, J. G. (2003). African American and European American therapists' experiences of addressing race in cross-racial psychotherapy dyads. *Journal of Counseling Psychology, 50,* 466–481.

Madden-Derdich, D., Leonard, S. A., & Gunnell, G. A. (2002). Parents' and children's perceptions of family processes inner-city families with delinquent youths: A qualitative investigation. *Journal of Marital and Family therapy, 28,* 355–369.

McLeod, J. (1996). Qualitative approaches to research in counseling and psychotherapy: Issues and challenges. *British Journal of Guidance and Counselling, 24,* 309–316.

Nevid, J. S., & Sta Maria, N. L. (1999). Multicultural issues in qualitative research. *Psychology and Marketing, 16,* 305–326.

Olesen, V. (1994). Feminisms and models of qualitative research. In N. K. Densin & Y. S. Lincoln (Eds.), *Handbook of qualitative research* (pp. 158–174). Thousand Oaks, CA: Sage.

Patton, M. Q. (1990). *Qualitative evaluation and research methods.* Newbury Park, CA: Sage.

Ponterotto, J. G. (1998). Charting a course for research in multicultural counseling training. *Counseling Psychologist, 26,* 43–68.

Ponterotto, J. G. (2002). Qualitative research methods: The fifth force in psychology. *Counseling Psychologist, 30,* 394–406.

Reber, A. S. (Ed.). (1995). *Dictionary of psychology* (2nd ed.). London: Penguin.

Rennie, D. L. (1996). Fifteen years of doing qualitative research on psychotherapy. *British Journal of Guidance and Counselling, 24,* 317–327.

Robinson, T., & Ginter, E. (Eds.). (1999). Racism: Healing its effects [Special issue]. *Journal of Counseling and Development, 77,* 4–72.

Said, E. I. (1979). *Orientalism.* New York: Vintage.

Stephenson, P. H., Wolfe, N. K., Coughlan, R., & Koehn, S. D. (1999). A methodological discourse on gender, independence, and frailty: Applied dimensions of identity construction in old age. *Journal of Aging Studies, 13,* 391–401.

Strauss, A., & Corbin, J. (1990). *Basics of qualitative research: Grounded theory procedures and techniques.* Newbury Park, CA: Sage.

Stubben, J. D. (2001). Working with and conducting research among American Indian families. *The American Behavioral Scientist, 44,* 1466–1483.

Thompson, C. E., & Jenal, S. T. (1994). Interracial and intraracial quasi-counseling interactions when counselors avoid discussing race. *Journal of Counseling Psychology, 41,* 484–491.

Thompson, C. E., Worthington, R., & Atkinson, D. R. (1994). Counselor content orientation, counselor race, and Black women's cultural mistrust and self-disclosures. *Journal of Counseling Psychology, 41,* 484–491.

Walsh-Bowers, R. (2002). Constructing qualitative knowledge in psychology. *Canadian Psychology, 43,* 163–179.

PART V

Concluding Thoughts

CHAPTER 17

Future Considerations for Fostering Multicultural Competence in Mental Health and Educational Settings: Social Justice Implications

SALLY M. HAGE

> We must be trained to do public policy work and to advocate for social justice. This work can and must be done by us as citizens, not just as mental health professionals.
>
> Dworkin and Yi (2003, p. 277)

> Multicultural counseling competence must be about social justice—providing equal access and opportunity, being inclusive, and removing individual and systemic barriers to fair mental health services.
>
> Sue (2001, p. 801)

THROUGHOUT THIS BOOK, experts in the field of multicultural counseling have shared strategies, critical incidents, and case examples with the aim of bringing to light the practical implications of each of the "Guidelines on Multicultural Education, Training, Research, Practice, and Organizational Change for Psychologists" (American Psychological Association [APA], 2003) for various areas in psychology. The collective writings of these well-known scholars, researchers, and practitioners provide a critical bridge for psychologists and mental health professionals between the broader, aspirational objectives of the Multicultural Guidelines ("knowing that") and the specific knowledge and skills necessary for carrying out the multicultural competencies model ("knowing how"; Johnson, 1987). Sue (2001) notes two specific outcomes that are sought when implementing multicultural competence. The first goal is "providing relevant treatment to all populations," that is, clients of diverse cultural, ethnic, and racial backgrounds (p. 800). To a large extent, the focus of this book is about accomplishing this first goal through the concrete application of the aspirations of the Multicultural Guidelines to various settings in psychology. The second desired outcome suggested by Sue for implementing multicultural competence is the development of theories, practices, policies, and organizational structures that are responsive to all groups. This second goal recognizes the importance of working collaboratively with members of marginalized communities to generate strategies to intervene at a systemic level, not just a micro level. Such strategies are ultimately aimed at preventing the negative consequences of oppression in the lives of people of color and other groups who share unequal power in society because of their immigration, age, socioeconomic status, religious heritage, physical ability, or sexual orientation. As Sue indicates, both of these levels of involvement—providing relevant treatment for diverse populations and developing theories, policies, and structures responsive to all groups—are "truly about social justice" (p. 800).

In this final chapter, future considerations for fostering multicultural competencies by expanding the social justice efforts of psychologists and mental health professionals in organizations, institutions, and society are presented. A definition of social justice is also provided. In addition, this chapter discusses specific strategies that mental health professionals may use to develop their competence in addressing social justice issues in their work.

DEFINING SOCIAL JUSTICE

Social justice refers to the fair and equitable distribution of power, resources, and obligations in society (Prilleltensky & Nelson, 1997). Social justice concerns include issues related to the justice of processes and procedures as well as issues related to the justice of outcomes (Van den Bos, 2003). Fundamental principles underlying this definition include values of inclusion, collaboration, cooperation, equal access, and equal opportunity. Such values are also the foundation of a democratic and egalitarian society (Sue, 2001). Finally, although social justice has not ordinarily been associated with issues of health, it is important to recognize the crucial link that exists between social justice and well-being. For individuals, the absence of justice often represents increased physical and emotional suffering as well as greater vulnerability to illness. But social justice issues and access to resources are also inexorably tied to the collective well-being (e.g., relationships and political welfare) of families, communities, and society (Prilleltensky & Nelson, 2002).

THE MULTICULTURAL GUIDELINES AND SOCIAL JUSTICE

Although the focus of the Multicultural Guidelines is not explicitly social justice, issues of justice and fairness are the backdrop and foundation to these competencies. In essence, the Multicultural Guidelines provide a framework for doing social justice in the domains of education, research, practice, and organizations (Speight & Vera, 2004). The Multicultural Guidelines address the need to take a broad and systemic approach by addressing varied roles of mental health practitioners, including addressing concerns at the organizational and systemic levels. In addition, they offer a clear statement in favor of involvement by psychologists in social change processes:

> Psychologists are in a position to provide leadership as agents of prosocial change, advocacy, and social justice, thereby promoting societal under-standing, affirmation, and appreciation of multiculturalism against the damaging effects of individual, institutional, and societal racism, prejudice, and all forms of oppression based on stereotyping and discrimination. (APA, 2003, p. 382)

Further, the Multicultural Guidelines refer to Principle F of the APA (1992) code of ethics: that our work should contribute to social justice. The last section of the Multicultural Guidelines is noteworthy in that it explicitly addresses the role of psychology in social and organizational change and policy development. In this section, the authors point to the "multiple opportunities" psychologists have to lead change and influence policy at a systemic level.

Notably, less attention in the multicultural competencies literature has been devoted to intervening at a systemic or macro level (Vera & Speight, 2003). This point is not to minimize the considerable contribution of the multicultural competencies in maximizing "the optimal development of clients and client systems" (Sue, 2001, p. 802). Ivey and Collins (2003) clearly express this point when they assert that the multicultural competencies themselves are a "major organizational intervention" to further social justice in the profession (p. 294). However, as suggested by Prilleltensky and Nelson (2002), what those committed to social justice "are able to achieve within micro and mesolevel settings is constrained by macro-level

social structures, processes and policies" (p. 167). For example, constructions of race are expressed and supported through macro systems that
help shape public discourse, language, and institutional practices
(Thompson & Neville, 1999). Hence, while it is critical to support the ongoing efforts of the multicultural competencies movement to transform
the traditional practice of psychology (i.e., in individual counseling and
small group interventions) to be more culturally relevant, it is also imperative to explore potential pathways to expand psychology's commitment and ability to engage in broader social change. Such work, including
efforts at social justice and social policy change, has been identified as
the "next frontier" for psychology (Prilleltensky & Nelson, 2002, p. 176).

THE SOCIOPOLITICAL CONTEXT FOR EXPANDING THE COMMITMENT TO SOCIAL JUSTICE

Several changes in the sociopolitical context itself necessitate that the
field of psychology give increased emphasis to social justice issues. One
of the most significant of these changes, addressed in the Multicultural
Guidelines, relates to the increasing racial and ethnic diversity of the
United States. Despite changes in the composition of the U.S. population,
people of color and women continue to be significantly underrepresented in positions of power in business, educational, and governmental
organizations and institutions. This imbalance in the allocation of power
and resources is likely to continue unless there is a concerted effort to
bring about widespread changes in society to eliminate bigotry and prejudice (Sue, 2003).

A second change in the sociopolitical context that calls for greater emphasis on social justice issues is the increasing economic disparity that
exists between people who are rich and people who are poor. About 35
million people (12.1%) in the U.S. population live below the official
poverty line, with about 16% of individuals under age 18 living in poverty
(Bureau of the Census, 2002). More than 43 million adults lack health insurance, and more than 33% of Hispanic citizens have no health insurance (U.S. Department of Health and Human Services [USDHHS], 2000).
People of color, women, immigrants, those without a high school education, and residents in rural and urban areas are disproportionately represented among those who live in poverty (Haveman, 1994). Further, the
"new poor" include those who do have access to information technology
and the education and skills to use technology (McNutt, 1998).

In his book *The Working Poor: Invisible in America,* David Shipler (2004)
chronicles the daily lives of the working poor, who make up the majority of
low-income Americans. Due to their lack of income, such families typically

live in lower-quality housing and are without adequate health insurance. Such housing may contain lead paint and be infested with mold, dust mites, and roaches. The infestation translates to lower IQ, attention deficits, and frequent illness among children. Frequently ill children are often absent from school, which means missed work and, ultimately, lost employment and income for the families. These children also tend to do poorly in school, which makes their chances of escaping a life similar to that of their parents seem insurmountable without intervention by concerned groups of individuals who are willing to take a stand and enact widespread changes to interrupt this cycle.

A critical question offered by Shipler (2004) and others (e.g., Speight & Vera, 2004) is whether concerned professionals have both the skills and the motivation (i.e., the will) to do what is needed to alter the inequities. The task of intervening in unjust systems is largely about creating access—access to education, resources, information, technology, health care, and opportunity (Jackson, 2000). Yet, a number of significant obstacles continue to stand in the way of increased involvement by mental health professionals in such social justice efforts. Briefly, these obstacles include institutional resistance by mainstream psychology, insistence on individual-level explanations and individual remedies for social problems, training and interventions devoid of social and cultural issues, traditional conceptions of value-free science, institutional career pressures and the need for economic survival, and human service delivery systems that are unresponsive to social justice interventions (Fox, 2003; Helms, 2003). Preparing our field to overcome these obstacles will require a transformation in both our thinking and the way we do our work. An important question to explore is what such a transformation would look like for mental health professionals.

STRENGTHENING THE COMMITMENT OF MENTAL HEALTH PROFESSIONALS TO SOCIAL JUSTICE

This section will discuss several changes that are needed in the training and orientation of mental health professionals in order to strengthen psychology's commitment to social justice.

SYSTEMS INTERVENTION

The first change is for mental health professionals to receive specific training in how to intervene at a systems level, not just with individual clients (Atkinson, Thompson, & Grant, 1993; Helms, 2003; Lewis, Lewis, Daniels, & D'Andrea, 1998). This training needs to include an emphasis on understanding human behavior through an ecological or contextual framework, that is, that human behavior is multiply determined by a series of dynamic interactions between social systems (Bronfenbrenner, 1979; Neville & Mobley, 2001).

The integration of social justice principles at the macro or systems level may require looking for theoretical frameworks and interventions that have been found to work in other disciplines, such as public health, sociology, law, and consulting psychology (Baluch, Pieterse, & Bolden, 2004; Helms, 2003; Prilleltensky & Nelson, 1997). As reflected in the Multicultural Guidelines, the "path to cultural competence requires a broad and integrated approach" (p. 816).

COLLABORATION

Mental health professionals also need to develop collaborations among multiple areas within psychology, particularly as a number of these fields already are oriented toward social change or social justice. "We do not need to reinvent the wheel; we just need to find those that are well oiled" (Prilleltensky & Prilleltensky, 2003, p. 279). Perhaps one avenue to further develop collaboration is for the nine divisions within APA to form a coalition of divisions for social justice. Prilleltensky and Prilleltensky (2003) also suggest creating alliances with the people we seek to help and with other professionals, so as to reconcile the roles of healers and social change agents. As noted by Brazilian educator Paulo Freire (1979), collective activism by members of oppressed groups is essential because they will not gain liberation by chance, "but through the praxis of their quest for it, through their recognition of the necessity to fight for it" (p. 27).

The disabilities rights movement, following the model of the 1960s civil rights movement, is a recent example of a collaborative network of clients, advocates, and service providers who organized themselves to create a powerful force for social change. Working together, they changed the perceptions of what it means to be considered disabled. Increasingly, professional services are now based on the belief that the medical model is ineffective and that oppressive institutions, not their victims, must be changed. This transformation has happened because persons with disabilities and their supporters learned the value of advocating for their rights, including the right to certain income and medical benefits, and how to influence legislation (Middleton, Rollins, & Harley, 1999).

INTERNATIONAL PERSPECTIVE

Mental health professionals also need to be trained to understand social justice issues from an international perspective (Lee, 1997). An experience that educator Michael Apple (1997) had while traveling in an Asian country illustrates this point. He noticed numerous signs advertising a U.S.-based fast food restaurant and asked his traveling companion, a local villager, about them. His companion told him that they represented vast tracts of land the military-dominated government had given over at a very low cost to a supplier of a U.S. based fast food restaurant to grow potatoes for the restaurant's french fries. From the local villager's perspective, the government's objective of attracting foreign capital came at an enormous cost. Whole communities of people had been displaced into large slums in the cities, which lacked schools, hospitals, running water, and housing, so that people in the "developed" world could have inexpensive french fries. Apple reflects on the meaning of this story for our educational efforts:

> The denial of basic rights, the destruction of the environment, the deadly conditions under which people (barely) survive, the lack of a meaningful future for the thousands of children I noted in my story—all of this is not only or primarily a "text" to be deciphered in our academic volumes as we pursue our postmodern themes. It is a reality millions of people experience in their bodies every day. Educational work that is not connected to a powerful understanding of these realities . . . is in danger of losing its soul. The lives of our children demand no less. (p. 124)

Too often, the countless stresses related to our work as psychologists and mental health professionals lead to a kind of tunnel vision, making it possible to ignore the global context of our times. This story illustrates the importance of connecting the work we do with what is happening in the larger community. If indeed power is about defining reality, and what is true or valued (Sue & Sue, 2003), then a social justice orientation demands that we be aware of how the numerous systems that are part of U.S. society, including economic, governmental, and educational systems, define truth for the global community (Douce, 2004; Dworkin & Yi, 2003). Such work can and should begin in the local context (as we also need to apply the social justice model in our own communities), but it also needs to be thoughtfully concerned with social justice practices and the state of power and oppression around the world.

HOLISTIC APPROACH

Holistic remedies are also vital to the social change process and to creating a just society. Unjust conditions, such as poverty, result from a "constellation of difficulties that magnify one another" (Shipler, 2004, p. 285). Hence, all of the social problems contributing to an unjust society (e.g., education, housing, employment, health care) need to be tackled at once. Too often, human services organizations, such as educational, psychological, and medical services, deal only with the particular problem clients present to them. Without more holistic efforts, mental health professionals, "despite good intentions, too often reinforce oppression even when they think they are working to ameliorate its consequences" (Fox, 2003, pp. 299–300).

An example of the kind of social justice efforts that need to take place is beginning to surface in a small number of settings across the United States. Collaborative partnerships are being created among medical clinics, counselors, social workers, and legal services. When a child enters a clinic with a medical condition, such as asthma, a counselor advocate or nurse conducts a home visit to assess the presence of environmental factors, such as rundown housing, and may also visit the child's school. Following the assessment, the advocate may contact the landlord to request that needed repairs be made and, if necessary, work with the client to utilize attorneys and social workers employed by the clinic to press for safe housing and other benefits, such as Medicaid. Without such an intensive, holistic approach, the impact any one organization or professional can make would likely be shallow and leave people vulnerable to the next crisis (Shipler, 2004).

Focus on Prevention

Last, a focus on prevention needs to be a key component of our social justice efforts. Although prevention has a long tradition as a specialty in the field of psychology, it has not enjoyed a very influential position (Romano & Hage, 2000). Intervention has been "primarily remedial when a strong need exists for preventive measures" (Sue, 2001, p. 816). Significant barriers, such as a focus on individual remediation, the influence of the medical model, and training requirements, have hindered further development of a prevention focus. One reason prevention is critical is the low remedial service use rates and options for mental health services in the United States. For example, Hoagwood and Koretz (1996) estimate that 60% to 80% of children in need of mental health treatment do not receive it. If we are to commit ourselves to addressing the needs of the most vulnerable (e.g., children, youth, people living in poverty, older adults), then we must search for ways to collaborate with schools and governmental and community organizations to prevent hardship, not just at the level of providing individuals with life skills or better coping mechanisms for dealing with existing problems, but at the level of systemic change (Hage, 2003).

Conyne (1997) aptly describes the characteristics of a prevention orientation, including an approach that is "before the fact," ecological, multidisciplinary, collaborative, and aimed at empowerment. A preventive orientation also starts with a vision of people as fundamentally healthy, resilient, and growth-oriented (Romano & Hage, 2000). It is significant that the majority of the work in primary prevention has adopted a person-centered approach at the micro levels (e.g., teaching life skills). Few attempts at macro-level social system change exist. The danger in pursuing only person-centered interventions is that unjust social conditions are ignored. One needs to ask whether our prevention work addresses the "causes of the causes" or only the surface of the causes (Prilleltensky & Nelson, 1997).

The question of how to infuse a prevention orientation into training programs and guidelines is an important one. The task is much like and intersects with efforts to integrate multicultural competence training into counseling training. It is not simply about adding one or even two more courses to the curriculum, or about tacking on extra reading or lecture material to course outlines. It is about fundamentally changing the lens and context for our training efforts, shifting from a remedial, individually focused, adaptation approach to one focused on before-the-fact intervention involving groups, communities, and social systems and ultimately aimed at social change. Further, the voices, experiences, and leadership of members of traditionally disenfranchised groups need to be represented and integrated into our prevention training and intervention efforts (Eddy, Martinez, Morgan-Lopez, Smith, & Fisher, 2002). In sum, the goal of such training is to orient psychologists and mental health professionals to a broader application of their counseling work to more effectively and sensitively respond to the tremendous social needs that exist in our communities.

SPECIFIC STRATEGIES FOR PSYCHOLOGISTS AND MENTAL HEALTH PROFESSIONALS TO DEVELOP COMPETENCE IN ADDRESSING SOCIAL JUSTICE IN EDUCATION, RESEARCH, AND PRACTICE

This section will discuss specific strategies psychologists and other mental health professionals might utilize to give greater focus to social justice in educational, research and practice settings.

EDUCATION

Much of the specific content of training programs for psychologists and mental health professionals has historically been directed by accreditation standards and guidelines. To prepare future mental health professionals to give greater emphasis to social justice concerns, classrooms must also become "laboratories for studying social justice issues" and social concerns (Rabow, Stein, & Conley, 1999). Giving more emphasis to social justice issues has several advantages over traditional approaches. A social justice training focus involves us in the principal issues of our increasingly multicultural society, while embracing education as a form of liberation (Freire, 1979). In addition, giving attention to social issues in the classroom makes students' educational experience more meaningful and deeply impacts their lives (Tatum, 1994).

Several aspects of a "liberating" education have been identified in the literature, including the development of critical thinking skills, collaborative and multidisciplinary methods, and stronger community involvement. Before giving attention to each of these aspects, it is important to briefly address one of the central objections to a social justice focus in the classroom, that is, that it is too political. To counter this objection, some have argued that counseling and, in general, the helping professions are not solely an intellectual task, but are also inherently a political one, to the extent that one takes account of the social and cultural context in which clients live (e.g., Varenne, 2003). In fact, it is argued that no education is politically neutral (hooks, 1994). Further some have argued, as educators we need to help students make a connection between the personal and the political. In such a framework, students (and, by extension, clients and research participants) see that their individual experiences do not occur in a vacuum, but are part of the social and cultural context, the lived version of political reality (Brown, 1994).

Critical Thinking Skills

Teaching a social justice model is about integrating a worldview in which the value of social justice plays a central role. It involves teaching others how to critically analyze inequality and oppression in society, along with privileges and experiences in their own life circumstances as they relate to forms of social and historical oppression (Arredondo, 1999; McGoldrick et al., 1999; Middleton et al., 1999). Freire (1979) identifies this process of critical awareness and engagement as "conscientization." The emphasis of this approach is on praxis, or "reflection and action upon the world in order to transform it" (p. 66). Students are active participants in their own education, for "education can only be liberatory when everyone claims knowledge as a field in which we all labor" (hooks, 1994, p. 14). Further, this model assumes that issues of oppression and injustice are relevant whether students are studying human development, ethical standards, or counseling theory (Middleton et al., 1999).

Collaboration

A related aspect of pedagogy oriented toward social justice is that learning is a collaborative process (McGoldrick et al., 1999). Freire (1979) uses the terms "learner-teacher" (referring to the instructor) and "teacher-learner" (referring to the student) to highlight the interaction that is a vital part of educational activities. This model assumes that teachers and students grow together and are mutually empowered in the educational process (hooks, 1994). Teachers and students engage in a "co-intentional" education process and, as such, are both participants "not only in the task of unveiling reality, and thereby coming to know it critically, but in the task of re-creating that knowledge" (Freire, 1979, p. 56). This "engaged pedagogy" (hooks, 1994) is the foundation for later active involvement in a social change process. These active learning methods would also likely support the development of needed skills "for negotiating across administrative levels for the purpose of obtaining high-level commitments and concessions to communitarian social justice goals from the power and resource holders" (Helms, 2003, p. 311).

Interdisciplinary Methods

A social justice approach to education is a challenging task partly because it involves an interdisciplinary focus (Rabow et al., 1999). Graduate students need basic counseling skills and an understanding of the professional helping literature, along with knowledge about power disparities within and across marginalized groups and procedures to alter the distribution of power. Such procedural knowledge includes awareness of laws, regulations, legislation (e.g., RBP Associates, Inc., 1964), and programs that affect diverse groups of people, particularly groups marginalized due to race, ethnicity, or other status. Trainees also need an understanding of policy issues so as to be aware of valuable resources and alternatives available to marginalized groups (Middleton et al., 1999). In sum, educators for social change need to "read and teach broadly" (Arredondo & Perez, 2003, p. 288) to prepare students for the multiple roles connected with social justice advocacy (Atkinson et al., 1993; Lewis et al., 1998).

Community Involvement

A social justice model of education also includes a strong experiential base, which informs students' critical analysis of social problems and social change. Immersion in settings with a transformative and macro-level orientation helps develop one's political literacy about social issues. Examples of such settings include labor unions, environmental organizations, public interest groups, and antipoverty organizations (Prilleltensky &

Nelson, 1997). One approach to strengthening the experiential component of an existing course is to include a service-learning experience (Vera & Speight, 2003). Service learning has been shown to foster a sense of community activism (Hondagneu-Sotelo & Raskoff, 1994), to promote students' moral development (Delve, Mintz, & Stewart, 1990), and to strengthen a commitment to social justice (Roschelle, Turpin, & Elias, 2000). Practica and internships outside the United States are another way to broaden students' experiences and awareness of social justice (Lee, 1997). Such experiences assist students with "looking at America through the eyes of others," as recommended by the Race Advisory Board created by President Clinton (as cited in Sue, 2001, p. 808). In addition, a broad base of experience helps students draw parallels between "particular" (e.g., racism) and general processes of oppression (Thompson, Murry, Harris, & Annan, 2003).

RESEARCH

Research training has traditionally focused on statistics and experimental or quasi-experimental research methods. To prepare psychologists and mental health professionals to give greater emphasis to social justice concerns in their research, they should also be exposed to methods that are particularly oriented toward social change (Prilleltensky & Nelson, 2002). Several principles of social change–oriented research have been identified in the literature, including the importance of attending to the researcher's values and cultural context, an emphasis on working collaboratively with members of marginalized communities, and the significance of additional methodologies (e.g., qualitative methods) in furthering a social justice agenda.

Value-Attentive Context

To give greater emphasis to social justice concerns in research, psychologists and mental health professionals need to carefully consider the context of their scientific work. Serious doubts have been raised about the assumption that it is possible for research to be value-neutral and objective. Some have argued that a researcher who claims such neutrality "runs the risk of reinforcing the societal status quo" (Prilleltensky & Nelson, 2002, p. 50). For example, Chesler (1989) offered a powerful critique of research that presented depictions of women as inferior to men as "truth." The point is to acknowledge that research findings emerge from the interaction of the values and assumptions of the investigator with the unique historical representation of the phenomenon under study (Prilleltensky & Nelson, 2002). Similarly, Fine (1994) encourages researchers to acknowledge the realities of "Self" and "Other" in our work, with whom we are "knottily entangled" (p. 71). What we need to do, writes Fine, is acknowledge the tension existing at the hyphen between these two realities and recognize our position as classed, gendered, raced, and sexual subjects who construct our own locations.

Collaboration

Research that is oriented toward social justice is guided by an awareness of power dynamics and is aimed at social change that benefits people who are marginalized (Kirby & McKenna, 1989). The authentic voices and experiences of people who are alienated in our society (e.g., people in poverty) are at the center of the research efforts. As reflected in the APA (2003) Multicultural Guidelines, such efforts recognize the importance of working collaboratively with members of marginalized communities from the earliest phases of the research (e.g., conceptualization) to ensure that the research is of benefit to participants' communities (Council of National Psychologists for the Advancement of Ethnic Minority Interests, 2000). The goal, as much as possible, is to construct knowledge collaboratively and make ethical and conscious decisions about how much we involve ourselves in social struggles with those who have been exploited (Fine, 1994).

Additional Methodologies

Research that examines processes that facilitate or impede social change often does not fit neatly into experimental or quasi-experimental designs. As a result, some have advocated for a naturalistic case study or qualitative approach (Prilleltensky & Nelson, 1997). A significant advantage of qualitative approaches is that the perceptions and experiences of those frequently ignored in traditional scholarship (e.g., people of color, women of low social power) are highlighted. Qualitative approaches recognize the importance of understanding experience from the participants' point of view and regard each participant as an expert in naming her or his reality. In sum, methodological diversity is consistent with an emphasis on respect for the personal, subjective experience of participants and multifaceted approaches to knowing (Hage, 2003).

Participatory action research (PAR) is one type of research that deserves further consideration in the effort to give greater emphasis to social justice concerns (Prilleltensky & Nelson, 2002). With a long history that originated with oppressed groups in Central and South America, PAR draws on both quantitative and qualitative methods. At its core, PAR is a method that recognizes that knowledge is coproduced in collaboration and in action with those who have traditionally been left out of research and whose lives are most affected by the problem under study. The research process becomes a means to empower participants in the quest to understand reasons for events or circumstances in their world. PAR is most often practiced in community-based social action projects committed to understanding, documenting, and evaluating the impact that social programs, social problems, and social movements have on individuals and communities (Fine et al., 2003).

Practice

Psychologists and mental health practitioners often find themselves in the midst of service delivery systems that fail to value social justice interventions (Helms, 2003). Several reasons have been suggested for this lack of attention to social justice issues, including that these issues are "critical, controversial, political, and perhaps quite removed from our typical counseling psychology practice" (Speight & Vera, 2004, p. 110). To prepare mental health practitioners to give greater emphasis to social justice concerns, clarity regarding specific ways that these professionals can confront issues of oppression in their existing work is needed (Vera & Speight, 2003). The APA (2003) Multicultural Guidelines, similar to the multicultural counseling competencies (Sue, Arredondo, & McDavis, 1992) and the "Operationalization of the Multicultural Competencies" (Arredondo et al., 1996), offer numerous suggestions for addressing racism and oppression in the explanatory statements that support these competencies (Arredondo, 1999; Ridley, Baker, & Hill, 2001).

Specific examples of social justice interventions that can be integrated into existing psychological services may be gleaned from this literature. For example, to broaden the base of clients served, practitioners can offer a sliding fee scale and provide transportation vouchers for clients of low income; they can identify concrete institutional barriers that prevent ethnic minority clients from using psychological services and work with decision-making entities to eliminate these barriers (Arredondo et al., 1996). To serve linguistically diverse clients, counseling centers can make a strong commitment to hiring bilingual counselors (Ridley et al., 2001). To prevent bias when using assessment instruments, practitioners need to interpret findings with specific awareness of the cultural and linguistic characteristics of their clients (Arredondo et al., 1996; Sue et al., 1992).

CONCLUSION

Psychologists and mental health professionals must embrace social justice as a central part of their identity as educators, researchers, and practitioners. They must be leaders in creating the change they wish to see in the world and, in doing so, bring "people to a place they could not imagine"

(Couto, 2000, p. 8). To strengthen the commitment to social justice, mental health professionals must confront their own participation in systems of privilege and oppression. As suggested by the Multicultural Guidelines, when people work through their own conscious and unconscious biases and negative attitudes toward ethnic and racial minority groups as well as other groups (e.g., gay, lesbian, and bisexual), they increase their resolve to eradicate not only racism but all forms of oppression (Helms, 1995; Thompson et al., 2003). Psychologists and mental health professionals also need to create a healthy, just climate within their own programs and institutions (e.g., employment and pay equity, policies and programs to prevent campus violence), thus creating a congruent base from which to engage in broader social change (Prilleltensky & Nelson, 2002). Finally, mental health professionals must recognize that there will be contradictions and tensions between their professional roles and commitment to social justice. Support networks are necessary for young professionals who may be in "precarious positions" due to their social justice leadership efforts (Helms, 2003; Prilleltensky & Nelson, 1997).

REFERENCES

American Psychological Association. (1992). *Ethical principles of psychologists and code of conduct.* Retrieved June 17, 2004, from http://www.apa.org/ethics/code2002.html.

American Psychological Association. (2003). Guidelines on multicultural education, training, research, practice, and organizational change for psychologists. *American Psychologist, 58,* 377–402.

Apple, M. W. (1997). Consuming the other: Whiteness, education, and cheap French fries. In M. Fine, L. Weis, L. C. Powell, & L. M. Wong. *Off White: Readings on race, power, and society.* New York: Routledge.

Arredondo, P. (1999). Multicultural counseling competencies as tools to address oppression and racism. *Journal of Counseling & Development, 77,* 102–108.

Arredondo, P., & Perez, P. (2003). Expanding multicultural competence through social justice leadership. *Counseling Psychologist, 31,* 305–313.

Arredondo, P., Toporek, R., Brown, S. P., Jones, J., Locke, D. C., Sanchez, J., et al. (1996). Operationalization of the multicultural counseling competencies. *Journal of Multicultural Counseling and Development, 24,* 42–78.

Atkinson, D. R., Thompson, C. E., & Grant, S. K. (1993). A three-dimensional model for counseling racial/ethnic minorities. *Counseling Psychologist, 21,* 257–277.

Baluch, S. P., Pieterse, A. L., & Bolden, M. A. (2004). Counseling psychology and social justice: Houston . . . We have a problem. *Counseling Psychologist, 32,* 89–98.

Bronfenbrenner, U. (1979). *The ecology of human development: Experiments by nature and design.* Cambridge, MA: Harvard University Press.

Brown, L. (1994). *Subversive dialogues: Theory in feminist therapy.* New York: Basic Books.

Chesler, P. (1989). *Women and madness.* New York: Harcourt Brace Jovanovich.

Conyne, R. (1997). Educating students in preventive counseling. *Counselor Education and Supervision, 36,* 259–269.

Council of National Psychologists for the Advancement of Ethnic Minority Interests. (2000). *Guidelines for research in ethnic minority communities.* Washington, DC: American Psychological Association.

Couto, R. A. (2000). Community health as social justice: Lessons on leadership. *Family and Community Health, 23,* 1–17.

Delve, C. I., Mintz, S. D., & Stewart, G. M. (1990). Promoting values development through community service: A design. *Directions for Student Services, 50,* 7–29.

Douce, L. (2004). Society of Counseling Psychology Division 17 of APA presidential address 2003: Globalization of counseling psychology. *Counseling Psychologist, 32,* 142–152.

Dworkin, S. H., & Yi, H. (2003). LGBT identity, violence, and social justice: The psychological is political. *International Journal for the Advancement of Counselling, 25,* 269–279.

Eddy, J. M., Martinez, C., Morgan-Lopez, A., Smith, P., & Fisher, P. A. (2002). Diversifying the ranks of prevention scientists through a community collaborative approach to education. *Prevention and Treatment, 5.* Retrieved June 15, 2003, from http://journals.apa.org/prevention/volume5/pre0050003a.html.

Fine, M. (1994). Working the hyphens: Reinventing self and other in qualitative research. In N. Denzin & Y. Lincoln (Eds.), *Handbook of qualitative research* (pp. 70–82). Thousand Oaks, CA: Sage.

Fine, M., Torre, M. E., Boudin, K., Bown, I., Clark, J., Hylton, D., et al. (2003). Participatory action research: From within and beyond prison bars. In P. Camic, J. E. Rhodes, & L. Yardley (Eds.), *Qualitative research in psychology: Expanding perspectives in methodology and design.* Washington, DC: American Psychological Association.

Fox, D. (2003). Awareness is good, but action is better. *Counseling Psychologist, 31,* 299–304.

Freire, P. (1979). *Pedagogy of the oppressed.* New York: Herder & Herder.

Hage, S. M. (2003). Reaffirming the unique identity of counseling psychology: Opting for the "Road Less Traveled By." *Counseling Psychologist, 31,* 555–563.

Haveman, R. (1994). The nature, causes and cures of poverty: Accomplishments from three decades of policy research and poverty. In S. H. Danzriger, G. D. Saudefer, & D. H. Weinberg (Eds.), *Confronting poverty: Prescriptions for change* (pp. 438–450). Cambridge, MA: Harvard University Press.

Helms, J. E. (1995). An update on Helm's White and People of Color racial identity models. In J. Ponterotto, J. M. Casas, L. A. Suzuki, & C. M. Alexander (Eds.), *Handbook of multicultural counseling* (pp. 181–198). Thousand Oaks, CA: Sage.

Helms, J. E. (2003). A pragmatic view of social justice. *Counseling Psychologist, 31,* 305–313.

Hoagwood, K., & Koretz, D. (1996). Embedding prevention services within systems of care: Strengthening the nexus for children. *Applied and Preventive Psychology, 5,* 225–234.

Hondagneu-Sotelo, P., & Raskoff, S. (1994). Community service-learning: Promises and problems. *Teaching Sociology, 22,* 248–254.

hooks, b. (1994). *Teaching to transgress: Education as the practice of freedom.* New York: Routledge.

Ivey, A. E., & Collins, N. M. (2003). Social justice: A long-term challenge for counseling psychology. *Counseling Psychologist, 31,* 290–298.

Jackson, J. (2000). What ought psychology to do? *American Psychologist, 55,* 328–330.

Johnson, S. D. (1987). Knowing that versus knowing how: Toward achieving expertise through multicultural training for counseling. *Counseling Psychologist, 15,* 320–331.

Kirby, S. L., & McKenna, K. (1989). *Experience, research, social change: Methods from the margins.* Toronto, Ontario, Canada: Garamond Press.

Lee, C. C. (1997). The global future of professional counseling: Collaboration for international change. *International Journal of Intercultural Relations, 21,* 279–285.

Lewis, J. A., Lewis, M. D., Daniels, J. A., & D'Andrea, M. J. (1998). *Community counseling: Empowerment strategies for a diverse society.* Pacific Grove, CA: Brooks/Cole.

McGoldrick, M., Almeida, R., Preto, N. G., Bibb, A., Sutton, C., Hudak, J., et al. (1999). Efforts to incorporate social justice perspectives into a family training program. *Journal of Marital and Family Therapy, 25,* 191–209.

McNutt, J. G. (1998). Ensuring social justice for the new underclass: Community interventions to meet the needs of the new poor. In B. Ebo (Ed.), *Cyberghetto or cybertopia: Race, class, and gender on the internet.* Westport, CN: Praeger.

Middleton, R. A., Rollins, C. W., & Harley, D. A. (1999). The historical and political context of the civil rights of persons with disabilities: A multicultural perspective for counselors. *Journal of Multicultural Counseling and Development, 27,* 105–120.

Neville, H. A., & Mobley, M. (2001). Social identities in context: An ecological model of multicultural counseling psychology processes. *Counseling Psychologist, 29,* 273–281.

Prilleltensky, I., & Nelson, G. (1997). Community psychology: Reclaiming social justice. In D. Fox & I. Prilleltensky (Eds.), *Critical psychology: An introduction.* Thousand Oaks, CA: Sage.

Prilleltensky, I., & Nelson, G. (2002). *Doing psychology critically: Making a difference in diverse settings.* New York: Macmillan.

Prilleltensky, I., & Prilleltensky, O. (2003). Synergies for wellness and liberation in Counseling Psychology. *Counseling Psychologist, 31,* 273–281.

Rabow, J., Stein, J. M., & Conley, T. D. (1999). Teaching social justice and encountering society: The pink triangle experiment. *Youth and Society, 30,* 483–514.

RBP Associates, Inc. (1996, August 13). *Civil rights act of 1964.* Retrieved June 17, 2004, from http://usinfo.state.gov/usa/infousa/laws/majorlaw/civilr19.htm.

Ridley, C. R., Baker, D. M., & Hill, C. L. (2001). Critical issues concerning cultural competence. *Counseling Psychologist, 29,* 822–832.

Romano, J., & Hage, S. (2000). Prevention and counseling psychology: Revitalizing commitments for the 21st century. *Counseling Psychologist, 28,* 733–763.

Roschelle, A. R., Turpin, J., & Elias, R. (2000). Who learns from service learning? *American Behavioral Scientist, 43,* 839–847.

Shipler, D. (2004). *The working poor: Invisible in America.* New York: Knopf.

Speight, S. L., & Vera, E. M. (2004). A social justice agenda: Ready, or not? *Counseling Psychologist, 32,* 109–118.

Sue, D. W. (2001). Multidimensional facets of cultural competence. *Counseling Psychologist, 29,* 790–821.

Sue, D. W. (2003). *Overcoming our racism: The journey to liberation.* San Francisco: Jossey-Bass.

Sue, D. W., Arredondo, P., & McDavis, R. J. (1992). Multicultural counseling competencies: A call to the profession. *Journal of Counseling and Development, 70,* 477–486.

Sue, D. W., & Sue, D. (2003). *Counseling the culturally diverse: Theory and practice* (4th ed.). New York: Wiley.

Tatum, B. D. (1994). Teaching White students about racism: The search for White allies and the restoration of hope. *Teachers College Record, 95,* 4.

Thompson, C. E., Murry, S. L., Harris, D., & Annan, J. R. (2003). Healing inside and out: Promoting social justice and peace in a racially divided, U.S. community. *International Journal for the Advancement of Counselling, 25,* 215–223.

Thompson, C. E., & Neville, H. A. (1999). Racism, mental health, and mental health practice. *Counseling Psychologist, 27,* 155–223.

U.S. Bureau of the Census. (2002). *Poverty in the United States: 2002* (P-60, No. 222). Washington, DC: U.S. Government Printing Office.

U.S. Department of Health and Human Services. (2000). *Healthy people, 2010* (Conference ed., Vols. 1 & 2). Washington, DC: Author.

Van den Bos, K. (2003). On the subjective quality of social justice: The role of affect as information in the psychology of justice judgments. *Journal of Personality and Social Psychology, 85,* 482–498.

Varenne, H. (2003). On internationalizing counseling psychology: A view from cultural anthropology. *Counseling Psychologist, 31,* 404–411.

Vera, E. M., & Speight, S. L. (2003). Multicultural competence, social justice, and counseling psychology: Expanding our roles. *Counseling Psychologist, 31,* 253–272.

Author Index

A

Abreu, J. M., 152
Adams, E. M., 10
Adan, A. M., 187
Ajamu, A., 258
Ajei, M., 114, 122
Akbar, N., 247
Aldarondo, F. J., 43
Alegria, M., 147, 150
Alexander, C. M., 77, 170
Alexander, C. N., 117
Allport, G. W., 95
Almeida, R., 294, 295
Alvarez, A. N., 43
Amazigo, U. O., 118
Anago-Manze, C. I., 118
Ancis, J. R., 193, 194, 195, 196, 198, 199, 200, 203
Annan, J. R., 296, 299
Aponte, H., 58
Apple, M. W., 290
Applewhite, S. L., 114
Arbona, C., 77
Archer, J., 161
Arciniega, G. M., 48
Arean, P., 252
Arnold, M. S., 183
Aronson, E., 231, 232, 243
Arorash, T. J., 213, 217
Arredondo, P., 5, 9, 11, 12, 20, 32, 40, 43, 48, 71, 83, 85, 102, 153, 161, 181, 182, 294, 295, 298
Arrindell, W. A., 256
Asay, P. A., 82, 276

Atkinson, D. R., 5, 9, 10, 12, 29, 59, 163, 164, 212, 222, 271, 289, 295
Auletta, G. S., 220
Aviles, R. M. D., 48
Awakuni, G. I., 131, 133, 135
Azocar, F., 252

B

Baer, J., 58
Baker, D. M., 44, 298
Baker, D. W., 149
Baluch, S. P., 290
Bámaca, M. Y., 270, 271
Banaji, M. R., 163, 237
Banks, A., 59
Banks, C. A. M., 213
Banks, J. A., 213
Baptiste, L., 180, 183
Barker-Hackett, L., 138
Barr, D. J., 220
Barraclough, D. J., 78
Bartolomeo, M., 44
Barton, C., 186
Batten, S., 263, 264
Baumann, K., 78
Baysden, M. F., 77, 78
Bazron, B. J., 220
Bean, R. A., 59
Beck, A. T., 252
Bedell, T. M., 59
Behrens, J. T., 29
Bellini, J., 43
Bemak, F., 148

303

C

Subject Index

315

N

O